ALSO BY
SARA MOULTON

Sara's Secrets for Weeknight Meals

Sara Moulton Cooks at Home

The *Good Morning America* Cut the Calories Cookbook

To Sherry
Happy Cooking!

SARA MOULTON'S
EVERYDAY
FAMILY
DINNERS

Sara Moulton

Sara Moulton

with *Photographs by* JAMIE TIAMPO

SIMON & SCHUSTER

NEW YORK LONDON TORONTO SYDNEY

Simon & Schuster
1230 Avenue of the Americas
New York, NY 10020

Copyright © 2010 by Sara Moulton Enterprises, Inc.

First Simon & Schuster hardcover edition April 2010

SIMON & SCHUSTER and colophon are registered trademarks of Simon & Schuster, Inc.

For information about special discounts for bulk purchases,
please contact Simon & Schuster Special Sales at
1-866-506-1949 or business@simonandschuster.com.

The Simon & Schuster Speakers Bureau can bring authors
to your live event. For more information or to book an event,
contact the Simon & Schuster Speakers Bureau at
1-866-248-3049 or visit our website at www.simonspeakers.com.

Designed by Jaime Putorti

Manufactured in the United States of America

10   9   8   7   6   5   4   3   2   1

Library of Congress Cataloging-in-Publication Data
Moulton, Sara.
Sara Moulton's everyday family dinners / by Sara Moulton ; with photographs by Jamie Tiampo.
p.   cm.
1. Dinners and dining. 2. Quick and easy cookery. I. Title.
TX737.M66 2009
641.5'4—dc22   2009041666

ISBN 978-1-4391-0251-0
ISBN 978-1-4391-0990-8 (ebook)

ACKNOWLEDGMENTS

In addition to the greater Moulton and Adler families, who contributed many ideas and recipes to this book, there's a battle-tested squad of important people I have to thank:

Joanne Lamb Hayes, my partner and the hardest-working woman in the cookbook business.

Judith Weber, my agent, who suggested I write this book.

Sydny Miner, my wonderful editor.

Jennifer Day, my *chef de cuisine* at *Gourmet* and the creator of several great recipes in this book.

Helen Baldus, my stalwart publicist.

Jamie Tiampo, a hardworking, meticulous, and creative photographer.

Bill, Ruth, and Sam, my part-time tasting panel and full-time family.

Finally, I must acknowledge *Gourmet* magazine, which was shuttered as I was finishing this book. There's no way for me to quantify how much I learned during my twenty-five years as a member of the team, except to say that my culinary education continued there until the very last day. More particularly, it is because of my years in *Gourmet*'s test kitchen that I can say with confidence and pride that the recipes in this book work.

TO RUTH HUMPHREY MOULTON,
MY FIRST COOKING TEACHER

CONTENTS

FACING PAGE: *Kalustyan's on Lexington Avenue in New York, my favorite store for international ingredients.*

SARA MOULTON'S
EVERYDAY
FAMILY
DINNERS

INTRODUCTION

As the title indicates, this book is dedicated to cooking dinner for the family on a weeknight. Now, as ever, I believe that few things are as beneficial to our health, both body and soul, as a home-cooked meal eaten at the table with family and friends.

I've spent a lot of time thinking about what constitutes dinner. Most of us tend to make the same ten recipes over and over again. This is boring, and when you're bored, you're disinclined to make any dinner at all. Broadly, this book is a compendium of strategies to wriggle free of the straitjacket that stipulates starch / vegetable / protein at every meal.

My continuing quest to rethink dinner has resulted in several new strategies. The chapter called "Appetizers for Dinner" formalizes my frequent preference for a meal's starters to its "main" course. "Two for One" spells out how to make a great new meal with the leftovers from the night before, simply by making sure that there will be leftovers. In "Five-Ingredient Mains," the challenge was to come up with recipes that are as delicious as they are quick to make. Also, there's "Whole Grain and Hearty," a sign of my growing appreciation for the healthfulness, variety, and flexibility of whole grains.

This book has a vegetarian chapter, as well as a number of vegetarian recipes in the nonvegetarian chapters. (These are marked with a Ⓥ icon.) Vegetarian entrées are greener than meat entrées, after all, and they're less expensive, too, which is not a small consideration during a recession. Most persuasive, perhaps, the variety, freshness, and flavor of the vegetables available to us now are greater than at any other time in history. Think of how hard Julia Child had to work a generation ago to get leeks and shallots into her local supermarket. Today we take leeks and shallots for granted—along with tomatillos, fresh fennel, and edamame.

Most of the recipes in this book contain suggested variations: how to make it lighter, how to make it vegetarian, what to exchange for ingredients you hate or simply can't find in your hometown. But I'm hoping to do more than provide you with options; I'd like to spark your creativity. Real cooks don't need a recipe. They can look at their ingredients, consider their options, and make a meal.

Things have changed since I published

my last book in 2005. I rely more on local and seasonal ingredients because more Americans are interested in cooking with them. (They're tastier than the mass-produced kind and friendlier to the environment, too.) I make use of a greater variety of international ingredients because they're more widely available here both in stores and on the Internet. The current recession has inspired me to substitute less-expensive, but equally flavorful, ingredients for the ones I might have called for in my previous books. I rely less on the supermarket in general and on prepared ingredients in particular.

People often tell me that the hardest part of preparing a meal is timing. Accordingly, this book incorporates several new ideas about how to cook smarter, faster, and cleaner. The most important is concerned with *mise en place;* the term literally translates from the French as "put in place." The idea is that all the ingredients of a recipe should be diced, sliced, and prepped before you start cooking. At the risk of banishment from my alma mater, the Culinary Institute of America, I've dispensed with *mise en place* almost entirely. I agree that this method makes perfect sense for most Asian recipes, which call for the ingredients to get in and out of the pan in twenty seconds, but it's a waste of time when you're cooking most other cuisines. In those cases, why not take advantage of the time required to cook an onion—about five minutes—to slice your red pepper? On the other hand, I do recommend pulling all of the ingredients for a recipe out of the fridge and the cupboard and setting them on the counter before you start cooking. That is a time-saving move.

This kind of thinking is reflected in the way the recipes are written. Instead of including instructions about how to prep an ingredient in the list of ingredients itself—"1 cup finely chopped onions," for example—I list the ingredient as you'd buy it at the market—"1 medium onion." The instructions about how to prep that onion have been moved to the body of the recipe.

I also recommend keeping a bowl for garbage (including potato and onion peels and the like) within arm's reach. It saves you from running back and forth to the garbage pail and from cluttering up your counter. (For all of my classical training, I find that if I'm not consciously focused on working neatly and cleaning up as I go, the mess stacks up around me, and I end up cooking in a space the size of a postage stamp. This slows me down.)

No recipe was included if it didn't pass muster with my "tasting panel," which included The Husband; Joanne Lamb Hayes, my official recipe tester; and my kids. Now fully grown, my kids both possess more than a passing interest in food. Ruthie worked for several summers at a farmers' market and currently works as the hostess at a restaurant here in New York City. Sam, the founder of the Fine Dining Club at his high school, moved out of his college dorm after a single semester because he couldn't stand the dorm food.

I'd never claim that my little panel is a perfect microcosm of the country at large, but I would say that I had to run a pretty tricky obstacle course before arriving at a dish that pleased all of them. The Husband and Sam like meat; Ruthie prefers vegetables. Sam doesn't care for vegetables, but he's crazy about carbs. The Husband and Sam like it spicy; Ruthie does not. Neither kid likes fish, although both are fine with shellfish. Ruthie loves all herbs except for parsley and cilantro; Sam won't touch an herb except for basil. The Husband can't stand sweet with his savory. Ruthie is the only one of us who cares deeply about dessert.

Me? I'm the umpire, although I'm hardly impartial. Looking over all the recipes, I couldn't help but notice that some of my favorite ingredients pop up over and over again: garlic, chiles, cheese, mayonnaise, and mustard. Of course, you're not required to like, or use, any of them. You can delete whichever ones you want without serious damage to any recipe in question.

Ultimately, it seems to me that there are several reasons why the need for a weeknight cookbook has increased in recent years. First, the recession is chasing more and more people into the kitchen; it's cheaper to eat at home than to eat out. Second, although there's now a world of recipes available on the Internet, how does the home cook know which ones to trust? If you search on Google for a macaroni and cheese recipe, you'll find literally more than a million in 0.51 seconds. But how many of those have been tested? I'm all for the de-mocratization of information, but with it comes an increasing need for critical thinking, editorial insight, and professional expertise, none of which automatically drops into the lap of everyone who owns a knife, a pan, an oven, and a computer. Finally, although food television is more popular today than ever, it is also more about entertainment than instruction. If someone actually wants to learn how to cook, he or she needs a cookbook devoted to that purpose. Americans, in general, still eat too much fast food and too much processed food. Indeed, we often eat too much, period. This isn't just unhealthful, it's expensive.

Still, I've never been into what used to be called health food, just as I've never liked the idea of food as nothing more than fuel for the body. There's simply not enough pleasure in it. When I was much younger, the Aristotelian ideal, everything in moderation, didn't appeal to me at all. There was nothing about my appetites then that was moderate. When I got to know Julia Child, I acquired a different understanding of this credo: not everything *in moderation,* but *everything* in moderation. There's no reason to deny yourself the pleasures of this life; just don't overdo it.

That said, I'll confess that the making of this book required The Husband and me to road test three entrées a night for nine months. As I sign off, I look forward in the short term to a little less everything and a little more moderation.

HOW TO USE THIS BOOK

I've included an icon throughout the book for recipes that are vegetarian. Look for ⓥ for vegetarian choices.

Avocados are Hass avocados.

Bay leaves are from Turkey.

Black pepper is freshly ground.

Bread crumbs: I like to make my own bread crumbs, but on a weeknight, there is nothing wrong with using packaged. Fresh are made by grinding fresh bread in a food processor fitted with the chopping blade. Dried bread crumbs are made by toasting broken pieces of bread in a low oven until they just begin to color, then allowing them to continue to dry out in the oven as it cools. Once they are dry and cool, they are ground in a food processor.

Brown sugar is firmly packed when measured.

Butter is unsalted.

Canned tomatoes are fire roasted, if possible. I love the way the process intensifies the flavor. I find Muir Glen in my local stores, but you may substitute another brand if that isn't available.

Cheeses are freshly grated. For most types of cheese, when I was coarsely grating, I grated a weighed piece of cheese on a box grater to get the measurement. When I was finely grating Parmigiano-Reggiano and other hard cheeses, I grated a weighed piece of cheese on a Microplane. However, I have given measurements for both Microplane (see Sources, page 359) grating and grating on a box grater. While a Microplane is easy to use and does a nice job of finely grating hard cheeses, the same weight of cheese will measure about twice as much as when it is grated on a box grater. I also found that grated coarsely on the box grater, 3 ounces of a hard cheese, such as Parmigiano-Reggiano, made 1 cup grated, while 4 ounces of a semihard cheese, such as Cheddar, made 1 cup grated.

Chorizo is Spanish. I especially like the Palacios brand. If you can't find it in your supermarket, check out the Sources section, page 359, in the back of this book.

Cream cheese and sour cream are whole milk or low-fat, not nonfat or fat-free.

FACING PAGE: *Some of my favorite tools. Clockwise from top left: tongs, bench scraper, smooth-edge can opener, fish spatula, swivel blade vegetable peeler, tortilla press, lemon/lime squeezer, Microplane.*

Eggs are large. There are a few recipes in this book where egg yolks are not cooked completely; they are left runny. Although the risk of salmonella is real, it is minuscule. If you are cooking for someone in a high-risk group—the immune impaired, the elderly, or the very young (under five years old)—consider cooking the yolks until they are cooked through.

Fish are not endangered. Overfishing, wasteful practices, and habitat destruction have endangered many species of fish. The fish I chose to use were not in the high-risk category at the time I was writing this book. But the situation keeps changing. It's not always easy to know if a fish is or isn't endangered. For up-to-date information on the status of any fish, please go to the Seafood Choices Alliance Web site at www.seafoodchoices.com or the Monterey Bay Aquarium (www.mbayaq.org). If the fish you desire is, indeed, endangered, the Seafood Choices Alliance will provide you with alternative choices.

Flour is unbleached all-purpose, unless otherwise noted.

Garlic is peeled and pressed. A garlic press is easy to use and much faster than hand chopping garlic when you are in a hurry.

Heavy cream is pasteurized, not ultra-pasteurized. To me, the latter tastes cooked and tends to break faster than the pasteurized when whipped.

Herbs: Use fresh whenever possible; if fresh are not available, 1 tablespoon chopped fresh herbs equals 1 teaspoon dried herbs. I have found that chopping reduces the volume of fresh herbs by half, so where I give dried as an alternative, the amount is based on the fresh chopped measure.

Herb substitutions: I know the world is divided between people who love cilantro and those who are genetically programmed to hate it. If you hate cilantro or cook for someone who does, just substitute basil, mint, or parsley or skip the herb.

Jalapeño chiles should have heat. There is this nutcase scientist in Texas who is breeding jalapeños that have no heat. Just cut off a thin slice, rub your finger over it, and lick your finger to see what kind of heat the jalapeño has. Pickled jalapeños miraculously seem always to have heat, so they are a safe bet. You can include the seeds and ribs to increase the heat. Unless it is noted otherwise, I removed the seeds and ribs when I tested the recipes.

Lemon, lime, and orange juices are freshly squeezed.

Since lemons, limes, and oranges differ so much in size, I have listed the exact juice amount in the ingredient list.

Lemon, lime, and orange zests are freshly grated. The best tool for this job is a Microplane. It is sold in many kitchenwares stores, or see Sources, page 359. I have also listed the exact amount of grated zest in the ingredient list. See note above.

Mayonnaise is original, full-fat for all cooked dishes. Reduced-fat can be used in cold dishes, if you like the flavor.

Meat is "natural" (minimally processed and raised without antibiotics and hormones), or organic, if possible.

Milk is whole. If you want to slim down the recipe, you can use lower-fat alternatives. (Do not use nonfat or skim milk here. I think it has no flavor.)

Olive oil is extra virgin. If you find it too costly, go ahead and use plain old olive oil, but hunt for one that has a flavor you like.

Poultry is organic, "natural" (minimally processed and raised without antibiotics and hormones), or kosher, if possible.

Rice vinegar comes in two varieties: seasoned and unseasoned. Seasoned has sugar and salt added to it. If all you have in the house is unseasoned, and a recipe calls for seasoned, just add a pinch of sugar and salt to it.

Sake is my preferred wine to add to Asian dishes, but dry sherry or rice wine (sweeter than the other two) will work just fine, too.

Salt is kosher except for baked goods, where it is table salt.

Spinach and lettuce are prewashed and dried.

Vanilla extract is pure.

Vegetable oil is whichever brand you prefer.

Wine must be drinkable. Don't ever use "cooking wine."

Yogurt: In most recipes, you can use whole milk, low-fat, or fat-free yogurt. I use Greek-style strained yogurt in some recipes. Fage is a good brand that is widely available in the dairy section of most supermarkets.

1
HEAD STARTS

One way to make it easier to cook dinner at home on a weeknight is to prepare some basic make-ahead, freeze-ahead recipes on the weekend. This chapter includes my favorite chicken and vegetable stocks, several fun salad dressings (with one low-fat variation), a variety of basic sauces and flavored butters, and a spice mix. There are also a couple of quick pickle recipes and a salsa, all of which make great toppings for any number of dishes. There are three recipes for all-purpose doughs or batters and two techniques: how to hard-cook/hard-boil an egg and how to poach a chicken breast.

All these recipes are called for in other recipes found in this book, but they're also versatile enough to be incorporated into recipes of your own invention. The point is, with a store of these basics at hand, you're much better prepared to throw together a meal that's delicious and nourishing, even if you begin without a plan. Think of them as "head starts."

FACING PAGE: *Still life with jars. Clockwise from top: Dill Pickle Cucumber Slices, Quick Tomato Sauce, Flavored Butters—Steak, Citrus and Herb— Tomatillo Salsa, Quick Kimchi.*

Homemade Chicken Stock

MAKES ABOUT 8 CUPS ▪ HANDS-ON TIME: 10 MINUTES ▪ TOTAL PREPARATION TIME: 3½ HOURS

Why bother making homemade chicken stock when there are so many respectable versions at the supermarket? Flavor, of course. At the end of the day the stock you pour out of a can or a box just can't touch the stock you make at home. The difference is gelatin, which adds unbeatable body to a stock. Gelatin comes into a stock from the long, slow simmering of bones. Homemade has it. Store-bought doesn't. You can see for yourself if you ever boil them down side by side. A homemade stock becomes thick and viscous, its flavor very concentrated. A store-bought stock simply disappears into thin air. (Makes you wonder what the heck it's made from in the first place.)

Of course, I'm not a snob and I'm not a purist. I use good store-bought chicken stock or broth all the time. But for a special occasion—let's say I'm making matzo ball soup for Passover—I start from scratch with chicken wings. It's part of what makes the occasion special.

Chicken stock freezes beautifully and can be stored in the freezer (I use 1-cup containers for convenience) for up to 6 months.

5 pounds chicken wings
2 medium onions
2 small carrots
2 medium celery stalks
4 fresh flat-leaf parsley sprigs
2 fresh thyme sprigs
1 teaspoon whole black peppercorns
1 Turkish bay leaf
Kosher salt and freshly ground black pepper

1. Put the chicken wings in a large stockpot and add enough cold water to cover them by 2 inches. Bring the mixture just to a boil over high heat, skimming the surface with a slotted spoon. Reduce the heat to medium-low immediately and simmer, skimming frequently, for 20 minutes.

2. Meanwhile, quarter the onions and halve the carrots and celery. Add to the stockpot along with the parsley, thyme, peppercorns, and bay leaf. Return the mixture just to a boil over high heat; reduce the heat to medium-low and simmer for 2½ hours.

3. Strain the stock through a colander into a bowl and discard the solids. Skim off all the fat that rises to the surface of the stock. (Or let the stock cool and refrigerate it overnight. The fat will harden on top of the stock and is much easier to remove.)

4. Return the stock to the pot and simmer until reduced by one-third, about 30 minutes. Add salt and pepper to taste.

Homemade Vegetable Stock (V)

Since I'm basically a carnivore and not remotely a fan of canned or boxed vegetable stocks, I always reach for chicken stock when a recipe calls for some liquid. Obviously, that's not an option when the recipe is vegetarian.

Faced with the need to come up with a vegetable stock of my own, I consulted all of my favorite vegetarian cookbooks. Many contained several different vegetable stocks, each for a specific use. I decided I wanted a one-size-fits-all stock, so I kept it simple. The very first time I tested this recipe I was very pleasantly surprised at its full body and taste. I'm thinking that if I always keep some at hand in the fridge or freezer, vegetable stock might start to make its way into all of my recipes, not just the vegetarian ones.

If you don't use the stock within 2 days, you can freeze it for up to 6 months.

8 medium mushrooms (preferably cremini)
3 medium onions
6 garlic cloves
2 tablespoons vegetable oil
2 tablespoons tomato paste
4 medium celery stalks
3 medium carrots
1 medium russet potato
2 fresh flat-leaf parsley sprigs
1 tablespoon soy sauce (low sodium, if you prefer)
2 teaspoons whole black peppercorns
2 Turkish bay leaves
Kosher salt and freshly ground black pepper

1. Clean, trim, and coarsely chop the mushrooms (about 2⅔ cups). Coarsely chop the onions (about 3 cups) and garlic (about 2 tablespoons). Heat the vegetable oil over medium heat in a large stockpot until hot. Add the mushrooms, onions, and garlic and cook, stirring, for about 10 minutes, or until golden. Add the tomato paste and cook, stirring, for 1 minute.

2. Meanwhile, very coarsely chop the celery (about 1½ cups) and carrots (about 1½ cups). Scrub and coarsely chop the potato with the skin on (about 1¾ cups). Add 10 cups cold water, the celery, carrots, potato, parsley, soy sauce, peppercorns, and bay leaves to the stockpot. Bring the mixture to a boil over high heat; reduce the heat to medium-low immediately and simmer for 1 hour, adding water as necessary to keep the vegetables covered.

3. Strain the stock through a colander into a bowl. Discard the solids and return the liquid to the stockpot; bring to a boil over high heat and cook until reduced to 4 cups. Add salt and pepper to taste.

Creamy Garlic Dressing Two Ways: Rich and Slim (v)

MAKES ABOUT ⅔ CUP   HANDS-ON TIME: 10 MINUTES   TOTAL PREPARATION TIME: 10 MINUTES

This is my adaptation of a dressing for grilled quail that I first encountered in *Gourmet* magazine. Generally, I steer clear of creamy dressings because of the extra calories they pack, but this one is so delicious that I couldn't leave it alone. Even so, I present it to you here in full-fat and lighter versions. The lower-fat alternative swaps out the cream for yogurt, which subtracts calories, adds tang, and is still plenty creamy.

2 tablespoons sherry
  vinegar
2 teaspoons Dijon
  mustard
¼ teaspoon kosher salt
⅛ teaspoon freshly
  ground black pepper
1 garlic clove
¼ cup heavy cream or
  plain low-fat or full-
  fat Greek-style yogurt
  (see page 49)
¼ cup extra virgin olive
  oil

Whisk together the vinegar, mustard, salt, and pepper in a small bowl until the salt has dissolved. Press the garlic (about 1 teaspoon) into the mixture. Gradually whisk in the cream and then the olive oil. Store in the refrigerator for a day or two.

$\mathcal{W}$arm Roasted-Tomato Vinaigrette (v)

MAKES ABOUT 1 CUP ■ HANDS-ON TIME: 10 MINUTES ■ TOTAL PREPARATION TIME: 45 MINUTES

Roasted tomatoes not only bring tremendous depth of flavor to this vinaigrette, they also help to reduce the amount of olive oil required. Normally, you'd need 6 to 8 tablespoons of olive oil to make 1 cup of vinaigrette; here, 4 tablespoons (¼ cup) do the trick. The result doubles as a great dressing for salad and a great sauce for fish or chicken.

1 pound plum tomatoes (about 4 medium)
¼ cup extra virgin olive oil
Kosher salt and freshly ground black pepper
1 tablespoon sherry vinegar

1. Place an oven rack in the upper third of the oven and preheat the oven to 425°F.

2. Core and quarter the tomatoes; arrange them, cut side up, in one layer in a 13 × 9 × 2-inch baking dish or pan. Drizzle them with 2 tablespoons of the olive oil and sprinkle them with ¾ teaspoon salt and ¼ teaspoon pepper. Roast the tomatoes for 30 minutes.

3. When the tomatoes have roasted, transfer them along with any liquid in the baking dish to a blender; add the remaining 2 tablespoons olive oil and the vinegar and puree until smooth. Season the vinaigrette with salt and pepper to taste. Store in the refrigerator for a day or two.

$\mathcal{Q}$uick Tomato Sauce

MAKES ABOUT 3 CUPS · HANDS-ON TIME: 5 MINUTES · TOTAL PREPARATION TIME: 30 MINUTES

Every time I make this recipe, which I do frequently, I marvel at its simplicity and tastiness. Why buy prepared tomato sauce, which is often loaded with all sorts of ingredients none of us needs (like high-fructose corn syrup), when you can make a much better sauce at home in about twenty-five minutes?

1 small onion
2 tablespoons extra
    virgin olive oil
2 garlic cloves
One 28-ounce can
    whole plum tomatoes
    (preferably fire
    roasted)
¼ to ½ teaspoon
    crushed red pepper
    flakes (optional)
Kosher salt and freshly
    ground black pepper

1. Finely chop the onion (about ½ cup). Heat the olive oil in a medium saucepan over medium heat until hot. Reduce the heat to medium-low; add the onion and cook for 5 minutes, or until it has softened. Press the garlic (about 2 teaspoons) into the saucepan and cook for 1 minute more.

2. While the onion and garlic are cooking, empty the canned tomatoes and their juices into a large bowl and break them into pieces with your hands, cut them with kitchen scissors, or pulse them in a food processor until medium chopped. Transfer them to the saucepan along with the red pepper flakes, if using. Bring the mixture to a boil over high heat. Reduce the heat to low and simmer the sauce, stirring occasionally, for about 20 minutes, or until it has thickened. Add salt and black pepper to taste.

Basic Barbecue Sauce

MAKES ABOUT 2 CUPS ■ HANDS-ON TIME: 7 MINUTES ■ TOTAL PREPARATION TIME: 27 MINUTES

Your basic barbecue fiend tends to make a fetish out of his or her sauce, just as he or she does every other aspect of the dish's preparation. Me, I'm not so choosy, and especially not if the sauce in question takes hours to make and it's a weeknight. That said, I'm not a fan of most supermarket sauces, either. I find that almost all of them are way too sweet for my taste. This sauce is quick and easy to make at home. It's not too hot and it's not too sweet—it's just right.

1 tablespoon vegetable oil
1 garlic clove
2 cups ketchup
¼ cup cider vinegar
¼ cup Worcestershire sauce
2 tablespoons packed dark brown sugar
1 tablespoon Creole Seasoning (page 20, add preparation time) or use store-bought seasoning
2 teaspoons dry mustard
Kosher salt and freshly ground black pepper

1. Heat the vegetable oil in a medium saucepan over medium heat until hot; reduce the heat to low and press the garlic (about 1 teaspoon) into the oil. Sauté it for about 1 minute, or until it just begins to turn golden.

2. Add the ketchup, vinegar, Worcestershire sauce, brown sugar, Creole Seasoning, and mustard. Bring the mixture to a boil over medium heat; reduce the heat to low and simmer the sauce, partially covered to reduce spattering, for 20 minutes, stirring occasionally.

3. Add salt and pepper to taste. Use as directed in a recipe or transfer to a nonreactive jar or bowl, cover, and refrigerate until you are ready to use it.

$\mathcal{P}$eanut Sesame Sauce Ⓥ

MAKES ABOUT 1¾ CUPS   HANDS-ON TIME: 10 MINUTES   TOTAL PREPARATION TIME: 10 MINUTES

I featured this recipe in the sauce chapter of my last cookbook, but I just can't leave it alone. The creation of my friend Rosa Ross, a cookbook author, it is hands down the best peanut sesame sauce on the planet. Believe me, I know, because I tried to surpass it with a recipe of my own. Her secret? Whole scallions, the white part *and* the green part, give her sauce that certain something.

This is the peanut sauce that goes into Warm Sesame Noodles with Mushrooms and Peas (page 234) and Ground Turkey and Mint Lettuce Wraps (page 64). It would work equally well as a sauce on grilled chicken, fish, or vegetables. It's addictive.

3 medium scallions
¾ cup smooth unsalted peanut butter
½ cup hoisin sauce
2 tablespoons fresh lemon juice
1 tablespoon soy sauce (low sodium, if you prefer)
2 teaspoons toasted sesame oil
Tabasco or your favorite hot sauce

1. Trim and coarsely chop the scallions (a heaping ⅓ cup). Combine them with the peanut butter, hoisin sauce, lemon juice, soy sauce, sesame oil, and Tabasco to taste in a food processor fitted with the chopping blade.

2. Process until pureed. Add water, 1 tablespoon at a time (up to ¼ cup), if needed to thin the sauce.

3. Use as directed in a recipe, or store, covered, in the refrigerator for up to 5 days.

how do i
SELECT A GOOD SOY SAUCE?

The taste of soy sauce varies a lot from brand to brand; you want one with flavor as well as saltiness. The key is natural fermentation. If the ingredient label contains anything other than soybeans, water, salt, sometimes wheat, and a preservative, you don't want it. Kikkoman and Eden Organic are good supermarket brands. If you're allergic to wheat, try tamari soy sauce, which is made without it. Lite soy sauce is lower in sodium than the regular kind, but it's also lower in flavor. Using it is a balancing act.

Foolproof Egg Lemon Sauce

MAKES ABOUT 1½ CUPS ▪ HANDS-ON TIME: 10 MINUTES ▪ TOTAL PREPARATION TIME: 10 MINUTES

Egg lemon sauce, or avgolemono, is probably the best-known Greek sauce. Alone, it fancies up lamb, chicken, fish, and vegetable dishes, but it's also used to flavor and thicken a range of soups and stews. Its three main ingredients are egg and lemon, as advertised, and hot chicken stock. When making it, the tricky part is adding the hot stock to the eggs in such a way that the eggs don't curdle. This recipe includes a cute little cheat that solves that problem: cornstarch, which thickens the sauce and prevents curdling.

Although I've specified this sauce for two of the recipes in this book (Halibut or Cod on Chickpea Puree, page 213, and Roast Chicken Stuffed with Zucchini and Cheese, page 320), feel free to use it as the Greeks do, on top of almost any cooked protein or vegetable.

1½ cups Homemade Chicken Stock (page 10, add preparation time) or canned broth
1 large egg yolk
1 to 2 tablespoons fresh lemon juice
1 tablespoon cornstarch
Kosher salt and freshly ground black pepper

Heat the chicken stock in a small saucepan over low heat until simmering. Whisk the egg yolk, 1 tablespoon lemon juice, and cornstarch together. Add a little of the chicken stock to the mixture in a stream, whisking. Add the egg mixture to the pot of chicken stock and heat for about 1 minute, or just until the sauce starts to bubble. Taste and add additional lemon juice if desired and salt and pepper to taste.

$\mathcal{B}$roccoli or Broccoli Raab Pesto ⓥ

MAKES ABOUT 1⅔ CUPS ▪ HANDS-ON TIME: 15 MINUTES ▪ TOTAL PREPARATION TIME: 15 MINUTES

I learned about pesto sideways. In Ann Arbor in the early seventies my dear friend Cindy Browne, a member of a local food co-op, used to call me up at the end of a day with a seductive invitation. "I've got a refrigerator full of rotting vegetables," she'd say. "Why don't you come over for dinner?" Often, she'd proceed to deal with the overabundance by turning it into *soupe au pistou. Pistou* is the French twist on Italian pesto.

I didn't come face-to-face with pesto itself until a few years later, when I began devouring Marcella Hazan's *The Classic Italian Cook Book.* This scrumptious sauce of basil, garlic, pine nuts, Italian cheese (Parmigiano-Reggiano and/or pecorino), and extra virgin olive oil has been a staple in my life ever since.

Coincidentally, the inspiration for this recipe is distinctly Cindy-esque: how to deal with a drawerful of lettuce quickly going bad. Swap it for the basil in a pesto sauce. Unfortunately, this notion was much more appealing in the imagination than in reality. Take it from me: Lettuce pesto is not a winner. We were seated around the dinner table, pondering its awfulness, when The Husband suggested replacing the bland lettuce with robust broccoli raab. The retooled product not only boasts big flavor, it's healthful as can be. (Note: Broccoli makes the pesto sweeter. Broccoli raab makes it more bitter.)

¼ cup slivered blanched almonds or walnuts

6 ounces broccoli or broccoli raab

2 medium scallions

1 ounce Parmigiano-Reggiano or other hard grating cheese

3 tablespoons extra virgin olive oil

2 garlic cloves

Kosher salt and freshly ground black pepper

1. Preheat the oven to 350°F. Spread out the almonds on a rimmed baking sheet and toast until golden, 7 to 10 minutes. Remove to a cooling rack and let cool to room temperature.

2. Meanwhile, coarsely chop the broccoli (about 2 cups). Trim and slice the scallions crosswise into ½-inch pieces (about ¼ cup). Microplane-grate the cheese (about ⅔ cup) or grate on the fine side of a box grater (about ⅓ cup).

3. Combine the almonds, broccoli, scallions, cheese, and olive oil in the bowl of a food processor fitted with the chopping blade. Press the garlic (about 2 teaspoons) into the processor bowl. Pulse until the mixture is finely chopped but not pureed. Transfer the pesto to a bowl and stir in salt and pepper to taste. Use as directed in a recipe. This will keep in the refrigerator for 3 days or frozen for up to 3 months.

Flavored Butters

MAKES SIXTEEN 1-TABLESPOON SERVINGS PER VARIATION   HANDS-ON TIME: 10 MINUTES
TOTAL PREPARATION TIME: 10 MINUTES

In my book, the taste of food is its prime quality. Everything else—including its healthfulness—comes second. That's why I'm usually very reluctant to gild the lily, so to speak. Just get the best and freshest ingredients and let them speak, or sing, for themselves. Do not smother them in sauces.

Still, I like flavored butters because they allow me to easily and lightly (not to say diaphanously) dress up an otherwise plain piece of fish, chicken, pork, or beef, and they're just the thing to dress up a pot of steamed vegetables or cooked rice. Preparing them is a snap; you can speed up the process by using an electric mixer or a food processor. With a stash of these butters in the fridge or freezer, you'll have a secret "sauce" at the ready for any night of the week.

(V) HERB BUTTER
½ pound (2 sticks) unsalted butter, softened
2 garlic cloves, pressed (about 2 teaspoons)
3 tablespoons chopped fresh tarragon, dill, marjoram, or oregano leaves
1 teaspoon kosher salt
¼ teaspoon freshly ground black pepper

(V) CITRUS BUTTER
½ pound (2 sticks) unsalted butter, softened
1 teaspoon freshly grated lemon zest
1 teaspoon freshly grated lime zest
2 teaspoons fresh lemon juice
2 teaspoons fresh lime juice
½ teaspoon kosher salt

STEAK BUTTER
½ pound (2 sticks) unsalted butter
2 tablespoons Worcestershire sauce
1 tablespoon Dijon mustard
1 garlic clove, pressed
½ teaspoon kosher salt

1. Stir together the ingredients for the Flavored Butter variation that you are making in a small bowl until the mixture is well blended. Divide the mixture equally onto 4 sheets of plastic wrap; shape each portion into a flattened square.

2. Wrap the squares tightly in the wrap, pack them in a resealable plastic bag, and store them in the freezer until you are ready to use them. To use them, cut each square into quarters. Each quarter will measure about 1 tablespoon.

$\mathcal{C}$reole Seasoning Ⓥ

MAKES ABOUT ½ CUP ■ HANDS-ON TIME: 10 MINUTES ■ TOTAL PREPARATION TIME: 10 MINUTES

In general, I'm not a fan of garlic and onion in powdered form; I prefer them fresh. But I am a fan of the cooking of Paul Prudhomme and Emeril Lagasse. Both of these super-star chefs made their names at New Orleans's Commander's Palace restaurant and both have based their repertoires on a special spice blend that includes onion powder and garlic powder. What can I say? The proof is in the spice mix. When I developed the recipe for Red Beans and Rice Soup with Ham (page 96), I thought this spice mix might improve it a little. After adding it, I realized at once that the spice mix turned a good soup into a great soup. It is just as important in the Breaded Creole Chicken with Ranch-Dressed Coleslaw (page 124).

1 tablespoon plus
  1 teaspoon hot
  paprika
1 tablespoon kosher salt
1 tablespoon garlic
  powder
1½ teaspoons freshly
  ground black pepper
1½ teaspoons onion
  powder
1½ teaspoons cayenne
  pepper
1½ teaspoons dried
  oregano
1½ teaspoons dried
  thyme

Combine the paprika, salt, garlic powder, black pepper, onion powder, cayenne, oregano, and thyme in a small bowl. Transfer the mixture to a tight-lidded jar or tin and use it as directed in a recipe. It will keep for up to 6 months.

STORING SPICES AND DRIED HERBS

If spices and dried herbs are kept in a cool, dark place (away from the stove and sunlight), they should last for at least 6 months. After that, you can still use them, but you will have to use more in order to get the same potency. You can tell when their flavor is fading because their color fades: paprika and red spices go from bright red to dull brown, dried green herbs go from green to dull gray. When you buy dried herbs and spices, buy them in small quantities so you won't mind replacing them when they are past their prime. Write the date of purchase on the jar, so you'll know when to replace it.

$\mathcal{Q}$uick and Quicker Kimchi  Ⓥ

MAKES ABOUT 2 CUPS ■ **HANDS-ON TIME: 20 MINUTES** ■ **TOTAL PREPARATION TIME: 2 HOURS 30 MINUTES**

I love all things acidic and salty. If you add crunch and spicy heat to these qualities, you have the Korean cabbage pickle called kimchi. Like sauerkraut, which is also made of cabbage, kimchi takes days to make, so I'd resigned myself to eating it only in Korean restaurants.

Then inspiration struck. Once upon a time I never made dill pickles because that process is so detailed and painstaking; then I doped out a way to make a quick cucumber pickle. There had to be a way to make quick kimchi. In fact, I came up with two ways, one that has to sit at room temperature for 2 hours and one that's almost instant because it starts with sauerkraut. Both are absolutely delicious and will add a unique crunch and heat to any recipe.

1 small head napa cabbage (about 1 pound)
⅓ cup kosher salt
⅓ cup unseasoned rice vinegar
1 tablespoon sugar
1 teaspoon sweet or hot paprika
¼ teaspoon cayenne pepper
½ medium red bell pepper
3 medium scallions
One 3-inch piece fresh ginger
1 garlic clove

1. Trim off the core end of the cabbage. Split each leaf lengthwise and cut it crosswise into 1½-inch ribbons (about 4 cups). Combine the cabbage and salt in a nonreactive bowl and set aside at room temperature for 2 hours.

2. Bring the vinegar, sugar, paprika, and cayenne to a boil over high heat in a small saucepan.

3. Meanwhile, finely chop the bell pepper (about ½ cup) and transfer it to a medium bowl. Trim and thinly slice the scallions (a heaping ⅓ cup) and peel and Microplane-grate the ginger (about 1 tablespoon); transfer each to the bowl with the bell pepper as it is prepared. Press the garlic (about 1 teaspoon) into the bowl.

4. Drain, rinse, and thoroughly dry the cabbage; add it to the bell pepper mixture along with the vinegar mixture and stir until thoroughly combined. Pack the kimchi into a nonreactive bowl or jar, cover, and refrigerate until you are ready to use it. Kimchi will keep in the refrigerator for about 1 week.

MAKES ABOUT 2 CUPS ■ **HANDS-ON TIME: 10 MINUTES**
TOTAL PREPARATION TIME: 15 MINUTES

QUICKER KIMCHI: Drain, rinse, and thoroughly dry 1 cup sauerkraut. Prepare the recipe as above, substituting the sauerkraut for the salted cabbage with no standing time, and serve right away.

Dill Pickle Cucumber Slices Ⓥ

MAKES 1⅓ CUPS   HANDS-ON TIME: 10 MINUTES   TOTAL PREPARATION TIME: 10 MINUTES

Good old-fashioned pickling and canning scare me to death. All those Mason jars, the sterilization and special procedures—it seems to me there are just too many ways for some horrible bacteria to invade the process, and I'll end up killing someone. When I was on the Food Network, I agreed to a canning show exactly one time, and that was when we had an expert guest scheduled. Of course, the weather was terrible that day, and my guest's plane didn't even land until after the show ended. The only way I got through it was by enlisting the help of my viewers; somebody would call in with a question and another viewer would call in with the answer. Not one of my favorite shows.

Me, I'm a quick pickle gal. The cucumber pickles in this recipe take a mere 10 minutes to "cure," but they emerge just as sweet and sour and crunchy as you please. They'd be a superb accompaniment to Pulled Chicken Barbecue on Beer Bread (page 100) and Barbecued Salmon (page 216), but you may be tempted to put them on everything.

One 5- to 6-inch piece seedless (English) cucumber
2 tablespoons fresh dill leaves or 1 teaspoon dried
2 tablespoons cider vinegar
1½ teaspoons sugar
½ teaspoon kosher salt
⅛ teaspoon freshly ground black pepper

Thinly slice enough of the cucumber to make 1⅓ cups. Finely chop the dill (about 1 tablespoon). Combine the cucumber with the vinegar, dill, sugar, salt, and pepper in a small nonreactive bowl. Set it aside at room temperature and use within an hour, or cover and refrigerate for later use.

 Tomatillo Salsa Ⓥ

MAKES 1 CUP   HANDS-ON TIME: 10 MINUTES   TOTAL PREPARATION TIME: 10 MINUTES

Although both tomatoes and tomatillos come from Mexico, both fit the definition of the Aztec word *tomatl* (which means "plump thing with a navel"), and both belong to the same scientific family, the two fruits have very different tastes. The tomatillo has a pleasingly sour, faintly lemony flavor. It is a key ingredient in the Mexican green salsa that is often served alongside red (or tomato-based) salsa.

This recipe is the base of several of the recipes in this book, including Kimchi or Tomatillo Salsa Clams (page 222), Chicken and Tomatillo Salsa Nachos (page 302), and the Mexican Salmon Salad Sandwiches (page 116). It also works perfectly well on its own with a side of chips.

2 large tomatillos (about
   6 to 7 ounces)
2 medium scallions
1 small jalapeño chile
   (make sure it has
   heat; see page 6)
¼ cup firmly packed
   fresh cilantro leaves
   and stems
2 tablespoons
   vegetable oil
2 teaspoons fresh lime
   juice
2 small garlic cloves
¼ teaspoon kosher salt
Freshly ground black
   pepper

1. Remove the papery husk, rinse, and thickly slice the tomatillos (about 1½ cups). Trim and thickly slice the white and light green parts of the scallions (about ¼ cup) and coarsely chop the jalapeño (about 2 teaspoons). Transfer the tomatillos, scallions, jalapeño, and cilantro to a food processor fitted with the chopping blade. Add the vegetable oil and lime juice and press in the garlic (about 2 teaspoons).

2. Pulse until the mixture is finely chopped. Add the salt and pepper to taste. Transfer to a bowl; cover and refrigerate until ready to use. Or freeze in ¼-cup packages for later use.

 *B*asic Crêpes **V**

MAKES EIGHT TO TEN 8-INCH CRÊPES ■ **HANDS-ON TIME: 20 MINUTES** ■ **TOTAL PREPARATION TIME: 50 MINUTES**

Many Americans of a certain age (my mother-in-law, Esther Adler, for instance) first encountered crêpes at the 1939 World's Fair, where crêpes Suzette was one of the smash hits of the restaurant at the French Pavilion. What wasn't to love? This dessert had everything: great flavor and great theater. You took the paper-thin French pancake; doused it with a sauce of sugar, orange juice, lightly grated orange peel, and liqueur (usually Grand Marnier); served it in a chafing dish; and set it aflame at tableside. The alcohol quickly burned off, leaving the sauce caramelized. *Ummmm-hmm!* The whole concoction was so dazzlingly exotic that Esther probably didn't notice how similar the crêpe was to the Eastern European blintz, a wrapping far more familiar to her.

Although crêpes were old hat by the time I encountered them in cooking school, it wasn't easy to master them. Crêpes are delicate, and they tended to stick to the pan, which meant that you tended to butcher them in the process of removing them from the pan. The key, then, was to find a pan that was "well seasoned," which is another way of saying "permanently greasy." If you made crêpes and omelets every day, your pan would stay well seasoned. If, like me, you didn't make crêpes and omelets every day, you were in trouble.

Then one day progress arrived in the form of the nonstick pan. Yay! Now making crêpes is a breeze. So is freezing and then defrosting them at will. Indeed, a batch of crêpes in your freezer, along with a few items in your pantry or fridge, spells instant dinner. Crêpes, after all, are like omelets (or blintzes or burritos): an all-purpose wrapping into which you can stuff just about anything, savory or sweet, freshly made or left over.

By the way, when I was first making crêpes, I was taught to slip a piece of wax paper between the individual crêpes before I froze them so they wouldn't stick together. Jeez, it was tedious. Turns out, it's unnecessary. Go ahead and stack them; they don't stick together.

5 tablespoons unsalted
butter
1 cup whole milk
¾ cup unbleached all-
purpose flour
2 large eggs
¼ teaspoon table salt

1. Melt the butter; set aside 2 tablespoons and combine the remaining 3 tablespoons, the milk, flour, eggs, and salt in a blender. Blend until smooth. Transfer to a bowl, cover, and set aside at room temperature for 30 minutes.

2. Lightly brush a 10-inch crêpe pan with some of the reserved melted butter and heat over medium-high heat until hot but not smoking. Reduce the heat to medium.

3. Stir the batter and ladle a scant ¼ cup into the pan, tilting and rotating the pan until the batter coats the bottom. Cook for 30 to 45 seconds, or until the surface of the crêpe looks set and the bottom is barely golden. Turn the crêpe and cook for 30 seconds more on the second side.

4. Transfer the crêpes to a cooling rack as they are cooked. Once they are cool, stack them until you are ready to use them. Wrap and freeze any extra crêpes for later use.

can you substitute
LIGHTLY SALTED BUTTER FOR UNSALTED BUTTER?

Although most of the butter sold in the United States is lightly salted, pastry chefs tend to use unsalted butter because of its pure flavor and because it gives them complete control over the amount of salt in the recipe. Also, salt tends to cover up rancidity, so it is easier to tell how fresh the butter is if it isn't salted. However, there really isn't much salt in lightly salted butter. If you want to use salted butter in a recipe that calls for unsalted, just cut ¼ to ⅜ teaspoon of salt per stick (½ cup) of butter from the amount of salt called for in the recipe. I'd say not to bother to adjust the salt if you are just using a few tablespoons of butter, but do if you are using a stick or more. By the way, it is important to have some salt in sweet recipes to balance the flavors.

$\mathcal{B}$asic Pizza Dough Ⓥ

This is one of those recipes for which the lickety-split hands-on time necessary to make the dough should outweigh the relatively lengthy amount of time it takes for the dough to rise. Just remember that at the end of it all, you'll have an absolutely delicious homemade pizza.

Exactly how much time passes from the moment you start to measure the ingredients to make the dough until the moment you put the ball of dough into an oiled bowl? Six minutes. Incredible, but true. The dough then needs 40 to 45 minutes to rise, but you'll use at least part of that time to make your toppings. You may even have time left over to read the newspaper. I'm telling you, this one's a snap.

2 to 2½ cups unbleached all-purpose flour
One 1¼-ounce envelope quick-rising yeast
1 teaspoon sugar
1 teaspoon table salt
¾ cup very warm water (120° to 130°F)
1 tablespoon extra virgin olive oil plus more for oiling the bowl

1. Combine 1¾ cups flour, the yeast, sugar, and salt in the bowl of a food processor fitted with the chopping blade; pulse until well blended. Add the warm water and 1 tablespoon olive oil. Process the mixture until it forms a ball, adding more flour, as needed, to make a soft but not sticky dough.

2. Shape the dough into a ball and place it in an oiled medium bowl. Turn the dough to make sure all sides are very lightly coated with oil. Cover the bowl with plastic wrap and set it aside in a warm place until the dough is double in size, 40 to 45 minutes.

3. When the dough has risen, roll out, top, and bake it as directed in the recipe you are using.

YEAST PRIMER

Fresh yeast was used through the middle of the twentieth century, and it is still available in some supermarkets; look for it in the dairy section near the butter. It is less available these days because it has a relatively short shelf life. Active dry yeast was the first convenient yeast on the market. If you're substituting active dry yeast for fresh, sprinkle it over the same amount of liquid used in a recipe that calls for fresh yeast, but make the liquid slightly warmer (100° to 110°F). Set the mixture aside for about 10 minutes. Follow the rest of the recipe as it is written, but you might find that you need to add a bit less flour because the fresh yeast contains a little water. Quick yeast is the easiest form of yeast to use. Just stir it into the flour mixture in the recipe and add liquid that is between 120° and 130°F. The rising times can be reduced by about half, depending upon the warmth of the rising location. If you have a recipe that was written for fresh yeast, the conversion is very easy. One ¼-ounce packet of active dry yeast or of quick yeast is formulated to equal one .6-ounce cake of fresh or compressed yeast.

$\mathcal{B}$asic Butter Pastry with Variations Ⓥ

MAKES ENOUGH PASTRY FOR TWO 9-INCH PIE SHELLS OR 1 DOUBLE-CRUST PIE
HANDS-ON TIME: 20 MINUTES   TOTAL PREPARATION TIME: 20 MINUTES

If, like me, you are pastry impaired, this is the dough for you because you just mix all of the ingredients very quickly in a food processor. It is used in several of the recipes in this book: Joanne's New-and-Improved Blueberry Tart (page 342), Raspberry Almond Ruge-lach (page 347), and the Rustic Potato and Greens Pie (page 229).

2 cups unbleached all-purpose flour
½ teaspoon table salt
12 tablespoons (1½ sticks) cold unsalted butter
2 large egg yolks

1. Combine the flour and salt in the bowl of a food processor fitted with the chopping blade. Cut the butter into ⅛-inch-thick slices and add to the flour mixture. Pulse 10 to 12 times, until the mixture resembles coarse crumbs.

2. Beat the yolks with 2 tablespoons ice water and add to the mixture; pulse 4 to 5 times, until a crumbly mixture forms. Press the mixture together to form a ball, adding more water, if necessary, to make it manageable.

3. You can immediately roll out the dough between lightly floured sheets of plastic wrap or, if you have the time, chill the dough for 1 hour before rolling it out. That allows the gluten in the flour to relax, ensuring a tender crust.

4. Use the pastry as directed in a recipe or divide it in half, shape it into balls, and flatten slightly. Wrap the flattened rounds tightly in freezer wrap and freeze until firm for later use. Use within 3 months.

SWEET VARIATION: Add ¼ cup sugar to the flour mixture and ½ to 1 teaspoon pure vanilla or almond extract to the egg mixture.

SAVORY VARIATION: Add ½ teaspoon dried basil, oregano, thyme, dill, or your favorite dried herb mixture to the flour mixture.

$\mathcal{H}$omemade Baked Tortilla Chips Ⓥ

MAKES 64 TORTILLA CHIPS, 4 SERVINGS ■ HANDS-ON TIME: 10 MINUTES ■
TOTAL PREPARATION TIME: 20 MINUTES

Everyone loves fried tortilla chips. Like potato chips, they're crispy and salty and full of flavor from the frying oil. But like potato chips, fried tortilla chips are pretty caloric. Baked tortilla chips are less caloric, but they're also flavorless and sawdust-y.

So I spent some time in the "lab" and came up with a recipe that boasts the appeal of both versions: the spice and oil of the fried tortilla chip and the healthfulness of the baked tortilla chip. They're also so easy to make that you may find yourself doing so all the time. "Bet you can't eat just one."

2 tablespoons
    vegetable oil
1 teaspoon ground
    cumin
1 teaspoon chili powder
½ teaspoon kosher salt
Eight 6-inch corn
    tortillas

1. Place an oven rack in the middle of the oven and preheat the oven to 400°F.

2. Combine the vegetable oil, cumin, chili powder, and salt in a small bowl and whisk until the salt has dissolved. Brush one side of each tortilla with the oil mixture; cut each tortilla into 8 wedges.

3. Arrange the tortilla wedges in one layer on 1 or 2 rimmed baking sheets. Bake for 10 to 12 minutes, or until crisp and golden. (If you need 2 baking sheets and both don't fit on one shelf, switch the sheets midway through baking.) Set aside to cool slightly.

$\mathscr{S}$ara's Hard-Cooked Eggs Ⓥ

HANDS-ON TIME: 5 MINUTES   TOTAL PREPARATION TIME: 18 MINUTES

This is my streamlined version of Julia Child's foolproof method of hard-cooking (hard-boiling) eggs. Julia figured out that the way to hard-boil an egg is to stop short of actually boiling it. Boil it, and all you'll do is guarantee that the thing ends up damn near as hard and rubbery as a hockey puck.

Instead, you start the eggs in cold water, bring them almost to a boil, pull them off the heat, and then cover and set them aside to finish cooking in the hot water. Finally, you plunge them into ice water and let them cool completely before peeling, a little trick that eliminates the nasty green line that would otherwise appear between the whites and the yolk.

Do it this way and you'll turn out perfect hard-cooked eggs every time.

Large eggs, at room
temperature

1. Place the desired number of eggs in a saucepan large enough for them to fit in a single layer and add enough cold water to cover them by 2 inches. Bring the water to a boil over medium heat.

2. Remove the saucepan from the heat, cover it, and set it aside for 13 minutes. Transfer the eggs to a bowl of half ice and half water. Let cool completely, peel, then refrigerate or use as directed in a recipe.

$\mathcal{C}$an't Overcook 'Em Chicken Breasts

MAKES 4 SERVINGS   HANDS-ON TIME: 3 MINUTES   TOTAL PREPARATION TIME: 20 TO 25 MINUTES

I'm asked this question over and over again: "Why do my chicken breasts turn out so dry?" The answer? You overcooked them. But this simple answer masks a tough problem. Salmonella is present in a huge percentage of raw chicken, including organic chicken. The only way to kill it is by cooking your chicken until it is well done. Unfortunately, it's a thin line between well done and overdone.

If you poach your chicken breasts briefly, turn off the heat, cover, and then leave the breasts in the pan to finish cooking, they will turn out moist and tender every time; plus, you'll be left with a broth to use in other recipes. Follow this recipe exactly and you can't go wrong.

3 cups Homemade Chicken Stock (page 10, add preparation time) or canned broth
1 to 1½ pounds boneless, skinless chicken breast halves

1. Bring the chicken stock to a boil over high heat in a saucepan just large enough to hold the chicken breasts in one layer; add the chicken breasts, making sure they are covered by the chicken stock. Simmer them very gently, uncovered, for 7 minutes. Remove the pan from the heat, cover it, and let it stand for 10 minutes.

2. Remove 1 chicken breast to a plate and cut into the center to make sure the breast is cooked through. If it is, remove the remaining breasts to the plate. If it is not, return it to the saucepan, cover the pan, and simmer it for 2 minutes more, then remove the chicken to the plate and set it aside to cool. Reserve the chicken stock for another use. After the chicken has cooled slightly, use it as directed in a recipe.

2
EGG-STRA SPECIALS

Like most of us, I used to think of eggs as breakfast food. These days, when I really have no time to make dinner, the first thing I reach for is a carton of eggs. Eggs are inexpensive, fast cooking, and nutritious, and they can more than hold their own as the star attraction in the center of your plate.

I know, of course, that the food police have been demonizing eggs for a generation. They told us that the cholesterol in eggs raised our blood cholesterol. (Now they tell us that the villain isn't so much cholesterol, but saturated fat.)

Me, I tend to side with the American Egg Board. Their Web site quotes a report concluding that "eating one or more eggs a day [does] not increase the risk of heart disease or stroke among healthy adults, and that eating eggs may be associated with a decrease in blood pressure." They further note that "one egg has 13 essential nutrients in varying amounts for only 75 calories" and that eggs "play a [positive] role in weight management, muscle strength, healthy pregnancy, brain function, eye health, and more."

Worried about salmonella? Although only one egg in twenty thousand is contaminated, high-risk groups such as the elderly, children under five, and the immune impaired should eat their eggs well done. The rest of us are good to go. Eggs are a global ingredient, and the recipes in this chapter incorporate any number of tasty international influences.

FACING PAGE: *Indian Scrambled Eggs.*

$\mathcal{P}$oached Eggs on Cheesy Grits with Corn

MAKES 4 SERVINGS ■ HANDS-ON TIME: 20 MINUTES ■ TOTAL PREPARATION TIME: 20 MINUTES

Poaching eggs can be an ordeal. I was taught the following method:

1. Bring a pot of water with a hefty amount of vinegar to a bare simmer. (The vinegar is there to help the egg whites set up.)
2. Create a whirlpool in the water by frantically twirling around a spoon in it.
3. Crack a raw egg into the center of the whirlpool to get the white to wrap neatly around the yolk.
4. Cook the egg to the desired degree of doneness, making sure that the water never comes to a boil, which would break up that damned white.

The method above requires skill, coordination, and supernatural patience. It takes time to create the perfect whirlpool for each egg. Sometimes the whirlpool peters out before you place the egg exactly in its center. Sometimes you miss the center, and the whirlpool scatters your white in the water instead of making it circle the yolk. That's how I always did it until this cute Australian chef named Bill Granger—aka the "egg master of Sydney"—visited my show one day and showed me something new.

Here's Bill's method:

1. Bring a pot of water to a boil. (What, no vinegar?)
2. Turn off the heat, add the eggs, cover, and leave them there until they're cooked to the desired degree of doneness.

I didn't believe it. Way too simple. But it works. So now I poach eggs the cute Australian chef way.

I decided to combine the poached eggs with grits, a bit of cheese, and some fresh summer corn. If you have time on your hands and some stone-ground grits, cook up those instead of the quick-cooking variety. If it's winter, use frozen corn instead of fresh.

1 small onion
3 ounces Canadian
    bacon
1 tablespoon
    vegetable oil
1¼ cups whole milk
Kosher salt and freshly
    ground black pepper
½ cup quick-cooking
    grits
1 large ear fresh corn
2 ounces sharp Cheddar
    cheese
2 tablespoons fresh flat-
    leaf parsley leaves
8 large eggs

1. Finely chop the onion (about ½ cup) and the bacon (about ½ cup). Heat the vegetable oil in a heavy 2-quart saucepan over medium heat until hot; add the bacon and cook for 3 minutes. Reduce the heat to medium-low; add the onion and cook for 5 minutes, or until softened.

2. Add the milk, ¾ cup water, ½ teaspoon salt, and ¼ teaspoon pepper to the onion mixture and bring to a boil over high heat. Very gradually whisk in the grits. Reduce the heat to low, cover, and simmer gently for 5 minutes.

3. Meanwhile, cut the kernels from the corn (about 1 cup), coarsely grate the cheese (about ½ cup), and chop the parsley (about 1 tablespoon).

4. Bring 4 inches salted water to a boil in a large saucepan over high heat. When the water has come to a boil, turn off the heat. Crack the eggs, one at a time, into a cup or ramekin and add each egg quickly to the water. Cover the saucepan and set it aside for 4 to 5 minutes, or until the egg whites are just cooked and the yolks are a bit runny. Lift the eggs from the water with a slotted spoon and drain them well.

5. When the grits have cooked, stir in the corn and cheese. Heat just until the cheese melts. Divide the grits among 4 soup plates; top each with 2 poached eggs and a sprinkle of parsley.

$\mathcal{J}$ndian Scrambled Eggs with Pappadams Ⓥ

MAKES 4 SERVINGS   HANDS-ON TIME: 20 MINUTES   TOTAL PREPARATION TIME: 20 MINUTES

My favorite eggs are poached or fried (I love those runny yolks), but scrambled eggs are a close second, as long as they're properly cooked. The right way to do it is slowly and at a very low temperature; this guarantees the eggs' creaminess, but it also requires a measure of Zen-like patience. Properly scrambled eggs constitute the entirety of my dad's culinary repertoire. He takes his time cooking them up for the whole family on Christmas morning and drives us nuts in the process, because no one's allowed to open presents until after we eat.

What's so Indian about these scrambled eggs? The flavorings—chile, ginger, cumin, turmeric, and cilantro—and the pappadams. Pappadam is an East Indian bread made with lentil flour: wide as a good-size pancake, but thin, crispy, and flavorful as a potato chip. Usually, pappadams are deep-fried, but I figured out that you can sauté them in much less oil, cutting way down on their calories while maintaining their crispiness.

If you can't find pappadams locally and don't want to order them online (see Sources, page 359), you can substitute pita crisps. Just take some pitas, split them crosswise, brush them with a little vegetable oil, sprinkle on some salt, and bake them at 400°F for 5 minutes, or until golden and, yes, crispy.

¼ cup vegetable oil
Four 8-inch pappadams
½ small onion
One 1-inch piece fresh ginger
3 tablespoons unsalted butter
1 large serrano chile
¾ teaspoon ground cumin
½ teaspoon ground turmeric
8 large eggs
⅓ cup plain low-fat or full-fat Greek-style yogurt (see page 49)
Kosher salt
½ pound plum tomatoes (about 2 medium)
½ cup fresh cilantro or basil leaves
Freshly ground black pepper

1. Heat 1 tablespoon vegetable oil in a large heavy skillet over medium-high heat until hot; add 1 pappadam, press it down with a metal spatula, and sauté for about 30 seconds, or until it begins to brown and puff slightly. Turn the pappadam and repeat the procedure for about 30 seconds more, until it is bubbly and opaque. Transfer to a plate and repeat with the remaining pappadams, adding vegetable oil as needed.

2. Finely chop the onion (about ¼ cup) and peel and Microplane-grate the ginger (about 1 teaspoon). Heat the butter in a medium skillet over medium heat until hot. Reduce the heat to medium-low; add the onion and ginger and cook for 5 minutes, or until the onion has softened. Finely chop the chile (about 1 tablespoon). Add the chile, cumin, and turmeric; cook, stirring, for 1 minute.

3. Lightly beat the eggs with the yogurt and ½ teaspoon salt; reduce the heat to low. Add the eggs to the onion mixture and cook, stirring frequently, until the eggs are creamy and just set, about 12 minutes.

4. Meanwhile, seed and finely chop the tomatoes (about 1 cup). Chop the cilantro (about ¼ cup). Stir in the cilantro, tomatoes, and salt and pepper to taste. Mound one-quarter of the scrambled eggs onto each pappadam and serve.

$\mathcal{B}$reakfast for Dinner Pizza

MAKES 4 SERVINGS ■ **HANDS-ON TIME: 20 MINUTES** ■ **TOTAL PREPARATION TIME: 65 MINUTES**

Years ago, when *Gourmet* ran a recipe for potato and rosemary pizza, it seemed so odd to me. Potato on bread? Then I tasted it. It worked perfectly, sort of like The Husband's idea of the perfect sandwich: stuffing and gravy on a kaiser roll. (Actually, potato pizza is not uncommon in Italy, so I shouldn't have been a doubter.) Think of this recipe as a natural extension of the potato pizza. Add eggs and bacon and voilà—breakfast for dinner pizza.

You might worry that it'll take too long to make pizza dough from scratch when you're trying to get dinner on the table. I've streamlined the process by mixing the dough in a food processor (so for all you nonbakers that means, hooray, no kneading!) and using quick-rising yeast. I made it exactly this way on my public television show, *Sara's Weeknight Meals,* one night, and it took me just six minutes from start to finish, including measuring all the ingredients. Indeed, this is the kind of recipe you can decide to make at the last minute because you probably already have all the ingredients in the house.

Note: Please read important pizza-making tricks (see headnote, page 191).

Basic Pizza Dough (page 26, add preparation time) or use store-bought dough
1 tablespoon cornmeal
1 pound boiling potatoes, such as Yukon gold or Red Bliss
1 tablespoon extra virgin olive oil, plus more for oiling the pan and rolling out the dough
Kosher salt and freshly ground black pepper
6 ounces bacon

1. Prepare the Basic Pizza Dough or take the store-bought dough out of the fridge. Place a rack in the bottom of the oven and preheat the oven to 500°F. Sprinkle the cornmeal onto a 14-inch round pizza pan or a baking sheet.

2. While the dough is rising, scrub and thinly slice the potatoes. Heat 1 tablespoon olive oil in a large skillet over high heat until hot. Add the potatoes, sprinkle them with salt and pepper, and reduce the heat to medium-low. Cover the skillet and cook until the potatoes are just tender, turning them several times, about 12 to 15 minutes. Transfer the potatoes to a bowl and set aside.

3. Quarter the bacon strips crosswise and add them to the same skillet. Cook over medium heat, turning occasionally, until the bacon is firm and just beginning to brown but is slightly undercooked, 5 to 7 minutes. Remove it to paper towels to drain.

4. Meanwhile, coarsely grate the cheese (about 1 cup) and chop the rosemary (about 1 teaspoon).

4 ounces Gruyère
cheese
2 teaspoons fresh
rosemary leaves or
½ teaspoon dried
1 tablespoon extra virgin
olive oil
4 large eggs

5. Roll out the dough on a lightly oiled surface to a ⅛ inch thickness in the shape of the pan you are using. Transfer the dough to the pan and pat it out until it fits. Bake on the bottom rack of the oven for 3 minutes, or until set but not browned. Let the crust cool for 5 minutes before topping.

6. Arrange the potatoes on the crust and sprinkle with the cheese, bacon, and rosemary. Bake on the bottom rack of the oven for 8 to 10 minutes, or until the cheese has melted and the crust is well browned.

7. Meanwhile, heat the olive oil in a large skillet. Crack the eggs, one at a time, into a small cup or ramekin and pour each egg into the pan. Season with salt and pepper to taste. Cook until the eggs are almost done, 2 to 3 minutes. Flip them over easy and cook for 1 minute more.

8. When the pizza has baked, cut it into quarters and transfer the quarters to 4 large dinner plates. Top each piece of pizza with a fried egg and serve.

$\mathcal{F}$ried Eggs with Crispy Kimchi Rice

MAKES 4 SERVINGS ▪ **HANDS-ON TIME: 20 MINUTES** ▪ **TOTAL PREPARATION TIME: 20 MINUTES**

This dish takes a tip from the people of Asia, who often eat rice in some form for breakfast. And why not? How big a leap is it for us, whose breakfasts can include bread, cereal, or potatoes? All I've done here is place an egg or two on some panfried rice flavored with kimchi, the garlicky cabbage pickle from Korea. I suggest beefing it up with Canadian bacon, but you're welcome to substitute prosciutto or regular bacon, or leave it out altogether.

4 ounces Canadian bacon
3 tablespoons vegetable oil
1 cup Quick or Quicker Kimchi (page 21, add preparation time) or store-bought kimchi
2 cups cooked short-grain white rice
2 tablespoons unseasoned rice vinegar
1 tablespoon unsalted butter
4 large eggs (see Note)
Kosher salt and freshly ground black pepper
⅓ cup fresh cilantro, basil, or mint leaves
2 medium scallions

1. Medium chop the Canadian bacon (about a scant cup). Heat 1 tablespoon vegetable oil in a 10-inch nonstick skillet over medium heat until hot. Add the Canadian bacon and cook until it begins to brown, about 2 minutes. While the bacon is cooking, coarsely chop the kimchi. Remove the bacon to a medium bowl, setting aside the skillet and any fat remaining in it. Add the kimchi, rice, and rice vinegar to the bacon in the bowl; stir with a fork until combined, separating any lumps of rice.

2. Add 1 tablespoon vegetable oil to the skillet and heat over medium heat until hot. Add the rice mixture and press firmly to fill the skillet. Cook until golden on the bottom, 3 to 5 minutes. Invert the rice cake onto an oiled flat baking sheet or large lid. Add the remaining 1 tablespoon oil to the skillet and slide the rice cake, browned side up, back into the skillet. Cook the rice cake until it is golden on the bottom, 3 to 5 minutes; invert it onto a plate and keep warm.

3. Heat the butter in a large skillet. Crack the eggs, one at a time, into a small cup or ramekin and pour each egg into the pan. Season with salt and pepper to taste. Cook until the eggs are almost done, 3 to 5 minutes. Flip them over easy and cook for 1 minute more.

4. Coarsely chop the cilantro (about 3 tablespoons) and scallions (about ¼ cup). Cut the rice cake into quarters and transfer the quarters to 4 large dinner plates. Top each with an egg. Sprinkle with the cilantro and scallions and serve.

NOTE: If desired, double the number of eggs and use 2 for each serving.

Toad-in-the-Hole Italiano

MAKES 4 SERVINGS   HANDS-ON TIME: 30 MINUTES   TOTAL PREPARATION TIME: 60 MINUTES

Say what you will about traditional British cuisine, you can't accuse the Brits themselves of being snobby about it. On the contrary, they're very funny. Name another country that festoons its traditional dishes with names like bubble and squeak, deviled bones, spotted dick, cock-a-leekie soup, clouty dumplings, and toad-in-the-hole.

Toad-in-the-hole is so dubbed because some comedian, squinting at a casserole of sausages covered in the same pancakelike batter as is used for popovers, thought it resembled a gang of toads sticking their little heads out of a hole. Whether he then proceeded to dig in with knife and fork is a mystery lost to time.

In fact, it tastes much better than it sounds. In this version, I've swapped an Italian sausage for the English variety used in a traditional recipe, and bulked up the recipe with bell peppers and cheese to make it more of a one-dish meal.

¼ cup extra virgin olive oil

1¼ pounds sweet or hot Italian sausages or a mixture

1 medium red bell pepper

1 medium green bell pepper

1½ ounces Parmigiano-Reggiano

Kosher salt and freshly ground black pepper

1 tablespoon fresh oregano leaves or ½ teaspoon dried

4 garlic cloves

1 cup unbleached all-purpose flour

2 large eggs

¾ cup whole milk

1. Preheat the oven to 375°F. Heat 1 tablespoon olive oil in a large skillet with an ovenproof handle over medium heat until hot. Add the sausages and cook until browned, about 5 to 7 minutes. Meanwhile, slice the red and green bell peppers (about 1 cup each). Microplane-grate the cheese (about 1 cup) or grate on the fine side of a box grater (about ½ cup) and chop the oregano (about 1½ teaspoons).

2. Remove the sausages to a plate and let cool; reserve the drippings in the skillet. Add 1 tablespoon olive oil, the bell peppers, and ½ teaspoon salt and cook, stirring, for 3 minutes. Press in the garlic (about 1 tablespoon plus 1 teaspoon); cook for 1 minute more. Cut the sausages into 1-inch chunks and stir into the mixture.

3. Combine the flour, cheese, oregano, ½ teaspoon salt, and ¼ teaspoon black pepper in a medium bowl. Whisk the eggs in a large glass measuring cup until frothy; whisk in the milk, ⅓ cup water, and the remaining 2 tablespoons olive oil. Gradually whisk the milk mixture into the flour mixture just until the batter is combined. It can still be slightly lumpy.

4. Pour the batter over the sausage mixture and bake until puffed and golden, 30 to 40 minutes. Serve immediately.

Open-Faced Zucchini Omelet with Tomato Sauce and Feta (V)

MAKES 4 TO 6 SERVINGS ▪ HANDS-ON TIME: 30 MINUTES ▪ TOTAL PREPARATION TIME: 35 MINUTES

For someone who doesn't like zucchini very much, I find myself using them in all sorts of recipes. What's wrong with zucchini? They're watery and boring. That's not even to talk about what a drag they are before they get to the dinner table. I feel about the zucchini grown in the garden on our family farm the way that Lucille Ball felt about those candies on the conveyor belt: They're endless, they keep on coming, and, ultimately, they will defeat you. But at least Lucy had the pleasure of stuffing the overflow into her mouth. Zucchini are like B-movie mutants. One day they're sweet little four-inch babies, the next they're ten-pound zeppelins, and we're hauling them straight from the garden to the compost heap.

Actually, I figured out how to redeem that humble squash a while ago. Grate and salt it, squeeze out the excess water, and sauté it. Voilà! You've concentrated the flavor, and it's sweet and delicious, which is why in this omelet zucchini stars with two of its best friends, tomato sauce and feta cheese.

½ recipe Quick Tomato Sauce (page 14, add preparation time) or 1½ cups store-bought sauce
3 medium zucchini (about 1 pound)
Kosher salt
1 medium onion
¼ cup extra virgin olive oil
10 large eggs
½ teaspoon freshly grated lemon zest
1 teaspoon fresh lemon juice
¼ teaspoon freshly ground black pepper
4 ounces feta cheese
¼ cup fresh dill or basil leaves

1. Start preparing the Quick Tomato Sauce, if using.

2. Coarsely grate the zucchini using the shredding disc of a food processor or the coarse side of a box grater (about 5 cups). Toss the zucchini with 1¼ teaspoons salt; transfer to a colander placed over a bowl and set aside to drain for 15 minutes.

3. Meanwhile, finely chop the onion (about 1 cup). Heat 2 tablespoons olive oil in a large nonstick skillet with an ovenproof handle over medium heat until hot. Add the onion and cook until golden, about 5 minutes.

4. Using your hands, gently but firmly squeeze the zucchini mixture to get out as much moisture as possible. Stir the zucchini into the onion and cook until hot, about 2 minutes.

5. Preheat the oven to 350°F. Beat the eggs lightly in a large bowl, adding the lemon zest and lemon juice, ½ teaspoon salt, and the pepper. Heat the store-bought tomato sauce, if using.

6. Add the egg mixture to the zucchini mixture and cook, lifting up the edges of the omelet to let uncooked egg mixture flow underneath until the omelet is mostly set, 4 to 5 minutes. Finely crumble the feta (about 1 cup) and sprinkle it over the omelet. Transfer the omelet to the oven; bake it for about 5 minutes, or until the top is just set. Finely chop the dill (about 2 tablespoons).

7. To serve, cut the omelet into quarters or sixths and transfer the pieces to large dinner plates. Top each portion with some of the tomato sauce and the dill. Pass any remaining sauce.

what is FETA CHEESE?

Feta cheese is a curd cheese that is pressed into a cake, sliced (the name *feta* comes from the Greek word for "slices" or "pieces"), salted, and set to age in a 7 percent solution of salt and either water or whey. That is about all the many fetas on the market have in common. Whether feta arrives in your market still protected by the liquid it aged in, vacuum packed, or both is determined by the producer and doesn't have a lot to do with quality. However, once the package is opened, drained feta will dry out quickly and will attract mold faster than that packed in liquid.

In addition to differences in the way it is packaged, there are great differences in the flavor of feta cheeses, depending upon the type of milk used, the length of aging, and the country of origin. Originally, feta was made from sheep's milk and goat's milk in countries bordering the eastern Mediterranean; when it comes from those areas, it usually still is. Today it is also made from cow's milk in northern Europe and the United States.

Eggs and Creamed Spinach in Phyllo Cups ⓥ

MAKES 4 SERVINGS   HANDS-ON TIME: 25 MINUTES   TOTAL PREPARATION TIME: 45 MINUTES

Flaky little phyllo cups are a great container for almost any ingredient, but they're just perfect for creamed spinach and softly poached eggs brushed with herb butter. "Wait a minute," you say? "Working with phyllo dough is just too tricky." It doesn't have to be. If you make a point of keeping it covered with plastic at all times, so that it doesn't dry out, the phyllo will do just what you want it to do.

You can find phyllo dough in the frozen food section of most supermarkets. If you defrost it overnight in the fridge, it's good to go the next day. After you've taken out the three sheets called for in this recipe, you can rewrap and refreeze the rest.

All sorts of other fillings would work well with this recipe, including sautéed mushrooms or leeks. Why not try mozzarella or Cheddar instead of Gruyère, and scrambled eggs instead of poached?

2 tablespoons Herb Butter (preferably with dill; page 19, add preparation time) or salted butter
Three 16 x 12-inch phyllo dough sheets
1 small onion
2 tablespoons extra virgin olive oil
4 ounces baby spinach (about 6 cups, packed)
2 ounces ⅓-less-fat cream cheese (Neufchâtel)
¼ cup fresh dill leaves
Kosher salt and freshly ground black pepper
8 large eggs
2 ounces Gruyère cheese

1. Preheat the oven to 350°F. Melt the Herb Butter.

2. Place 1 sheet of phyllo on a work surface and brush the sheet with melted butter; top it with 2 more sheets, brushing each with butter. Cut the stack of sheets into four 4-inch strips; cut each strip in half. Fold over enough of each piece to make it a 4-inch square.

3. Brush 8 large muffin pan cups with any remaining butter. Ease the phyllo squares gently into the cups and press to fit. Bake the phyllo cups for 6 to 8 minutes, or until they are golden and crisp. Carefully remove the pan to a cooling rack and set aside to cool.

4. Finely chop the onion (about ½ cup). Heat the olive oil in a large skillet over medium heat until hot; add the onion and cook until golden, about 7 minutes.

5. Turn the heat up to medium-high, add the spinach to the skillet, and cook until it has wilted, 2 to 3 minutes; stir in the Neufchâtel and cook, stirring, until it melts. Chop the dill (about 2 tablespoons). Add the dill and salt and pepper to taste.

6. Meanwhile, bring 4 inches salted water to a boil in a large saucepan over high heat. When the water has come to a boil, turn off the heat. Crack the eggs, one at a time, into a cup or ramekin and add each egg quickly to the water. Cover the saucepan and set it aside for 4 to 5 minutes, or until the egg whites are just cooked and the yolks are a bit runny. Lift the eggs from the water with a slotted spoon and drain them well. Coarsely grate the Gruyère (about ½ cup).

7. Place 2 phyllo cups on each of 4 plates; spoon one-eighth of the spinach mixture into each of the phyllo cups. Top each with one-eighth of the Gruyère and a poached egg.

$\mathcal{I}$ndividual Huevos Rancheros Ⓥ

MAKES 4 SERVINGS   HANDS-ON TIME: 15 MINUTES   TOTAL PREPARATION TIME: 25 MINUTES

With all the huevos rancheros recipes in the world, why did I have to include one in this book? It's just that I love this combination of flavors so much that I had to help spread the word. What makes mine different? The eggs are poached in salsa, a method that is faster and lighter than the traditional. The refried beans are cooked in vegetable oil (with onion and spices) instead of lard, which makes them less caloric but no less tasty. Finally, everybody gets his or her own personal huevos rancheros on 2 tortillas.

1 small onion
1½ tablespoons
    vegetable oil
1 teaspoon ground
    cumin
½ teaspoon chili powder
One 15½-ounce can
    pinto beans
Kosher salt and freshly
    ground black pepper
4 ounces pepper Jack
    cheese
Eight 6-inch corn
    tortillas
One 16-ounce jar
    prepared salsa
8 large eggs
1 ripe Hass avocado
1 tablespoon fresh lime
    juice

1. Preheat the oven to 375°F. Coarsely chop the onion (about ½ cup). Heat ½ tablespoon vegetable oil in a large skillet over medium heat until hot. Reduce the heat to medium-low; add the onion and cook for 5 minutes, or until it has softened. Add the cumin and chili powder and cook for 1 minute.

2. Rinse and drain the pinto beans; add them to the onion mixture along with ½ cup water. Cook, covered, for 5 minutes, or until most of the water has evaporated. Remove from the heat and mash the beans with a potato masher or fork until they are smooth, with some lumps; add salt and pepper to taste.

3. Coarsely grate the cheese (about 1 cup). Brush both sides of each tortilla with the remaining 1 tablespoon vegetable oil; arrange the tortillas on two unrimmed baking sheets. Toast in the oven until the edges begin to brown, about 8 minutes. Divide the refried beans among the tortillas; reserve the skillet. Spread the beans to within ¼ inch of the edges of each tortilla. Divide the cheese among the tortillas and bake until the cheese melts, about 4 minutes.

4. Meanwhile, add the salsa to the skillet in which the beans were cooked and bring it to a boil. Remove the skillet from the heat and make 8 shallow wells in the salsa with the back of a spoon; crack the eggs, one at a time, into a cup or ramekin and pour each egg into a well. Season the eggs with salt and pepper, cover the skillet, and cook over medium heat until the eggs reach the desired doneness, 5 to 7 minutes.

5. To serve, place 2 tortillas on each plate; top each tortilla with an egg and some of the salsa. Quarter, seed, and peel the avocado. Cut each quarter into 6 slices, brush the slices with the lime juice, and arrange them on the eggs.

RIPENING A HASS AVOCADO

Did you know that avocados don't start to ripen until they are picked? That means they should be on their way to perfection by the time they arrive in your market, and some markets these days will have a separate display of those that are ready to use. If you want to use it right away, it should feel firm, yet give slightly when pressed. To speed up ripening, place a firm avocado in a paper bag with a banana or an apple and store at room temperature. It should be ripe in several days. If you aren't ready to use it when it reaches the ripeness you want, refrigerate it and the ripening process will slow down.

In Florida and the Caribbean, growers raise large, shiny, medium green avocados that are lower in fat, and the natives just love them. However, most chefs will go out of their way to find a Hass avocado because its higher fat content brings with it a more robust flavor.

Turkish Poached Eggs with Yogurt and Sage Oil

MAKES 4 SERVINGS · HANDS-ON TIME: 10 MINUTES · TOTAL PREPARATION TIME: 20 MINUTES

I was researching paprika on the Web when I came across a recipe for Turkish poached eggs. I was intrigued. I'd never heard of this dish, but all sorts of folks were weighing in with their versions of it. It looked so simple that I couldn't imagine what all the fuss was about.

Until I tried it. This is a classic less-is-more recipe. The garlicky yogurt and egg match up beautifully with the oil or butter flavored with sage, crushed red pepper flakes, and, yes, paprika. It's cool and hot, creamy and sour and crispy. Prep-wise, this dish is simple. Flavor-wise, it's satisfyingly complex.

1⅓ cups plain low-fat or full-fat Greek-style yogurt (see page 49)
½ to 1 garlic clove
Kosher salt
¼ cup extra virgin olive oil or 4 tablespoons (½ stick) unsalted butter
8 large fresh sage leaves
1 teaspoon plain or smoked sweet paprika
¼ teaspoon crushed red pepper flakes
8 large eggs
Toasted whole grain bread slices

1. Bring 4 inches salted water to a boil in a large saucepan over high heat to poach the eggs. Place the yogurt in a small skillet. Press the garlic (½ to 1 teaspoon) into the yogurt and add salt to taste; heat over very low heat for about 1 minute, or until barely warm. Do not overheat or the yogurt will curdle.

2. Meanwhile, heat the olive oil in a small deep saucepan until hot. Add the sage a few leaves at a time (the oil will bubble up) and fry for about 10 seconds, or until they are crispy. Transfer the sage leaves to paper towels to drain. Remove the pan from the heat, let the oil cool slightly, and stir in the paprika, red pepper flakes, and a pinch of salt.

3. When the water has come to a boil, turn off the heat. Crack the eggs, one at a time, into a cup or ramekin and add each egg quickly to the water. Cover the saucepan and set aside for 4 to 5 minutes, or until the egg whites are just cooked and the yolks are a bit runny. Lift the eggs from the water with a slotted spoon and drain well.

4. To serve, divide the warmed yogurt among 4 shallow soup bowls. Place 2 poached eggs on top of the yogurt in each bowl. Pour the hot sage oil over the eggs, top with the fried sage leaves, and serve with the toasted bread.

what is GREEK-STYLE YOGURT?

These days most supermarkets carry Greek-style strained yogurt as well as the regular yogurt; one brand I like is called Fage. Greek-style yogurt is much thicker in texture than your usual supermarket varieties and even the no-fat version is delicious. (I know I usually say no fat, no flavor. I am contradicting myself, but in this case no fat *does* have flavor.) If you can't find Greek yogurt, you can simulate your own: Purchase about one-third more regular yogurt than the amount of Greek yogurt called for in the recipe and allow it to drain in a coffee filter–lined strainer in the refrigerator for about 4 hours, or until it has reduced to the necessary amount. For example, drain 1 cup regular yogurt to get ⅔ cup or 3 cups regular yogurt to get 2 cups.

Fried Eggs with Warm Lentils and Roasted-Tomato Vinaigrette

MAKES 4 SERVINGS ■ HANDS-ON TIME: 30 MINUTES ■ TOTAL PREPARATION TIME: 50 MINUTES

Left to my own devices, I'm tempted to finish off just about every recipe with a fried or poached egg. When pierced, the yolk seeps into the food on which the egg is sitting, a rich and instant no-effort sauce.

In this case, the beneficiaries are lentils. Lentils are damn near a superfood. They're tasty, they cook up quickly (in only 20 minutes), and they boast the highest protein content of any bean or legume.

The combo of fried egg and lentils is wonderful all by itself, but the tomato vinaigrette pulls it all together. You may find yourself reaching for a piece of toast or crusty bread to mop up the bits that elude a fork.

Warm Roasted-Tomato
  Vinaigrette (page 13,
  preparation time
  included in recipe)
1 cup green lentils
  (preferably *lentilles
  du Puy*, see Note)
2 ounces pancetta
3 tablespoons extra
  virgin olive oil
1 small onion
1 garlic clove
½ cup Homemade
  Chicken Stock (page
  10, add preparation
  time) or canned broth
1 to 2 teaspoons sherry
  vinegar
1 teaspoon Dijon
  mustard
Kosher salt and freshly
  ground black pepper
8 large eggs

1. Start the Warm Roasted-Tomato Vinaigrette. Bring 3 cups salted water to a boil over high heat. Rinse the lentils in cold water; add them to the boiling water and return the water to a boil. Reduce the heat to medium, cover the pot, and simmer until the lentils are just tender, 20 to 25 minutes.

2. Meanwhile, finely chop the pancetta (about ¼ cup). Heat 1 tablespoon olive oil in a large skillet over medium heat; add the pancetta and cook, stirring often, until it is crisp, 3 to 5 minutes. Chop the onion (about ½ cup).

3. Remove the pancetta from the pan with a slotted spoon and drain on paper towels. Reduce the heat to medium-low; add the onion and cook for 5 minutes, or until it has softened. Press the garlic (about 1 teaspoon) into the pan and cook for 1 minute more. Drain the lentils and add to the skillet along with the chicken stock. Bring the mixture to a boil, scraping up the brown bits at the bottom of the pan, and simmer until the stock has mostly evaporated. Stir in the pancetta, sherry vinegar to taste, and the mustard. Add salt and pepper to taste. Finish the Warm Roasted-Tomato Vinaigrette.

4. Heat the remaining 2 tablespoons olive oil in a large nonstick skillet over medium heat until hot. Crack the eggs, one at a time, into a small cup or ramekin and pour each egg into the pan. Season with salt and pepper to taste. Cook until the eggs are almost done, 2 to 3 minutes. Flip them over easy and cook for 1 minute more.

5. Divide the lentils among 4 large dinner plates. Top each with 2 fried eggs and some of the vinaigrette.

NOTE: *Lentilles du Puy* are small green lentils from France. I like them because they hold their shape better than regular green lentils. You can find them in specialty food shops or see Sources (page 359).

Scrambled Egg and Smoked Salmon Crêpes

MAKES 8 WRAPS, 4 SERVINGS   HANDS-ON TIME: 25 MINUTES   TOTAL PREPARATION TIME: 35 MINUTES

Several years ago *Gourmet* ran a recipe by Eric Ripert, one of my all-time favorite chefs. (It helps that aside from being a great chef, he happens to look like a rock star.) He'd embellished a simple croque monsieur—the French grilled cheese sandwich—with the addition of smoked salmon. I was shocked, just shocked. As a proper food snob, I'd always believed that fish and cheese don't mix. Well, I was wrong. We served this little appetizer in the *Gourmet* dining room and killed with it.

In this recipe I've added all of Eric's happy ingredients (including a little freshly grated lemon zest) to some softly scrambled eggs and wrapped it all up in a crêpe, sort of like a French breakfast burrito. Take the time to cook the scrambled eggs very slowly and over low heat. They turn out wonderfully creamy that way.

8 Basic Crêpes (page 24, add preparation time) or store-bought crêpes

2 tablespoons unsalted butter

8 large eggs

2 tablespoons whole milk

1 teaspoon freshly grated lemon zest

Kosher salt and freshly ground black pepper

4 ounces Gruyère cheese

8 ounces thinly sliced smoked salmon

1. Prepare the crêpes if making homemade.

2. Preheat the oven to 350°F. Lightly oil a rimmed baking sheet.

3. Melt the butter in a large skillet over medium heat. Lightly beat the eggs with the milk, lemon zest, ¼ teaspoon salt, and ¼ teaspoon pepper. Add the egg mixture to the pan and cook, stirring frequently, until the eggs are creamy and just set, about 12 minutes.

4. Meanwhile, coarsely grate the cheese (about 1 cup). Divide the salmon into 8 equal pieces. Spread out the crêpes on a work surface. Sprinkle the cheese onto the crêpes; top with the salmon.

5. Divide the eggs among the crêpes, making a log near one edge of each. Roll up the crêpes halfway, tuck in the ends, and finish rolling. Place the crêpes, seam side down, on the baking sheet and bake for 10 minutes. Transfer 2 crêpes to each of 4 plates and serve right away.

Tahini Crab Omelet Wraps

MAKES 8 OMELETS, 4 SERVINGS   HANDS-ON TIME: 30 MINUTES   TOTAL PREPARATION TIME: 35 MINUTES

This is not your typical diner omelet; it's more of a delicate egg pancake wrapped around a creamy Middle Eastern–flavored crab salad. It's filling, but it's not heavy.

Actually, these thin omelets are great wrappers for all sorts of ingredients. You can make them ahead and stack them up. When you're ready for dinner, roll them up with leftovers from the fridge and a little grated cheese, then heat gently in the oven, covered, until hot. Or stuff them with a salad as I have here, and eat them cold or at room temperature.

6 large eggs
Kosher salt
Vegetable oil
3 large radishes
2 medium scallions
¼ cup well-stirred tahini
2 tablespoons fresh
   lemon juice
1 tablespoon extra virgin
   olive oil
1 garlic clove
Freshly ground black
   pepper
¼ pound lump crabmeat
   (about 1 cup)

1. Beat the eggs with 1 tablespoon water and ¼ teaspoon salt. Lightly brush a 10-inch nonstick skillet with vegetable oil and heat over medium heat until hot but not smoking.

2. Ladle about ¼ cup egg mixture into the pan, tilting and rotating the pan to coat the bottom. Cook until the surface of the egg looks set and the bottom is barely golden, 1 to 2 minutes. Turn over the omelet and cook for 1 minute more on the second side. Transfer to a cooling rack. Repeat to cook 8 omelets. Let the omelets cool to room temperature.

3. Finely chop the radishes (about ½ cup) and trim and finely chop the scallions (about ¼ cup). Whisk together the tahini, lemon juice, and olive oil in a medium bowl. Press in the garlic (about 1 teaspoon) and add salt and pepper to taste. Pick through the crab and remove any bits of shell; gently fold the crab into the tahini mixture along with a little water if the mixture seems dry. Gently fold in the radishes and scallions.

4. To serve, place the omelets flat on a work surface; divide the filling among them (a generous ⅛ cup for each), spread to cover the omelet, and roll up. Transfer 2 wraps to each of 4 large dinner plates.

BLT and Egg Pie

MAKES 6 SERVINGS ■ HANDS-ON TIME: 30 MINUTES ■ TOTAL PREPARATION TIME: 65 MINUTES

Everyone loves the BLT, that all-American classic, especially during the height of tomato season. It was Joanne Lamb Hayes, my partner on this book, who thought that there might be a way to turn this lunchtime sandwich into a dinner pie. How big a stretch is it, really? Bacon, eggs, and tomato go together at least as well as bacon, lettuce, tomato, and toast, and the mayo that moistens a BLT also adds creaminess to the filling of an egg tart (a little trick Joanne discovered when judging a cooking contest for *Country Living* magazine years ago). The BLT's lettuce moves from between two slices of bread to the top of this pie as a kind of simple salad tossed with a tart garlic dressing.

You might be tempted to substitute low-fat mayo for the regular kind. Don't do it; it will separate and ruin the pie.

Basic Butter Pastry (page 28, add preparation time; you'll need just ½ recipe) or store-bought pastry for a single-crust pie

1 pound small ripe tomatoes

Kosher salt

8 slices bacon

1 medium onion

3 large eggs

¾ cup whole milk

½ cup mayonnaise

¼ teaspoon freshly ground black pepper

Pinch of cayenne pepper

3 cups Boston lettuce leaves

Creamy Garlic Dressing Two Ways (page 12) or store-bought dressing

1. Prepare the Basic Butter Pastry and set half aside while you make the filling. (Freeze the remaining half for another use.)

2. Preheat the oven to 375°F. Slice the tomatoes ¼ inch thick and sprinkle the slices on both sides with 1 teaspoon salt. Arrange them on a rack over a rimmed baking sheet to drain.

3. Heat a large skillet over medium heat until hot. Add the bacon and cook for about 7 minutes, or until crisp. Meanwhile, thinly slice the onion (about 1 cup). Roll out the pastry between lightly floured sheets of plastic wrap to make an 11-inch round. Fit the round into a 9-inch pie plate. Fold the edges in; press firmly, forming a double-thick edge, and flute.

4. Transfer the bacon to paper towels to drain. Remove all but 1 tablespoon of the bacon fat from the skillet and reserve it for another use. Add the onion to the fat in the skillet and cook, stirring occasionally, until it begins to brown, about 5 minutes.

5. Pat the tomatoes dry with paper towels. Layer half of the onion into the crust. Crumble half the bacon over the onion and top with half the tomatoes. Repeat the layering with the remaining onion, bacon, and tomatoes.

6. Beat the eggs, milk, mayonnaise, ½ teaspoon salt, the black pepper, and cayenne in a small bowl to blend; pour the mixture over the tomato slices.

7. Bake the pie until the filling is set in the center, about 35 minutes.

8. While the pie is baking, break the lettuce into bite-size pieces. Prepare the dressing.

9. To serve, cut the pie into 6 wedges, place each wedge on a serving plate, and top with about ½ cup greens drizzled with some of the dressing.

what is the best way

TO STORE EGGS?

Although we've all been taught to store eggs in that little open egg container on the door of the fridge, don't do it. The door is the warmest place in the fridge and should house only high salt/acid/sugar items like jams, hot sauces, and pickles. And forget Grandma's bowl of eggs on the kitchen counter. Eggs stored at room temperature age four times as fast as when they're refrigerated.

When you're cooking with eggs, fresher is better: the yolks are firmer and the whites more viscous. Fresh eggs don't spread out in the fry pan; they stand up high. In desserts and soufflés, fresh eggs produce more volume than old eggs. So it's very important to keep your eggs well chilled. After you bring them home from the supermarket, put them in their closed carton in the back of the fridge. (The only time you want an old egg is if you intend to hard-cook it. An old egg has more air between the shell and the membrane, which makes it easier to peel.)

3
APPETIZERS FOR DINNER

When I go out for dinner these days, I lean more toward the appetizers than toward the entrées, if only because I find it more interesting to eat smaller portions of several different dishes than a large portion of one dish. This chapter applies the same strategy to dinner at home. The recipes are so easy that you can make three or four of them in the time it would ordinarily take to prepare a single entrée. Serve them family style and dazzle one and all with the variety. Some are protein based, some vegetable based, and some starch based; team them up thoughtfully, and you'll cover all your food groups in one meal.

FACING PAGE: *Clockwise from top: Guacamole Eggs, Marinated White Bean Toasts, Guacamole Eggs, Ground Turkey and Mint Lettuce Wraps.*

Chorizo-Stuffed Mushrooms

MAKES 20 MUSHROOMS, 4 SERVINGS   HANDS-ON TIME: 25 MINUTES   TOTAL PREPARATION TIME: 40 MINUTES

My mom used to make stuffed mushrooms on a regular basis when I was a kid. (She probably found the recipe in *The New York Times Cookbook,* her bible then.) I've taken the basic components and methods of that dish and souped them up with sausage and cheese. Ideally, you should use Spanish sausage (preferably Palacios chorizo) and Spanish cheese (Manchego). If you can't find Palacios (see Sources, page 359), you can use any chorizo. Just keep in mind that fresh chorizo from Mexico hasn't been cured and will have to be cooked thoroughly before you add it to this recipe. If you can't find Manchego, just substitute Parmigiano-Reggiano.

¼ pound Spanish chorizo
20 large (1½ to 2½ inches in diameter) white mushrooms (about 1 pound)
2 tablespoons extra virgin olive oil
1 medium onion
1 slice firm white bread
1 ounce Manchego cheese
¼ cup fresh flat-leaf parsley leaves
Kosher salt and freshly ground black pepper

1. Place an oven rack in the middle of the oven and preheat the oven to 400°F. Lightly oil a large shallow baking pan. Remove the casing from the sausage and finely chop the sausage (about ⅔ cup).

2. Clean the mushrooms; trim off and discard the dry ends of the stems. Remove the stems from the mushroom caps; finely chop the stems. Arrange the mushroom caps, stem side down, in the oiled pan and bake for about 10 minutes, or until they release their liquid.

3. Meanwhile, heat the olive oil in a medium skillet over medium heat until hot. Add the chorizo and cook it until it begins to brown, about 3 minutes. Transfer the chorizo to a medium bowl with a slotted spoon. While the chorizo is cooking, chop the onion (about 1 cup).

4. Reduce the heat to medium-low; add the onion and cook for 5 minutes, or until it has softened. Add the chopped mushroom stems to the onion and cook until they release all their liquid, about 3 minutes. Transfer the vegetable mixture to the bowl with the chorizo and set it aside to cool slightly.

5. Cut the bread into ¼-inch squares (about ½ cup), coarsely grate the cheese (about ¼ cup), and chop the parsley (about 2 tablespoons). Stir the bread, cheese, and parsley into the chorizo mixture; add salt and pepper to taste.

6. Turn over the mushroom caps and divide the chorizo mixture among them, mounding slightly. Bake the stuffed caps for about 15 minutes, or until the mushrooms are tender and the stuffing is golden brown.

what should you look for

WHEN SELECTING CHORIZO?

There are two kinds of chorizo on the market, dried and fresh. While both can add lots of flavor to a dish, they are very different products. I am partial to the Spanish kind and the Portuguese *chouriço,* which are spicy, fermented, cured sausages that add a smoky flavor to the dish and a red blush to the sauce because of the dried red peppers in the mix. They usually can be used without cooking (be sure to check the label).

In Mexico and the southwestern United States, chorizo is a mixture of ground fresh pork seasoned with chiles and spices. It can be purchased either in skins or in bulk and is usually found in the fresh meat section of the supermarket. It is fresh meat and needs to be thoroughly cooked just as you would cook ground pork. Unless a recipe calls for Mexican or fresh chorizo by name, fresh chorizo is probably not what the author had in mind.

Pork Sliders, Asian Style

MAKES 8 SLIDERS, 4 SERVINGS HANDS-ON TIME: 30 MINUTES TOTAL PREPARATION TIME: 30 MINUTES

Every fan of burgers is also a fan of mini burgers, aka sliders—especially mini me. I know, of course, that your basic hairy-chested carnivore loves sliders because he can eat more of them at one sitting than he can of a standard-size burger. (This character is impervious to "the psychology of serving," which suggests that people eat less if you serve them less.) Me, I find even one standard-size burger too much to polish off at a sitting, but I'm delighted to dig in to a smaller version.

I've added a bunch of chopped vegetables to these burgers to provide not just flavor and crunch, but moisture. The soy sauce and sesame oil add Asian flavors. These little devils are great right out of the pan, but if you lather 'em up with Cilantro Mayo, they become down-right decadent—or at least mini decadent.

⅛ small green cabbage
¼ small red bell pepper
¼ cup fresh basil leaves
1 medium scallion
One 1-inch piece fresh ginger
1 garlic clove
½ pound lean ground pork
2 teaspoons soy sauce
½ teaspoon kosher salt
⅛ teaspoon sesame oil
2 tablespoons vegetable oil
Cilantro Mayo (recipe follows)
Mini pitas or small rolls (see Note)

1. Finely chop the cabbage (about ⅓ cup), bell pepper (about ¼ cup), basil (about 2 tablespoons), and scallion (about 2 tablespoons); peel and Microplane-grate the ginger (1 teaspoon). Combine the cabbage, bell pepper, basil, scallion, and ginger in a large bowl and press in the garlic (about 1 teaspoon). Gently stir in the pork, soy sauce, salt, and sesame oil and shape the mixture into 8 mini burgers.

2. Heat the vegetable oil over medium heat until hot. Add the burgers and cook for 2 minutes per side, or until just cooked through. Meanwhile, prepare the Cilantro Mayo.

3. Serve the sliders in mini pitas or on small rolls, topped with Cilantro Mayo.

NOTE: Both Sahara's mini pitas and Martin's Famous Dinner Potato Rolls are just the right size for these sliders. You can find either product at most supermarkets.

CILANTRO MAYO: Stir together ¼ cup mayonnaise, 1 tablespoon finely chopped fresh cilantro, 1 teaspoon lime juice, and salt and pepper to taste.

$\mathcal{M}$anchego-Stuffed Figs Wrapped in Bacon

MAKES 16 STUFFED FIGS, 4 SERVINGS   HANDS-ON TIME: 15 MINUTES   TOTAL PREPARATION TIME: 25 MINUTES

We never failed to make friends when we served Baked Dates Stuffed with Parmesan in the *Gourmet* dining room. Supersimple and supertasty, this appetizer is the brainchild of Suzanne Goin, chef at Los Angeles's Lucques and AOC.

I've substituted figs for the dates and Manchego (one of my favorite Spanish cheeses) for the Parmesan. Be sure to use a high-quality brand of bacon. (I recommend Niman Ranch.) When your recipe is made of only three ingredients, each of them should be top-notch.

16 dried Calimyrna figs
    (8 to 9 ounces)
2 ounces aged
    Manchego cheese
8 slices bacon (about
    7 ounces)

1. Place a rack in the middle of the oven and preheat the oven to 450°F.

2. Cut a small lengthwise slit in one side of each fig; cut the cheese into thirty-two ½-inch cubes. Gently stuff 2 cubes of cheese into each fig and press the fig around the cheese to cover it.

3. Cut the bacon slices in half crosswise and wrap them lightly around the stuffed figs. Place the figs, seam side down, in a shallow baking pan and bake for 10 minutes, or until the bacon is cooked. Remove the figs to paper towels to drain and serve warm.

how do i

ADD SEASONINGS TO RAW GROUND MEAT MIXTURES?

I love to add a variety of seasonings to my burgers, as well as to meat mixtures for my homemade sausages. The trouble is that you can't just taste the meat raw. To check the seasonings in any raw ground meat mixture, I make what I refer to as a test pilot. I sauté a small patty of the mixture until it is cooked through and then taste it. That way, corrections can be made before the flavor combination is set in the cooked burgers or sausages.

Quick Baked Littleneck Clams

MAKES ABOUT 24 BAKED CLAMS, 6 TO 8 SERVINGS   HANDS-ON TIME: 20 MINUTES   TOTAL PREPARATION TIME: 24 MINUTES

I love clams in any recipe. The only challenge is getting them open. My first job right out of cooking school was "womaning" the raw bar at a restaurant in Cambridge, Massachusetts. Some nights I would shuck dozens and dozens of raw clams and oysters. You would think that I would have mastered the technique. No way! Now my favorite way to shuck shellfish is to get someone else to do it (my brother, a cousin, or the fishmonger), or I just steam them open in a pot with garlic, shallots, olive oil, and white wine, which not only opens them, but also creates the most delicious liquid. (Toss it all with linguine, and you have pasta with clam sauce.)

The first time I made this recipe, I steamed the clams, but it seemed like too much work just to get them open. I had read a recipe that suggested broiling them, so I gave it a try. I don't know if I have an especially hot broiler, but suddenly not only were the clams opening, their shells were shattering all over the oven. I decided to try the more gentle heat of a hot oven. It worked beautifully.

2 dozen littleneck clams
2 ounces pancetta
¼ cup fresh flat-leaf
    parsley leaves
2 slices firm white bread
1 tablespoon extra virgin
    olive oil
1 garlic clove

1. Place a rack in the middle of the oven and preheat the oven to 475°F. Scrub the clams, discarding any that won't close, and arrange them on a broiler pan or on a rack in a roasting pan.

2. Bake the clams for 8 to 10 minutes, or until all have opened. Discard any clams that don't open. Set the clams aside until they are cool enough to handle. Remove the top shell, leaving the clam and juice in the bottom shell.

3. Meanwhile, finely chop the pancetta (about ¼ cup) and chop the parsley (about 2 tablespoons). Pulse the bread in a blender or food processor to make 1 cup fresh bread crumbs. Heat the olive oil in a medium skillet over medium heat until hot. Add the pancetta and cook, stirring occasionally, for about 5 minutes, or until it begins to brown. Press the garlic (about 1 teaspoon) into the skillet and cook for 1 minute more. Transfer the mixture to a medium bowl and stir in the bread crumbs and parsley.

4. Divide the crumb mixture among the clams. Put the clams on a rimmed baking sheet and bake for 3 to 5 minutes, or until the crumbs brown. (Or broil the clams 8 inches from the heat source for 1 to 2 minutes, just until browned and heated through.)

how do i

SELECT, HANDLE, AND COOK FRESH CLAMS?

Many people would love to cook clams, but they are not comfortable selecting and handling them. The most important things to remember are that clams must be purchased alive, as close to use as possible, like to stay cool, and need oxygen (no plastic bags!). Selecting the right clam for your recipe often depends upon availability, but if you are given a choice, certain varieties are better for some dishes than for others.

In the Northeast, where I usually shop for clams, there are two main types of clam, quahogs (pronounced "*ko*-hogs") and soft-shells. Quahogs are classified by size. Littlenecks are 1¼ to 1½ inches across, and you get seven to ten per pound. They are tender and have a sweet taste. Cherrystones are 2¼ to 3 inches across and come five to seven to a pound. They are chewier than the littlenecks. The largest clams are simply called quahogs or chowder clams and are chopped up and used for just that. Soft-shells, also known as steamers, fryers, or long necks (after the black siphon that protrudes from their shells), are usually steamed or shucked and turned into fried clams. If you live in another area of the country, your fishmonger should be able to recommend a variety that will work in the dish you want to make.

Clams should be scrubbed just before cooking. If any shells are open and don't close during scrubbing, discard them. No matter how you cook them, if the shells don't open within about 8 minutes, toss them out.

$\mathscr{G}$round Turkey and Mint Lettuce Wraps

MAKES 12 WRAPS, 4 SERVINGS   HANDS-ON TIME: 20 MINUTES   TOTAL PREPARATION TIME: 20 MINUTES

Any number of Asian cultures work out variations on this theme: ground and seasoned meat wrapped in lettuce. As you might imagine, the lettuce makes for a lighter and more refreshing wrap than one made with starchy products. This recipe features ground turkey, but you can substitute pork or beef.

1 medium onion
1 tablespoon
  vegetable oil
1 pound ground turkey
½ cup Peanut Sesame
  Sauce (page 16, add
  preparation time) or
  store-bought sauce
One 4- to 5-inch piece
  seedless (English)
  cucumber
½ cup fresh mint or
  cilantro leaves
12 large butter lettuce
  leaves
Soy sauce, as an
  accompaniment

1. Finely chop the onion (about 1 cup). Heat the vegetable oil in a large heavy skillet over medium heat until hot. Reduce the heat to medium-low; add the onion and cook for about 5 minutes, or until it has softened. Add the turkey to the skillet and sauté it, stirring with a fork to break it into pieces, for about 7 minutes, or until it is cooked through.

2. Meanwhile, make the Peanut Sesame Sauce. Add ½ cup of the sauce to the turkey mixture. (Refrigerate the remaining Peanut Sesame Sauce for another use.) Heat the turkey mixture just until the sauce bubbles.

3. Meanwhile, finely chop the cucumber (about 1 cup) and half the mint leaves (about ¼ cup); stir them into the hot turkey filling. Divide the filling and the remaining mint leaves among the lettuce leaves. Fold the sides of the leaves over the filling and roll up the leaves to enclose the filling. Serve with soy sauce for dipping.

Smoked Trout or Salmon Rillettes

MAKES ABOUT 1½ CUPS, 4 SERVINGS   HANDS-ON TIME: 15 MINUTES   TOTAL PREPARATION TIME: 15 MINUTES

In *The Food of France,* Waverley Root describes rillettes as being "made of finely shredded pork cooked in lard and eaten cold." He then suggests, "Spread a little of it on a piece of French bread, accompany it with a swallow of Vouvray from its own neighborhood, and you have an excellent start for a meal."

Sounds civilized, doesn't it? My first encounter with rillettes was a little more decadent. I was at the tail end of my *stagiaire* ("apprenticeship") in Chartres, France, and The Husband and I were staying in a fifteenth-century farmhouse, the home of the daughter of the woman in whose house I'd been rooming. Breakfast was unlike anything I've ever seen before or since. The daughter's husband was a proud native of the Auvergne region of France, and he wanted us to see how they chowed down in his neck of the woods. Our first meal of the day consisted not only of rillettes, but of pork chops, stinky cheese, mustard, pickles, crusty bread, and plenty of wine. I suppose there's a way to be presented with a spread like that and maintain one's composure, but we were young and went hog wild. Finally, we pushed ourselves away from the table, staggered outside, and began gulping down huge drafts of country air in a pitiful attempt to clear our heads.

Thirty years later our appetites are a little more moderate. We still love rillettes—pork, rabbit, goose, duck, or other poultry—but we're also happy to dig into the seafood variety, which is lower in fat than the other kinds but still full of flavor. This version includes radishes, shallots, and capers for crunch, and lemon to brighten it up.

8 ounces smoked trout or salmon fillets

6 large radishes

1 medium shallot

¼ cup sour cream or plain low-fat or full-fat Greek-style yogurt (see page 49)

2 tablespoons well-drained capers

1 tablespoon fresh lemon juice

2 teaspoons Dijon mustard

Kosher salt and freshly ground black pepper

Crackers, as an accompaniment

1. If using trout, remove and discard the skin. Finely chop the trout or salmon (about 1⅓ cups). Coarsely shred the radishes (about 1 cup), and trim and finely chop the shallot (about 2 tablespoons).

2. Combine the fish, radishes, shallot, sour cream, capers, lemon juice, mustard, and salt and pepper to taste. Transfer to a bowl and serve with crackers. The rillettes will keep, covered and refrigerated, for 4 days.

Panko Scallops with Wasabi Mayonnaise

MAKES 4 SERVINGS   HANDS-ON TIME: ABOUT 30 MINUTES   TOTAL PREPARATION TIME: ABOUT 30 MINUTES

Sweet and silky bay scallops make the perfect one-bite appetizer. They're simple, too, if only because they're so complete in themselves that you'd be a fool to mess with them too much.

Years ago *Gourmet* published a great little recipe for Panko Scallops with Green Chile Chutney. We often served it in the *Gourmet* dining room, and it was always a hit. The not-so-secret ingredient is the panko bread crumbs. Large and coarse, they provide a crunchy exterior that contrasts beautifully with the soft scallop inside.

In this recipe, I've paired up the sweet and crunchy scallops with a spicy (and easy-to-make) wasabi dipping sauce. They play very nicely together.

⅓ cup mayonnaise or sour cream
2 teaspoons fresh lemon juice
1½ teaspoons prepared wasabi
1 teaspoon soy sauce (low sodium, if you prefer)
1 large egg
¼ cup low-fat milk
1¼ cups panko bread crumbs
Kosher salt and freshly ground black pepper
2 to 3 tablespoons vegetable oil
¾ pound bay or small sea scallops

1. Stir together the mayonnaise, lemon juice, wasabi, and soy sauce in a small bowl. Cover and refrigerate until ready to use.

2. Whisk the egg in a medium bowl until frothy; gradually whisk in the milk. Combine the crumbs with ½ teaspoon salt and ¼ teaspoon pepper in a pie plate or shallow baking dish.

3. Heat the vegetable oil in a large skillet over medium heat until hot; reduce the heat to medium-low. Working quickly, dip the scallops into the egg mixture, shaking off any excess. Then dip them into the crumbs to coat them completely.

4. Add the scallops to the vegetable oil; sauté them, turning once, for 3 to 4 minutes per side, or until they are golden. Drain the scallops on paper towels briefly, sprinkle them with salt and pepper to taste, then divide them among 4 plates. Top each with a dollop of wasabi mayonnaise and serve.

what is WASABI?

One of the great things about sushi is the hot wasabi paste that's served with it. Americans love wasabi. Weirdly enough, though, the so-called wasabi that we eat here isn't wasabi at all. Rather, it is a combination of dried and ground horseradish, Chinese mustard powder, cornstarch, and artificial coloring. The problem is that real wasabi happens to be highly perishable. It's a rhizome, or aboveground root, like ginger, and its heat and flavor evaporate within 15 to 20 minutes of being peeled and finely grated. Even in Japan, then, where most of the world's supply is grown, wasabi is a pretty rare delicacy. Once the fresh root is prepared, it is the lucky few to whom the condiment is served immediately.

Happily, we've begun growing wasabi in America. There's not a huge amount of it, and it's expensive, but it is available (see Sources, page 359). If you're willing to splurge, I recommend it. It has a more subtle heat than the powdered or paste versions.

Meanwhile, like most folks, I'll keep eating the "wasabi" we're served here. It may not be authentic, but it is unique and I like it.

Guacamole Eggs (V)

MAKES 12 STUFFED EGG HALVES, 4 TO 6 SERVINGS   HANDS-ON TIME: 10 MINUTES
TOTAL PREPARATION TIME: 22 MINUTES, PLUS COOLING TIME

I've always been a fan of stuffed eggs, even the retro kind with paprika sprinkled all over the filling. Cookshop, one of my neighborhood haunts in New York, offers deviled eggs as a starter snack alongside such other perfect little tastes as chicken wings and fried hominy. When dining there, I'm often content to order several snacks and a salad and call it a meal. I'm never hungry afterward.

As for this recipe, the title says it all. Everything required to make guacamole goes into the stuffing for these eggs, plus a little mayo. Eggs and avocados are a happy match, and because avocados are so naturally creamy, I was able to cut back on the usual amount of mayo, which is part of what makes a stuffed egg so stuffing.

6 large eggs
⅛ small white onion
½ small jalapeño chile (make sure it has heat; see page 6)
1 ripe medium Hass avocado
1 tablespoon mayonnaise
2 to 3 teaspoons fresh lime juice
Kosher salt and freshly ground black pepper

1. Cook the eggs following the directions for Sara's Hard-Cooked Eggs (page 30). Meanwhile, mince enough onion and jalapeño to make 1 tablespoon of each.

2. When the eggs have cooked and cooled, peel them under cold running water and halve them lengthwise. Remove the egg yolks to a small bowl; place the whites on a serving plate.

3. Halve, seed, peel, and coarsely chop the avocado. Add the avocado, mayonnaise, and lime juice to taste to the yolks and mash with a fork to make a chunky mixture. Stir in the onion and jalapeño; season with salt and pepper to taste. Spoon the mixture into a resealable plastic bag, pressing out as much air as possible before zipping.

4. To serve: Cut ¼ inch from one corner of the plastic bag. Pipe the avocado mixture into the egg whites using 1 slightly rounded tablespoon filling per egg.

A Summer Salad from Paris ⓥ

MAKES 4 SERVINGS   HANDS-ON TIME: 15 MINUTES   TOTAL PREPARATION TIME: 15 MINUTES

Janis Adler is my sister-in-law. When I went to France to do an apprenticeship in the late seventies, Jan made the trip with me and we had a lot of fun banging around for a few days in Paris and Chartres before I had to start my job. We're both still huge Francophiles, although I know, all these years later, that her command of the language remains much surer than my own, which has shrunk to kitchen French.

In 1997, when Jan and her husband were settled in Portland, Oregon, and their kids were young, they took in a young French student for the summer. I'll let Jan herself take it from here:

> This Parisian teenager was foisted on us by well-meaning friends who had no inkling about the perpetual bedlam involved in running a household with a three- and a five-year-old. I had a naive pipe dream this young woman would be some sort of mother's helper, maybe even a sometime babysitter. I was wrong. She had no interest in the children. But she did like to cook, and so a deal was struck. I was just as thrilled to have her help with the cooking as I would have been to have her help with the kids. Sure enough, she was a good cook and prepared meals for us about twice a week. This salad was one of her recipes.

Of course, a tomato, mozzarella, and basil salad is a well-known classic of Italian cuisine—Italians call it *insalata caprese* (a tip of the hat to the Isle of Capri)—but the addition of avocado makes it new and even more delicious. Every summer when the Adlers reunite, Jan and I make this salad for ourselves nearly every day for lunch. It resides in this book's appetizer chapter, however, because I know most carnivores wouldn't consider it a meal in itself.

2 large ripe beefsteak tomatoes, or 5 plum tomatoes, or 2 cups cherry tomatoes

Kosher salt

8 ounces lightly salted mozzarella (preferably fresh)

2 ripe Hass avocados

1 cup fresh basil leaves

Extra virgin olive oil

1. Slice the tomatoes ⅓ inch thick and salt them on both sides. Set aside for 10 minutes and then gently pat them dry with paper towels.

2. Slice the mozzarella ⅓ inch thick and cut the slices in half, if large. Halve, seed, peel, and slice the avocados ⅓ inch thick. Coarsely shred the basil leaves or leave them whole. Layer all the ingredients decoratively on a serving plate and drizzle liberally with olive oil.

$\mathcal{M}$arinated White Bean Toasts ⓥ

MAKES 24 TOASTS, 4 SERVINGS (ABOUT 1⅔ CUPS BEAN MIXTURE)   HANDS-ON TIME: 25 MINUTES
TOTAL PREPARATION TIME: 25 MINUTES

One of my favorite parts of a meal at Esca, one of my favorite restaurants in New York, is when a little plate of lightly dressed white beans and fresh herbs on toast comes out to whet your appetite for the thrills to come. This is my interpretation of that dish (theirs usually has some kind of fish in it; I left it out). I'm sure that Esca uses very fancy extra virgin olive oil because it's that kind of restaurant. I just reached for my supermarket extra virgin olive oil. The dish still turned out very, very well.

1 small red onion
One 12-inch baguette or 6 thin slices country-style bread
¼ cup extra virgin olive oil
1 garlic clove
One 15½-ounce can small white beans
1 tablespoon plus 1 teaspoon fresh oregano leaves (plus 24 leaves for garnish, optional)
2 tablespoons fresh lemon juice
Kosher salt and freshly ground black pepper

1. Place an oven rack in the middle of the oven and preheat the oven to 400°F. Finely chop the onion (about ½ cup) and transfer it to a small bowl; add ice and water to cover and set it aside for 10 minutes.

2. Trim off and discard the ends of the baguette; cut the remaining baguette diagonally to make 24 slices or cut the country bread slices into quarters. Brush the slices on both sides with 2 tablespoons olive oil and arrange them on a rimmed baking sheet. Toast them for 8 to 10 minutes, turning once, until they are golden. Remove the toasts from the oven and set them aside to cool slightly. Split the garlic lengthwise. Rub the toast slices with the cut sides of the garlic.

3. Rinse and thoroughly drain the beans. Chop the oregano (about 2 teaspoons). Combine the beans, the remaining 2 tablespoons olive oil, the lemon juice, and oregano in a medium bowl. Mash with a potato masher or fork, leaving some large pieces.

4. Drain the onion, pat it dry, and stir it into the bean mixture along with salt and pepper to taste. Divide the bean mixture among the toast slices and spread the mixture to the edges. Garnish each toast with an oregano leaf, if using, and serve.

COOKING BEANS

Although I have called only for canned beans in this book because they are ready to go right into a dish, it is also easy and economical to cook dried beans when you have a little time on your hands. You can freeze them in 1-cup containers and add them still frozen to soups and stews; they thaw quickly as the dish comes back to a boil.

To soak or not to soak? Many cookbooks recommend soaking your beans overnight in water to cover. They also suggest the quick-soak method if you don't have time for the overnight soak: Cover the beans with cold water, bring the water to a boil, cover, and let the beans sit for 1 hour. Either way, you drain off the water and then proceed with the recipe. Soaking the beans is supposed to cut down on cooking time, but in the end, it saves you only about 30 minutes. So, it is your choice.

To cook beans, follow the instructions on the package. Or pick through them to remove any small stones, rinse them thoroughly, and simmer for 40 to 60 minutes, until they are tender. You will need about 2 quarts of water to cook a pound of beans.

Don't keep that bag of beans in your cupboard a long time. The longer beans are stored, the drier they become and the longer it will take for them to get tender. For years people thought that salt added to the bean cooking water kept the beans from becoming tender. In an article in the *Los Angeles Times,* food writer Russ Parsons dispelled that myth but confirmed another one. The presence of acid in the cooking liquid can double the cooking time for dried beans, and if the concentration is high enough, it can even prevent them from ever becoming tender. Although it may sound like a good idea as far as flavor is concerned, never try to cook dried beans in tomato juice, canned tomatoes, citrus juices, or wine. Cook the beans completely in water and then add them to flavorful sauces.

$\mathcal{P}$olenta Crostini with Tapenade Ⓥ

| MAKES 16 CROSTINI, 4 SERVINGS | HANDS-ON TIME: 20 MINUTES | TOTAL PREPARATION TIME: 20 MINUTES |

Although it's known today chiefly as a delicious puree of olives, usually served as an appetizer on crackers or bread, tapenade started out as a puree of capers. (The word *tapenade* comes from *tapeno,* the Provençal word for "capers.") The original spread contained capers, black olives, and anchovies, all pureed with olive oil.

In this recipe, the tapenade goes on top of cooked polenta rounds. Available at your local supermarket, cooked polenta is a great "cheat," which I also use in Polenta Lasagne (page 157). I place polenta in the same category as potatoes, pasta, and rice: a great backdrop for all sorts of toppings and sauces. By the way, the supermarket also sells tapenade. I'd leave it alone. With this recipe, yours will be so much fresher and more delicious.

One 16- or 17-ounce log cooked plain polenta
¼ cup extra virgin olive oil (or 2 tablespoons butter to brown the polenta and 2 tablespoons olive oil for the tapenade)
1 cup pitted kalamata olives (about 5 ounces)
½ cup fresh flat-leaf parsley leaves, plus 16 leaves for garnish
2 flat anchovy fillets (optional)
1 tablespoon well-drained capers
½ teaspoon freshly grated lemon zest
1 tablespoon fresh lemon juice
¼ teaspoon freshly ground black pepper
8 grape tomatoes

1. Preheat the oven to 250°F. Lightly oil a rimmed baking sheet. Trim off and discard the crinkled ends of the polenta log; cut the remaining polenta crosswise into 16 slices.

2. Heat 1 tablespoon olive oil or butter in a large nonstick skillet over medium heat until hot. Add as many polenta slices as will fit in one layer and sauté, turning once, for about 5 minutes per side, or until crisp and browned. Remove the polenta slices to the baking sheet and keep them warm in the oven. Repeat, adding another tablespoon olive oil or butter as needed, until all the slices have been browned.

3. Meanwhile, combine the olives, parsley, anchovies (if using), capers, lemon zest, lemon juice, and pepper in a food processor fitted with the chopping blade. Pulse until coarsely chopped. Add the remaining 2 tablespoons olive oil and continue to pulse until the mixture is finely chopped but not pureed.

4. Halve the grape tomatoes. To serve, divide the olive mixture among the polenta rounds. Top each with a grape tomato half and a parsley leaf.

sparagus or Broccoli Calzones Ⓥ

MAKE 12 CALZONES, 6 SERVINGS ▪ **HANDS-ON TIME: 20 MINUTES** ▪ **TOTAL PREPARATION TIME: 55 MINUTES**

One of the great things about being able to make homemade pizza dough in no time at all is that you can also make calzones in no time at all. (Calzones are turnovers made with pizza dough.) As you rummage around in the refrigerator for a suitable filling, the only tricky part is figuring out how long you need to cook a given ingredient before wrapping it in the round of dough and cooking it some more. In this case, I thought I might have to blanch the asparagus or broccoli before I wrapped it up, but I was wrong.

Basic Pizza Dough
(page 26, add
preparation time) or
use store-bought
dough
2 tablespoons cornmeal
½ pound medium
asparagus or broccoli
florets or florets and
trimmed stems
Extra virgin olive oil for
the dough
One 5.2-ounce package
spreadable garlic-
herb cheese
(preferably Boursin)

1. Prepare the Basic Pizza Dough or take the store-bought dough out of the fridge. Sprinkle the cornmeal onto 2 baking sheets. Place 2 racks 5 inches apart in the middle of the oven and preheat the oven to 375°F.

2. Trim the asparagus. Peel the bottom half of the stems if the stems are thicker than ⅓ inch; slice the asparagus crosswise into ½-inch pieces (about 1⅓ cups) and place in a medium bowl. If using broccoli, cut into ½-inch pieces (about 1⅓ cups).

3. When the dough has risen, divide it into 12 balls. Working with 1 ball at a time, roll it out into a 4-inch round on a lightly oiled surface. Crumble the cheese; sprinkle one-twelfth on each dough round, patting it gently into the surface and leaving a ½-inch border.

4. Divide the asparagus among the dough rounds. Moisten the edges of each round with water and fold half of the round over the filling. Pinch the edges together very tightly and place the calzones on the baking sheets.

5. When the calzones have risen, bake them for 7 minutes; switch the pans on the racks. Bake the calzones for 6 to 7 minutes more, or until they are nicely browned. Serve right away.

4

SOUP SUPPERS

There's nothing I enjoy cooking and eating more than soup. The possibilities are infinite. Working at the Del Rio in Ann Arbor, Michigan, in the early seventies and then with Rebecca Caras in Boston later in the decade, I learned how easy it is to come up with a new soup every day. You don't need a recipe, but you do need a formula. Here is mine:

1. Sauté aromatic vegetables such as garlic and onions to provide depth of flavor.

2. Add the remaining solid ingredients (unless you're holding back some of them as a garnish).

3. Add liquid to cover the solid ingredients by about 1 inch. It can be chicken, beef, or vegetable broth; water; wine; or a tomato product.

4. Simmer until the ingredients are tender.

5. If you want to thicken the soup, puree some or all of it. I rarely use flour or cream to thicken a soup. I think they dull the flavor of the other ingredients and add unnecessary calories.

6. Heat the soup until hot or chill it until cold and then serve it right away. There's nothing worse than tepid soup.

7. Garnish.

All of the recipes in this chapter are substantial enough to constitute a meal with nothing more than a simple salad on the side. Most of them are equipped with a starch garnish: croutons, tortilla chips, quesadillas, or toasts. In the remaining cases, you'd do well to supplement the soup with salad and some rustic bread.

FACING PAGE: *Seafood Gazpacho.*

Seafood Gazpacho

MAKES 6½ CUPS, 4 SERVINGS ■ HANDS-ON TIME: 20 MINUTES ■ TOTAL PREPARATION TIME: 30 MINUTES

The inspiration for this dish came from a *Gourmet* magazine recipe called Mexican Seafood Cocktail that we often served to guests as an appetizer in the dining room at the magazine. You could substitute any kind of seafood for the shrimp and crabmeat or replace them with cooked fish, or any cooked protein, such as chicken, pork, or beef, for that matter.

¼ cup Garlic Croutons (recipe follows, add preparation time) or store-brought garlic-flavored croutons

6-inch piece seedless (English) cucumber

1 large green bell pepper

1 garlic clove

3 cups canned tomato-clam juice, chilled

3 tablespoons fresh lemon juice

2 tablespoons extra virgin olive oil

1 tablespoon sherry vinegar

1 teaspoon sugar

½ teaspoon Tabasco

Kosher salt and freshly ground black pepper

½ pound cooked, shelled, and deveined medium shrimp (see Jenn's "Boiled" Shrimp, page 111)

½ pound lump crabmeat

1. Make the Garlic Croutons. Coarsely chop enough of the cucumber, with the skin left on, and the bell pepper to make ½ cup of each. Finely chop the rest (about 1 cup of each). Smash the garlic and remove the skin.

2. Combine 1 cup tomato-clam juice, the coarsely chopped cucumber and bell pepper, the lemon juice, olive oil, vinegar, sugar, garlic, and hot sauce in a blender. Blend until the vegetables are pureed. Stir in the remaining 2 cups tomato-clam juice. Add 1 teaspoon salt and black pepper to taste.

3. Quarter the shrimp crosswise. Combine the tomato mixture, shrimp, crabmeat, and the remaining cucumber and bell pepper in a glass or metal bowl. Set the bowl into a bowl of ice and water for 10 minutes to quick-chill the soup.

4. To serve, divide the chilled soup among 4 large chilled seafood cocktail glasses or soup plates and top with the croutons.

MAKES 1½ CUPS ■ HANDS-ON TIME: 10 MINUTES ■
TOTAL PREPARATION TIME: 25 TO 30 MINUTES

GARLIC CROUTONS: Preheat the oven to 300°F. Trim the crusts from 2 slices firm white bread (about 3 ounces) and cut the bread into ¾-inch squares. Combine 2 tablespoons extra virgin olive oil, 2 pressed garlic cloves (about 2 teaspoons), ½ teaspoon sweet paprika, and ⅛ teaspoon kosher salt in a small bowl. Add the bread and toss until the pieces are evenly coated. Spread out the croutons on a large, ungreased rimmed baking sheet and bake for 15 to 20 minutes, or until the bread squares are crisp and beginning to brown. Let cool.

Chilled Guacamole Soup
with Smoked Salmon and Chopped Egg

MAKES 6¼ CUPS, 4 SERVINGS ■ HANDS-ON TIME: 35 MINUTES ■ TOTAL PREPARATION TIME: 35 MINUTES

This is a swell little hot-weather no-cook meal that will refresh you and fill you up. The avocados provide the base flavor and creamy texture; the salmon and eggs supply the protein; the buttermilk and lime keep it bright and light. It's great with baked tortilla chips.

2 large eggs
Homemade Baked Tortilla Chips (page 29, add preparation time) or store-bought chips
4 medium scallions
1 cup fresh cilantro leaves
2 small serrano chiles
1 pint cherry or grape tomatoes
¼ pound smoked salmon
3 small ripe Hass avocados
1½ cups buttermilk
2 teaspoons fresh lime juice
Kosher salt and freshly ground black pepper

1. Cook the eggs following the directions for Sara's Hard-Cooked Eggs (page 30); let cool and chop them (see Note, page 115). Prepare the Homemade Baked Tortilla Chips.

2. Meanwhile, trim and chop the scallions (about ½ cup), cilantro (about ½ cup), and chiles (about 1 tablespoon), keeping them all separate. Quarter the tomatoes (about 1⅔ cups) and cut the salmon into ¼-inch ribbons. Quarter, seed, and peel the avocados.

3. Combine the avocados, buttermilk, 1½ cups cold water, ¼ cup scallions, ¼ cup cilantro, the lime juice, 2 teaspoons chiles, and 1 teaspoon salt in a blender. Blend until smooth. Transfer to a glass or metal bowl and stir in the tomatoes, the remaining ¼ cup scallions, ¼ cup cilantro, 1 teaspoon chiles, and salt and pepper to taste. Set the bowl into a bowl of ice and water to quick-chill the soup.

4. To serve, divide the soup among 4 soup plates. Place some of the salmon and eggs in the center of each plate. Serve with the Homemade Tortilla Chips.

Really Quick Borscht

MAKES 12 CUPS, 6 SERVINGS ▪ HANDS-ON TIME: 38 MINUTES ▪ TOTAL PREPARATION TIME: 38 MINUTES

A classic borscht is delicious, substantial, and nourishing as hell, but it can take hours to prepare. By grating the beets before boiling them and substituting a tender cut of pork for stew meat, I've figured out how to cut the cooking time way down, making this great dish entirely doable for dinner on a weeknight.

Although this recipe was designed to be served hot, my notoriously beet-loving husband has no problem scarfing it down cold. When I expressed some astonishment at his wanton ways, he reminded me about Barney Greengrass, the great deli on Manhattan's Upper West Side, where bright pink borscht mixed with sour cream is brought to the table in milk glasses as a super-refreshing complement to the house's signature sturgeon, eggs, and onion. I stood corrected. You can serve this borscht hot or cold.

1 large onion
3 garlic cloves
3 tablespoons
    vegetable oil
6 cups Homemade
    Chicken Stock
    (page 10, add
    preparation time) or one
    48-ounce can broth
One 16-ounce package
    coleslaw mix (about
    8 cups) or 7 cups
    shredded cabbage plus
    1 cup shredded carrots
¼ cup plus 2 tablespoons
    balsamic vinegar
1 pound plum tomatoes
    (about 4 medium)
5 medium beets (about
    1 pound)
Kosher salt and freshly
    ground black pepper
4 boneless pork chops
    (about ¾ inch thick;
    1¼ to 1½ pounds)
½ cup sour cream
¼ cup chopped fresh
    dill leaves

1. Slice the onion into ¼-inch wedges (about 2 cups); thinly slice the garlic (about 1 tablespoon). Place the onion and garlic in the bowl of a food processor fitted with the chopping blade. Pulse 4 to 5 times until chopped (about 2 cups).

2. Heat 2 tablespoons vegetable oil in a large saucepan over medium heat until hot. Reduce the heat to medium-low; add the onion and garlic and cook for 5 minutes, or until the onion has softened. Add the chicken stock, coleslaw mix, and vinegar; cover and bring to a boil over high heat while preparing the remaining vegetables.

3. Cut each tomato into 8 chunks and peel the beets. Add the tomatoes to the food processor and pulse 3 to 4 times until coarsely chopped. Remove the chopping blade from the processor and change to the coarse shredding blade. Shred the beets onto the tomatoes in the processor bowl. Add the beets and tomatoes to the chicken stock mixture as soon as they are processed; cover and bring the mixture to a boil over high heat. Reduce the heat to medium and cook for 6 to 8 minutes, or until the beets are tender. Add salt and pepper to taste.

4. Meanwhile, heat the remaining 1 tablespoon vegetable oil in a large skillet over high heat until hot. Season the pork chops on all sides with salt and pepper to taste. Add the pork chops to the skil-

let and cook for 2 minutes per side (they will still be pink inside). Transfer them to a plate and loosely cover with aluminum foil; set aside to rest for 5 minutes.

5. Scoop 1 cup borscht into the skillet; bring it to a boil, scraping up the brown bits at the bottom of the pan. Return the borscht to the saucepan and cook until hot. Cut the chops crosswise in half and then slice thinly; add any juices that have collected on the plate to the soup.

6. To serve, divide the sliced meat among 6 soup plates. Ladle the soup onto it and top each portion with some of the sour cream and dill.

CHOOSING A BALSAMIC VINEGAR

Real balsamic vinegar contains only grapes (usually white Trebbiano grapes) that have been crushed and fermented to make a "must," then reduced, combined with some older balsamic vinegar, and aged in a series of barrels made from different woods. The vinegar is transferred to a different, smaller barrel each year as it concentrates and the volume gets smaller. Genuine balsamic vinegar can be made only in the regions of Modena and Reggio in Italy. The vinegar must be aged for ten years, and the better ones are aged for twenty-five to fifty years. Balsamic vinegars are dark, thick, silky, and sweet, with a hit of fruity acid; they can be very expensive. A drop or two of these vinegars on fresh summer tomatoes, fresh fruit, or chunks of Parmigiano-Reggiano is a memorable experience.

Factory-made balsamic vinegars are a mixture of red wine vinegar and brown sugar or caramel; occasionally, some grape "must" has been added. They are lighter in color and will have a strong vinegar bite and aroma. Far less expensive than genuine balsamic, these are a good choice if you are using a lot in a sauce or simmering down a cup of it to use as a garnish. To choose the right balsamic vinegar, read the label: Look at the ingredient list, find out where the vinegar was made, and see how long it was aged.

Spicy Sweet Potato Soup with Garlic Rye Croutons

MAKES ABOUT 8 CUPS, 4 SERVINGS ■ HANDS-ON TIME: 25 MINUTES USING PACKAGED CROUTONS ■
TOTAL PREPARATION TIME: 1 HOUR 15 MINUTES USING PACKAGED CROUTONS

One of my favorite *Gourmet* side dishes was Whipped Chipotle Sweet Potatoes. This recipe turns that side dish into a wonderful soup. As in the original recipe, the crux here is the hot-meets-sweet alchemy between the chipotle in adobo sauce and the sweet potatoes. Chipotles, or smoked jalapeños, bring both heat and smoke to a dish, while the adobo sauce, made of tomato, vinegar, and garlic, adds depth of flavor.

I bulked up the soup with Canadian bacon, another of the sweet potato's natural partners, but you could easily make a vegetarian version of this dish simply by leaving out the bacon and using vegetable stock instead of chicken stock.

4 medium sweet potatoes (about 2 pounds)
2 large onions
3 tablespoons unsalted butter
Kosher salt and freshly ground black pepper
3 garlic cloves
8 ounces Canadian bacon
2 medium celery stalks plus ¼ cup celery leaves for garnish
5 cups Homemade Chicken Stock (page 10, add preparation time) or canned broth
½ to 1 chipotle in adobo sauce with 1 tablespoon adobo sauce
1½ cups Garlic Rye Croutons (recipe follows, add preparation time) or packaged croutons

1. Preheat the oven to 400°F. Pierce the sweet potatoes several times with the tines of a fork. Place them on a rimmed baking sheet and bake them for 60 to 75 minutes, or until they are very tender. Remove them to a cooling rack to cool slightly.

2. Meanwhile, halve the onions and slice thinly (about 4 cups). Melt 2 tablespoons butter in a 3-quart saucepan over medium heat until hot. Reduce the heat to medium-low; add the onions and cook for 5 minutes, or until they have softened.

3. Remove 1 cup onions, season with salt and pepper to taste, and set aside. Press the garlic (about 1 tablespoon) into the onions in the saucepan and cook for 1 minute. Transfer the onion-garlic mixture to a blender. Reserve the saucepan.

4. Meanwhile, chop the Canadian bacon (about 1½ cups) and the celery stalks (about 1 cup). Melt the remaining 1 tablespoon butter in the saucepan over medium heat. Add the bacon and celery and cook, stirring occasionally, until both begin to brown, about 5 minutes.

5. When the sweet potatoes are cool enough to handle, split them in half lengthwise and scoop the flesh into the blender along with 2 cups chicken stock, the chipotle, and adobo sauce. Blend until pureed, adding more chicken stock, if necessary, to thin the mixture enough to blend.

6. Transfer the soup to the saucepan with the bacon and celery. Add the remaining chicken stock and bring to a boil over high heat, stirring frequently. Reduce the heat to low and simmer until the celery is tender, about 3 minutes. Coarsely chop the celery leaves. Top the soup with the reserved onions and the croutons, and garnish with the celery leaves.

MAKES ABOUT 1½ CUPS ▪ **HANDS-ON TIME: 10 MINUTES** ▪
TOTAL PREPARATION TIME: 25 TO 30 MINUTES

GARLIC RYE CROUTONS: Preheat the oven to 300°F. Trim the crusts from 2 slices rye bread (about 3 ounces) and cut the bread into ¾-inch squares. Combine 2 tablespoons extra virgin olive oil, 2 pressed garlic cloves (about 2 teaspoons), ½ teaspoon sweet paprika, and ⅛ teaspoon kosher salt in a small bowl. Add the bread and toss until the pieces are evenly coated. Spread out the croutons on a large, ungreased rimmed baking sheet and bake for 15 to 20 minutes, or until the bread squares are crisp and beginning to brown. Let cool.

is their a difference
BETWEEN SWEET POTATOES AND YAMS?

Americans are a little confused about sweet potatoes and yams. Unless you are shopping in a Caribbean market, it doesn't matter whether the sign says SWEET POTATOES or YAMS; they are all sweet potatoes. Native to America, these orange-, golden-, or white-fleshed roots were misnamed from the beginning. They aren't even related to potatoes (which are tubers, not roots), much less to yams.

True yams are a part of the diet in tropical areas and can be found in the United States only in ethnic markets. They are hard, rough skinned, and not very sweet, and they must be cooked (usually for a long time) before they can be eaten. We don't serve them for Thanksgiving. To confuse the issue even more, sweet potato producers in some parts of the South raise a variety of sweet potato that is larger, darker orange, and moister than the ones raised in other parts of the country, and they market these as yams.

Sweet potatoes are harvested in the fall, but they are in the market year-round. Look for ones that are smooth, plump, firm, and blemish free. Store them at room temperature, as the moisture in the refrigerator can cause them to spoil faster.

$\mathcal{S}$outhern Manhattan Corn Chowder with Fried Pickles

MAKES ABOUT 9½ CUPS, 4 SERVINGS ▪ HANDS-ON TIME: 50 MINUTES (SUMMER) ▪
TOTAL PREPARATION TIME: 50 MINUTES (SUMMER)

Everyone knows that summer corn and tomatoes go together like love and marriage. Adding pickles to the mix is my own little twist. Originally, I wanted to create a Manhattan corn chowder on the model of a Manhattan clam chowder. But when I thought of Manhattan, I thought of delis. When I thought of delis, I thought of pickles. And when I thought of pickles, I thought of the American South, where they slice, bread, and fry the sour little suckers—a fate that's never befallen one of New York's proud kosher dills. Too bad for them. A fried pickle is a happy pickle, and the ones in this recipe (actually, they're sautéed) add a delightful tang and crunch to every spoonful of this soup.

Note: I have given both a summer version (fresh tomatoes and corn) and a winter variation (canned tomatoes and frozen corn) so you can make this soup all year long.

4 ounces bacon (about 6 slices)
1 medium onion
2 medium celery stalks
1 small green bell pepper
1 large garlic clove
1 teaspoon fresh thyme leaves or ⅓ teaspoon dried
1 pound boiling potatoes, such as Yukon gold or Red Bliss
3 cups Homemade Chicken Stock (page 10, add preparation time) or canned broth
3 large ears fresh corn
2 pints (about 4 cups) cherry tomatoes
1 cup dill pickle slices
¼ cup stone-ground cornmeal

1. Heat a large stockpot over high heat. Reduce the heat to medium; add the bacon and cook until crisp, about 7 minutes.

2. Meanwhile, slice the onion (about 1 cup), celery (about ¾ cup), and bell pepper (about ¾ cup) into 1-inch pieces. Thinly slice the garlic (about 1 teaspoon). Combine the onion, celery, bell pepper, garlic, and thyme in the bowl of a food processor fitted with the chopping blade; pulse 4 to 5 times until coarsely chopped. Scrub the potatoes and cut into ½-inch dice.

3. Remove the cooked bacon to paper towels to drain; remove and reserve all but 1 tablespoon bacon fat in the stockpot. Reduce the heat to medium-low; scrape the onion mixture into the bacon fat in the stockpot and cook for 5 minutes, or until the vegetables have softened. Set aside the food processor bowl. Add the chicken stock and potatoes to the stockpot; bring to a boil over high heat, reduce the heat to low, and simmer until the potatoes are almost tender, about 12 minutes.

4. Meanwhile, husk the corn and remove the kernels from the cobs (about 3 cups). Scrape the cobs with the back of a knife to get the corn milk and add it to the corn kernels. Combine 1 cup corn kernels and ½ cup chicken stock from the pot in the food processor

Kosher salt and freshly
ground black pepper
2 ounces Swiss cheese
1 to 4 tablespoons
pickle juice

fitted with the chopping blade and process until pureed. Transfer the puree to a bowl. Add the tomatoes to the food processor; pulse 5 to 6 times until coarsely chopped.

5. Heat 2 tablespoons reserved bacon fat in a large skillet over medium heat. Toss the pickle slices with the cornmeal in a plastic bag, and place the pickles in the skillet in a single layer. Fry until golden, about 5 minutes; turn and fry the other side until golden, adding more fat if necessary, 3 to 4 minutes more. Sprinkle with salt and black pepper to taste and remove to a small plate. Coarsely shred the Swiss cheese (½ cup). Crumble the bacon.

6. When the potatoes are almost tender, add the remaining 2 cups corn kernels, the tomatoes, and pureed corn mixture to the pot and simmer for 5 minutes. Taste the soup and add pickle juice, salt, and pepper as desired. Divide the chowder among 4 soup plates and serve topped with the Swiss cheese, fried pickles, and bacon.

MAKES ABOUT 8½ CUPS, 4 SERVINGS ▪ HANDS-ON TIME: 40 MINUTES ▪
TOTAL PREPARATION TIME: 40 MINUTES (WINTER)

WINTER VERSION: Substitute one 15½-ounce can chopped tomatoes (preferably fire roasted) and 3 cups thawed frozen corn for the fresh tomatoes and corn.

$\mathcal{B}$lack Bean Soup with Quesadillas Ⓥ

MAKES 7 CUPS, 4 SERVINGS ▪ HANDS-ON TIME: 35 MINUTES ▪ TOTAL PREPARATION TIME: 35 MINUTES

This is the ultimate vegetarian soup-and-sandwich duo. Bean soup is plenty hearty by nature. Combine it with a substantial "sandwich" like this quesadilla and you're good to go.

1 large onion
3 tablespoons vegetable oil
5 garlic cloves
Three 15½-ounce cans black beans
2 tablespoons fresh oregano leaves or 1 teaspoon dried
One 28-ounce can chopped tomatoes (preferably fire roasted)
1 Turkish bay leaf
1 teaspoon ground cumin
Four 8-inch flour tortillas
¼ cup Basic Barbecue Sauce (page 15, add preparation time) or store-bought sauce
2 teaspoons fresh lime juice
1 ripe Hass avocado
Kosher salt
4 ounces sharp Cheddar cheese
Freshly ground black pepper

1. Chop the onion (about 2 cups). Heat 2 tablespoons vegetable oil in a large saucepan over high heat until hot. Add the onion, reduce the heat to medium, and sauté the onion until it is tender and begins to brown, about 7 minutes. Press the garlic (about 5 teaspoons) into the onion and cook for 1 minute more.

2. Rinse and drain the beans and chop the oregano (about 1 tablespoon). Add the beans to the onion in the saucepan along with the tomatoes and their liquid, 2 cups water, the oregano, bay leaf, and cumin. Bring to a boil over high heat, stirring frequently. Reduce the heat to medium-low, cover the saucepan, and simmer for 20 minutes.

3. Meanwhile, make the quesadillas. Place 2 tortillas on a work surface. Combine the barbecue sauce and 1 teaspoon lime juice; divide the mixture between the tortillas and spread to within ½ inch of the edges.

4. Halve, seed, peel, and thinly slice the avocado; toss the slices with 1 teaspoon lime juice and sprinkle with salt. Divide half the slices between the tortillas. Coarsely chop, cover, and set aside the remaining avocado slices. Coarsely grate the cheese (about 1 cup) and divide it between the tortillas: top each filled tortilla with another tortilla to make 2 quesadillas. Press the edges of the quesadillas together well to seal them before you put them in the skillet.

5. Brush the top of 1 quesadilla with some of the remaining 1 tablespoon vegetable oil. Heat a large skillet over medium heat until hot. Brush the skillet with some more of the vegetable oil and invert the quesadilla, oil side down, into the pan; cook for 3 minutes, or until nicely browned. Brush the top tortilla with more of

the oil; turn the quesadilla and cook for 2 minutes more, or until browned. Remove the quesadilla to a plate and keep warm. Repeat with the remaining quesadilla. Cut each quesadilla into 6 pieces.

6. When the soup has cooked, remove and discard the bay leaf. Transfer 2 cups soup to a blender or food processor fitted with the chopping blade and puree until smooth. Stir the puree into the remaining soup along with salt, pepper, and lime juice to taste. Reheat to a boil. Divide the soup among 4 soup plates, top with the reserved avocado, and serve with the quesadillas.

what is the best way
TO CHILL A BIG POT OF SOUP?

I'm often asked if it is all right to put a pot of warm soup in the fridge to chill. It's not a great idea to put a large amount of *anything* hot in the refrigerator; it can raise the overall temperature of the fridge and cause other foods to lose quality and even spoil. The best way to chill food quickly is to put the hot food in a bowl (preferably metal or heatproof glass), then immerse that bowl in a bowl of ice and water and stir the food every now and then until it reaches room temperature. In the case of soups and sauces, it is even faster if you transfer the liquid from the pot to a large shallow pan and set it inside another pan of ice and water. The added surface area will allow the heat to escape faster. Once the soup or sauce has reached room temperature, it can be returned to a container that will fit in the fridge, covered, and allowed to chill further.

$\mathcal{S}$pring Soup with Bread Dumplings

MAKES ABOUT 8 CUPS (WITHOUT DUMPLINGS), 4 SERVINGS ■ HANDS-ON TIME: 35 MINUTES ■
TOTAL PREPARATION TIME: 40 MINUTES

First things first: This is a spring soup. It's meant to be made when asparagus and fava beans are in season. Just because you can find these items in the supermarket in November, when they have been flown in from the other half of the world, doesn't mean you should give them a second thought. Eat this soup when our half of the planet is awakening from its long winter nap and you'll feel renewed, too.

That said, when I was finished preparing it, I worried that this light little soup might not be substantial enough to satisfy The Husband. Poring over the Italian cookbooks in my library, I came across several recipes for "bread dumplings." Now, I have never met a dumpling I didn't like, from gnocchi to pierogi, but these were news to me. Most dumplings require some sort of batter and a bit of prep time. I couldn't believe you could get away with using bread as the batter. Turns out that bread dumplings are a snap to make and, even better, when I added them to the soup, they absorbed a ton of flavor from the broth and puffed up like little balloons. The Husband was happy.

Bread Dumplings (recipe follows)

½ pound shelled fresh fava beans or shelled fresh lima beans, or 1⅔ cups thawed frozen limas or favas, or a combo

3 leeks (about 1½ pounds)

2 tablespoons unsalted butter

4 cups Homemade Chicken Stock (page 10, add preparation time) or canned broth

½ pound asparagus

½ pound small white mushrooms

2 ounces Parmigiano-Reggiano

1 cup shelled fresh or thawed frozen green peas

1. Prepare the Bread Dumplings.

2. If using fava beans, bring 1 quart salted water to a boil over high heat. Add the shelled fava beans and blanch for 1 minute; immediately transfer them with a slotted spoon to a bowl of ice and water to cool. When they are cool enough to handle, gently peel the skins from the beans.

3. Trim off and discard the green parts of the leeks, leaving about 5 inches. Cut the white parts in half lengthwise and then into 1-inch pieces (about 3½ cups); rinse them well and pat them dry.

4. Melt the butter in a large skillet over medium heat. Reduce the heat to medium-low; add the leeks and cook for 5 minutes, or until they have softened.

continued on next page

5. Meanwhile, bring the chicken stock to a boil in a 4-quart sauce-pan. Trim the asparagus. Peel the bottom half of the stems if the stems are thicker than ⅓ inch; slice the asparagus crosswise into 1-inch pieces (about 1⅓ cups). Clean, trim, and quarter the mush-rooms (about 2⅔ cups). Add the asparagus and mushrooms to the leeks and cook for 2 to 3 minutes more, or until almost tender. Microplane-grate the cheese (about 1⅓ cups) or grate on the fine side of a box grater (about ⅔ cup).

6. Add the leek mixture to the chicken stock along with the favas and peas. Bring to a boil over high heat. Reduce the heat to low; add the dumplings and cook for 8 to 10 minutes, until they are cooked through. Stir in the cheese and serve.

BREAD DUMPLINGS: Beat 2 large eggs in a medium bowl until frothy. Stir in 2 cups fresh white or whole wheat bread crumbs, 2 ounces Parmigiano-Reggiano (about 1⅓ cups Microplane-grated or ⅔ cup grated on the fine side of a box grater), and 2 tablespoons chopped fresh flat-leaf parsley leaves. Roll into 12 balls. Cook in the soup as directed above.

$\mathcal{C}$reamy Tomato Basil Soup and "Grilled" Cheese Slices Ⓥ

MAKES ABOUT 7 CUPS, 4 SERVINGS ▪ HANDS-ON TIME: 25 MINUTES ▪ TOTAL PREPARATION TIME: 30 MINUTES

This is the first recipe I thought of when it came time to write this book. I'm not sure if it was because of my lingering affection for the canned cream of tomato soup of my childhood or my present-day love of the freshly made tomato and basil soup served by the Così sandwich shop in my neighborhood. I do know that nothing beats the huge, bursting flavor of ripe tomatoes—raw, cooked, or canned—just as there are few things as deadly and disappointing as genetically engineered supermarket tomatoes.

I wanted this soup to be satisfying, but not too heavy. The "grilled" cheese is actually broiled cheese, and broiling the cheese-covered baguette slices cuts calories, too. As the cheese melts, the bread gets crusty—perfect for dipping into the soup.

2 medium carrots
1 medium onion
3 tablespoons extra virgin olive oil
2 tablespoons tomato paste
One 28-ounce can plus one 15-ounce can whole tomatoes (preferably fire roasted)
20 large fresh basil leaves
2 ounces Parmigiano-Reggiano
1½ cups whole milk
Kosher salt and freshly ground black pepper
4 ounces good melting cheese, such as fontina, Gruyère, or smoked Cheddar
Eight ½-inch-thick baguette slices

1. Thinly slice the carrots (about 1 cup) and onion (about 1 cup). Heat 1½ tablespoons olive oil in a large saucepan over medium heat until hot. Reduce the heat to medium-low; add the carrots and onion and cook for 5 minutes, or until the onion has softened. Stir in the tomato paste and cook for 1 minute. Add the tomatoes and their juices to the saucepan along with 10 basil leaves. Bring the mixture to a boil over high heat; reduce the heat to low and simmer for 15 minutes.

2. Meanwhile, coarsely grate the Parmigiano-Reggiano (about ⅔ cup). Working in batches, transfer the soup to a blender (reserve the saucepan) and puree until smooth. Add the Parmigiano-Reggiano to the last batch before pureeing.

3. Return the soup to the saucepan and bring it to a boil over high heat. Whisk in the milk and salt and pepper to taste. Cook just until hot. Coarsely grate the melting cheese (about 1 cup) and cut the remaining 10 basil leaves crosswise into thin ribbons (about 2 tablespoons).

4. Preheat the broiler. Arrange the baguette slices on a rimmed baking sheet and brush both sides of the slices with the remaining 1½ tablespoons olive oil. Broil for about 1 minute, just until they begin to brown. Turn and broil for about 30 seconds, or until barely golden. Divide the melting cheese among the slices and broil for about 1 minute, or until the cheese has melted and begins to brown.

5. Ladle the soup into 4 individual onion soup bowls or large ramekins. Top each bowl with 2 baguette slices, cheese side up; sprinkle with basil; and serve.

$\mathcal{S}$unny Summer Soup with Zucchini Crisps ⓥ

MAKES ABOUT 10 CUPS, 4 TO 6 SERVINGS ▪ HANDS-ON TIME: 50 MINUTES ▪ TOTAL PREPARATION TIME: 60 MINUTES

When *Gourmet* ran a recipe for a yellow squash soup several years ago, I rejected the very idea of it. Bor-ing. But one of my old pals from the test kitchen told me that I was wrong and I had to try it. I did and I was very pleasantly surprised.

This is my adaptation of that soup. I've amped up the yellow color, creamy texture, and sunny flavor by adding Yukon gold potatoes, a yellow bell pepper, and carrots. I've also en-listed Cousin Zucchini as a crispy garnish. A bowl of this soup is a perfect ode to summer.

Note: If this looks like too much dicing for you, cut the vegetables instead into large chunks and pulse them in a food processor until they are medium chopped.

2 pounds yellow summer squash (about 6 medium)

1 large yellow bell pepper (about 10 ounces)

4 medium carrots

½ pound Yukon gold potatoes (about 2 medium)

1 medium onion

2 tablespoons unsalted butter

Kosher salt

4 cups Homemade Vegetable or Chicken Stock (pages 11 and 10, add preparation time) or canned broth

Zucchini Crisps (recipe follows)

12 large fresh basil leaves

Freshly ground black pepper

1. Cut the squash in half and then into ½-inch dice (about 8 cups); cut the bell pepper into ½-inch dice (about 1½ cups); cut the carrots into ½-inch dice (about 1¼ cups); cut the potatoes into ½-inch dice (scant 1 cup).

2. Medium chop the onion (about 1 cup). Melt the butter in a large saucepan over medium heat. Reduce the heat to medium-low; add the onion and ½ teaspoon salt and cook for 5 minutes, or until the onion has softened.

3. Add the squash, bell pepper, carrots, and potatoes to the sauce-pan along with the vegetable stock; bring to a boil over high heat. Reduce the heat to low and simmer, partially covered, until the vegetables are tender, about 15 minutes. Remove from the heat and let cool, 10 minutes.

4. Meanwhile, make the Zucchini Crisps. Thinly slice the basil crosswise (a scant ¼ cup).

5. Transfer 3 cups of the vegetables from the soup to a small bowl using a slotted spoon and reserve. Working in small batches, puree the remaining soup in a blender until smooth; transfer to a bowl. Return the soup to the saucepan along with the reserved vegetables and add water, if necessary, to reach the desired consistency; add salt and black pepper to taste. Heat just to a boil. Divide the soup among 4 to 6 soup bowls; top each serving with some Zucchini Crisps and basil.

ZUCCHINI CRISPS: Preheat the oven to 250°F. Cut 1 medium zucchini crosswise into ¼-inch-thick slices (about 1¾ cups). Pulse 1½ slices firm white bread in a blender or food processor to make fresh bread crumbs. Combine ⅔ cup of the bread crumbs and 1½ ounces Parmigiano-Reggiano (1 cup Microplane-grated or ½ cup grated on the fine side of a box grater) in a medium bowl. Mix ⅓ cup Wondra or unbleached all-purpose flour with ½ teaspoon kosher salt and ¼ teaspoon freshly ground black pepper in a pie plate or shallow baking dish. Beat 1 large egg with ½ teaspoon water in a small bowl. Heat 2 tablespoons extra virgin olive oil in a large nonstick skillet over high heat until hot. Dredge the zucchini slices in the flour, shaking off any excess. Dip them into the egg and then into the crumbs. Reduce the heat to medium-low. Fry the zucchini in several batches for 4 to 5 minutes, or until browned on both sides. Add more olive oil as needed. Drain the crisps on paper towels and sprinkle with salt. Transfer them to a rimmed baking sheet and keep them warm in the oven.

Indian Red Lentil and Chicken Soup

MAKES ABOUT 6 CUPS, 4 SERVINGS ▪ HANDS-ON TIME: 30 MINUTES ▪ TOTAL PREPARATION TIME: 50 MINUTES

This is my quick version of mulligatawny soup, a well-known standard of Indian cuisine. I've swapped in light coconut milk for the full-fat version. These days both are usually available in the international aisle of your local supermarket (or make your own coconut milk from scratch; see page 353). To save time, I've called for already-cooked rotisserie chicken, but you're certainly welcome to make your own.

What with the lentils, chicken, and coconut milk, this rich and hearty soup is sure to fill you up, and make you happy.

2 medium carrots
1 medium onion
1 Golden Delicious apple
2 medium celery stalks
1 tablespoon vegetable oil
1 tablespoon garam masala (see Note)
One 1½-inch piece fresh ginger
4 cups Homemade Chicken Stock (page 10, add preparation time) or canned broth
1 cup light coconut milk
1 cup red lentils
2 cups packed skinless cooked chicken from a large store-bought rotisserie chicken, or leftovers
½ cup fresh cilantro leaves (optional)

1. Finely chop the carrots and onion (about 1 cup each); peel and finely chop the apple (about 1 cup); and finely chop the celery (about ¾ cup).

2. Heat the vegetable oil in a 3-quart saucepan over high heat; reduce the heat to medium. Add 1 teaspoon garam masala; cook for 1 minute, or until it starts to smell fragrant. Add the carrots, onion, apple, and celery; cook, stirring frequently, until the mixture has softened, about 8 minutes. Meanwhile, peel and Microplane-grate the ginger (about 1½ teaspoons).

3. Add the chicken stock, coconut milk, ginger, and 1 teaspoon garam masala to the saucepan. Rinse the lentils in cold water and immediately stir into the soup. Bring the soup to a boil over high heat, reduce the heat to low, and simmer for 20 to 25 minutes, or until the lentils are just tender.

4. While the soup is cooking, cut the chicken into ¼-inch pieces. Coarsely chop the cilantro (about ¼ cup), if using.

5. Add the chicken and remaining 1 teaspoon garam masala to the soup; return it to a boil. Serve the soup sprinkled with the chopped cilantro, if desired.

NOTE: Garam masala is a spice blend from India. You can find it in specialty food stores or see Sources (page 359).

MARROM GLACE

KALUSTYAN'S
SINCE 1944

TOP GRADE
LENTIL MIX
BLEND OF MOONG & MASOOR DAL

14 OZ.

$2.99

Chicken Potpie Soup

MAKES ABOUT 9 CUPS, 4 SERVINGS ▪ HANDS-ON TIME: 35 MINUTES ▪ TOTAL PREPARATION TIME: 35 MINUTES

Although the men in my family love chicken potpie, I don't make it at home because it seems like too much work on a weeknight. You have to poach the chicken and vegetables, thicken the broth, and make pastry. However, as consolation, I thought I could take the same elements and turn them into a soup.

The only tricky part of this recipe was figuring out the pastry. I tried several different possibilities—from store-bought puff pastry to homemade biscuits to actual pie dough—but none of them was quite right. Finally, my cooking partner, Joanne, came up with the lavash croutons made from the soft, thin flat bread (not the lavash crackers). They have unbeatable crunch and flavor and require nothing more than toasting. If you can't find lavash in your supermarket, flour tortillas are an acceptable substitute.

The final recipe is win-win; it delivers deep potpie comfort with weeknight ease.

6 cups Homemade
   Chicken Stock
   (page 10; add
   preparation time) or
   canned broth
1 pound boneless,
   skinless chicken
   breast halves
Lavash Croutons (recipe
   follows)
2 medium celery stalks
2 large leeks
2 large carrots
6 tablespoons (¾ stick)
   unsalted butter
6 tablespoons
   unbleached all-
   purpose flour
1 cup dry white wine
1 tablespoon fresh
   thyme leaves or
   ½ teaspoon dried
2 teaspoons fresh sage
   leaves or ⅓ teaspoon
   dried

1. Bring the chicken stock to a boil in a large saucepan over high heat; add the chicken breasts and simmer them very gently for 7 minutes. Remove the pan from the heat, cover, and let stand for 10 minutes. Remove the chicken breasts to a plate and cut into one to make sure it is cooked through. If it is not, return the chicken to the saucepan, cover, and simmer for 2 minutes more. After the chicken has cooled slightly, cut it into bite-size pieces.

2. Meanwhile, make the Lavash Croutons.

3. Cut the celery crosswise into ½-inch pieces (about 1 cup). Trim off and discard the green parts of the leeks, leaving about 5 inches. Cut the white parts in half lengthwise, and then into ½-inch lengths (about 2¼ cups); rinse them well and pat dry. Split the carrots lengthwise and cut them into ½-inch pieces (about 1¾ cups).

4. Melt the butter in a large skillet over medium heat. Reduce the heat to medium-low; add the celery, leeks, and carrots and cook for 8 minutes, stirring frequently, until they have softened.

5. Add the flour and cook, stirring, for 3 minutes. Add the wine, whisking constantly, and bring to a boil over high heat. Add 2 cups hot chicken stock from the saucepan, whisking constantly. Bring

1 tablespoon fresh
lemon juice
Kosher salt and freshly
ground black pepper

to a boil over high heat, stirring constantly. Whisk the vegetable–chicken stock mixture into the remaining stock in the saucepan.

6. Finely chop the thyme (about 1½ teaspoons) and the sage (about 1 teaspoon). Add the thyme and sage to the saucepan; return to a boil, reduce the heat to low, and simmer until the vegetables are tender, about 3 minutes. Add the chicken, lemon juice, and salt and pepper to taste. Return just to a boil. Divide the soup among 4 soup plates; top each serving with some Lavash Croutons.

LAVASH CROUTONS: Preheat the oven to 425°F. Melt 1 tablespoon butter with ½ teaspoon pressed garlic. Brush a 9-inch square lavash flat bread on both sides with the butter, sprinkle with kosher salt, and cut into 1-inch squares. Bake until crisp, 5 to 6 minutes.

Red Beans and Rice Soup with Ham

MAKES ABOUT 10 CUPS, 6 SERVINGS ■ HANDS-ON TIME: 25 MINUTES ■ TOTAL PREPARATION TIME: 40 MINUTES

Red beans and rice is one of the signature dishes of New Orleans, a city rich with the influences of Latin America and the Caribbean. Indeed, that's why Louis Armstrong, New Orleans's pioneering cultural ambassador to the world, used to sign off his letters, "Red beans and ricely yours. . . ."

Now that virtually all of us everywhere enjoy red beans and rice, I didn't see why I couldn't turn this classic into a delicious soup. All it took was the addition of celery, onion, and bell pepper (aka the holy trinity of New Orleans, Cajun, and Creole cooking), a little Creole seasoning, and some chicken stock. I loved it the very first time I made it.

Leave out the sausage and ham and substitute vegetable stock for the chicken stock, and you've got a lean vegetarian version of this winner.

2 tablespoons
    vegetable oil
6 ounces ham
1 large onion
4 medium celery stalks
1 large green bell
    pepper
3 garlic cloves
1 tablespoon Creole
    Seasoning (page
    20, add preparation
    time) or store-bought
    Creole seasoning
1 pound fully cooked
    smoked andouille
    sausage
Two 15½-ounce cans
    red kidney beans
6 cups Homemade
    Chicken Stock (page
    10, add preparation
    time) or canned broth
1 Turkish bay leaf
1½ cups cooked white
    or brown rice (*Note*:
    ½ cup uncooked
    rice equals 1½ cups
    cooked.)

1. Heat the vegetable oil in a 3-quart saucepan over medium heat. Medium chop the ham (about 1⅓ cups) and add to the saucepan; cook until the ham is lightly browned, about 5 minutes. Transfer with a slotted spoon to a small bowl and set aside.

2. Meanwhile, medium chop the onion (about 2 cups), celery (about 2 cups), and bell pepper (about 1½ cups). Add the onion to the saucepan and cook, stirring occasionally, for about 5 minutes, or until it is lightly browned. Add the celery and bell pepper and cook for 2 to 3 minutes. Press the garlic (about 1 tablespoon) into the vegetables in the saucepan; stir in the Creole Seasoning and cook for 1 minute more.

3. Halve the sausage lengthwise and slice it crosswise into ¼-inch-thick pieces (about 3 cups); rinse and drain the beans. Add the chicken stock, sausage, beans, ham, and bay leaf to the vegetable mixture and simmer for 15 minutes. Discard the bay leaf, stir in the rice, heat, and serve.

Smoky Fish Chowder

Is it a stretch to suggest that what we like about smoked food is the same thing that we like about open fires, namely, the scent of the hearth and the suggestion of the intimate comforts of home? It's why no one can resist the smell of bacon cooking.

This recipe combines two of my favorite smoked foods: Canadian bacon and trout. The rest of the ingredients—potatoes, celery, onion, and milk—are all chowder regulars. The finished product is the ultimate cold-weather comfort soup.

4 tablespoons (½ stick) unsalted butter
8 ounces Canadian bacon
1 medium onion
2 medium celery stalks
1 pound boiling potatoes, such as Yukon gold or Red Bliss
1 tablespoon plus 1 teaspoon fresh thyme leaves or ⅔ teaspoon dried
3 tablespoons all-purpose flour
2½ cups Homemade Chicken Stock (page 10, add preparation time) or canned broth
3 cups whole milk
12 ounces smoked trout fillets
Smoked paprika, for garnish
Chopped fresh dill leaves or parsley, or chopped chiles, for garnish (optional)

1. Melt the butter in a large saucepan over medium heat. Medium chop the Canadian bacon (about 1¾ cups) and add it to the saucepan; cook it until it turns light brown, about 5 minutes. Remove it with a slotted spoon to a bowl and set aside.

2. Finely chop the onion (about 1 cup) and celery (about 1 cup). Reduce the heat to medium-low; add the onion and celery to the saucepan and cook for 5 minutes, or until the onion has softened. Meanwhile, scrub the potatoes and cut them into ⅓-inch cubes; finely chop the thyme (about 2 teaspoons).

3. Add the flour to the saucepan and cook, stirring, for 2 minutes. Add the chicken stock and milk and bring to a boil over high heat, whisking constantly. Add the potatoes and thyme and simmer, stirring occasionally, for 12 to 15 minutes, or until the potatoes are tender.

4. Remove and discard the skin from the trout. Break the flesh into bite-size pieces (a little more than 2 cups) and add them to the pan along with the reserved bacon; cook until heated through. Serve the soup sprinkled with paprika and chopped herbs or chiles, if using.

5

SANDWICH NIGHT

It wasn't so long ago that the food police declared that carbohydrates were the devil. All too many people went along with the decree, sheepishly purging bread, potatoes, and pasta from their kitchens. Horrified, some of us fought back, saying, "Wait! You can't throw out all carbs!" and stood up for whole grains, including slices of whole wheat white bread, which allow you to have your white bread and eat it, too. But, really, you can put any number of healthy foods between two slices of bread, no matter what kind of bread it is. So why throw out the baby with the bathwater?

In my book, bread remains the staff of life. Who doesn't love a sandwich? For dinner purposes, the kind of sandwich I propose is not peanut butter and jelly on Wonder bread, but a heartier and more flavorful thing that is also a snap to prepare and serve. The menu in this chapter includes a sandwich for every taste: chicken, beef, pork, duck, seafood, fish, and vegetarian. I recommend a particular type of bread for each sandwich, but you're welcome to substitute whatever you want.

FACING PAGE: *Peking Duck Wraps.*

$\mathcal{P}$ulled Chicken Barbecue on Beer Bread with Pickled Cucumbers

MAKES 4 SERVINGS ■ HANDS-ON TIME: 20 MINUTES ■ TOTAL PREPARATION TIME: 20 MINUTES

This recipe probably has more "cheats" in it than any other in the book. You shred a supermarket rotisserie chicken (or leftover chicken) and toss it with barbecue sauce. I suggest topping it with Dill Pickle Cucumber Slices and serving it on Beer Bread, but you can certainly top it with chopped-up dill pickles from the store and serve it on your favorite commercial rolls or hamburger buns. For that matter, you can also buy the barbecue sauce at the supermarket if you don't want to whip up my quick version. In short, it doesn't get much simpler. And it's delicious, too.

1 recipe Beer Bread
   (page 264, add
   preparation time) or
   use 4 large rolls or
   hamburger buns
1 recipe Basic Barbecue
   Sauce (page 15, add
   preparation time) or
   2 cups store-bought
   sauce
1 recipe Dill Pickle
   Cucumber Slices
   (page 22, add
   preparation time;
   optional)
4 cups packed
   shredded skinless
   cooked chicken
   from a large store-
   bought rotisserie
   chicken, or leftovers,
   or Can't Overcook
   'Em Chicken Breasts
   (page 31, add
   preparation time)

1. Prepare the Beer Bread, Basic Barbecue Sauce, and Dill Pickle Cucumber Slices, if using, or bring the prepared sauce to a boil in a medium saucepan and warm the store-bought buns.

2. Add the chicken to the sauce and heat until hot.

3. Cut the Beer Bread, if using, into 8 pieces (about 4 by 3 inches each). Place pieces of bread on each of 4 serving plates and divide the chicken mixture among them. Top the chicken with the pickled cucumbers, if using, and another piece of bread.

$\mathcal{C}$hicken Parmigiana Heros

MAKES 4 SERVINGS ■ HANDS-ON TIME: 25 MINUTES ■
TOTAL PREPARATION TIME: 35 MINUTES

When I told The Husband that I was going to develop a recipe for a chicken Parm hero, he said, "Why bother when you can buy one at any sub shop in the country?" I said, "Because mine will be homemade from fresh ingredients, taste much better, and cost less." That shut him up. Then he tasted it and got real happy.

1 small onion
24 large fresh basil
  leaves
¼ cup extra virgin
  olive oil
One 14.5-ounce can
  chopped tomatoes
  (preferably fire
  roasted)
Kosher salt and freshly
  ground black pepper
3 tablespoons whole
  milk
4 thin-sliced chicken
  breast cutlets (about
  ¾ pound)
½ ounce Parmigiano-
  Reggiano
⅓ cup prepared Italian
  bread crumbs
Four 6-inch hero rolls
  or one 24-inch
  loaf Italian bread,
  quartered
1 garlic clove
3 ounces lightly
  salted mozzarella
  (preferably fresh)

1. Finely chop the onion. Slice 12 basil leaves crosswise into ribbons (about 1 tablespoon). Heat 1 tablespoon olive oil in a large skillet over medium heat until hot. Reduce the heat to medium-low; add the onion and cook for 5 minutes, or until it has softened. Add the tomatoes and sliced basil; bring the mixture to a boil and simmer until it is thick and saucy, about 10 minutes. Season the sauce with salt and pepper to taste and keep warm.

2. Meanwhile, combine the milk, ¼ teaspoon salt, and ⅛ teaspoon pepper in a resealable plastic bag. Add the chicken and knead until it is coated with the milk. Microplane-grate the Parmigiano-Reggiano (about ⅓ cup), or grate on the fine side of a box grater (about ⅙ cup). Combine the cheese and the crumbs. Heat another 1 tablespoon olive oil in a large skillet with an ovenproof handle. Dip the chicken cutlets into the crumbs, coating them well. Add them to the skillet and fry, turning once and adding 1 tablespoon of olive oil, about 5 minutes per side, until they are golden on both sides.

3. Preheat the broiler to high. Split the rolls lengthwise; brush the cut sides with the remaining 1 tablespoon olive oil and toast them under the broiler for 30 to 45 seconds, or just until they begin to brown. Split the garlic and rub the toasted bread with the cut sides of the garlic.

4. Slice the mozzarella into 12 pieces and place the slices over the chicken pieces in the skillet; place the skillet under the broiler for about 1 minute, or just until the cheese melts and starts to brown.

5. Place a roll on each of 4 serving plates. Spoon one-quarter of the sauce onto each roll; add the chicken, top with the remaining basil leaves, and serve.

Hot Ploughman's Sandwiches

MAKES 4 SERVINGS ■ HANDS-ON TIME: 25 MINUTES ■ TOTAL PREPARATION TIME: 25 MINUTES

The ploughman's lunch originated in England, where fieldworkers have been called plough-men or ploughboys since at least the middle of the fourteenth century. Indeed, as www .wisegeek.com points out, "The name and ingredients of the ploughman's lunch [bread, cheese, and pickled vegetables] are meant to evoke a bygone era, when a ploughman would have packed his lunch to the field so that it would be ready to hand when he wanted to take a break." Amusingly, the ploughman's lunch per se appears to be of much more recent vin-tage, the mid-twentieth-century invention of an English advisory board to promote the eating of more English cheese. Cheap, filling, and flavorful, the ploughman's lunch, washed down with a pint of beer, remains a staple of rural pubs throughout the United Kingdom.

When I was growing up, my mom used to make a ploughman's sandwich, although she substituted chutney for the Brits' Branston Pickle. (You can find Branston Pickle at www .ethnicgrocer.com and use it in place of the chutney and onions in this recipe.) The deli-ciousness of that sandwich has burned in my brain for a lifetime. Accordingly, I thought I'd turn it into a hot weeknight supper entrée by literally beefing it up and adding my own ver-sion of pickled onions.

Pickled Red Onion
  (recipe follows)
⅓ cup mango chutney
  (preferably Major
  Grey's)
1 tablespoon Dijon
  mustard
8 slices rustic white
  bread
8 thin slices sharp
  Cheddar cheese
  (about 6 ounces)
8 ounces thinly sliced
  deli roast beef
2 tablespoons unsalted
  butter

1. Prepare the Pickled Red Onion. Chop the chutney if the pieces are large; stir in the mustard.

2. Place 4 bread slices on a work surface. Arrange 1 slice of the cheese on each of the bread slices. Divide the roast beef, chutney, pickled onion, and remaining cheese among the bread slices and top each with one of the remaining bread slices.

3. Heat 1 tablespoon butter in a large cast-iron skillet over medium-low heat; add the sandwiches and place something heavy (such as a heavy skillet, flat saucepan lid, or heatproof plate and a weight such as a food can or full teakettle) on top to firmly press the sandwiches down. Cook for 4 or 5 minutes, or until golden; add remaining 1 tablespoon butter, turn the sandwiches, weight down, and cook for 4 or 5 minutes more, or until the cheese has melted. Cut the sandwiches in half and serve.

PICKLED RED ONION: Slice 1 medium red onion ¼ inch thick (about 1 cup); split 1 garlic clove lengthwise. Combine the onion, ¾ cup cider vinegar, 1½ tablespoons sugar, 1½ teaspoons pickling spice, the garlic, and ¾ teaspoon kosher salt in a very small saucepan. Bring the mixture to a boil over high heat. Reduce the heat to medium and simmer for 2 minutes. Remove the pan from the heat and let cool for 10 minutes. Drain well; remove the garlic and any large pieces of spice, and use as directed above.

Texas Cheesesteak Sandwiches

MAKES 4 SERVINGS ▪ HANDS-ON TIME: 25 MINUTES ▪ TOTAL PREPARATION TIME: 25 MINUTES

Everybody loves a Philly cheesesteak, yours truly certainly included. I tried and failed to create a cheesesteak recipe for the home cook in time for my last book—when I started with sliced deli beef, the cheesesteak turned out dry. The results were much better when I began with very thinly sliced raw beef, but that figured to be too much trouble for the home cook.

Finally, I had my eureka moment. If you start by cooking up a tender steak, then slice it, add sautéed bell pepper, and quickly melt the cheese on top, the meat will turn out pink and succulent. Inspired, I added my own little twist—Ro*Tel canned tomatoes. A Tex-Mex fave that emerged out of a tiny south Texas border town named Elsa in the early 1940s, Ro*Tel boasts chopped green chile peppers and a special blend of spices. It's been widely available since the 1990s, which was when I was turned on to it by Marie Ostrosky, a proud and tasteful Texan who worked with me on *Cooking Live*.

One 10-ounce can chopped tomatoes with green chiles (preferably Ro*Tel) or one 10-ounce can chopped tomatoes plus 1 tablespoon chopped jalapeño chile (make sure it has heat; see page 6)
6 ounces sharp Cheddar cheese
1 medium onion
1 small green bell pepper
1¼ pounds skirt steak
Kosher salt and freshly ground black pepper
3 tablespoons vegetable oil
4 slices rustic white bread (¾ inch thick)
1 garlic clove

1. Bring the tomatoes to a boil in a medium saucepan over high heat; cook, stirring frequently, for about 7 minutes, or until there is very little juice in the pan. Remove from the heat.

2. Meanwhile, coarsely grate the cheese (about 1½ cups). Slice the onion (about 1 cup) and bell pepper (about ¾ cup). Trim the steak and cut it into 6-inch lengths; season them with salt and black pepper to taste. Heat 2 tablespoons vegetable oil in a large skillet over high heat until hot; reduce the heat to medium-high and add the steak in batches. Cook for 2 to 3 minutes on each side for medium rare. Remove the steak to a platter and cover loosely with aluminum foil.

3. Heat the remaining 1 tablespoon vegetable oil in the same skillet over medium heat until hot; add the onion, bell pepper, and a pinch of salt. Cook for 5 minutes, or until the onion has charred slightly, adding water, if necessary, to keep the onion from burning.

4. Toast the bread until just golden. Split the garlic and rub one side of each slice of toast with the cut sides of the garlic.

5. Return the reduced tomatoes to a boil over low heat; slowly add the cheese, stirring constantly, until all the cheese has melted. Thinly slice the steak against the grain. Add the meat juices to the tomato and cheese sauce and season the sauce with salt and pepper to taste.

6. Place 1 toasted bread slice, garlicky side up, on each of 4 dinner plates. Divide the steak and vegetables among the slices and top with the cheese sauce. *Note:* You will need a steak knife and fork to eat this sandwich.

Picadillo Sloppy Joes

MAKES 4 SERVINGS (3½ CUPS FILLING) ■ HANDS-ON TIME: 30 MINUTES ■ TOTAL PREPARATION TIME: 30 MINUTES

A traditional dish found in many Latin American countries, picadillo consists of shredded or ground beef, tomatoes, and a variety of regional ingredients, often including olives and raisins. The ingredients I've used here, starting with the chili sauce, are so assertive that you don't have to cook them very long to develop the flavor. This makes it an ideal recipe for a weeknight.

Usually, picadillo is used as a filling in turnovers or served on top of rice. I thought it would be tasty on a bun, sort of like a Latin sloppy joe.

1 medium onion
2 tablespoons extra virgin olive oil
3 garlic cloves
1 pound ground chuck, round, or sirloin
One 4½-ounce can chopped green chiles
½ cup pimiento-stuffed green olives
1 cup chili sauce
¼ cup dark seedless raisins
Kosher salt and freshly ground black pepper
1 to 2 tablespoons fresh lemon or lime juice
Hot sauce
Hot dogs buns

1. Finely chop the onion (about 1 cup). Heat the olive oil in a large skillet over medium heat until hot. Reduce the heat to medium-low; add the onion and cook for 5 minutes, or until it has softened. Press the garlic (about 1 tablespoon) into the pan and cook for 1 minute more.

2. Turn the heat up to medium-high. Add the ground chuck and cook, stirring and breaking up the lumps, for about 5 minutes, or until it is no longer pink.

3. Drain the chiles; finely chop the olives (about ⅓ cup). Add 1 cup water, the chili sauce, chiles, olives, raisins, 1 teaspoon salt, and ¼ teaspoon pepper to the skillet; simmer for 10 minutes, or until most of the liquid has evaporated. Stir in the lemon juice, hot sauce to taste, and salt and pepper to taste. Divide the mixture among the buns and serve.

is there a difference
BETWEEN HAMBURGER AND GROUND BEEF?

There is. Government regulations specify that a package of beef that is ground and labeled "hamburger" in a USDA-inspected plant may have additional beef fat (not a part of the meat that was ground) added to it, and one labeled "ground beef" may not. Both hamburger and ground beef may have no more than 30 percent fat by weight. The cut of meat used does not have to be specified and it can have seasonings but not water, phosphates, extenders, or binders added. Actually, I don't recommend buying either "hamburger" or "ground beef." I prefer to buy beef that has been ground from a single cut and is labeled "ground chuck," "ground round," or "ground sirloin," or, better yet, buy your favorite cut of meat and grind it yourself.

Kielbasa Sandwiches with Kimchi and Cheddar

MAKES 4 SERVINGS ▪ HANDS-ON TIME: 20 MINUTES ▪ TOTAL PREPARATION TIME: 20 MINUTES

Given the enduring popularity of hot dogs and sauerkraut, I thought it might make sense to pair up kielbasa and kimchi. Call it the attempt of a not-so-mad scientist to create a Polish-Korean love child from a couple of all-American parents. (Truthfully, ever since I figured out how to make a quick and delicious kimchi, I've had to restrain myself from putting it into everything.)

This recipe was a big hit with the family from the very first time I tried it. The acid and heat in the kimchi provide a refreshing contrast to the richness of the kielbasa. The Cheddar cheese just gilds the lily; it's great, but you can leave it off and it won't hurt the sandwich.

This sandwich should be a crowd-pleaser not only on a weeknight, but served up to the sports-watching crew on a weekend as well. (I can't pretend that I follow sports, but I am interested in food for sports watching.)

1 cup well-drained Quick or Quicker Kimchi (page 21, add preparation time) or use store-bought kimchi
4 hero rolls
2 tablespoons extra virgin olive oil
1½ pounds kielbasa (about 1½ kielbasas)
2 ounces sharp Cheddar cheese

1. Prepare Quick or Quicker Kimchi.

2. Heat a large skillet over medium heat until hot. Split the rolls horizontally to within ½ inch of the other side. Brush the cut surfaces with the olive oil. Reduce the heat to medium-low; place the rolls, cut side down, in the skillet, 2 at a time, and cook for about 1 minute, or until they just begin to brown. Transfer to a platter and set aside.

3. Meanwhile, cut the kielbasa crosswise into 4 pieces and split it horizontally. Thinly slice the cheese.

4. Add the kielbasa, cut side down, to the same skillet and cook over medium-low heat for about 5 minutes, or until browned. Turn and cook for about 5 minutes more, or until the other sides have browned.

5. Top the kielbasa with the kimchi and cheese; cover the skillet and cook for about 1 minute, or just until the cheese has melted. Transfer the kielbasa pieces to the rolls and serve.

Peking Duck Wraps

MAKES 8 WRAPS, 4 SERVINGS ■ HANDS-ON TIME: 25 MINUTES ■ TOTAL PREPARATION TIME: 25 MINUTES

One evening recently I was cooking sautéed duck breasts, a favorite at our house, when I thought of Peking duck and wondered if I couldn't dream up a version for this book. Peking duck is a great classic of Chinese cuisine, "a dish fit for an emperor," according to writer Emily Hahn, but making it damn near requires an emperor's kitchen staff. Ms. Hahn, writing in Time-Life's *The Cooking of China* (1968), laid out some of the details:

> The traditional version calls for the choicest fowl, brought to the exact degree of plumpness and tenderness through force-feeding, and got ready for the table by a many-staged process [including air-drying it for a full day]. The birds are roasted in a mud-lined oven, suspended from hooks to ensure even heat on all sides.

In short, no home cook in his or her right mind is ever going to make traditional Peking duck—at least not on a weeknight.

Think of this recipe, then, as Peking duck light. (That's light on procedure, not on flavor.) You use the same kind of duck, but the breasts only, and you sauté them, which takes only about 15 minutes. (The skin won't turn out quite as crispy as if you had roasted the duck, but it's plenty crispy enough.) The Asian-style coleslaw with which I've supplemented the classic recipe provides acidic contrast to the sweet hoisin and fatty skin. Roll it all up in my cheating nonhomemade pancakes (aka flour tortillas) and you have a feast in every bite. Best of all, you can measure the hands-on cooking time in minutes (about 25 of them), not days.

4 Pekin duck breast halves
Kosher salt and freshly ground black pepper
Ginger Hoisin Sauce (recipe follows)
½ medium napa cabbage
1 medium jicama
1 medium red bell pepper
4 medium scallions

1. Heat a large skillet over medium-high heat until hot. Score the skin on each breast half in a crisscross pattern. Season the duck on all sides with salt and black pepper to taste and place, skin side down, in the skillet. Cook until the skin looks very crispy, 6 to 8 minutes. Do not remove the fat as you go; the liquid fat in the pan helps to render out the fat in the skin.

2. When the duck skin is crisp, remove the duck to a plate, skin side down; pour off almost all the fat from the pan and reserve it for another use or discard it. Return the duck to the skillet, meat side down, and cook for 2 to 3 minutes more for medium-rare.

3 tablespoons seasoned
rice vinegar
¼ teaspoon crushed red
pepper flakes
Eight 8-inch flour
tortillas

Return the duck to the plate, skin side up, cover it loosely with aluminum foil, and set it aside for 5 minutes.

3. Meanwhile, make the Ginger Hoisin Sauce.

4. Shred the cabbage (about 2 cups). Peel the jicama; finely chop both the jicama and bell pepper either by hand or in a food processor fitted with the chopping blade (about 1 cup each). Trim and thinly slice the scallions crosswise (about ½ cup). Stir together the vinegar, ½ teaspoon salt, and the crushed red pepper flakes in a medium bowl until the salt dissolves. Add the cabbage, jicama, bell pepper, and scallions and toss until the salad is well mixed.

5. Spread out the tortillas on a work surface. Spread them with sauce, dividing it equally. Thinly slice the duck at an angle into ¼-inch-thick slices and arrange the slices on the tortillas; top with the cabbage salad. Fold in the sides of the tortillas and roll up. Place 2, seam side down, on each of 4 plates.

GINGER HOISIN SAUCE: Combine 3 tablespoons soy sauce (low sodium, if you prefer), 3 tablespoons hoisin sauce, 2 teaspoons grated fresh ginger, 2 teaspoons unseasoned rice vinegar, ½ garlic clove, pressed (about ½ teaspoon), and a pinch of cayenne pepper in a small saucepan and simmer for 2 minutes.

Southwestern Caesar Shrimp Sandwiches

MAKES 4 SERVINGS ■ HANDS-ON TIME: 25 MINUTES ■ TOTAL PREPARATION TIME: 25 MINUTES

This recipe is all about the dressing. These days you can order a Caesar salad at virtually every restaurant in the country, but the dressing's often missing the single most important ingredient: anchovies. "That's not a problem for me," you say. "I hate anchovies." Well, the role of an anchovy in the Caesar dressing is not to add anchovy taste, but to provide depth of flavor and saltiness. If the anchovy is in balance with the rest of the ingredients, you won't even taste it, but you will love the dressing. (This "balance" is of no interest to people like The Husband, who orders a small plate of anchovies to eat with his Caesar salad whenever possible.) I threw a chipotle (smoked jalapeño) into the dressing for added spice and heat, but you can leave it out if you're not a fan. This recipe would work equally well with cooked chicken, pork, or beef replacing the shrimp.

1½ ounces Parmigiano-Reggiano
¼ cup fresh lemon juice
1 tablespoon Dijon mustard
6 flat anchovies (optional)
1 tablespoon drained capers
1 small chipotle chile in adobo sauce
1 teaspoon Worcestershire sauce
1 garlic clove
½ cup extra virgin olive oil
Kosher salt and freshly ground black pepper
¾ pound cooked, shelled, and deveined medium shrimp (see Jenn's "Boiled" Shrimp, opposite)
8 large romaine lettuce leaves
2 cups tortilla chips
Four 7- to 8-inch flour tortillas

1. Microplane-grate the cheese (about 1 cup) or grate on the fine side of a box grater (about ½ cup). Combine ¼ cup cheese with the lemon juice, mustard, anchovies (if using), capers, chipotle, and Worcestershire sauce in a blender. Press the garlic (about 1 teaspoon) into the mixture and blend until pureed. With the blender running, gradually drizzle in the olive oil until combined. Transfer the dressing to a medium bowl and add salt and pepper to taste.

2. Cut the shrimp crosswise into ½-inch pieces and stir them into the dressing. Halve the lettuce leaves lengthwise and cut them crosswise into ½-inch ribbons. Coarsely crush the tortilla chips (about 1 cup). Add the lettuce, tortilla chips, and the remaining cheese to the shrimp mixture and toss to combine.

3. Spread out the tortillas on a work surface. Divide the shrimp mixture among the tortillas, covering one-half of each tortilla. Starting with the side covered with filling, roll up the tortillas halfway; fold in the ends of the roll and continue rolling. To serve, place a filled tortilla, seam side down, on each of 4 serving plates and cut diagonally in half.

how can i
COOK SHRIMP TO KEEP THEM FROM GETTING TOUGH?

Whether you deep-fry, sauté, stir-fry, steam, or boil shrimp, they cook to tender, juicy perfection very, very quickly and then overcook. Shrimp should be cooked just until they turn color and then removed before they are cooked through; the stored heat will complete the cooking. If shrimp are going to be a part of a mixed dish, it is best to cook them first, remove them from the heat, and stir them into the finished dish just before serving. My *chef de cuisine* at *Gourmet,* Jennifer Day, made the best "boiled" shrimp. They, like my hard-cooked eggs, are not really boiled. Jenn's shrimp are tender, unlike the usual rubbery boiled shrimp you find at bar mitzvahs and weddings, and well seasoned. Here is her recipe:

JENN'S "BOILED" SHRIMP

Bring a pot of highly salted water to a boil. Add fresh peeled and deveined shrimp and simmer until the shrimp turn color and are just cooked through (cut one open to make sure it is not translucent in the center), 3 to 4 minutes. (We usually cook what are referred to as large shrimp, so adjust the timing if your shrimp are smaller or larger.) Drain the shrimp and transfer immediately to a bowl of ice and water and let chill for 10 minutes. Drain, pat dry, and use in whatever recipe you are making.

"Fried" Catfish BLTs

MAKES 4 SERVINGS ■ HANDS-ON TIME: 30 MINUTES ■ TOTAL PREPARATION TIME: 30 MINUTES

The Husband tends to scorn the BLT as an "air sandwich." Of course, it's delicious—how can it not be as long as bacon is involved—but it's hardly what you'd call filling. That's why I've bulked up the traditional BLT with some "fried" fish. I've also tricked up the standard-issue mayo with some fresh basil and a little lemon zest. The result is a sandwich buff enough to kick sand in the face of the skinny little BLT. Indeed, this is a sandwich worthy of dinner entrée status.

8 slices bacon (about 7 ounces)
2 plum tomatoes
Kosher salt
¾ cup mayonnaise
¼ cup fresh basil leaves
½ teaspoon freshly grated lemon zest
Freshly ground black pepper
4 slices firm white bread
¼ cup Wondra or unbleached all-purpose flour
1 large egg
Four 4-ounce catfish fillets
¼ cup extra virgin olive oil
8 slices rustic bread
4 large romaine lettuce leaves

1. Preheat the oven to 400°F. Arrange the bacon on a rack on a rimmed baking sheet and bake for 12 to 15 minutes or until crisp. Drain on paper towels.

2. Meanwhile, slice the tomatoes ⅓ inch thick. Lightly salt them on both sides and set them aside for 10 minutes; pat them dry. Combine the mayonnaise, basil, lemon zest, ¼ teaspoon salt, and ⅛ teaspoon pepper in a blender and puree. Pulse the bread in a blender or food processor to make 2 cups fresh bread crumbs.

3. Spread out the flour and bread crumbs in separate pie plates lined with wax paper or parchment; beat the egg in a bowl. Season the catfish fillets with salt and pepper to taste; working with 1 fillet at a time, toss them in the flour, lifting the wax paper on both sides to move them around; shake off the excess flour. Dip them into the egg, letting the excess drip off, and finally into the crumbs, shaking off any excess.

4. Heat 2 tablespoons olive oil in a large nonstick skillet over medium heat until hot. Sauté the catfish for about 5 minutes per side or until golden and just cooked through. Add the remaining 2 tablespoons olive oil when you turn the pieces.

5. Toast the bread. Place 4 slices on serving plates and spread the top sides with some of the mayonnaise mixture; top each with lettuce, bacon, tomatoes, and a catfish fillet. Spread one side of the remaining toast slices with the mayonnaise mixture and place them, mayo side down, on the sandwiches. Cut each sandwich in half and serve.

COOKING CATFISH

These days, the catfish you consume aren't like the ones your grandpa used to catch in local ponds and streams. The farm-raised catfish you will find in today's markets have been trained to feast on a special diet that floats on the surface of the water and reduces the off flavors that once marred catfish's popularity. Farm-raised catfish come to market in a uniform size, filleted, boned, and skinned, all ready to go in the pan, under the broiler, or on the grill. In the store, select fresh fillets that look moist, almost translucent, and vary from pure white to pink in color. As with all fish, catfish should have no fishy odor.

Catfish have several areas that are fattier than the rest of the fillet, and removing those areas not only makes the fish leaner, it reduces the possibility of the fish's having the "muddy" flavor that wild catfish are known for. The largest fatty area is a layer right under the skin. This is sometimes removed in processing, and the fish is labeled "double skinned." If the fatty area is still visible, it can be easily scraped off with the blade of a knife. Removing the gray line that runs lengthwise down the center of the fillet will also improve the flavor. You can either split the fillet and trim off the gray area or cut a V down the center of the fillet to remove it.

$\mathcal{T}$una Niçoise Sandwiches

MAKES 4 SERVINGS (ABOUT 2⅓ CUPS FILLING) ■ HANDS-ON TIME: 25 MINUTES ■ TOTAL PREPARATION TIME: 35 MINUTES

This luxe tuna salad sandwich combines almost all of the components of the French *salade niçoise* with an olive dipping sauce from the *Gourmet* dining room that was a huge hit with our guests for years. From the *salade niçoise* I borrowed tuna, hard-cooked eggs, green beans, and tomatoes. (Boiled potatoes didn't make the cut—too much starch.) I tossed them with a simple sauce consisting of store-bought mayo, chopped kalamata olives, and a little lemon juice and tucked the mix into a toasted pita pocket, which provides a nice contrasting crunch.

2 large eggs
¼ pound haricots verts or regular green beans
1 cup cherry or grape tomatoes
¼ cup fresh dill leaves
6 large Boston lettuce leaves
½ cup mayonnaise
⅓ cup drained pitted kalamata olives
1 tablespoon plus 1 teaspoon fresh lemon juice
One 12-ounce can solid tuna in water
Kosher salt and freshly ground black pepper
4 large pitas with pockets

1. Cook the eggs following the directions for Sara's Hard-Cooked Eggs (page 30). When the eggs have cooked and cooled, peel them under cold running water and coarsely chop them or use an egg slicer to chop them (see Note).

2. Meanwhile, bring a medium pot of salted water to a boil. Trim the haricots verts; quarter the tomatoes (about ¾ cup). Finely chop the dill (about 2 tablespoons). Coarsely chop the lettuce (about 2 cups).

3. When the water comes to a boil, add the haricots verts; return the water just to a boil. Remove the haricots verts to a bowl of ice and water using a slotted spoon. When they are cool, thoroughly drain them, pat them dry, and coarsely chop them (about ¾ cup).

4. Combine the mayonnaise, olives, and lemon juice in a mini food processor fitted with the chopping blade and process until almost smooth. Transfer the mixture to a medium bowl. (Or finely chop the olives and mix the ingredients in a medium bowl.) Thoroughly drain the tuna and finely crumble it into the mayonnaise mixture; add the eggs, tomatoes, haricots verts, dill, and salt and pepper to taste, and stir gently.

5. Cut the pitas in half and toast them in a toaster until they are warm and lightly browned. Divide the tuna mixture and lettuce among the pita halves.

NOTE: An easy way to chop hard-cooked eggs is to slice them in both directions using an egg slicer.

Mexican Salmon Salad Sandwiches

MAKES 4 SERVINGS ■ HANDS-ON TIME: 15 MINUTES ■ TOTAL PREPARATION TIME: 15 MINUTES

How so many of us grew up eating canned tuna while never even encountering canned salmon is a mystery to me. All I know is that ever since I "discovered" canned salmon for myself, I've been making up for lost time, but bringing the word to the world at large remains an uphill battle. I remember having to almost literally twist the arms of two of the cameramen on my PBS show, *Sara's Weeknight Meals,* to get them to try a canned salmon burger with corn salsa. One bite, and they were believers.

Besides its flavor, canned salmon is: 1. Very affordable. 2. Almost always wild salmon, which is sustainable. 3. A great source of omega-3 fatty acids. 4. "Shelf stable" (a choice item to stock in the pantry for a rainy day).

This sandwich is brightened up considerably by the tomatillo salsa in the mayo. If you want to lose the cilantro in the salsa, just use parsley instead. Finally, given that you don't need to turn on the stove to make this recipe, it's a very good candidate for dinner on a hot summer night.

½ recipe Tomatillo Salsa (page 23, add preparation time) or ½ cup store-bought salsa
⅓ cup mayonnaise
2 teaspoons fresh lemon juice
One 14¾-ounce can salmon
1 ripe Hass avocado
Kosher salt and freshly ground black pepper
Four 7-inch pitas
2 cups baby romaine lettuce leaves

1. Prepare the Tomatillo Salsa in a medium bowl; stir in the mayonnaise and lemon juice.

2. Thoroughly drain the salmon and remove the bones. Flake the salmon into the salsa mixture, leaving the pieces large. Halve, seed, and peel the avocado. Cut it into ½-inch cubes (about 1 cup) and fold it into the salmon mixture. Add salt and pepper to taste.

3. Slice open the tops of the pitas. Divide the salmon mixture and baby romaine among the pitas and serve.

NOTE: If you have the time, you can make corn tortilla shells for serving the salad instead of using pita bread: Preheat the oven to 400°F. Brush both sides of eight 6-inch corn tortillas with vegetable oil and sprinkle with kosher salt. Fold them in half, put them on a rimmed baking sheet, and prop them up using foil so they stay propped up. Bake for 10 minutes or until crisp.

Moroccan Carrots and Goat Cheese on Whole Grain V

MAKES 4 SERVINGS ■ HANDS-ON TIME: 30 MINUTES ■ TOTAL PREPARATION TIME: 30 MINUTES

Truthfully, you probably won't be able to sell this sandwich on its own to the terminal carnivores in your clan, but team it up with a hearty salad or side vegetable and you might just be all right. Then again, even your meatheads should be able to appreciate the dazzling variety of textures and flavors here: tart, crispy shredded carrots combined with salty olive relish and creamy goat cheese on whole grain bread. Delicious.

3 medium carrots

2 tablespoons fresh lemon juice

1 teaspoon sugar

½ teaspoon kosher salt

½ teaspoon ground cumin

¼ teaspoon paprika (sweet, hot, or smoked)

1 cup pitted green olives

½ cup fresh flat-leaf parsley leaves

2 tablespoons extra virgin olive oil

1 tablespoon well-drained capers

½ teaspoon freshly grated lemon zest

¼ teaspoon freshly ground black pepper

One 4-ounce log fresh goat cheese, softened

⅛ teaspoon cayenne pepper

8 slices rustic whole grain or white bread

1. Coarsely grate the carrots in a food processor fitted with the shredding disc (about 1⅓ cups). Transfer the carrots to a small bowl and stir in 1 tablespoon lemon juice, the sugar, salt, cumin, and paprika.

2. Remove the shredding disc from the processor and insert the chopping blade. Combine the olives, parsley, olive oil, capers, the remaining 1 tablespoon lemon juice, lemon zest, and black pepper in the food processor and pulse until the mixture is finely chopped but not pureed (about ¾ cup).

3. Combine the cheese and cayenne in a small bowl. Place 1 slice of bread on each of 4 serving plates; spread the cheese mixture onto the slices. Divide the carrot mixture on top of the cheese; top with the olive mixture and the remaining bread slices. Gently press the sandwiches together and cut each diagonally in half before serving.

what are CAPERS?

Although capers are native to the Mediterranean and Asia, they have been imported to America for more than a century. They are the preserved flower buds of a prickly shrub of the Capparidaceae family, ranging in size from the tiny nonpareils of France to plump capers larger than ¼ inch. You can purchase capers either pickled in a vinegar brine or dry salted. Salted capers need to be rinsed to reduce the saltiness. Capers of all kinds remind me of tiny little pickles and add a delicious crunch and saltiness to any dish. While some people prefer salted over pickled, I like them all.

Roasted Vegetable and Fresh Ricotta Sandwiches Ⓥ

MAKES 4 SERVINGS ▪ HANDS-ON TIME: 35 MINUTES ▪ TOTAL PREPARATION TIME: 35 MINUTES

The star of this sandwich is the fresh ricotta cheese. A family recipe from Richard Ferretti, the creative director at *Gourmet,* it was published in the magazine several years ago. In the dining room we were delighted and astonished to discover how simple it was, and how delicious. The flavor and texture are much better than anything you can buy at the supermarket.

In the beginning we served this recipe as directed by the magazine: on top of rigatoni with marinara sauce. But this creamy homemade ricotta is capable of starring in all sorts of recipes, including this sandwich. You'll really impress your family and friends when you tell them you made the cheese from scratch.

1 small eggplant (about 10 ounces)
1 large zucchini (about 12 ounces)
1½ pounds plum tomatoes (about 6 medium)
3 tablespoons extra virgin olive oil
Kosher salt and freshly ground black pepper
8 garlic cloves
1 quart whole milk
½ cup heavy cream
1½ tablespoons fresh lemon juice
8 slices whole grain bread

1. Preheat the oven to 425°F. Generously oil 2 rimmed baking sheets.

2. Cut the eggplant (about 2⅔ cups), zucchini (about 3 cups), and tomatoes (about 3¾ cups) crosswise into ¼-inch-thick slices.

3. Combine the olive oil, ¾ teaspoon salt, and ¼ teaspoon pepper in a small dish. Brush the oil mixture on both sides of the eggplant, zucchini, tomatoes, and garlic and arrange them on the baking sheets. Roast the vegetables for 30 minutes, turning the eggplant and zucchini and removing the garlic after 15 minutes.

4. Meanwhile, line a strainer with a double layer of cheesecloth or dampened paper towels and place it over a bowl. Slowly bring the milk, cream, and ¼ teaspoon salt to a rolling boil in a heavy 4-quart pot over medium heat, stirring occasionally.

5. Stir the lemon juice into the milk mixture; reduce the heat to low; simmer, stirring constantly, until the mixture curdles, about 2 minutes. Pour the mixture into the cheesecloth-lined strainer and let it drain for 10 to 15 minutes; discard the liquid. Transfer the ricotta to a bowl. Mash the roasted garlic cloves and stir them into the ricotta along with salt and pepper to taste.

6. Divide the warm ricotta among 4 slices of bread and top with the hot roasted vegetables, and the remaining 4 slices of bread. Cut the sandwiches in half and serve.

6

SPECTACULAR SALADS

Salads are so versatile and easy to make that you could serve a different one every night of the year, a particularly tempting option when the weather is warm. Each of the salads in this chapter was designed to have enough ingredients to make up a satisfying meal, but not so many that putting it together eats up a bunch of your time.

All contain protein (yes, chickpeas have protein in them) with a huge supporting cast of vegetables. They are tossed with a variety of dressings, and there are two more in the "Head Starts" chapter that you can swap out for one of these dressings if you prefer. You can also change the lettuce component if you are not a fan of watercress or arugula, for instance. You have a choice here of three chicken salads; two beef, including one hearty warm salad; two seafood salads; and a ham, a kielbasa, a mixed Italian cold cuts, and a vegetarian salad.

FACING PAGE: *Rice , Radish, and Snap Pea Salad with Seared Beef.*

Asian Chicken Salad with Carrot Ginger Sauce

MAKES 4 TO 6 SERVINGS ■ HANDS-ON TIME: 55 MINUTES ■ TOTAL PREPARATION TIME: 55 MINUTES

This recipe was an excuse for me to repurpose the super-refreshing carrot salad dressing served at sushi restaurants. You're welcome to substitute peanuts for the almonds, and cooked broccoli for the sugar snap peas.

The "uncooked" ramen noodles add crunch, sort of like an Asian crouton. Many people don't know it, but there's no reason not to eat these noodles straight out of the bag, as they've already been cooked (fried, actually) before you buy them. If you'd prefer an ingredient that has not been fried, use baked tortilla chips in place of the ramen noodles.

1 cup slivered almonds

3 tablespoons sesame seeds

4 ounces sugar snap peas

2 medium carrots

One 3-inch piece fresh ginger

4 medium scallions

⅓ cup vegetable oil

3 tablespoons seasoned rice vinegar

2 teaspoons toasted sesame oil

2 teaspoons soy sauce (low sodium, if you prefer)

¾ teaspoon hot chili sauce (preferably sriracha; see opposite)

Kosher salt

½ small head napa cabbage

1 small romaine lettuce heart

6 large radishes (optional)

1. Preheat the oven to 350°F. Spread out the almonds in a shallow baking dish and bake for about 5 minutes, or until golden. Spread the sesame seeds in a pie plate and bake for about 3 minutes, or until golden.

2. Meanwhile, bring a large saucepan of salted water to a boil over high heat; prepare a medium bowl of ice and water. Remove the strings from the peas and cut the peas diagonally in half. Stir them into the boiling water; return the water to a boil, remove and drain the peas, and plunge them into the ice and water. When the peas have cooled, drain them thoroughly and pat them dry.

3. Make the dressing: Coarsely chop the carrots (about 1 cup) and peel and chop the ginger (about 1 tablespoon). Trim and thinly slice the scallions, keeping the green and white parts separate (about ¼ cup of each). Combine the carrots, ginger, white parts of the scallions, vegetable oil, ¼ cup water, rice vinegar, sesame oil, soy sauce, and hot chili sauce in a blender. Blend until smooth; season with salt to taste.

4. Cut enough of the cabbage and romaine crosswise into ½-inch ribbons to make 2 cups of each. Coarsely shred the radishes, if using (about 1 cup). Coarsely crumble the ramen noodles.

1 package ramen
 noodles
3 cups packed
 shredded skinned
 cooked chicken
 from a large store-
 bought rotisserie
 chicken, or leftovers,
 or Can't Overcook
 'Em Chicken Breasts
 (page 31, add
 preparation time)

5. Combine the chicken, cabbage, romaine, peas, radishes (if using), almonds, sesame seeds, and green parts of the scallions in a large bowl. Toss with half the dressing. Sprinkle the ramen noodles over the top and serve; pass the remaining dressing.

what is SRIRACHA?

A few years ago this flavorful Thai chili sauce suddenly started appearing in dishes on restaurant menus all over the country. The best-known brand, Huy Fong, was developed by a Vietnamese hot-sauce maker who moved to Los Angeles and brought his craft with him. Named for a town in Vietnam that is famous for hot sauce, Sriracha Hot Chili Sauce was aimed at American tastes. Made from red jalapeño chiles and supplemented by sugar and garlic, in addition to vinegar and salt, it boasts a thick, smooth, nearly ketchuplike texture. No wonder it's a smash. Adding just a splash is a surprisingly easy way to give new life to sauces, soups, salad dressings, and vegetable dishes. Different sriracha brands have entered the market, so try small bottles and choose your favorite, or just pick up the one with the rooster on the bottle and "Huy Fong" on the label.

Breaded Creole Chicken
with Ranch-Dressed Coleslaw

MAKES 4 SERVINGS ■ HANDS-ON TIME: 45 MINUTES ■ TOTAL PREPARATION TIME: 1 HOUR

There's a lot going on in this salad and it does require more than the usual amount of hands-on prep. I think it's worth it, but you can speed up the process by using coleslaw mix from the produce section of your supermarket and, if you're really in a pinch, store-bought ranch dressing. However you get there, the result is a very hearty and satisfying salad.

1 cup buttermilk
Kosher salt and freshly ground black pepper
1 pound boneless, skinless chicken breast halves
½ small cabbage
2 large carrots
1 small red bell pepper
1 large dill pickle
Ranch Dressing (recipe follows)
6 tablespoons extra virgin olive oil
1⅓ cups dry bread crumbs
2 teaspoons Creole Seasoning (page 20, add preparation time) or store-bought seasoning

1. Combine the buttermilk, 1 teaspoon salt, and ¼ teaspoon black pepper in a resealable plastic bag. Add the chicken, seal the bag, and knead until the chicken is evenly coated with the marinade; set aside at room temperature to marinate for 20 minutes while you prepare the rest of the ingredients.

2. Trim and shred the cabbage, preferably using the slicing disc of a food processor (about 4 cups). Coarsely grate the carrots, preferably using the shredding disc of a food processor (about 1½ cups). Cut the bell pepper into matchsticks (about 1 cup); chop the pickle (about 1 cup). Toss together the cabbage, carrots, bell pepper, pickle, and a hefty pinch of salt in a large bowl.

3. Prepare the Ranch Dressing.

4. Heat 2 tablespoons olive oil in a large nonstick skillet over medium heat until hot. Combine the bread crumbs and Creole Seasoning and spread out the mixture on a pie plate lined with wax paper or parchment; remove the chicken from the buttermilk, letting the excess drip off. Dip the pieces, one at a time, into the bread crumbs to coat well, lifting the wax paper on both sides to move them around; shake off any excess.

5. Add half the chicken to the skillet and cook, turning once and adding another 1 tablespoon olive oil, for 2 to 3 minutes per side, until golden and just cooked through. Remove to a plate and set aside for 10 minutes before cutting. Repeat with the remaining chicken and olive oil. Slice the chicken into ½-inch strips.

6. Just before serving, stir ½ cup Ranch Dressing into the cabbage mixture; add salt and pepper to taste. Divide the slaw among 4 dinner plates; top it with the chicken. Pass the remaining dressing.

MAKES SCANT 1 CUP

RANCH DRESSING: Whisk together ½ cup buttermilk, ⅓ cup mayonnaise, 2 tablespoons finely chopped mixed fresh herbs (such as tarragon, chives, and parsley), and 1 tablespoon fresh lemon juice. Press in 1 small garlic clove (about 1 teaspoon) and add kosher salt and freshly ground black pepper to taste.

$\mathcal{C}$hicken, Green Bean, and Potato Salad with Broccoli Pesto

MAKES 6 SERVINGS ■ HANDS-ON TIME: 30 MINUTES ■ TOTAL PREPARATION TIME: 45 MINUTES

The Italians, who know a thing or two about good food, have never shied away from pairing up starch with starch. The Romans, for example, like to glorify their pizza with potatoes. Similarly, there's a Ligurian classic that combines pasta and potatoes with green beans and pesto.

For this recipe, I borrowed the potatoes, green beans, and pesto from the Ligurian starchfest. My "pesto," however, is based not on basil, but on broccoli, which gives the sauce a peppery kick. I've added poached chicken and olives to make the dish more substantial, as well as a little chicken broth, which thins out the pesto, ensuring that all of this salad's parts are properly coated. In retrospect, I must confess that this dish bears very little resemblance to the Ligurian original, but I don't think you'll be disappointed.

2 large boneless, skinless chicken breast halves (about 1½ pounds total) or 3⅔ cups skinned cubed rotisserie chicken

½ pound small boiling potatoes, such as Yukon gold or Red Bliss

½ pound green beans or haricots verts

¾ cup Broccoli or Broccoli Raab Pesto (page 18, add preparation time) or 1 cup store-bought basil pesto

6 tablespoons extra virgin olive oil, if using Broccoli or Broccoli Raab Pesto

2 tablespoons fresh lemon juice

1. Cook the chicken following the directions for Can't Overcook 'Em Chicken Breasts (page 31). Set it aside until cool enough to handle, then cut it into ½-inch cubes. Strain and reserve the chicken cooking liquid.

2. While the chicken is cooking, scrub the potatoes and combine with cold salted water to cover by 1 inch in a small saucepan and bring the water to a boil over high heat. Reduce the heat to medium-low and simmer for about 10 minutes, or until the potatoes are just tender (can be pierced easily with a knife). Drain the potatoes and let them cool until they can be quartered. (If using rotisserie chicken, reserve ¼ cup of the potato cooking liquid.) Meanwhile, trim the green beans.

3. Bring another large saucepan of salted water to a boil over high heat; prepare a medium bowl of ice and water. Add the green beans to the boiling water and cook until just tender (about 4 minutes for green beans, 3 minutes for haricots verts). Transfer them to the bowl of ice and water with a slotted spoon and let cool. Remove the beans, drain, and lay out on paper towels. Cut the beans into

¾ cup pitted kalamata
olives
One 3½- to 4-ounce jar
capers
Kosher salt and freshly
ground black pepper

1-inch lengths. Chop the olives and drain and rinse the capers (a scant ½ cup).

4. Prepare the Broccoli or Broccoli Raab Pesto. Whisk together the pesto, olive oil (if using broccoli pesto), and lemon juice in a large bowl. Whisk in some of the reserved chicken or potato cooking liquid, a little at a time, until the dressing reaches the desired consistency (1 to 2 tablespoons is about right). Add the chicken, potatoes, beans, olives, and capers and toss until they are well coated with the dressing. Add salt and pepper to taste and serve.

Rice, Radish, and Snap Pea Salad with Seared Beef

**MAKES 4 SERVINGS   HANDS-ON TIME: 30 MINUTES   TOTAL PREPARATION TIME: 30 MINUTES WITH WHITE RICE,
55 MINUTES WITH BROWN RICE**

Back in the seventies I worked for a catering company in Cambridge, Massachusetts, called Caras & Rowe, run by the estimable and talented Ms. Rebecca Caras. Besides preparing food for events in and around Boston, we also made food to be sold at several of the area's takeout shops. One of my favorites of these recipes was a rice salad with peas, radishes, scallions, and dill.

I've taken that salad in an Asian direction with a light rice vinegar and toasted sesame oil dressing. I've also added some seared and sliced steak and topped it all off with a dollop of wasabi sour cream. If the cuts of beef I recommend don't fit your budget, just use a less expensive cut, like flank steak. The resulting dish is both refreshing and substantial.

1 cup raw brown or white rice or 3 cups cooked rice
Sesame Dressing (recipe follows)
1 to 1½ pounds top loin or sirloin steak, cut 1½ inches thick
Kosher salt and freshly ground black pepper
1 tablespoon vegetable oil
¼ pound sugar snap peas (unshelled) or 1 cup thawed frozen peas
4 large radishes
4 medium scallions
½ cup sour cream
1½ to 2 teaspoons prepared wasabi
1 teaspoon soy sauce (low sodium, if you prefer)

1. Bring a large pot of salted water to a boil over high heat. Stir in the rice; reduce the heat to medium and cook, uncovered, for about 45 minutes for brown rice or 17 minutes for white, or until tender. Meanwhile, prepare the Sesame Dressing. When the rice is tender, drain it, rinse it in cold water, thoroughly drain it again, and toss it with the Sesame Dressing in a medium bowl.

2. Meanwhile, season the steak on all sides with salt and pepper. Heat the vegetable oil in a large skillet (preferably cast iron) over medium heat until very hot. Cook the steak, turning once, for about 3 to 5 minutes per side for medium-rare. Remove the steak to a plate and set it aside for 5 minutes; cover and chill it for at least 20 minutes, or until the rice has cooked.

3. While the steak is chilling, bring a large saucepan of salted water to a boil over high heat; prepare a medium bowl of ice and water. Add the whole pea pods to the boiling water; return the water to a boil, remove and drain the peas, and plunge them into the ice and water. When the peas have cooled, drain them thoroughly and pat them dry. Cut them crosswise into ½-inch-thick slices (about 1 cup). Halve the radishes through the root, lay them flat, and

thinly slice them (about 1 cup). Trim and thinly slice the scallions (about ½ cup). Add the cut pea pods (or thawed peas, if using), radishes, and scallions to the rice and toss to combine.

4. Make the wasabi dressing: Whisk together the sour cream, steak juices from the steak plate, wasabi, and soy sauce in a small bowl.

5. To serve, mound some of the rice salad mixture in the center of each of 4 plates. Thinly slice the meat and arrange some slices on top of each portion of rice salad. Drizzle with the wasabi dressing.

MAKES ½ CUP

SESAME DRESSING: Whisk together ¼ cup unseasoned rice vinegar and 1 teaspoon sugar until the sugar has dissolved. Whisk in 3 tablespoons vegetable oil, 2 tablespoons soy sauce (low sodium, if you prefer), and 1 teaspoon toasted sesame oil.

Warm Steak House Salad with Blue Cheese Dressing

MAKES 4 SERVINGS ■ HANDS-ON TIME: 30 MINUTES ■ TOTAL PREPARATION TIME: 35 MINUTES

It is an article of faith with The Husband that salads are rabbit food. This salad, as "manly" as I could make it, is my attempt to prove him wrong. On the bottom is a crusty shredded potato pancake. On top is hot sliced steak. The finished product is drizzled with a creamy blue cheese dressing finished with Worcestershire sauce and steak juices. Sure, there's a mound of spinach in the middle of it all, but that's hardly going to spoil the party. (Sometimes I think that the only thing that'll truly satisfy a meathead is to serve up a cheeseburger, wave my magic wand over it, and say, "Shazam! It's a salad!")

1 pound russet potatoes (2 medium)
5 tablespoons extra virgin olive oil
Kosher salt and freshly ground black pepper
One 1¼- to 1½-pound beef sirloin steak (about 1½ inches thick)
1 large onion
Blue Cheese Dressing (recipe follows) or store-bought dressing
5 ounces baby spinach (about 8 cups, packed)

1. Scrub and peel the potatoes. Grate using the shredding disc of a food processor. Heat 2 tablespoons olive oil in a 12-inch non-stick skillet over medium heat until hot. Add the potatoes and press down to make one big potato pancake. Cook for 10 to 12 minutes on the first side, pressing down frequently with a spatula, or until golden. Invert the pancake onto a baking sheet, add ½ tablespoon olive oil to the skillet, and slide the pancake back into the skillet, uncooked side down. Reduce the heat to medium-low and cook for 10 to 12 minutes, or until golden. Season both sides of the pancake with salt and pepper to taste once they have been cooked.

2. At the same time, in a separate medium skillet, heat 1 tablespoon olive oil over high heat until hot. Season the steak with salt and pepper to taste. Reduce the heat to medium-high, add the steak to the skillet, and cook for 3 to 5 minutes per side for medium rare. Transfer the steak to a plate, cover loosely with aluminum foil, and set aside. Set aside the skillet.

3. While the steak is cooking, halve and thinly slice the onion (about 2 cups). Add 1½ tablespoons olive oil and the onion to the steak drippings in the pan; reduce the heat to medium-low and cook for 5 minutes, or until the onion has softened. Stir the steak juices from the steak plate into the onion.

4. While the onion is cooking, prepare the Blue Cheese Dressing. To serve, cut the potato pancake into 4 wedges and place each on a dinner plate. Top each wedge with sliced steak, onion, spinach, and Blue Cheese Dressing.

MAKES ABOUT 1⅔ CUPS

BLUE CHEESE DRESSING: Combine 2 tablespoons sherry vinegar, 1 tablespoon fresh lemon juice, 1 tablespoon Worcestershire sauce, and 2 teaspoons Dijon mustard in a blender; press in ½ garlic clove (about ½ teaspoon). With the blender running, add ⅓ cup extra virgin olive oil in a stream until the mixture has emulsified. Add 3 ounces crumbled blue cheese (about ¾ cup) and ⅓ cup sour cream; blend until the mixture is well mixed. Add water, if necessary, to reach the desired consistency and add salt and pepper to taste. Stir in extra blue cheese to taste, if desired.

Ham and Beet Salad
with Crispy Johnnycake and Goat Cheese Toasts

MAKES 4 SERVINGS ■ HANDS-ON TIME: 25 MINUTES ■ TOTAL PREPARATION TIME: 45 MINUTES

I'm a New Englander at heart; my family has been rooted there for more generations than I care to count. My brother, my sister, and I were born and grew up in New York City only because my parents decided to take a little thirty-five-year break from Milton and Cambridge, Massachusetts, a move that baffled just about everyone in both of their families.

Even in New York, however, I grew up eating such traditional New England fare as fish chowder, Indian pudding, plum pudding, roast beef with Yorkshire pudding (pudding is kind of a big deal in New England), and johnnycakes. You'll also find johnnycakes in the American South and the Caribbean, but those are a different breed. Mine are made of cornmeal (preferably stone ground), combined with a little salt and warm water to make a batter, and then cooked up like pancakes. They should be crispy on the outside and creamy on the inside. In this salad, they play the crouton role, alongside a cozy little trio of beets, goat cheese, and orange dressing. I tossed in some ham for protein.

3 medium beets (1 to 1¼ pounds)

12 to 14 johnnycakes (recipe follows)

¾ cup walnut pieces

½ cup fresh orange juice

2 medium shallots

1 teaspoon freshly grated orange zest

2 tablespoons sherry vinegar

1 teaspoon Dijon mustard

½ teaspoon kosher salt

5 tablespoons vegetable oil

4 ounces soft goat cheese

8 ounces ready-to-eat ham, cut ⅓ to ½ inch thick

5 ounces arugula (about 7½ cups, packed)

1. Steam the beets in a steamer or in a steaming basket or strainer set in a saucepan for 30 to 45 minutes until just tender. Set them aside until they are cool enough to handle, then peel and slice them (a sturdy egg slicer is a good tool here).

2. While the beets are cooking, preheat the oven to 350°F and make the johnnycakes. Chop the walnuts, spread them out on a rimmed baking sheet, and toast until golden, 7 to 10 minutes. Set aside to cool. Transfer the johnnycakes as they are done to the rimmed baking sheet.

3. Make the dressing: Put the orange juice in a small saucepan and simmer it for about 5 minutes, or until it has been reduced by half. Finely chop the shallots (about ¼ cup). Transfer the reduced orange juice to a bowl; whisk in the orange zest, shallots, vinegar, mustard, and salt until the salt has dissolved. Gradually whisk in the oil.

4. Crumble the goat cheese (about 1 cup). Cut the ham into bite-size pieces (about 2¾ cups). Top each of the johnnycakes with some of the goat cheese. Bake the johnnycakes for 5 minutes or until the cheese is nicely melted. Remove the johnnycakes from

the oven and quickly spread the cheese evenly on each one using a butter knife.

5. While the johnnycakes are in the oven, combine the beets, walnuts, ham, and arugula in a bowl; add the orange dressing and toss well. Divide the salad among 4 plates and put 3 warm johnnycakes on the side of each plate.

MAKES 12 TO 14

JOHNNYCAKES: Bring 1¼ cups water to a boil. Mix together 1 cup johnnycake meal or cornmeal, preferably stone ground (see Sources, page 359), 1 teaspoon sugar, and ½ teaspoon table salt in a large bowl. Whisk in 1 cup of the boiling water. Mix well. Add additional water if necessary to make a very loose batter. Heat 1 tablespoon vegetable oil per batch in a frying pan or griddle over medium heat. Working in batches, drop 2 tablespoons of the cornmeal mixture into the heated pan or griddle. Press down gently to form a very thin pancake. Cook for 6 minutes per side. Repeat until all the batter has been fried, adding up to 2 tablespoons more oil, as needed.

Bean and Kielbasa Salad
with Creamy Chipotle Dressing

MAKES 4 SERVINGS ■ HANDS-ON TIME: 25 MINUTES ■ TOTAL PREPARATION TIME: 25 MINUTES

I was a happy little butterball of a kid, subsisting on a fairly strict diet of hot dogs smothered in ketchup and hot fudge sundaes. It wasn't until puberty kicked in and I realized that this regimen simply would not do that I started eating more mindfully and investigating the non–hot dog food groups. But I'll always have a soft spot for hot dogs, and what are kielbasas if not spicier and more refined hot dogs?

For the purpose of this salad, I tried not to douse the kielbasa in ketchup, opting instead for a mayo-yogurt dressing flavored with some chipotle and a little of the adobo sauce in which the chipotle is packed. The heat in the dressing is nicely counterbalanced by the sweetness of the fresh corn in the salad. Nostalgic for pork and beans, I added pinto beans, as well as celery, red bell pepper, and scallions. In this scheme, the kielbasa is more flavoring than main ingredient. It's more healthful that way.

½ pound kielbasa
1 tablespoon
vegetable oil
One 15½-ounce can
pinto beans
1 small red bell pepper
2 small ears fresh corn
or 1 cup thawed
frozen corn kernals
4 medium celery stalks
3 medium scallions
1 small chipotle chile in
adobo sauce, plus
½ teaspoon adobo
sauce
½ cup mayonnaise
¼ cup plain low-fat or
full-fat Greek-style
yogurt (see page 49)
Kosher salt

1. Quarter the kielbasa lengthwise and cut crosswise into ¼-inch pieces (about 1¾ cups). Heat the vegetable oil in a medium skillet over medium heat until hot. Add the kielbasa and cook, stirring occasionally, for 4 minutes, or until it begins to brown. Transfer with a slotted spoon to a medium bowl and set aside to cool slightly.

2. Meanwhile, rinse, drain, and pat dry the beans. Medium chop the bell pepper (about 1 cup), cut the corn kernels from the cobs (about 1 cup), slice the celery crosswise into ¼-inch-thick pieces (about 2 cups), and trim and thinly slice the scallions (a heaping ⅓ cup). Add the beans, bell pepper, corn, celery, and scallions to the kielbasa in the bowl.

3. Mince the chipotle and combine it and the adobo sauce with the mayonnaise, yogurt, and salt to taste in a small bowl (about ¾ cup). Add the chipotle dressing to the kielbasa mixture, toss well, and serve.

what are CHIPOTLES?

Chipotles are smoked jalapeño chiles. They are available dried whole, powdered, pickled, or canned in adobo sauce (a tomato-based sauce that includes onions, bay leaves, other spices, and vinegar). My favorite is this last version—chipotles in adobo. They're available in Latin markets and many supermarkets these days; little cans of these fiery morsels have recently become best sellers around the country. If you can't find them in your area, try one of the sources (page 359). Because a little goes a long way, you aren't likely to use the whole can quickly. Here's an easy way to freeze the chiles: Spoon each chipotle with a little bit of the sauce individually onto a cookie sheet lined with wax paper or parchment. Put the cookie sheet into the freezer and freeze the chiles until they are hard. Once they are hard, they will peel off the paper easily, and you can transfer them to a resealable plastic bag and freeze them for future recipes.

what is KIELBASA?

Kielbasa is traditionally a lightly smoked, herb- and garlic-flavored pork sausage. Often called Polish sausage in the market, it plays a part in the cuisines of most Eastern European countries, although the name may be spelled differently. In the American supermarket, these days you can find kielbasa made from a variety of meats. It is usually fully cooked so that it can be prepared quickly; it adds a lot of flavor wherever it is used.

Muffuletta Salad

MAKES ABOUT 6 SERVINGS ▪ HANDS-ON TIME: 40 MINUTES ▪ TOTAL PREPARATION TIME: 40 MINUTES

In *Crescent City Cooking,* Susan Spicer describes the muffuletta sandwich—"fragrant, filling, and dripping with oil"—as New Orleans's answer to a hero or a hoagie. It was invented in 1906 by a Sicilian immigrant named Salvatore Lupo at his Central Grocery and is still sold there, more than a century later. Although cold cuts and cheese are crucial parts of the sandwich, the sandwich is truly defined by the muffuletta bread ("a sesame seed–speckled round loaf of crusty Italian bread") and the olive salad ("which ranks alongside hot sauce and beignet mix as the best souvenirs from the Quarter").

This recipe turns the classic muffuletta sandwich inside out by featuring the olive salad, cold cuts, and cheese and dispensing with the muffuletta loaf in favor of croutons, which serve the same purpose as the sandwich bread: soaking up the flavorful oil in the salad. You can find all the ingredients at the supermarket.

Note: If you're not a fan of pork or if you can't find the Italian cold cuts at your supermarket, you're welcome to substitute turkey or roast beef or any of your favorite cold cuts instead.

1 small semolina bread
    (about 10 ounces)
    or any rustic white
    bread
2 garlic cloves
¼ cup plus
    2 tablespoons extra
    virgin olive oil
1 cup small broccoli
    florets
¼ cup red wine vinegar
2 tablespoons olive
    brine
2 teaspoons sugar
½ teaspoon kosher salt
1 cup pimiento-stuffed
    green olives
¾ cup drained
    giardiniera (Italian
    pickled vegetable
    salad)

1. Preheat the oven to 350°F. Bring a large saucepan of salted water to a boil.

2. Meanwhile, cut the bread into ¾-inch cubes (about 6 cups). Press the garlic (about 2 teaspoons) into a large bowl; whisk in 2 tablespoons olive oil. Toss the bread cubes in the olive oil mixture until evenly coated; arrange the cubes on a rimmed baking sheet and toast until golden on the edges, 7 to 9 minutes. Set aside the bowl.

3. Add the broccoli florets to the boiling water; return the water just to a boil. Remove the broccoli with a slotted spoon and drain; set aside to cool to room temperature.

4. In the same bowl in which you tossed the bread cubes, prepare the dressing: Whisk together the vinegar, olive brine, sugar, and salt until the sugar and salt have dissolved. Gradually whisk in the ¼ cup olive oil.

¼ pound sliced
    mortadella
¼ pound sliced cooked
    capocolla ham
¼ pound sliced
    provolone cheese
⅛ pound sliced salami
4 cups thinly sliced
    romaine lettuce

5. Combine the olives and giardiniera in the bowl of a food processor fitted with the chopping blade; pulse several times or until the pieces are about ½ inch. Add the olive mixture to the dressing.

6. Stack the mortadella, capocolla, provolone, and salami and cut into bite-size pieces; toss with the mixture in the bowl. Add the bread cubes, broccoli, and lettuce. Toss well and serve.

Seared Scallops and Butter Lettuce Salad with Grapefruit Vinaigrette

MAKES 4 SERVINGS ■ HANDS-ON TIME: 25 MINUTES ■ TOTAL PREPARATION TIME: 25 MINUTES

Scallops are so naturally sweet that they practically sit up and beg for an acid counterpoint. Lemon is the usual "go to" acid for fish and seafood, but in this case, I chose grapefruit instead because I thought that grapefruit juice, cooked down, would contribute body to the base of a vinaigrette. (I was right.) I added avocados to the scallops because basically I've got avocado on the brain these days. (I never looked twice at them until I was well into my thirties. Now I can't leave them alone.) Finally, I tossed in some sunflower seeds. Healthwise, of course, you can't beat them; they're a great source of vitamin E, thiamin, and magnesium. But I also love them for their crunch and their unique flavor. All together, this is an eminently refreshing summertime salad entrée.

1 cup Wondra or all-purpose flour
¾ pound medium sea scallops
Kosher salt and freshly ground black pepper
½ cup vegetable oil
⅓ cup fresh grapefruit juice
1 small shallot
1 tablespoon unseasoned rice vinegar
⅛ teaspoon sugar
1 small grapefruit (preferably pink)
2 small heads butter lettuce
1 ripe Hass avocado
20 medium chives or 1 medium scallion, green part only
¼ cup sunflower seeds

1. Spread out the flour in a pie plate lined with wax paper or parchment. Season the scallops with salt and pepper to taste. Working in batches, toss the scallops in the flour, lifting the wax paper on both sides to move the scallops around; transfer the scallops to a strainer and shake off the excess flour.

2. Heat 2 tablespoons vegetable oil in a large skillet over medium heat until hot. Add the scallops to the skillet and sauté for 2 to 3 minutes per side, or until just cooked through. Transfer the scallops to a plate using tongs and set aside to cool to room temperature.

3. Put the grapefruit juice in a small saucepan or skillet and simmer until it has reduced to 2 tablespoons; transfer it to a small bowl. Finely chop the shallot (about 2 tablespoons); add it to the reduced grapefruit juice along with the rice vinegar, ¼ teaspoon salt, and sugar. Whisk until the sugar and salt have dissolved. Gradually whisk in the remaining 6 tablespoons vegetable oil. Whisk in some of the juices that have accumulated on the scallop plate until the dressing reaches the desired consistency.

continued on next page

4. Peel and section the grapefruit; cut each section in half. Tear the lettuce into bite-size pieces (about 4 cups). Halve, seed, peel, and slice the avocado; thinly slice the chives crosswise (about 1 tablespoon). Toss the lettuce with ⅓ cup dressing.

5. Mound the lettuce on each of 4 plates and top with the scallops, avocado, and grapefruit. Sprinkle with the chives and sunflower seeds and drizzle with the remaining grapefruit dressing.

what are HEARTS OF PALM?

Hearts of palm are actually the inner rings of baby palm trees that are raised especially to produce this delicacy. While they are usually found fresh only in Florida and tropical areas where they are produced, they are available canned in supermarkets everywhere and have appeared on elegant menus for many years. In *Miami Spice,* author Steven Raichlen notes that hearts of the palmetto, "more prosaically known as swamp cabbage [are] harvested throughout the state, but especially around Lake Okeechobee. . . . The softly crunchy texture and sweet, mild taste are absolutely unique."

$\mathcal{S}$moked Salmon, Hearts of Palm, and Watercress Salad with Buttermilk Dressing

MAKES 4 SERVINGS   HANDS-ON TIME: 30 MINUTES   TOTAL PREPARATION TIME: 30 MINUTES

This recipe works because the richness of the salmon is beautifully offset by the pepperiness of the watercress, the heat of the chiles, and the acidity of the lemon and the buttermilk. The hearts of palm contribute their own unique flavor and crunch, as well as a final spritz of acid, courtesy of the canning liquid in which they've been immersed. (I've always been a fan of hearts of palm even though I've never tasted them fresh. I'm sure my chef pals in Florida will read this and shudder in disbelief.)

2 large eggs
6 small boiling potatoes, such as Yukon gold or Red Bliss
¼ cup fresh chives, tarragon or dill leaves, or a combination
¾ cup buttermilk
¼ cup mayonnaise
1 teaspoon freshly grated lemon zest
Kosher salt and freshly ground black pepper
One 14-ounce can hearts of palm
½ pound thinly sliced smoked salmon
1 bunch watercress
1 heart of romaine lettuce
6 peperoncini or 4 pickled cherry peppers

1. Cook the eggs following the directions in Sara's Hard-Cooked Eggs (page 30).

2. Meanwhile, combine the potatoes and cold salted water to cover by 1 inch in a small saucepan. Bring the water to a boil over high heat. Reduce the heat to medium-low and simmer for 15 minutes, or until the potatoes are just tender. Drain the potatoes, let cool, and slice (about 1½ cups).

3. While the potatoes cook, make the dressing: Chop the chives (about 2 tablespoons). Whisk together the buttermilk, mayonnaise, chives, lemon zest, and salt and pepper to taste.

4. Drain the hearts of palm and chop them (about 2 cups) and eggs (see Note, page 115); cut the salmon into strips (1 generous cup). Remove and discard the tough stems from the watercress (about 3 cups) and shred the romaine (about 3 cups). Finely chop the peperoncini (about ⅓ cup).

5. Toss together the hearts of palm, eggs, salmon, watercress, romaine, potatoes, peperoncini, and dressing and serve.

ℱalafel Salad with Creamy Garlic Dressing Ⓥ

MAKES 4 SERVINGS ■ HANDS-ON TIME: 40 MINUTES ■ TOTAL PREPARATION TIME: 50 MINUTES

"The hamburger of the Levantine Middle East" is how Martha Rose Shulman describes falafel in *Mediterranean Harvest*. "[It is] a street food and meze that is as popular in Lebanon, Syria, Israel, and Jordan as it is in Egypt, where it originated." A pita-pocketed sandwich built around deep-fried chickpeas or fava beans, falafel is also not exactly unknown in the United States of America.

In this recipe, I have streamlined and sped up the process of making falafel, sautéing large patties instead of deep-frying small balls. The Husband was horrified to learn that I was using iceberg lettuce in the salad. "It has no flavor," he complained. I patiently explained that I didn't choose iceberg for its flavor, but for its crunch and its cooling sweetness, a counterbalance to the hot chiles. Nonetheless, you, and The Husband, are welcome to substitute romaine or mesclun or any other of your favorite salad greens.

1 cup cherry tomatoes
3 pickled cherry peppers
½ seedless (English) cucumber
1 small head iceberg lettuce
1 small onion
5 tablespoons extra virgin olive oil
2 garlic cloves
¾ teaspoon ground cumin
½ teaspoon ground coriander
¼ teaspoon cayenne pepper
One 15½-ounce can chickpeas
1 large egg
2 tablespoons well-stirred tahini
½ teaspoon kosher salt
1 recipe Creamy Garlic Dressing Two Ways (page 12)
¾ cup panko bread crumbs

1. Place the tomatoes in a food processor fitted with the chopping blade; pulse until medium chopped (about ¾ cup); transfer them to a bowl. Remove the stems and seeds from the cherry peppers and chop them in the food processor (about ⅓ cup); add them to the bowl.

2. Remove the chopping blade and place the slicing disc on the food processor. Split the cucumber in half lengthwise and slice in the processor (about 2 cups); transfer the slices to the bowl. Discard the outer leaves of the lettuce and medium chop by hand or cut it into wedges and use the food processor with the slicing disc (about 6 cups). Add the lettuce to the bowl. Wipe out the food processor, fit the processor with the chopping blade, and set aside.

3. Chop the onion (about ½ cup.) Heat 2 tablespoons olive oil in a medium skillet over medium heat. Reduce the heat to medium-low; add the onion and cook for 5 minutes, or until it has softened. Press the garlic (about 2 teaspoons) into the pan and add the cumin, coriander, and cayenne; cook for 1 minute and then transfer to a medium bowl.

4. Rinse and drain the chickpeas (about 1⅓ cups). Pulse them in the food processor just until they are coarsely chopped; remove ½ cup chopped chickpeas and add it to the onion mixture. Add the egg, tahini, and salt to the chickpeas remaining in the processor and process them until they are very finely ground; stir them into the onion mixture. Cover the mixture and chill it for 10 minutes. Meanwhile, prepare the Creamy Garlic Dressing.

5. Shape the chilled chickpea mixture into 12 patties (the mixture will be loose). Spread out the panko on a pie plate lined with wax paper or parchment and dip the patties into it to coat on all sides, lifting the wax paper on both sides to move them around; shake off any excess.

6. Heat 2 tablespoons olive oil in a large nonstick skillet over medium heat until hot. Add the falafel patties and cook until crisp and golden on one side, about 3 minutes. Add the remaining 1 tablespoon olive oil and turn the patties; cook for 3 minutes, or until crisp and golden.

7. To serve, toss the chopped vegetables with ½ cup of the dressing and divide the mixture among 4 large salad bowls. Top each salad with 3 falafel patties and some of the remaining dressing.

7
WHOLE GRAIN AND HEARTY

Once upon a time, not so long ago, no one was allowed to eat carbohydrates . . . or at least no one who subscribed to the South Beach Diet or the Atkins Diet, aka the food police of their day. This sweeping ban had the ironic effect of inspiring many of us not to shun carbs, but to shower fresh attention on them, especially the whole grain varieties. The result was the rediscovery of some ancient grains like farro and wheat berries, a new appreciation of underutilized grains like barley, and the reembracing of old standbys like brown rice and grits. Don't worry about the food police. These recipes—inflected by the flavors of France, Italy, India, Israel, Japan, and the American South—are good and good for you.

If, on a weeknight, you feel daunted by the amount of time it takes to cook some of these grains, get into the habit of cooking the grains ahead in big batches on the weekend and then freezing them in measured amounts. It will significantly speed up the total cooking time on many of these recipes.

FACING PAGE: *Soba Noodles with Asian Clam Sauce.*

Mushroom Farro "Risotto" ⓥ

MAKES 4 SERVINGS ■ HANDS-ON TIME: 35 MINUTES ■ TOTAL PREPARATION TIME: 60 MINUTES

A kind of hulled wheat, farro was first cultivated in the ancient Near East some ten thousand years ago. Later it showed up in ancient Egypt and Israel. Today it's grown in Morocco, Spain, Albania, Turkey, Switzerland, Italy, and elsewhere. Recently, farro has also been gaining popularity in this country because it's so highly nutritious.

Farro also happens to be delicious. It has a full-bodied taste and a pleasant, slightly chewy texture. In this recipe, I've messed with it very little. It doesn't end up as creamy as traditional risotto because it isn't as starchy, but it's plenty creamy enough and it will stick to your ribs.

3 cups Homemade Vegetable or Chicken Stock (pages 11 and 10, add preparation time) or canned broth

1 ounce mixed dried exotic mushrooms, such as porcini, chanterelle, oyster, cremini, and shiitake

1½ cups farro

4 ounces mixed fresh exotic mushrooms, such as porcini, chanterelle, oyster, cremini, and shiitake

3 tablespoons unsalted butter

1 medium onion

1 tablespoon plus 1 teaspoon fresh thyme leaves

½ cup dry red wine

3 ounces Parmigiano-Reggiano

Kosher salt and freshly ground black pepper

1. Bring 1 cup vegetable stock and the dried mushrooms to a boil in a small saucepan over high heat. Remove from the heat and set aside to soak the mushrooms for 20 minutes. Combine the farro and cold water to cover by 1 inch in a medium bowl; set aside to soak the farro for 20 minutes.

2. Meanwhile, clean, trim, and chop the fresh mushrooms (about 1⅓ cups). Heat 1 tablespoon butter in a large skillet over medium heat until hot. Reduce the heat to medium-low; add the fresh mushrooms and sauté for about 5 minutes, stirring occasionally, or until they are tender. Remove to a bowl and set aside.

3. While the mushrooms are cooking, finely chop the onion (about 1 cup). Chop the thyme (about 2 teaspoons). Melt the remaining 2 tablespoons butter in a medium saucepan over medium heat. Reduce the heat to medium-low; add the onion and cook for 5 minutes, or until it has softened.

4. Bring the remaining 2 cups vegetable stock to a simmer in a medium saucepan.

5. Drain the farro and add it along with the thyme to the onion; cook, stirring constantly, for 1 minute. Add the red wine to the farro and simmer for 1 to 2 minutes, or until it is absorbed.

6. Meanwhile, gently lift the dried mushrooms out of the soaking liquid to let any sand sink to the bottom of the pan. Set aside. Pour the liquid through a strainer lined with a coffee filter or dampened paper towel into a measuring cup; add the liquid to the simmering stock.

7. Add the hot stock mixture to the farro in three increments, simmering until almost all the liquid has been absorbed before adding more. This should take about 25 minutes.

8. Meanwhile, rinse the soaked mushrooms thoroughly to remove any remaining sand and add them to the cooked fresh mushrooms. Microplane-grate the cheese (about 2 cups) or grate on the fine side of a box grater (about 1 cup).

9. When the farro has cooked, stir in the mushroom mixture along with the cheese; season with salt and pepper to taste and serve.

how do i know
I AM BUYING REAL PARMIGIANO-REGGIANO?

Parmigiano-Reggiano cheese has been manufactured and perfected in a small region of northern Italy for more than two thousand years. There are several hard cheeses you can find in stores that are similar in appearance and color to Parmigiano-Reggiano, but their flavor is very different. To make sure you are getting what you want, always look for the rind on the cheese. Parmigiano-Reggiano has its name, as well as the identification number of the dairy and production month and year, stenciled in bands of pin dots all around each wheel. Parmigiano-Reggiano is available in a range of ages. If it is not marked, you can tell the age of the cheese by the sprinkling of white crystals in it—the more crystals, the older the cheese. If you want to make Parmigiano-Reggiano curls, select a younger cheese with fewer crystals. If you want more flavor intensity, select a more mature one with more crystals.

arley Provençale Ⓥ

MAKES 4 SERVINGS ▪ **HANDS-ON TIME: 30 MINUTES** ▪ **TOTAL PREPARATION TIME: 1 HOUR 50 MINUTES**

For most of us, barley is not a soloist. We eat it in mushroom barley soup, but otherwise we rarely encounter it. This is a shame, as barley does just fine on its own.

There are all kinds of barley, but pearled barley is the most widely available in America because it doesn't take forever to cook. Although it's not quite as nutritious as whole grain barley, pearled barley is still plenty healthful and a dandy source of protein and fiber. I'm also a fan of its texture: not as chewy as wheat berries, but nonetheless nice and firm.

In this recipe, I've topped off the barley with ratatouille (the quick and tasty vegetable stew from the south of France), then finished it off with fresh basil and grated Parmigiano-Reggiano. Believe me, no one's going to miss the mushrooms.

1 cup pearled barley
Kosher salt
1 medium onion
¼ cup extra virgin olive oil
3 garlic cloves
1 small eggplant (about 1 pound)
1 medium zucchini
1 small red bell pepper
¾ pound plum tomatoes (about 3 medium)
2 tablespoons drained capers
20 large fresh basil leaves
Freshly ground black pepper
2 cups Homemade Vegetable or Chicken Stock (pages 11 and 10, add preparation time) or canned broth
2 ounces Parmigiano-Reggiano

1. Combine the barley and 3 cups cold water in a medium saucepan; cover and set aside to soak at room temperature for 1 hour.

2. Add 1 teaspoon salt to the barley and bring to a boil over high heat. Reduce the heat to low and simmer for about 40 minutes, or until the barley is tender and has absorbed all the liquid.

3. Meanwhile, prepare the ratatouille. Finely chop the onion (about 1 cup). Heat 2 tablespoons olive oil in a skillet over medium heat until hot. Reduce the heat to medium-low; add the onion and cook for 5 minutes, or until it has softened. Press the garlic (about 1 tablespoon) into the saucepan and cook for 1 minute more.

4. Peel the eggplant. Cut the eggplant, zucchini, and bell pepper into ¾-inch pieces (about 2¾ cups eggplant, 1¾ cups zucchini, and 1⅓ cups bell pepper). Add the remaining 2 tablespoons olive oil to the onion mixture along with the eggplant, zucchini, bell pepper, and ½ teaspoon salt. Cook for 5 minutes.

5. Cut the tomatoes into ¾-inch pieces (about 1½ cups). Add the tomatoes and capers to the skillet; cover and cook for 20 minutes over medium-low heat. Shred the basil (about ½ cup); stir it into the ratatouille. Add salt and black pepper to taste.

6. Combine the cooked barley with the vegetable stock in a small saucepan and heat over medium-high heat until hot. Microplane-grate the cheese (about 1⅓ cups) or grate on the fine side of a box grater (about ⅔ cup). To serve, spoon the barley into 4 pasta bowls; top with the ratatouille and Parmigiano-Reggiano.

how do i
SELECT A GOOD EGGPLANT?

Select medium to small eggplants that are very firm and have smooth, shiny skin. Avoid those that look wrinkled, dent when you press them, or feel light for their size. Use them shortly after purchase. While salting eggplant slices or cubes and allowing them to drain can reduce their tendency to absorb oil when they are being cooked, it doesn't really help to get rid of the bitterness. Japanese eggplants have fewer seeds and are always less likely to be bitter than Mediterranean eggplants. They are also smaller and easy to handle. Despite rumors to the contrary, there is no such thing as male and female eggplants. It has been alleged that female Mediterranean eggplants have more seeds, which make the eggplant bitter. The truth is that eggplants become bitter if they are very mature and full of seeds when harvested or if they have been stored too long in either the supermarket or your own refrigerator.

$\mathcal{W}$heat Berries with Creamy Cauliflower Sauce

MAKES 4 TO 6 SERVINGS   HANDS-ON TIME: 35 MINUTES   TOTAL PREPARATION TIME: 1 HOUR 5 MINUTES

I was introduced to wheat berries by my tenth-grade boyfriend, a hippie who took me to a vegetarian restaurant on New York's Lower East Side in a well-intentioned but futile attempt to expand my palate. The tofu was bland, the steamed vegetables were blander, and the room itself was dark and dour.

But I liked the wheat berries. A wheat berry is a grain of wheat stripped of its outer hull, leaving just the whole kernel. It's rich in niacin and B-complex vitamins. When cooked, wheat berries are pleasantly chewy, with a nutty taste.

1¾ cups wheat berries (about ¾ pound)
Kosher salt
1 small head cauliflower (about 1¾ pounds)
2 tablespoons extra virgin olive oil
Freshly ground black pepper
1 small boiling potato, such as Yukon gold or Red Bliss
2 cups Homemade Chicken Stock (page 10, add preparation time) or canned broth
½ cup pine nuts
¼ pound Spanish chorizo
1 medium onion
1 medium green bell pepper
2 garlic cloves

1. Rinse the wheat berries. Bring 1 quart water to a boil in a large saucepan over high heat; stir in the wheat berries, reduce the heat to low, and simmer, partially covered, for 45 minutes. Stir in 1 teaspoon salt and additional water, if needed; cook for about 15 minutes more, or until just tender; drain.

2. Meanwhile, preheat the oven to 450°F. Trim the cauliflower stalk even with the base of the crown. Discard the stalk and any leaves. Put the cauliflower, stalk side down, on a cutting board and cut into ¾-inch slices. Brush the cauliflower slices on both sides using 1 tablespoon olive oil; sprinkle the slices with ½ teaspoon salt and ¼ teaspoon pepper. Arrange them on a lightly oiled rimmed baking sheet and roast, turning once, for about 20 minutes, or until the cauliflower slices are tender and caramelized on both sides. Set aside to cool to room temperature, then coarsely chop them. Set aside ¾ cup.

3. While the cauliflower is roasting, peel and slice the potato. Combine it with the chicken stock in a small saucepan and cook it over medium heat for 10 to 12 minutes, or until it is tender. Drain the potato, reserving the chicken stock. Combine the potato, the remaining chopped cauliflower, and ¼ cup chicken stock in a blender. Puree until smooth, adding more chicken stock, if necessary, to make a thick sauce.

4. When the cauliflower sauce is finished, reduce the oven temperature to 350°F, spread out the pine nuts on a rimmed baking sheet, and toast, watching carefully, for 3 to 4 minutes, or until golden. Set aside.

5. Peel the chorizo and cut it into small pieces. Heat the remaining 1 tablespoon olive oil in a large skillet over medium heat until hot. Add the chorizo and cook, stirring constantly, for 5 minutes or until it is heated through.

6. Finely chop the onion (about 1 cup) and bell pepper (about 1 cup). Reduce the heat under the chorizo to medium-low; add the onion and bell pepper to the chorizo and cook for 5 minutes, or until the onion has softened. Press the garlic (about 2 teaspoons) into the skillet and cook for 1 minute more. Stir the cauliflower sauce and the reserved ¾ cup chopped cauliflower into the chorizo mixture. Add salt and black pepper to taste.

7. To serve, stir the cauliflower sauce into the wheat berries and top with the toasted pine nuts.

$\mathscr{I}$sraeli Couscous with Peas, Shiitakes, and Sweet Potato Sauce ⓥ

MAKES 4 SERVINGS   HANDS-ON TIME: 25 MINUTES   TOTAL PREPARATION TIME: 35 MINUTES

Although to the casual viewer it looks like a grain, couscous is actually tiny grains of pasta made from semolina flour. Israeli couscous (aka pearl couscous, supercouscous, Israeli toasted pasta, and *maftoul*) is larger, chewier, and nuttier than the kind usually found on supermarket shelves.

If you're feeling fancy, you can fry up some whole sage leaves for a garnish. Here's how: Heat about 1 inch of vegetable oil in a small deep saucepan until it is hot. (You'll know it's hot enough when bubbles rise to the surface as soon as you stick the handle of a wooden spoon into it.) Add 3 sage leaves and cook for 10 seconds. Using a slotted spoon, transfer the leaves to paper towels and sprinkle them with kosher salt. Repeat, frying any remaining leaves, 3 at a time.

1 medium sweet potato (about 8 ounces)
4 tablespoons (½ stick) unsalted butter
2¼ to 2½ cups Homemade Vegetable or Chicken Stock (pages 11 and 10, add preparation time) or canned broth
1 medium onion
1 garlic clove
4 ounces shiitake mushrooms
1 cup pearl or Israeli couscous
4 large sage leaves
1 cup thawed frozen green peas
Kosher salt and freshly ground black pepper
Freshly grated Parmigiano-Reggiano (optional)

1. Peel the sweet potato and grate using the shredding disc of a food processor. Melt 1 tablespoon butter in a medium saucepan over medium heat; add the sweet potato and cook, stirring, for 3 minutes. Add ¾ cup vegetable stock; cover and simmer for 10 minutes, or until the sweet potato is tender. Transfer the mixture to a mini food processor or blender and puree until smooth (about 1 cup).

2. Meanwhile, finely chop the onion (about 1 cup). Melt 2 tablespoons butter in a large saucepan over medium heat. Reduce the heat to medium-low; add the onion and cook for 5 minutes, or until it has softened. Press the garlic (about 1 teaspoon) into the pan; cook for 1 minute more.

3. Clean the shiitake mushrooms; remove and discard the stems and slice the caps into ½-inch strips (about 2½ cups). Add the remaining 1 tablespoon butter and the shiitakes to the onion mixture and cook, stirring occasionally, for 5 minutes or until the mushrooms are just tender.

4. Add the couscous to the saucepan and cook, stirring constantly, for 1 minute. Add 1½ cups vegetable stock. Bring the mixture to a boil over high heat; reduce the heat to medium-low and simmer, covered, for 10 minutes, or until tender. Finely chop the sage (about 1½ tablespoons).

5. Add the sweet potato puree and peas to the couscous. Cook just until heated through, adding more vegetable stock, if necessary, to achieve a creamy texture; add salt and pepper to taste. To serve, divide among 4 pasta plates; top with the chopped sage and Parmigiano-Reggiano, if using.

$\mathcal{B}$rown Rice with Broccoli Pesto

MAKES 4 SERVINGS HANDS-ON TIME: 25 MINUTES TOTAL PREPARATION TIME: 45 MINUTES

This dish is a perfect example of the way I think we should be eating most of the time: a substantial serving of whole grains and vegetables in the center of the plate with a modest portion of protein for flavor on the top.

In this recipe, the whole grain is brown rice, while the protein comes in the form of shrimp. Not only is this dish filling and economical (whole grains and vegetables are much cheaper than animal protein), it's also a very tasty combination of flavors and textures.

¾ cup brown rice
¾ cup Broccoli or Broccoli Raab Pesto (page 18) or 1 cup store-bought basil pesto
One 15½-ounce can white beans
¼ pound peeled and deveined medium shrimp
2 tablespoons unsalted butter
Kosher salt and freshly ground black pepper

1. Bring 1⅔ cups salted water to a boil over high heat. Stir in the rice and return to a boil; reduce the heat to low, cover the pan, and cook for 35 to 40 minutes, until the rice is tender.

2. Meanwhile, prepare the Broccoli or Broccoli Raab Pesto.

3. Rinse and drain the beans. Coarsely chop the shrimp. Melt the butter in a medium skillet over medium heat. Add the shrimp and a pinch of salt; sauté until the shrimp are just cooked through, 2 to 3 minutes.

4. When the rice is tender, stir in the pesto, beans, shrimp, and salt and pepper to taste. Add some water if desired to achieve a creamy consistency. Reheat just until hot. Divide the rice among 4 pasta bowls and serve.

$\mathcal{S}$moky Cheese Grits with Summer Succotash Ⓥ

MAKES 4 TO 6 SERVINGS   HANDS-ON TIME: 25 MINUTES   TOTAL PREPARATION TIME: 25 MINUTES

Long before Sylvester the Cat, of "Sufferin' succotash" fame—indeed, long before the arrival on these shores of the white man and his cartoons, the corn and lima bean dish known as succotash was a staple of American cuisine. (The word *succotash* itself is an anglicized version of a word from the Narragansett Indians.) And why not? Certainly there are few foods more delicious than fresh corn in season.

I'm a fan of lima beans, too, of both their taste and meaty texture, but I'm aware that not everyone feels the same way. So, in this recipe, I've replaced the limas with fresh soybeans, aka edamame, which taste milder than limas and have a more silky texture. This mixture is served on a bed of creamy cheese grits, which elevates a classic side dish to the status of light and flavorful vegetarian entrée, just right for summer.

1 cup frozen edamame

2 large ears fresh corn or 2 cups thawed frozen corn kernels

1 medium onion

1 tablespoon vegetable oil

1 garlic clove

2 cups cherry or grape tomatoes

1 tablespoon balsamic vinegar

Kosher salt and freshly ground black pepper

1 cup whole milk

1 cup quick-cooking grits

4 ounces smoked Gruyère, Gouda, or Cheddar cheese

1 tablespoon unsalted butter

2 tablespoons chopped fresh chives

1. Cook the edamame following the package directions; drain well. Cut the corn from the cobs (about 2 cups), if using fresh corn. Finely chop the onion (about 1 cup).

2. Heat the vegetable oil in a large skillet over medium heat until hot. Reduce the heat to medium-low; add the onion and cook for about 5 minutes, or until it has softened. Press the garlic (about 1 teaspoon) into the skillet and cook for 1 minute more.

3. Halve the tomatoes. Add the tomatoes and vinegar to the onion mixture and cook, stirring, for about 2 minutes, or until the tomatoes start to soften. Stir in the edamame and corn and cook for 3 minutes. Add salt and pepper to taste; set the succotash aside and keep warm.

4. Meanwhile, combine 2 cups water, the milk, ½ teaspoon salt, and ¼ teaspoon pepper in a large saucepan; bring to a boil over high heat. Very gradually whisk in the grits, reduce the heat to medium, and cook, stirring frequently, for about 8 minutes, or until the grits are thick and creamy.

5. Coarsely grate the cheese (about 1 cup). Remove the grits from the heat and stir in the cheese and butter. Add salt and pepper to taste. To serve, divide the grits among 4 to 6 soup plates; spoon the succotash into each bowl and sprinkle the chives over the top.

Polenta Lasagne

MAKES 4 SERVINGS • HANDS-ON TIME: 35 MINUTES • TOTAL PREPARATION TIME: 50 MINUTES

Classic lasagne is not the kind of dish you can just throw together on a weeknight, but you can pull it off if you start with flavorful shortcut ingredients, including precooked polenta and Italian sausage. You begin by slicing and sautéing the polenta, which gives it a little crunch and some toastiness—a nice change from the usual pasta noodles. The finished product tastes like the slow-cooking comfort food you expect to see only on a weekend or a special occasion.

1 medium onion
3 tablespoons extra virgin olive oil
½ pound sweet or hot Italian sausage
2 garlic cloves
One 14½-ounce can diced tomatoes (preferably fire roasted)
Kosher salt and freshly ground black pepper
One 16- to 18-ounce log cooked plain polenta
2 ounces Parmigiano-Reggiano
4 ounces sliced mozzarella

1. Place an oven rack in the top third of the oven and preheat the oven to 375°F. Lightly oil an 8-inch square pan.

2. Finely chop the onion (about 1 cup). Heat 1 tablespoon olive oil in a large skillet over medium heat. Slice the sausage into ½-inch pieces using a serrated knife; add the sausage to the pan. Cook, stirring occasionally, for 6 to 8 minutes, or until the sausage is no longer pink. Reduce the heat to medium-low; add the onion and cook for 5 minutes, or until it has softened. Press the garlic (about 2 teaspoons) into the pan and cook for 1 minute more. Add the tomatoes with their juice and cook for 4 to 5 minutes, or until most of the juice has evaporated and the mixture is saucy; season with salt and pepper to taste.

3. Meanwhile, cut the polenta into ⅓-inch-thick slices. Heat another 1 tablespoon olive oil in a large nonstick skillet over high heat until hot. Reduce the heat to medium and add half the polenta slices in one layer. Sauté the polenta for about 5 minutes, or until it begins to brown; turn the polenta and sauté for 4 to 5 minutes, or until the second side begins to brown. Remove the polenta slices and arrange them to cover the bottom of the oiled baking pan. Add the remaining 1 tablespoon olive oil to the skillet and repeat with the remaining polenta (remove the slices to a plate if the sauce has not finished cooking).

continued on next page

4. Microplane-grate the Parmigiano-Reggiano (about 1⅓ cups) or grate on the fine side of a box grater (about ⅔ cup). When the sauce has finished cooking, spoon half over the polenta in the pan. Top it with half the mozzarella and Parmigiano-Reggiano. Repeat layering the remaining polenta, sauce, mozzarella, and Parmigiano-Reggiano.

5. Bake the lasagne for 15 to 20 minutes, or until bubbly and lightly browned. Cut into 4 servings and transfer to dinner plates.

how can i make
CRÈME FRAÎCHE AT HOME?

In *Baking with Julia* (William Morrow, 1996), Julia Child describes crème fraîche as "similar in taste and texture to sour cream, but it has the added benefits of being able to be heated without separating and to be whipped when chilled." Crème fraîche is becoming easier to find, but if you plan ahead, you can make your own. You just whisk together 1 cup heavy cream (not ultrapasteurized) and ¼ cup buttermilk and transfer the mixture to a glass jar with no lid. Cover the top of the jar with a paper towel secured with a rubber band and set the mixture aside until it thickens, for up to 24 hours. Then you remove the paper towel, cover the jar tightly, and chill.

Whole Wheat Linguine with Salmon and Asparagus

MAKES 4 SERVINGS   HANDS-ON TIME: 20 MINUTES   TOTAL PREPARATION TIME: 25 MINUTES

This recipe, like my Mexican Salmon Salad Sandwiches (page 116), begins with canned salmon. I know it seems counterintuitive, but canned salmon is not only delicious and healthful, it is also more likely to be wild salmon instead of farmed. If you're worried about the fat content in the crème fraîche, you can turn to the lower-fat alternative.

½ cup walnut pieces
½ pound asparagus
12 ounces whole wheat linguine
1½ cups crème fraîche
1 cup Homemade Chicken Stock (page 10, add preparation time) or canned broth
One 14¾-ounce can salmon
1 tablespoon plus 1 teaspoon freshly grated lemon zest
2 tablespoons fresh lemon juice
Kosher salt and freshly ground black pepper

1. Bring a large pot of salted water to a boil over high heat. Preheat the oven to 350°F.

2. Medium chop the walnuts, spread them out on a rimmed baking sheet, and toast until golden, 7 to 10 minutes. Remove the pan to a cooling rack and let the walnuts cool to room temperature.

3. Meanwhile, trim the asparagus. Peel the bottom half of the stems if the stems are thicker than ⅓ inch and cut the asparagus diagonally into 1½-inch lengths (about 1½ cups). When the pot of water has come to a boil, add the asparagus and cook for 1 minute. Using a slotted spoon, remove the asparagus to a bowl. Stir the linguine into the same pot of boiling water and cook until al dente, following the timing directions on the package.

4. While the pasta is cooking, bring the crème fraîche and chicken stock to a boil in a medium saucepan; cook until reduced by half. Thoroughly drain the salmon, discard the bones, and flake the salmon into the bowl with the asparagus.

5. Drain the linguine well and return it to the cooking pot; add the reduced crème fraîche mixture, the lemon zest, and lemon juice. Bring the mixture to a boil and simmer over low heat for 2 minutes. Add the asparagus and salmon mixture and salt and pepper to taste; cook just until hot. Serve in 4 pasta bowls and top with the toasted walnuts.

LOW-FAT VERSION: Replace the crème fraîche with ¾ cup milk (full or low-fat). In step 4, whisk together the milk, just ½ cup chicken stock, and 2½ teaspoons cornstarch. Bring the mixture to a boil, whisking, and add to the linguine and remaining ingredients.

$\mathcal{I}$ndian Rice and Lentil Pilaf Ⓥ

MAKES 4 SERVINGS ▪ HANDS-ON TIME: 45 MINUTES ▪ TOTAL PREPARATION TIME: 55 MINUTES

I love the nutty taste of basmati rice, but I love it even more after it's been supercharged with a battery of whole spices toasted in oil until fragrant. Add lentils, which are high in protein, and potatoes, which score well on the satiation index, and you've produced a very satisfying and substantial dish. Whip up a salad like my Cucumber and Tomato Salad with Yogurt and Toasted Cumin Seed Dressing (page 262), for example, and dinner is good to go.

1 medium onion
¼ cup vegetable oil
One 1½-inch cinnamon stick
6 cardamom pods
1 Turkish bay leaf
½ teaspoon coriander seeds
½ teaspoon cumin seeds
2 dried red chiles (chiles de arbol)
3 whole cloves
¾ cup basmati rice
½ teaspoon ground turmeric
Kosher salt
⅔ cup lentils
½ pound boiling potatoes, such as Yukon gold or Red Bliss
3 medium carrots
Freshly ground black pepper

1. Finely chop the onion (about 1 cup). Heat 2 tablespoons vegetable oil in a medium saucepan over medium heat until hot. Add the cinnamon stick, cardamom pods, bay leaf, coriander seeds, cumin seeds, chiles, and cloves and cook, stirring constantly, for 1 minute, or until they become fragrant. Transfer the spices with a slotted spoon to a plate. Reduce the heat to medium-low and add the onion to the saucepan. Cook, stirring occasionally, for 10 minutes, or until the onion is golden. Set aside.

2. Rinse the basmati rice in a strainer until the water runs clear. Drain the rice and add it to the onion in the saucepan along with the sautéed spices and the turmeric; cook over medium heat, stirring, for 1 minute, or until the rice is coated with the oil. Add 1½ cups water and ½ teaspoon salt; bring the water to a boil over high heat. Cover the pan with a paper towel and the lid and simmer over low heat for 20 minutes, or until all the liquid has been absorbed. Remove the pan from the heat and set aside, covered, for 15 minutes.

3. Meanwhile, combine the lentils, 2 cups water, and ½ teaspoon salt in a medium saucepan; bring them to a boil over high heat, cover, and simmer over low heat for 25 minutes, or until the lentils are just tender.

continued on next page

FACING PAGE: *Some of my favorite Indian flavorings. Clockwise from top left: bay leaves, fresh ginger, cinnamon, coriander seeds, dried chiles, yellow mustard seeds, cumin seeds, sesame seeds, cardamom pods.*

4. Scrub the potatoes and cut them into ½-inch cubes (about 1 cup). Heat the remaining 2 tablespoons vegetable oil in a large nonstick skillet over medium heat. Add the potatoes and cook, stirring occasionally, for 10 to 12 minutes, or until they are nicely browned; reduce the heat to low and cook for 5 minutes more. Coarsely grate the carrots, preferably using the shredding disc of your food processor (about 2 cups); add them to the potatoes and cook for 3 minutes more, or until both are tender.

5. Fluff the rice with a fork; remove the bay leaf, cardamom pods, cinnamon sticks, cloves, and chiles. Drain the lentils and stir them gently into the rice along with the potato mixture; add salt and pepper to taste.

$\mathcal{S}$oba Noodles with Asian Clam Sauce

MAKES 4 SERVINGS   HANDS-ON TIME: 30 MINUTES   TOTAL PREPARATION TIME: 30 MINUTES

Soba noodles are thin Japanese buckwheat noodles that are rich in protein and fiber. The Japanese usually serve them cold, in salads, but they're also great served hot.

Anytime you steam clams, you get an instant full-flavored sauce in the form of clam broth. In this case, I've taken the broth in an Asian direction with the addition of ginger, cabbage, and cilantro. Pour it over the soba noodles and you have a wonderfully refreshing, yet totally filling, dinner entrée. By the way, if you were born with the anti-cilantro gene (yes, there really is such a thing), just substitute fresh basil or parsley.

3 pounds littleneck clams
4 medium scallions
One 1½-inch piece fresh ginger
8 ounces soba (buckwheat) noodles
1 pound bok choy or napa cabbage
¼ cup fresh cilantro sprigs
¼ cup vegetable oil
2 garlic cloves
⅓ cup dry white wine
Kosher salt and freshly ground black pepper
Crusty bread, as an accompaniment

1. Bring a very large pot of well-salted water to a boil over high heat. Scrub the clams, discarding any that won't close.

2. Trim and chop both the white (about ¼ cup) and the green (about ¼ cup) parts of the scallions, keeping them separate. Peel and Microplane-grate the ginger (about 1½ teaspoons).

3. When the water has come to a boil, add the noodles and cook following the package directions. Drain and rinse well; set aside.

4. Meanwhile, trim and thinly slice the bok choy (4 generous cups). Chop the cilantro (about 2 tablespoons).

5. Heat the vegetable oil in a large saucepan over medium heat. Add the chopped white parts of the scallions and cook until softened, about 1 minute. Add the ginger and press the garlic (about 2 teaspoons) into the pan; cook for 1 minute more.

6. Add the clams and white wine to the pan; turn the heat up to high. Cover the pan and cook for 5 to 7 minutes, or until the clams open; transfer the clams to a bowl as they open. Discard any clams that won't open after 6 to 8 minutes.

7. Add the bok choy to the saucepan; cover the pan and steam for 2 minutes or until the bok choy has wilted. Add the noodles, clams in their shells, chopped green parts of the scallions, the cilantro, and salt and pepper to taste; cook just until hot. Serve in 4 pasta bowls with crusty bread.

Some of the most dependably popular shows I did on the Food Network were those that featured chicken. I'm not sure if it's because chicken cooks so fast or because it's so lean (at least the white meat) or because it's neutral enough to work with so many other ingredients. I do know why I like it; I'm a huge sauce fan, and chicken is the perfect backdrop for sauces. I also know that most American families eat poultry for dinner several times a week, and I'm often asked for new ways to serve it.

This chapter, then, is all about toothsome alternatives to the usual chicken breast entrée. There are recipes here for dark meat chicken and white meat chicken; chicken with and without bones; sautéed, grilled, and baked chicken; as well as for chicken livers, turkey meatballs, and Cornish game hens. (I am also a huge fan of duck, but recipes for that scrumptious bird grace two other chapters, so I've kept them out of this one.)

FACING PAGE: *Chicken Saltimbocca with Artichoke Sauce.*

$\mathcal{C}$hicken Cassoulet

MAKES 6 TO 8 SERVINGS   HANDS-ON TIME: 35 MINUTES   TOTAL PREPARATION TIME: 45 MINUTES

Cassoulet is to southwest France as chili is to Texas or the baked bean is to Boston, a defining source of local pride. A rich, hearty stew consisting of white beans, roast pork, sausage, and duck or goose, cassoulet has been described by Paula Wolfert, a respected cookbook author and an authority on the food of southwest France, as "the ultimate slow food" because it can literally take days to make. Indeed, cooking the dish for so long is what gives it its tremendous depth of flavor. Seeing cassoulet listed on the menu of one of his favorite restaurants in Paris, Ernest Hemingway once wrote, "It made me hungry to read the name."

In this recipe, born out of my love for the traditional version, I did my best to capture as much as I could of the flavors of that version while keeping in mind that very few of us have days to invest in the making of a single dish. This is just right for a wintry weeknight here in twenty-first-century America.

2 tablespoons extra
   virgin olive oil
8 bone-in chicken thighs
   (2 to 2½ pounds)
Kosher salt and freshly
   ground black pepper
1 medium onion
1 tablespoon fresh
   rosemary leaves or
   ½ teaspoon dried
1 tablespoon fresh
   thyme leaves or
   ½ teaspoon dried
4 garlic cloves
Two 15½-ounce cans
   white beans
½ pound kielbasa,
   bratwurst, or high-
   quality hot dogs
½ cup dry red wine

1. Heat 1 tablespoon olive oil in a large skillet with an ovenproof handle over high heat until hot; reduce the heat to medium-high. Season the chicken with salt and pepper to taste and add it to the skillet, skin side down; cook for 3 to 4 minutes, or until browned. Turn the chicken and cook the remaining side for 3 to 4 minutes, or until browned.

2. Meanwhile, finely chop the onion (about 1 cup). Finely chop the rosemary (about 1½ teaspoons) and the thyme (about 1½ teaspoons); combine the rosemary and thyme in a small bowl. Press the garlic (about 1 tablespoon plus 1 teaspoon) into the bowl. Rinse and drain the beans; mash 1 cup beans in a small bowl with a fork. Cut the kielbasa in half lengthwise and then crosswise into ½-inch-thick pieces.

3. Remove the chicken to a plate using tongs; drain off and discard all but 1 tablespoon of the fat from the skillet. Reduce the heat to medium-low; add the onion and cook for 5 minutes, or until it has softened. Add the herb and garlic mixture and cook for 2 minutes. Add the red wine and simmer over low heat until it has reduced by half.

166   SARA MOULTON'S EVERYDAY FAMILY DINNERS

1 cup Homemade
Chicken Stock
(page 10, add
preparation time) or
canned broth
2 tablespoons Dijon
mustard
1 cup panko bread
crumbs

4. Return the chicken to the skillet along with any juices that have accumulated on the plate. Add the kielbasa, chicken stock, both the mashed and the whole beans, and the mustard; bring the mixture to a simmer. Cover the pan and simmer for 15 minutes, or until the chicken has just cooked through. While the chicken is cooking, preheat the broiler.

5. Toss the bread crumbs with the remaining 1 tablespoon olive oil. Remove the lid from the skillet; season the mixture with salt and pepper to taste. Sprinkle the bread crumbs evenly over the top. Put the skillet under the broiler, about 4 inches from the heat source, and broil for 45 to 60 seconds, or until the crumbs are golden.

Chicken with Fresh Tomato, Orange, and Olive Sauce

MAKES 4 SERVINGS ■ HANDS-ON TIME: 35 MINUTES ■ TOTAL PREPARATION TIME: 60 MINUTES

This is my favorite kind of chicken stew. Everything gets thrown into one pot and simmers slowly, exchanging flavors. The orange juice combines with the tomatoes, vinegar, and olives to produce a sweet-and-sour effect, and the light coating of flour on the chicken, which helps to keep the chicken moist, also slightly thickens the sauce. This is a very saucy dish, so I recommend serving it with rice, orzo, or couscous. A simple green salad would round out the meal nicely after that.

If you have a little extra time during the weekend, consider cooking this recipe ahead for a weeknight. It's tasty right out of the skillet, but even better a day or two later.

½ cup Wondra or unbleached all-purpose flour

3 to 3½ pounds cut-up chicken (about 8 pieces)

Kosher salt and freshly ground black pepper

¼ cup extra virgin olive oil

1 medium onion

5 medium plum tomatoes

2 garlic cloves

3 cups Homemade Chicken Stock (page 10, add preparation time) or canned broth

½ teaspoon freshly grated orange zest

⅓ cup fresh orange juice

32 small pimiento-stuffed olives

2 to 3 tablespoons olive brine

1 tablespoon sherry vinegar

1. Spread out the flour in a pie plate lined with wax paper or parchment. Season the chicken with salt and pepper. Toss half the chicken in the flour, lifting the wax paper on both sides to move the pieces around; shake off the excess flour.

2. Heat 1½ tablespoons olive oil in a large skillet over high heat until hot; place the floured chicken in the hot oil. Reduce the heat to medium. Sauté the chicken, turning once, until it is nicely browned on all sides, about 6 minutes. When it is done, transfer it to a large bowl. Flour the remaining chicken and brown in another 1½ tablespoons oil. Add it to the bowl when it is done.

3. Meanwhile, medium chop the onion (about 1 cup). Medium chop the tomatoes (about 2¼ cups). Add the remaining 1 tablespoon olive oil to the skillet and heat until hot. Reduce the heat to medium-low; add the onion and cook for 5 minutes, or until it has softened. Press the garlic (about 2 teaspoons) into the skillet and cook for 1 minute. Turn the heat up to medium-high, add the tomatoes, and cook for about 3 minutes, or until they begin to soften.

4. Add the chicken stock, orange zest, orange juice, olives, 2 tablespoons olive brine, and the vinegar to the skillet and bring the mixture to a boil over high heat. Add the chicken and any juices from the bowl to the pan; return to a boil. Reduce the heat to low and simmer, partially covered, turning once, for about 15 minutes, or until the chicken is just cooked through.

5. Remove the chicken to a serving platter. Cook the sauce on high heat until slightly thickened, 6 to 8 minutes. Add salt and pepper and additional olive brine to taste. Spoon the sauce over the chicken and serve.

Quick Chicken Gumbo

MAKES 4 SERVINGS   HANDS-ON TIME: 30 MINUTES   TOTAL PREPARATION TIME: 35 MINUTES

The key word here is *quick*. Everyone knows that it takes hours to make this Louisiana classic the right way. The roux alone should be stirred over low heat for a minimum of 45 minutes in order for it to develop a properly deep golden color and an equally deep flavor. But I've cut some corners because I'm looking to help you get a respectable approximation of this great dish on the table on a weeknight. I probably wouldn't serve this recipe to a Louisianan and call it gumbo, but I think everyone else will be very happy with it.

¼ cup vegetable oil
⅓ cup all-purpose flour
1 medium red bell pepper
1 medium green bell pepper
2 medium celery stalks
1 medium onion
4 garlic cloves
1 pound chicken tenders
8 ounces fully cooked smoked andouille sausage or any smoked or fresh sausage of your choice (see Note)
1 tablespoon Creole Seasoning (page 20, add preparation time) or store-bought Creole or Cajun spice
2 cups Homemade Chicken Stock (page 10, add preparation time) or canned broth
One 10-ounce package thawed frozen cut okra
Kosher salt and freshly ground black pepper
Cooked white rice, as an accompaniment

1. To make the roux, heat the vegetable oil in a Dutch oven over medium heat. Add the flour and cook, whisking occasionally, for 10 minutes, or until it is golden and smells like popcorn.

2. While the roux is cooking, finely chop the red and green bell peppers (about 1 cup each), celery (about 1 cup), and onion (about 1 cup) and put them in a medium bowl; press the garlic (about 1 tablespoon plus 1 teaspoon) into the mixture. Add the chopped vegetables to the roux and cook, stirring occasionally, for 10 minutes. The roux will clump on the vegetables, but it will disappear into the sauce once the chicken stock is added.

3. Meanwhile, cut the chicken into 1-inch pieces and slice the sausage crosswise 1 inch thick. Add the Creole Seasoning to the roux and cook, stirring, for 1 minute. Gradually stir in the chicken stock and ½ cup water, whisking until smooth; bring the mixture to a simmer.

4. Add the chicken to the sauce and cook for 4 minutes. Add the sausage and okra and cook until just heated through. Add salt and pepper to taste and serve over rice.

NOTE: If using fresh, uncooked sausage, it must be sliced ½ inch thick and added when the chicken is added to the gumbo.

Tandoori Chicken Wing Drummettes

MAKES 4 SERVINGS   HANDS-ON TIME: 20 MINUTES   TOTAL PREPARATION TIME: 8 TO 10 HOURS 20 MINUTES

Tandoori chicken, as everyone knows, is a Day-Glo orange staple of Indian restaurants everywhere. Originally from the Punjab region of India, this dish consists of chicken, usually skinless, that's marinated in yogurt and spices and then cooked at high heat in a clay oven known as a tandoor.

What is the source of the food's eye-burning color? The spices, originally: cayenne and turmeric. These days, however, many restaurants are not shy about lending nature a helping hand in the form of red and yellow food coloring. Visual pyrotechnics aside, tandoori chicken happens to be delicious. The yogurt acts as a tenderizer, and the spices give it a taste all its own.

This recipe makes use of my favorite part of the chicken, the wings. To me, the wings boast the perfect ratio of skin to meat to bone (with the bone and the skin teaming up to make the meat more flavorful). If you plan to get all the meat off the bone, you really have to eat these drummettes with your hands. Best, then, to consider this a fun, casual family meal.

Note: You'll have to plan ahead, because the wings need to marinate for 8 to 10 hours before cooking.

½ small onion
One 1-inch piece fresh ginger
2 garlic cloves
2 tablespoons fresh lime juice
1 cup plain low-fat or full-fat Greek-style yogurt (see page 49)
2 teaspoons vegetable oil
1 tablespoon ground cumin
1 tablespoon ground coriander
1½ teaspoons kosher salt
¾ teaspoon cayenne pepper
½ teaspoon ground turmeric
3 pounds chicken wing drummettes

1. Finely chop the onion (about ¼ cup) and peel and thinly slice the ginger (about 1 teaspoon) and garlic (about 2 teaspoons). Combine the onion, ginger, garlic, and lime juice with the yogurt, vegetable oil, cumin, coriander, salt, cayenne, and turmeric in a blender and blend until smooth. Transfer the mixture to a large resealable plastic bag or to a medium bowl. (This can be done the night before; close tightly or cover and refrigerate.)

2. The next morning or 8 to 10 hours before cooking, score each drummette twice about ¼ inch deep and add them to the marinade. Seal the bag and knead until the drummettes are evenly coated with the marinade. Refrigerate them until you are ready to cook them.

3. Place an oven rack in the middle of the oven and preheat the oven to 400°F. Arrange the drummettes in one layer on a rack on a rimmed baking sheet. Bake for 25 to 30 minutes, turning them halfway through the cooking time, until they are cooked through. Serve right away.

*C*hicken and Caramelized Fennel

MAKES 4 SERVINGS ▪ HANDS-ON TIME: 25 MINUTES ▪ TOTAL PREPARATION TIME: 55 MINUTES

This is an adaptation of the recipe for one of my favorite entrées at La Tulipe restaurant in New York, where I was *chef tournant* in the early eighties. I knew about raw fennel as a kid because my mom used to cut it into our salads. But it becomes a different vegetable when it's caramelized and braised, as it is in this dish. Raw fennel is very crunchy and tastes distinctly of licorice. Caramelized and braised, it becomes meltingly tender, the taste sweeter and more complex.

At La Tulipe we thickened the sauce for this recipe using veal stock pureed with garlic, which creates a texture like a milkshake; I guess you'd call it a garlic milk shake. (Any vegetable can perform this trick, but I'd never done it with garlic before I made this recipe.) As for the veal stock, which provides body to a recipe because it has so much natural gelatin, it's not the kind of ingredient most home cooks have kicking around, so I replaced it with chicken stock and leaned on the garlic milk shake to provide body. It does a great job here. Who needs veal stock?

2 medium fennel bulbs
Kosher salt and freshly
　ground black pepper
2 tablespoons unsalted
　butter
2 tablespoons extra
　virgin olive oil
6 garlic cloves
1 cup Homemade
　Chicken Stock
　(page 10, add
　preparation time) or
　canned broth
4 chicken breast halves
　with bones and skin
　(about 3 pounds)
⅓ cup sun-dried
　tomatoes or ½ cup
　sun-dried tomatoes
　packed in oil
1 teaspoon freshly
　grated lemon zest

1. Preheat the oven to 375°F. Trim the fennel; save some fronds for garnish, if desired. Slice the fennel bulbs lengthwise into ½-inch slices and season with salt and pepper to taste.

2. Heat 1 tablespoon butter and 1 tablespoon olive oil in a large skillet with an ovenproof handle over medium heat until hot; add the fennel and garlic. Cook for 12 minutes, turning the fennel slices once, until well browned on both sides. Add the chicken stock, bring it to a boil, cover the skillet tightly, and transfer it to the oven. Bake the fennel and garlic for about 30 minutes, or until the fennel is tender.

3. At the same time, heat the remaining 1 tablespoon butter and 1 tablespoon olive oil in another large skillet with an ovenproof handle over high heat until hot (see Note). Reduce the heat to medium. Season the chicken with salt and pepper and sauté, skin side down, for about 8 minutes, or until golden. Turn the chicken and transfer the skillet to the oven. Roast the chicken for 25 to 30 minutes, or until cooked through. Transfer the chicken to a platter, cover loosely with aluminum foil, and set aside for 10 minutes.

4. Meanwhile, if using sun-dried tomatoes not packed in oil, cover the tomatoes with hot water in a bowl; let stand until plumped, about 10 minutes, then drain them. Coarsely chop the tomatoes (about ½ cup). When the fennel has cooked, reserve a few pieces of the fennel and divide the rest among 4 dinner plates; keep warm. Transfer the chicken stock, garlic, and the reserved fennel to a blender and blend until smooth. Transfer to a saucepan, stir in the tomatoes, lemon zest, and salt and pepper to taste, and heat until hot.

5. When the chicken has rested, place 1 piece on top of the fennel on each plate. Add the drippings from the chicken platter to the sauce and spoon the sauce over the chicken and fennel; garnish with the reserved fennel fronds, if desired.

NOTE: If you don't have 2 large skillets, transfer the fennel, garlic, and chicken stock to a baking dish before transferring it to the oven and use the same skillet for the chicken.

what is FENNEL?

Bulb or Florence fennel is a sweet and mildly anise-flavored member of the carrot family. The bulb and celery-like stalks are used raw in salads or cooked as a side dish. The fluffy fronds can be used as garnish or snipped and added to dishes as you would dill. In the market, look for crisp, unblemished bulbs and stalks and fresh-looking fronds. Tightly wrapped, fennel will keep in the refrigerator for 4 or 5 days.

Wild fennel is also edible. It is foraged for use in cooking and dried for use as a grilling wood. Fennel seeds, which are produced by a variety of fennel other than the one that yields fresh fennel bulbs, offer more pungent flavor. A little added to soups and stews can contribute a delicate anise note, but start slow, as fennel seeds can overpower the dish if you add too much.

$\mathscr{C}$hicken Bouillabaisse with Rouille

MAKES 4 SERVINGS · HANDS-ON TIME: 35 MINUTES · TOTAL PREPARATION TIME: 1 HOUR

I'm taking some liberties by calling this recipe a bouillabaisse. The classic recipe, of course, is a venerable fish stew that originated in Marseille. It's flavored with saffron and garnished with a rouille sauce. Then again, I've held on to everything that goes into a traditional bouillabaisse but the fish, which I've replaced with chicken.

Rouille literally means "rust" in French, a reference to the sauce's color. It is made from one of two bases—ground bread crumbs and olive oil, or mayonnaise—to which is added garlic, red peppers, and chiles. It's perfect in this context, but it will improve virtually any dish on which it is drizzled.

1½ pounds boneless, skinless chicken thighs
Kosher salt and freshly ground black pepper
¼ cup extra virgin olive oil
1 medium onion
12 small boiling potatoes, such as Yukon gold or Red Bliss (about 1 pound)
2 garlic cloves
1 tablespoon fresh thyme leaves or ½ teaspoon dried
1¾ cups Homemade Chicken Stock (page 10, add preparation time) or canned broth
One 14½-ounce can chopped tomatoes (preferably fire roasted)
½ cup dry white wine
4 strips orange peel
½ teaspoon fennel seeds
¼ teaspoon saffron threads (optional)
Rouille (recipe follows)

1. Cut each chicken thigh into quarters. Toss half the chicken pieces with salt and pepper to taste. Heat 2 tablespoons olive oil in a large skillet over high heat; reduce the heat to medium. Add the seasoned chicken pieces and cook, turning frequently, for about 5 minutes, or until browned on all sides; transfer to a bowl with tongs or a slotted spoon. Repeat with the remaining chicken.

2. Meanwhile, halve and slice the onion (about 1 cup); scrub and quarter the potatoes. Heat the remaining 2 tablespoons olive oil in the same skillet over medium heat until hot; reduce the heat to medium-low. Add the onion and cook for 5 minutes, or until it has softened. Press the garlic (about 2 teaspoons) into the pan and cook for 1 minute. Chop the thyme (about 1½ teaspoons).

3. Add the potatoes to the skillet along with the chicken stock, tomatoes, white wine, orange peel, thyme, fennel seeds, and saffron, if using. Bring to a boil over high heat; reduce the heat to low and simmer for 10 minutes. Add the chicken and simmer for 25 minutes, or until the chicken and potatoes are tender. Taste the sauce, and if it seems watery, remove the chicken and boil the sauce until it reaches the desired consistency. Add salt and pepper to taste.

4. Meanwhile, prepare the Rouille.

5. To serve, divide the bouillabaisse among 4 soup plates and top with the Rouille.

ROUILLE: Combine 1 cup fresh bread crumbs, ½ cup bottled roasted peppers, ¼ cup extra virgin olive oil, 4 pressed garlic cloves (1 tablespoon plus 1 teaspoon), ¼ teaspoon kosher salt, and ¼ to ½ teaspoon cayenne pepper in a food processor fitted with the chopping blade. Process until smooth; add a little water, if necessary, to reach the desired consistency.

$\mathcal{C}$hicken Breasts in Creamy Poblano Sauce

MAKES 4 SERVINGS   HANDS-ON TIME: 25 MINUTES   TOTAL PREPARATION TIME: 40 TO 45 MINUTES

There's no better introduction to the wonderful world of chiles than the poblano. It's hot, but not too hot, and it boasts a marvelous smoky flavor, besides. In fact, the poblano's role in this recipe is less to make it spicy than to make it tasty. The chicken breast, bland as it is, provides the perfect backdrop for the flavorful ingredients. If you follow the recipe exactly, the chicken should turn out quite tender and juicy.

2 medium poblano
   chiles
3 tablespoons vegetable
   oil, plus extra for
   oiling the poblanos
4 boneless, skinless
   chicken breast halves
   (about 1¼ pounds)
Kosher salt and freshly
   ground black pepper
1 extra-large onion
4 ounces shiitake
   mushrooms
1 tablespoon fresh
   oregano leaves or
   ½ teaspoon dried
1 cup cherry tomatoes
2 garlic cloves
½ cup dry white wine
½ cup Homemade
   Chicken Stock
   (page 10, add
   preparation time) or
   canned broth
4 ounces ⅓-less-
   fat cream cheese
   (Neufchâtel)
1 tablespoon fresh
   lemon juice

1. Preheat the broiler to high. Rub the poblanos with vegetable oil and place them on the broiler pan. Broil them, 4 inches from the heat source, for about 10 minutes, turning several times until they have blackened on all sides. Transfer the poblanos to a medium bowl and cover them with plastic wrap. Set them aside until they are cool enough to handle, then remove and discard the skin and seeds. Finely slice the chiles (about ¾ cup). Reduce the oven temperature to 350°F.

2. Meanwhile, heat 2 tablespoons vegetable oil in a large ovenproof skillet over high heat until hot. Season the chicken with salt and pepper to taste. Add it to the pan and cook for 2 minutes per side, or until golden. Transfer the chicken to a bowl and set it aside.

3. Slice the onion (about 3 cups). Add the remaining 1 tablespoon vegetable oil to the skillet; reduce the heat to medium. Add the onion and cook for 7 minutes, stirring occasionally, or until golden.

4. Clean the mushrooms, remove and discard the stems, and coarsely chop the caps (about 2 cups). Chop the oregano (about 1½ teaspoons). Stir the mushrooms, oregano, and a pinch of salt into the onion in the skillet and cook for 2 minutes, stirring occasionally. Halve the cherry tomatoes (about 1 cup) and add them to the skillet. Press in the garlic (about 2 teaspoons) and cook, stirring, for 2 minutes.

5. Add the white wine and simmer over low heat until reduced by half. Add the chicken stock, sliced poblanos, and cheese; whisk until combined and bring just to a simmer. Return the chicken and any juices from the bowl to the skillet. Cover the skillet tightly with aluminum foil and bake for 15 to 20 minutes, or until the chicken has just cooked through. Season the sauce with salt and pepper to taste and stir in the lemon juice. Transfer the chicken to each of 4 plates and top with the sauce.

what is the best way
TO ROAST AND PEEL PEPPERS?

There are a number of ways to roast peppers; all are easy. If you have a gas stove, turn on one burner to a low flame for every four peppers that you want to roast. Arrange the peppers directly on the grate over the flame and use tongs to turn them often until they are blackened on all sides. If you have an electric stove, place a rack 4 inches from your broiler's heat source and preheat the broiler to high. Place the peppers on the rack and char them as directed above. Either method will take 10 to 15 minutes. Transfer the peppers to a bowl, cover it tightly with plastic wrap, and set it aside until the peppers are cool enough to touch. Working over a bowl to catch the juices, quarter each pepper and discard the stem and seeds; pull off and discard the skin and use the peppers as directed in your recipe. Don't rinse the peeled peppers, as that removes some of the flavor. The juices you have caught in the bowl are a delicious addition to soups and sauces.

Chicken Saltimbocca with Artichoke Sauce

MAKES 4 SERVINGS ▪ HANDS-ON TIME: 35 MINUTES ▪ TOTAL PREPARATION TIME: 45 MINUTES

Saltimbocca, which literally means "jump into the mouth" in Italian, is a no-brag-just-facts description of the wonderfulness of the classic recipe made with veal scaloppine, prosciutto, and sage. My version substitutes chicken for veal and adds an artichoke sauce. This recipe would work not only as a special treat for the family on a weeknight, but as a winning dinner entrée for guests on a weekend.

The only time-consuming part of this recipe is the pounding of the chicken breasts. But if you sprinkle the breasts with a little water before bashing away at them with a rolling pin, they won't stick to the plastic bag and shred. In any case, I tend to find the bashing part of the preparation strangely soothing, especially after a bad day at the office or a squabble with the kidlets.

4 boneless, skinless chicken breast halves (about 1¼ pounds; see Note)

12 large fresh sage or basil leaves

2 to 3 ounces thinly sliced prosciutto di Parma

⅓ cup Wondra or unbleached all-purpose flour

Kosher salt and freshly ground black pepper

3 tablespoons extra virgin olive oil

⅓ cup dry Marsala or sherry

One 14-ounce can artichoke hearts

1 cup Homemade Chicken Stock (page 10, add preparation time) or canned broth

1 tablespoon unsalted butter

1. Sprinkle a small amount of water into a large resealable plastic bag. Place a chicken breast half in the bag and close, leaving ½ inch open. Pound the bag with a rolling pin or meat pounder until the breast is about ¼ inch thick; remove and set aside. Repeat with the remaining chicken breasts.

2. Put 3 sage leaves on the less smooth side of each pounded chicken breast. Cover them with the prosciutto and press until they adhere. Cover the breasts and chill them for 10 minutes. Cut each breast crosswise in half.

3. Spread out the flour in a pie plate lined with wax paper or parchment. Season half the chicken pieces with salt and pepper to taste. Working with one piece at a time, coat the chicken with the flour, lifting the wax paper on both sides to move the piece around; shake off the excess flour.

4. Heat 1½ tablespoons olive oil in a large skillet over high heat until hot; reduce the heat to medium. Sauté the chicken for 2 minutes per side, or until the pieces are golden and just cooked through; remove them to a plate and cover them loosely with aluminum foil. Repeat with the remaining oil and chicken.

5. Add the Marsala to the skillet; bring it to a boil, scraping up the brown bits at the bottom of the pan, and simmer for about 1 minute, or until the pan is almost dry.

6. Drain and coarsely chop the artichoke hearts (about 1⅓ cups). Add them to the skillet along with the chicken stock and simmer until reduced by half. Return the chicken to the skillet and simmer just until reheated. Add the butter to the pan and swirl until it has melted. Divide the chicken among 4 dinner plates; spoon the sauce over the chicken and serve.

NOTE: Or use 1¼ pounds thin chicken cutlets (about 7), which will not need to be pounded or cut in half. Just make sure to distribute the sage leaves and prosciutto evenly among all the cutlets.

Hungarian Chicken Livers

MAKES 4 TO 6 SERVINGS   HANDS-ON TIME: 25 MINUTES   TOTAL PREPARATION TIME: 50 MINUTES

Every time I buy a whole chicken, I dig around for the little package of giblets and pick out the liver to sauté in olive oil as a weeknight appetizer for The Husband. It's the kind of thing a shiksa wife loves to do for her Hebrew mate.

It's hard to lose with chicken livers. They just have so much flavor all by themselves. In this recipe, I've glorified them with a Hungarian sauce composed of paprika, caraway seeds, red pepper, and sour cream. (You're welcome to lose the sour cream if you'd like. It makes an already rich dish that much richer.) If you decided to ladle this dish onto some egg noodles, you wouldn't be sorry for a second—and you could easily feed a party of eight.

1 pound chicken livers
1 cup whole milk
1 large onion
1 red bell pepper
1 cup plus 1 tablespoon Wondra or unbleached all-purpose flour
Kosher salt and freshly ground black pepper
5 tablespoons vegetable oil
1 tablespoon tomato paste
2 teaspoons sweet paprika
2 teaspoons caraway seeds
⅓ cup dry white wine
1 to 1½ cups Homemade Chicken Stock (page 10, add preparation time) or canned broth
½ cup sour cream (optional)

1. Trim the chicken livers and separate them into halves if they are still attached. Combine the livers and milk in a small bowl and chill for 30 minutes. Meanwhile, thinly slice the onion (about 2 cups) and bell pepper (about 1½ cups).

2. Spread out 1 cup flour in a pie plate lined with wax paper or parchment. Drain the livers and season them with salt and pepper to taste. Working in batches, toss the livers in the flour, lifting the wax paper on both sides to move the livers around; transfer to a strainer and shake off the excess flour.

3. Heat 3 tablespoons vegetable oil in a large skillet over high heat until hot. Sauté the livers for 4 to 5 minutes, turning frequently, until they are golden on all sides (watch out; they will spit). Transfer the livers to a bowl and set aside.

4. When the livers have been removed from the skillet, add the remaining 2 tablespoons vegetable oil along with the onion. Reduce the heat to medium and sauté the onion, stirring occasionally, for 5 to 7 minutes, or until it is golden; add the bell pepper and cook for 3 minutes more.

5. Add the tomato paste, paprika, caraway seeds, and ¼ teaspoon salt to the skillet and cook for 1 minute. Stir in 1 tablespoon flour and cook for 1 minute. Whisk in the white wine and bring the mixture to a boil; reduce the heat to low and simmer for 1 minute.

Whisk in 1 cup chicken stock and simmer for 3 minutes more; add more chicken stock if the sauce seems too thick. Return the livers to the skillet and cook just until they are hot and cooked through. Stir in the sour cream, if using, and salt and black pepper to taste, and serve.

what is INSTANTIZED FLOUR?

Instantized flour is the generic name for Wondra, the kind of flour my grandmother used for making gravies. You can still find it in most supermarkets in the baking section. It comes in a unique round blue can. According to *The Nutrition Bible,* by Jean Anderson and Barbara Deskins, instantized flour "has been moistened and dried into granules that blend instantly in hot and cold liquids." What this means is no lumps in your gravy. Hooray!

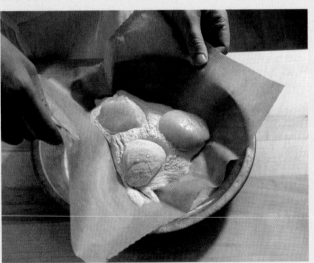

Wondra is one of my favorite coatings for foods that I am going to fry or sauté. I learned this from David Waltuck, the chef at a three-star restaurant in New York called Chanterelle (that re-

To dredge fish or meat in flour, place a piece of wax paper or parchment in a pie plate, fill with flour, and put your food in the flour. Hold the edges of the paper and use it to move the pieces of food around in the flour, which will help to coat the food, not your fingers.

cently closed, alas) when I went to visit the restaurant to do a story on the "family meal," the meal that restaurants serve to their staff right before service. He used Wondra to dip his fish in before he sautéed it. The fish was wonderfully crispy, much better than the result with regular old all-purpose flour.

ens Kotopoulo

MAKES 4 SERVINGS   HANDS-ON TIME: 20 MINUTES   TOTAL PREPARATION TIME: 1 HOUR 35 MINUTES

Kotopoulo is a Greek restaurant specialty. The chicken marinates for hours in a blend of lemon, herbs, and olive oil before it's roasted. In the end, the skin is crispy, the meat is succulent, and your taste buds are dancing.

Sadly, given how long it takes to make, *kotopoulo* is not the kind of dish any of us can pull off on a weeknight. But my brother-in-law Rick Adler, chillin' and grillin' at our most recent family reunion, gave me an idea about how to approximate it. He started with a cut-up chicken, marinated it *à la grecque* for several hours, and then grilled the pieces.

In this case, you start with a Cornish hen, which is smaller than the smallest roasting chicken you can find in a supermarket, and then split it in half, which helps to speed up both the marination and the cooking. You still have to marinate the halves for a full hour, but that's not hands-on time, and you will be delighted with the results, I promise.

¼ cup fresh oregano leaves

¼ cup fresh thyme leaves

¼ cup plus 2 tablespoons fresh lemon juice

¼ cup plus 2 tablespoons extra virgin olive oil

2 teaspoons kosher salt

2 Cornish hens (1 to 1¼ pounds each), rinsed, dried, and split

1. Chop the oregano (about 2 tablespoons) and thyme (about 2 tablespoons). Combine the lemon juice, oregano, thyme, olive oil, and salt in a resealable plastic bag, for the marinade. Add the hens, seal the bag, and knead until they are evenly coated with the marinade. Refrigerate for 1 hour.

2. Preheat the broiler to high. Arrange the hen halves, skin side up, on a broiler pan and broil 4 inches from the heat source for 10 minutes, or until they begin to brown.

3. Reduce the oven temperature to 300°F. Transfer the hens to the middle shelf of the oven and roast them for about 15 minutes, or until they are just cooked through; set aside at room temperature for 5 minutes before serving.

$\mathcal{C}$hicken Kiev Revisited

MAKES 4 SERVINGS ▪ HANDS-ON TIME: 25 MINUTES ▪ TOTAL PREPARATION TIME: 35 MINUTES

Talk about retro! The last time I made chicken Kiev was probably thirty years ago. I revived it at the suggestion of Joanne, who thought it might be a great way to use some of our flavored butters. Of course, the classic chicken Kiev, which surfaced in the Ukrainian capital in the early years of the twentieth century, was all about the butter. It wasn't enough that the breasts were breaded and deep-fried. There were also huge chunks of butter tucked into the meat. When you cut into the breast, the melted butter would shoot out, Vesuvius style, and spread across your plate, an instant and extravagant sauce. Of course, it was absolutely delicious, but afterward you tended to feel as if you yourself were breaded, stuffed, and swimming in butter.

This version is much lighter than the original. The chicken is sautéed and baked, not deep-fried, and there's only a tablespoon of butter per person. (If you haven't had time to make the Herb Butter, you can use regular old butter mixed with a little minced garlic.) Finally, though, it's hard to go wrong with crispy breaded chicken and melted butter. What's old is new.

4 boneless, skinless chicken breast halves (about 1¼ pounds)
4 tablespoons Herb Butter (see Flavored Butters; page 19, add preparation time)
Kosher salt and freshly ground black pepper
2 large eggs
½ cup Wondra or unbleached all-purpose flour
1 cup dry bread crumbs
2 tablespoons extra virgin olive oil
Lemon wedges, for garnish

1. Starting at the thick end, insert a knife horizontally into the center of each chicken breast to make a pocket. Fill each pocket with 1 tablespoon Herb Butter. Season the chicken with ½ teaspoon salt and ¼ teaspoon pepper. Lightly beat the eggs in a bowl.

2. Preheat the oven to 350°F. Line up 3 bowls: the first filled with the flour, the second with the beaten eggs, and the third with the bread crumbs. Coat the chicken lightly with the flour, shaking off the excess, then dip it into the eggs, letting the excess drip off. Coat well with the crumbs.

3. In an ovenproof skillet just large enough to hold the chicken breasts in one layer, heat 1 tablespoon olive oil over high heat until hot. Reduce the heat to medium; add the chicken breasts and sauté them for 3 minutes per side, or until they are golden, adding the remaining 1 tablespoon olive oil when they are turned.

4. Transfer the skillet to the oven and bake the breasts until they are just cooked through, 8 to 11 minutes, depending on their size. Serve with lemon wedges.

Turkey Meatballs with Broccoli Pesto and Orzo

MAKES 6 TO 8 SERVINGS ▪ HANDS-ON TIME: 35 MINUTES ▪ TOTAL PREPARATION TIME: 45 MINUTES

Although it's not obvious at first glance, this dish is a takeoff on spaghetti and meatballs, only I've replaced the spaghetti with orzo and the tomato sauce with broccoli pesto. Also, the meatballs are made with turkey (flavored with a little prosciutto), although you're welcome to make them with beef. I specify largish meatballs to speed up prep time, figuring it's quicker to make 20 large meatballs than 40 smaller ones.

¾ cup Broccoli or Broccoli Raab Pesto (page 18) or 1 cup store-bought basil pesto

1 medium onion

3 tablespoons extra virgin olive oil

4 ounces prosciutto

1 slice firm white bread

2 large eggs

1¼ pounds ground turkey

Kosher salt

½ teaspoon crushed red pepper flakes

8 ounces orzo

1. Prepare the Broccoli or Broccoli Raab Pesto.

2. Bring a large pot of salted water to a boil. Finely chop the onion (about 1 cup).

3. Heat 1 tablespoon olive oil in a large skillet over medium heat until hot. Reduce the heat to medium-low; add the onion and cook for 5 minutes, or until it has softened. Remove the onion and spread it out on a plate; cover it loosely with aluminum foil and put it in the freezer for 5 minutes to cool quickly.

4. Meanwhile, finely chop the prosciutto (about ¾ cup). Pulse the bread in a blender or food processor to make ½ cup bread crumbs.

5. Lightly beat the eggs in a large bowl; gently stir in the cooled onion, the turkey, prosciutto, bread crumbs, 1½ teaspoons salt, and the red pepper flakes. At this point, you might want to fully cook a little sample and taste it to see if you want to add any more seasoning (see How Do I Add Seasonings to Raw Ground Meat Mixtures?, page 61). Shape the soft mixture into 2-inch balls (about 20).

6. Heat the remaining 2 tablespoons olive oil in the large skillet over medium heat. Add the meatballs to the skillet and cook for 10 to 12 minutes, turning frequently, until they are almost cooked through.

7. Meanwhile, cook the orzo until al dente, following the package directions. Drain it, reserving 1 cup of the cooking liquid. Add the orzo to the meatball skillet along with the broccoli pesto and enough of the reserved cooking liquid to make a sauce. Cook until heated through. Divide the orzo among 6 to 8 pasta bowls and top with the meatballs and sauce.

9
TERRIFIC TURF

There's a bumper sticker given away to the patrons of Famous Dave's Bar-B-Que of Saint Paul, Minnesota. WE LIKE VEGETARIANS, it reads. THEY MAKE US LAUGH. Although I am hardly as meatheaded as Famous Dave, I understand that, by and large, America still runs on beef, pork, and chicken. Accordingly, this chapter is filled with lots of tasty possibilities: two recipes for steak and two for burgers, recipes for plain and smoked pork chops, and recipes for stir-fry beef, chorizo pork and beans, pizza with corned beef, and a lip-smacking ground lamb dish.

That said, the older I get, the more I feel that a little meat goes a long way. Accordingly, the portion sizes for the recipes here are relatively modest, and the recipes themselves are frequently bulked up with vegetables and herbs. Even so, most of these entrées will need a side dish or two, so look to "Side Dishes with Star Quality" (page 253) for inspiration along those lines.

FACING PAGE: *Seared Cuban-Style Steak.*

Pastrami-Spiced Steak

MAKES 4 SERVINGS   HANDS-ON TIME: 15 MINUTES   TOTAL PREPARATION TIME: 25 MINUTES PLUS MARINATING

Pastrami—smoked, spiced, and thinly sliced brisket of beef—isn't just a one-dish definition of Jewish delicatessen cuisine, it's also a shortcut definition of Jewish identity. The smallest deviation from the correct composition of a pastrami sandwich—it must be served on rye bread with mustard—is regarded as heresy. No less a figure than Milton Berle once declared, "Anytime a person goes into a delicatessen and orders a pastrami on white bread, somewhere a Jew dies."

However you eat it, pastrami is almost never homemade, but why shouldn't we feel free to apply that one-of-a-kind pastrami spice mix to a steak and cook it up in our very own kitchen? The steak needs to cure in the spice mix for quite a while, so get it going in the morning before you go to work. It'll be ready to cook up when you get home at night.

1½ pounds hanger, flank, or strip steak
¼ cup extra virgin olive oil
1 tablespoon fresh coarse-ground black pepper
1 tablespoon firmly packed dark brown sugar
2 teaspoons ground coriander
2 teaspoons dry mustard
1½ teaspoons ground allspice
Kosher salt
1 teaspoon sweet or hot paprika
1 teaspoon garlic powder

1. Cut the steak into 4 equal pieces; place the pieces in a resealable plastic bag with 2 tablespoons olive oil. Combine the pepper, brown sugar, coriander, mustard, allspice, 1 teaspoon salt, the paprika, and garlic powder in a small bowl; add the mixture to the bag with the steak. Seal the bag and knead until the pieces are evenly coated with the spice mixture. Refrigerate for at least 4 hours or up to 12 hours.

2. Preheat the oven to 375°F. Remove the steak from the bag; pat very dry with paper towels. This is very important; if the steak is not dry, it will not sear properly. Heat the remaining 2 tablespoons olive oil in an ovenproof skillet over medium heat. Add the steak pieces and sauté for 2 minutes per side. Transfer the skillet to the oven and cook for 6 to 8 minutes, depending on the thickness of the pieces, for medium-rare (135°F on an instant-read thermometer).

3. Remove the steak to a serving platter; cover loosely with aluminum foil and set aside for 10 minutes. Slice the pieces diagonally across the grain, season them with salt, if desired, drizzle them with the meat juices from the platter, and serve.

Seared Cuban-Style Steak

MAKES 4 SERVINGS   HANDS-ON TIME: 25 MINUTES   TOTAL PREPARATION TIME: 60 MINUTES

This recipe was inspired by Cuba's (and Miami's) ubiquitous *mojo*-marinated *palomilla* steak. The *mojo* (pronounced "mo-ho") is a combination of citrus and garlic. In Cuba the citrus comes courtesy of a *naranja agria,* or "sour orange," a fruit that looks like a bumpy green orange but tastes like a lime. Given the relative scarcity of the *naranja* in America, I've substituted a mixture of lime and orange. The meat—I have chosen skirt steak—picks up a lot of flavor from the *mojo* in a short amount of time. You can fit only half the steak at once in a large skillet, but it cooks very quickly. While the steak is resting for a few minutes, use the same skillet to sear the onion, which becomes the perfect crunchy topping for the tangy, garlicky meat.

½ cup plus
    2 tablespoons extra
    virgin olive oil
1 teaspoon cumin seeds
4 garlic cloves
1 tablespoon fresh
    oregano leaves or
    ½ teaspoon dried
    oregano
¼ cup fresh lime juice
1 teaspoon freshly
    grated orange zest
2 tablespoons fresh
    orange juice
Kosher salt
1½ pounds skirt steak
1 large onion
1 cup fresh flat-leaf
    parsley leaves

1. Combine ½ cup olive oil and the cumin seeds in a small saucepan; press in the garlic (about 1 tablespoon plus 1 teaspoon). Heat the mixture over medium heat until it is hot and set aside to cool slightly. Finely chop the oregano (about 1½ teaspoons). Add the oregano, lime juice, orange zest, orange juice, oregano, and ½ teaspoon salt to the oil.

2. Trim the steak and cut into 6-inch lengths; place the pieces in a resealable plastic bag. Pour the citrus marinade over the steak; seal the bag and knead until the steak pieces are evenly coated with the marinade. Set the steak aside to marinate at room temperature for 30 minutes. Then pat very dry with paper towels. This is very important; if the steak is not dry, it will not sear properly.

3. Meanwhile, slice the onion (about 2 cups); coarsely chop the parsley (about ½ cup).

4. Heat 1 tablespoon olive oil in each of 2 large skillets over high heat (if you don't have 2 large skillets, work in batches). Sear half the steak pieces for 1 minute per side in each of the 2 hot pans and transfer them to a plate; cover them loosely with a piece of aluminum foil.

5. Reduce the heat to medium-low; add half the onion (about 1 cup) to each of the pans with a pinch of salt and a little bit of water, if necessary (if the bottom of the pan has gotten too dark), and sauté for 5 minutes, or until the onion is tender. Add the juices from the meat plate to the skillets. Thinly slice the steak across the grain. Serve the steak topped with the onion and chopped parsley.

Reuben Pizza

When I was just getting started on this book, I asked Jennifer Day, my *chef de cuisine* at *Gourmet*, to put on her thinking cap and pass along her best recipe ideas. She and her husband, Matt, cook dinner at home almost every night, and they're always experimenting with new dishes. It wasn't too long before she came up with this gem: Transfer the ingredients of a Reuben sandwich onto a pizza. Well, why not?

Making this pizza is a breeze. The dough takes just 6 minutes to prepare, and while it's rising, you can throw together the quick cream sauce and measure out the rest of the ingredients. Please note the two unusual pizza-making tricks here:

1. Roll out the dough on a lightly oiled surface, not a lightly floured one.
2. Prebake the rolled-out dough before you put on the toppings. This will give you a much crisper crust.

Finally, if you want to put a dent in the calorie count here, use low-fat milk in place of whole milk and replace the corned beef with turkey, for a turkey Reuben pizza.

Basic Pizza Dough (page 26, add preparation time) or use store-bought dough
1 to 2 tablespoons cornmeal
Russian Dressing (recipe follows) or use store-bought dressing, optional
8 ounces thinly sliced cooked corned beef
6 ounces Swiss cheese
1 cup drained sauerkraut
2 tablespoons unsalted butter
2 tablespoons unbleached all-purpose flour
1 cup whole milk
1 tablespoon Dijon mustard
Kosher salt
Extra virgin olive oil

1. Prepare the Basic Pizza Dough or take the store-bought dough out of the fridge. Sprinkle the cornmeal onto 2 baking sheets. Place a rack in the bottom of the oven and preheat the oven to 500°F.

2. Prepare the Russian Dressing, if using.

3. Cut the corned beef crosswise into ½-inch strips (about 1¾ cups); coarsely grate the cheese (about 1½ cups). Rinse the sauerkraut in a strainer and press until dry.

4. Make the sauce: Melt the butter in a small saucepan over medium heat. Whisk in the flour and cook, whisking constantly, for 2 minutes. Gradually whisk in the milk and, whisking constantly, bring to a boil over high heat; reduce the heat to low and simmer for 2 minutes. Whisk in 1 cup of the cheese and the mustard; add salt to taste and set aside.

continued on next page

5. When the dough has almost risen, divide it into 4 balls; roll out each ball on a lightly oiled surface to make a 9½ × 7-inch rectangle that is about ⅛ inch thick. Transfer 2 rectangles to the baking sheets. Place 1 sheet on the bottom rack of the oven and bake for 3 minutes, or until set but not browned.

6. Remove the baking sheet from the oven and place the other baking sheet on the bottom rack of the oven. Bake the other 2 rectangles for 3 minutes, or until set but not browned. Let the crusts cool on the baking sheets for 5 minutes before topping.

7. Spoon one-quarter of the sauce onto each of the partially baked crusts, spreading it to within ¼ inch of the edges. Arrange one-quarter of the corned beef, sauerkraut, and the remaining cheese on top of each.

8. Place 1 baking sheet at a time on the bottom rack of the oven and bake each pizza for 7 to 8 minutes, or until the cheese melts and the crusts are golden and crisp on the bottom. Remove the baking sheet from the oven and cover loosely with aluminum foil to keep the pizza warm while the other sheet bakes. Serve the pizzas with Russian Dressing, if desired.

MAKES ABOUT 1 CUP   HANDS-ON TIME: 5 MINUTES
TOTAL PREPARATION TIME: 5 MINUTES

RUSSIAN DRESSING: Stir together ⅔ cup mayonnaise, 2 tablespoons chili sauce, and ¼ cup finely chopped dill pickles.

Thai-Style Beef Stir-fry with Chiles and Basil

MAKES 4 SERVINGS   HANDS-ON TIME: 25 MINUTES   TOTAL PREPARATION TIME: 25 MINUTES
(ADD 30 MINUTES IF FREEZING BEFORE CUTTING)

Although I've dispensed with *mise en place* in this book to allow you to prep and cook simultaneously, this dish is an exception. Here all the ingredients have to be prepped in advance because the actual cooking time is so brief. How painful is 25 minutes of prep, when it takes only 3 minutes to cook?

What makes this dish Thai? Shallots, lime juice, soy sauce, basil (use Thai basil, if you can find it), and fish sauce. I've substituted serranos for Thai bird chiles and brown sugar for palm sugar because the subs are more readily available than the Thai ingredients.

1 pound beef flank steak
½ cup fresh basil leaves (preferably Thai)
2 small shallots
2 serrano chiles
2 tablespoons soy sauce (low sodium, if you prefer)
1 tablespoon oyster sauce
1 tablespoon fish sauce
1 tablespoon fresh lime juice
2 teaspoons firmly packed brown sugar
5 tablespoons vegetable oil
2 garlic cloves
Cooked white rice, as an accompaniment

1. If time permits, freeze the steak for 30 minutes to make it easier to slice.

2. Meanwhile, finely chop the basil leaves (about ¼ cup), thinly slice the shallots (about ¼ cup), and very thinly slice the chiles crosswise, including their ribs and seeds for more heat, if desired (about ¼ cup). Whisk together ¼ cup water, the soy sauce, oyster sauce, fish sauce, lime juice, and brown sugar.

3. Cut the steak diagonally across the grain into ¼-inch-thick slices. Heat 2 tablespoons vegetable oil in a large skillet over medium high heat until hot. Add one-third of the beef and stir-fry for 1 to 2 minutes, or just until seared on both sides. Transfer the steak with tongs to a large plate. Repeat twice, adding 1 tablespoon vegetable oil and one-third of the meat each time.

4. Add the remaining 1 tablespoon vegetable oil to the skillet. Reduce the heat to medium; add the shallots and stir-fry for 1 minute, or until they start to turn golden. Add the chiles and press the garlic (about 2 teaspoons) into the pan. Stir-fry for 1 minute more. Add the soy sauce mixture and basil; bring to a boil over high heat. Return the beef and beef juices from the plate to the pan and cook for 30 seconds, or until just heated. Serve immediately over white rice.

Korean Burgers

This recipe is my all-Americanization of *bulgogi,* which is, along with kimchi, one of the most well known dishes of Korea. Literally translated as "fire meat," *bulgogi* is Korean barbecue. Although it is often made with grilled beef, marinated and thinly sliced, *bulgogi* can also be made with chicken, pork, or fish. In Korea it is usually served with lettuce or a leafy vegetable, on rice or stir-fried noodles, or in a Korean "sushi" roll. In Los Angeles, which these days is home to the largest Korean community outside of Korea itself, *bulgogi* is served on flour tortillas and sold by mobile vendors as *kogi,* aka "Korean barbecue tacos." Los Angeles, then, is where Korea meets Mexico.

My hybrid is more like Korea meets the American heartland. I took most of *bulgogi's* classic ingredients, mixed them with ground meat, shaped them into burgers, and topped them all off with kimchi. It works like a charm.

Quick or Quicker
  Kimchi (page 21, add
  preparation time) or
  store-bought kimchi
4 medium scallions
One ¾-inch piece fresh
  ginger
3 tablespoons soy
  sauce (low sodium,
  if you prefer)
1½ tablespoons
  unseasoned rice
  vinegar
1 tablespoon firmly
  packed dark brown
  sugar
1½ teaspoons toasted
  sesame oil
1 garlic clove
1½ pounds ground beef
  chuck, round, or
  sirloin, or bison
Kosher salt and freshly
  ground black pepper
2 tablespoons
  vegetable oil
4 hamburger buns

1. Prepare the kimchi.

2. Trim and thinly slice the scallions (about ½ cup); peel and Microplane-grate the ginger (about ¾ teaspoon). Combine the ginger, soy sauce, rice vinegar, brown sugar, and sesame oil in a small bowl; press the garlic (about 1 teaspoon) into the bowl.

3. Gently stir the scallions and the soy sauce mixture into the ground chuck in a bowl with a fork and shape the meat into 4 burgers, being careful not to overwork the meat. Season the burgers on both sides with salt and pepper to taste.

4. Heat the vegetable oil in a large skillet over high heat until hot; reduce the heat to medium and add the burgers. Cook for 5 minutes per side for medium-rare.

5. Meanwhile, split and toast the buns. To serve, place a burger on the bottom half of each bun, top with some kimchi, and close.

Quick Seared Beef and Scallions

MAKES 4 SERVINGS   HANDS-ON TIME: 25 MINUTES   TOTAL PREPARATION TIME: 25 MINUTES

This recipe started out as a weeknight version of beef negamaki, a succulent Japanese-American restaurant dish consisting of seared beef, scallions, soy sauce, sake, and ginger. Unfortunately, making negamaki turned out to be something of a chore. The meat has to be frozen and pounded before it is sliced, then the meat and scallions have to be tied up together in rolls. This is simply too much fuss on a weeknight.

So no more freezing and pounding, no more rolling and tying, but I kept the delicious and complementary components of the original dish. The resulting easy-to-make recipe could end up in your regular repertoire.

1 pound tri-tip beef or
   flank steak
12 medium scallions
One ½-inch piece fresh
   ginger
¼ cup soy sauce (low
   sodium, if you prefer)
2 tablespoons sake or
   dry sherry
¼ teaspoon sugar
2 tablespoons plus
   1½ teaspoons
   vegetable oil
¼ teaspoon kosher salt
Cooked white rice, as
   an accompaniment

1. Preheat the broiler to high. Cut the beef across the grain into ¼- to ⅓-inch-thick slices and cut the slices in half. Trim the scallions and cut the white and most of the green parts into 2-inch lengths (about 3 cups). Peel and Microplane-grate the ginger (about ½ teaspoon). Combine the ginger, soy sauce, sake, and sugar in a small bowl.

2. Toss the scallions with 1½ teaspoons vegetable oil and the salt. Arrange in one layer on a rimmed baking sheet and broil, 4 inches from the heat source, for about 5 minutes, or until slightly softened and charred at the edges. Set aside.

3. Heat 1 tablespoon vegetable oil in a large skillet over high heat until just smoking. Working in batches, sear the meat, turning once, for about 1 minute per side, or until nicely browned, adding more vegetable oil as necessary. Transfer the meat to a plate as it is cooked and cover it loosely with aluminum foil.

4. Add the soy sauce mixture to the skillet along with any juices from the plate where the meat was resting. Bring the mixture to a boil, scraping up the brown bits at the bottom of the pan. Add the meat and scallions and cook just until heated through, adding water, if necessary, to create more sauce. Spoon the meat, scallions, and sauce over hot rice and serve.

$\mathcal{B}$uttermilk "Fried" Pork Chops

MAKES 4 SERVINGS   HANDS-ON TIME: 30 MINUTES   TOTAL PREPARATION TIME: 1 HOUR
(ADD 30 MINUTES IF FREEZING BEFORE CUTTING)

After a single semester of college, my son, Sam, decided to move out of his dorm and into an apartment with his friends because he couldn't stand dorm food. Sam has always been a great eater—he founded the Fine Dining Club at his high school—but he never spent much time learning how to cook. Naturally, I was a little concerned at the thought that he or his roommates were suddenly going to have to make dinner every night. I gave him both of my own cookbooks with the Sam-friendly recipes clearly earmarked.

I expected Sam to start phoning me with minor questions, like how to double a recipe. Instead, several nights a week, usually when I was in the middle of cooking dinner, Sam would call and say, "Mom, I'm at the supermarket and I want to make a steak recipe for the eight of us. What do you suggest?" Suffering from empty-nest syndrome, I'd happily walk him through whole recipes. It quickly paid off. After a while Sam had mastered risotto, fried rice, veal francese, and skirt steak with red wine sauce.

When Sam came home for the summer, I tested these "fried" pork chops on him. Sure enough, they leaped right into his repertoire (minus the parsley). The key to this recipe is the buttermilk, a great tenderizer. On the inside the chops turn out very juicy. On the outside the panko bread crumbs create a wonderfully crispy crust. It's almost as if you had deep-fried them.

Four ½-inch-thick boneless pork chops (about 1 pound)
1 cup buttermilk
1 teaspoon Tabasco
Kosher salt
1 garlic clove
2½ cups panko bread crumbs
6 to 8 tablespoons extra virgin olive oil or vegetable oil
2 tablespoons fresh flat-leaf parsley leaves
4 lemon wedges, for garnish

1. If time permits, freeze the pork chops for 30 minutes to make them easier to cut. Carefully cut each horizontally to make 2 thin chops, for a total of 8 chops. Sprinkle a small amount of water into a large resealable plastic bag. Place a pork chop in the bag and close, leaving ½ inch open. Pound with a rolling pin or meat pounder until the chop is about ⅛ inch thick; remove and set aside. Repeat with the remaining chops.

2. Whisk together the buttermilk, Tabasco, and ½ teaspoon salt; press in the garlic (about 1 teaspoon). Transfer to a large resealable plastic bag. Place the pounded chops in the bag with the buttermilk mixture and marinate at room temperature, turning several times, for 30 minutes.

3. Spread out the bread crumbs in a pie plate lined with wax paper or parchment. Season the chops with salt. Working with one chop at a time, toss the chop in the bread crumbs, lifting the wax paper on both sides to move the chop around; shake off the excess crumbs.

4. Heat 3 tablespoons olive oil in a large nonstick skillet over medium heat until hot; add half the chops. Sauté them, turning once, for 3 minutes per side, or until golden and just cooked through. Remove to a plate and keep warm. Repeat with the remaining 3 tablespoons olive oil and the remaining chops, adding more oil if necessary. Chop the parsley (about 1 tablespoon).

5. Divide the pork chops among 4 dinner plates, top each portion with some chopped parsley, and serve with a wedge of lemon.

what does
"NATURAL" MEAN ON A MEAT PACKAGE?

According to the USDA, all fresh meat qualifies as "natural" as long as it doesn't contain "any artificial flavor, coloring ingredient, chemical preservative, or any other artificial or synthetic ingredient; and the product and its ingredients are not more than minimally processed (ground, for example)." The USDA suggests that all products with "natural" on their label should explain how they qualify for the term "natural."

$\mathcal{C}$horizo Pork and Beans

MAKES 4 TO 6 SERVINGS   HANDS-ON TIME: 30 MINUTES   TOTAL PREPARATION TIME: 45 MINUTES

Pork and beans is an American staple, but the canned product that you find in many supermarkets is made with salt pork (which is actually just salted pork fat) and way too much sugar. By contrast, think of French cassoulet, Italian *cotechino* with lentils, and Portuguese/Brazilian *feijoada*. In each of these dishes the pork comes from pork sausages, and there's no sugar added.

For this recipe, I started with pinto beans and added Spanish ingredients: chorizo sausages, Manchego cheese, and sherry. I mashed some of the beans to create a creamy texture and topped the finished casserole with crunchy, cheesy panko crumbs. No one's going to miss the sugar.

8 to 10 ounces Spanish chorizo

2 tablespoons extra virgin olive oil plus up to 1 tablespoon more, if needed

1 large onion

1 large red bell pepper

3 garlic cloves

⅓ cup dry sherry, vermouth, or white wine

Two 15-ounce cans pinto beans

One 14½-ounce can chopped tomatoes (preferably fire roasted)

1 cup Homemade Chicken Stock (page 10, add preparation time) or canned broth

Kosher salt and freshly ground black pepper

1 cup panko bread crumbs

1 ounce aged Manchego or Parmigiano-Reggiano cheese

1. Remove the skin from the chorizo; cut the chorizo in half lengthwise and then crosswise into ½-inch-thick pieces. Heat 2 tablespoons olive oil in a large saucepan over medium-high heat until hot. Add the chorizo and cook, stirring occasionally, for about 5 minutes, or until the pieces are lightly browned on both sides. Transfer the chorizo with a slotted spoon to a bowl.

2. Meanwhile, chop the onion (about 2 cups) and bell pepper (about 1½ cups). Remove and measure the chorizo-flavored oil from the saucepan; return 2 tablespoons to the pan, set aside 1 tablespoon for the panko, and discard any remaining. If there is not that much oil, use additional olive oil to make up the difference.

3. Heat the saucepan over medium heat, reduce the heat to medium-low, add the onion, and cook for 5 minutes, or until it has softened. Add the bell pepper and cook for 2 minutes; press the garlic (about 1 tablespoon) into the mixture and cook for 1 minute more. Add the sherry and simmer for 2 to 3 minutes, or until it has reduced by half.

4. Meanwhile, rinse and drain the beans. Add the beans, tomatoes, and chicken stock to the saucepan and simmer the mixture for 15 minutes, or until reduced by half. Mash the mixture in the saucepan with a potato masher to crush some of the beans; stir the chorizo into the mixture and season with salt and black pepper to taste.

5. While the beans are cooking, preheat the broiler. Toss the panko with the reserved 1 tablespoon chorizo-flavored oil. Microplane-grate the cheese (about ⅔ cup) or grate on the fine side of a box grater (about ⅓ cup). Transfer the bean mixture to a shallow metal baking pan and sprinkle the crumbs and cheese evenly over the top. Broil for 40 to 60 seconds, until golden. Spoon into shallow bowls and serve immediately.

Spanish-Style Burgers

MAKES 6 SERVINGS ■ HANDS-ON TIME: 25 MINUTES ■ TOTAL PREPARATION TIME: 35 MINUTES

I have no idea whether they actually eat burgers like this in Spain. I just named this dish as I did because all the condiments—green olives, paprika, and piquillo peppers—are Spanish.

Piquillo peppers (see Sources, page 359) come from the Ebro River valley in northern Spain. They're handpicked and slow-roasted over open wood fires. I first discovered them years ago at the Fancy Food Show in New York, where they impressed me immediately. If you can't find these sweet, hot, smoky peppers at your local supermarket, you're welcome to substitute regular jarred roasted red peppers.

I would have recommended a good Spanish melting cheese for the top of the burger—Idiazabal, for example—if I thought you could find it everywhere. You should definitely ask your local cheese shop if they stock it. Otherwise, Monterey Jack or Cheddar will work fine.

1 large onion
3 tablespoons extra
    virgin olive oil
2 garlic cloves
½ cup mayonnaise
½ teaspoon smoked
    sweet or hot paprika
2 pounds ground pork,
    beef, bison, or turkey
Kosher salt and freshly
    ground black pepper
½ cup whole bottled
    piquillo peppers
    (about 5) or small
    roasted red peppers
    (pimientos, about 2)
⅓ cup pitted green
    olives
6 slices Monterey Jack
    cheese (6 ounces)
6 hamburger buns

1. Finely chop one-half of the onion (about 1 cup) and slice the other half (about 1 cup). Heat 1 tablespoon olive oil in a large skillet over medium heat until hot. Reduce the heat to medium-low; add the chopped onion and cook for 5 minutes, or until it has softened. Press 1 garlic clove (about 1 teaspoon) into the skillet and cook for 1 minute. Transfer the onion and garlic with a slotted spoon to a large bowl and set aside to cool.

2. Heat 1 tablespoon olive oil in the same skillet over medium heat. Add the sliced onion and cook stirring occasionally, until the onion is slightly golden but still crisp, about 5 minutes. Transfer it to a small bowl and set aside to cool. Wipe out the skillet with a paper towel.

3. Meanwhile, combine the mayonnaise and paprika in small bowl; press in the remaining garlic clove (about 1 teaspoon).

4. Add the pork to the cooled chopped onion mixture; gently stir together with a fork. Shape the meat mixture into 6 burgers and season them on both sides with salt and black pepper to taste.

5. Heat the remaining 1 tablespoon olive oil in the skillet over medium heat. Add the burgers and cook for 6 minutes per side, or until they are almost cooked through. (I like them barely pink.

If you used beef or bison, cook them to the doneness you prefer. If you used turkey, cook them until they are completely cooked through.)

6. While the burgers are cooking, chop the piquillo peppers (about ½ cup) and the olives (about ¼ cup) and combine them with the sliced onion in a bowl; season with salt and black pepper to taste. Divide the mixture on top of the cooked burgers in the skillet and top each with a slice of cheese. Reduce the heat to low, cover the skillet, and cook for about 1 minute, or just until the cheese has melted.

7. Meanwhile, split and toast the hamburger buns. Spread the top and bottom of each bun generously with the mayonnaise mixture, place a burger on the bottom half of each bun, close, and serve.

how can i
KEEP BURGERS FROM PUFFING UP IN THE CENTER?

As burgers cook, the outer edges get done first and shrink, pushing the juices into the center of the burgers, reshaping the burgers into meatballs. My favorite trick to prevent this is to create an indentation in the center of each burger by pressing down with my thumb when I shape the burger. I also make them a bit bigger than the bun so that when they do what comes naturally, they turn out the size and shape I want.

MEAT SAFETY

Increased research into food-borne illnesses has made us more careful about the way we purchase and serve meats. It really isn't a lot of trouble for the cook to take extra precautions when shopping for and handling meats, and it's especially important when you are serving meat to the very young, the very old, or anyone with a compromised immune system. The USDA suggests the following guidelines:

- Pick up your fresh meats just before checking out in the supermarket.

- Put fresh meats in a plastic bag to prevent drips, and take them home right away.

- Be especially careful when handling ground meats. Because grinding exposes so much meat surface to the air, ground meats are more perishable than solid cuts.

- Refrigerate meats at 40°F and use them before the "sell-by" date or, for best quality, freeze them by the "sell-by" date at 0°F for up to 3 months for ground meat or 6 months for steaks and roasts.

- Never put cooked meats on a platter or work surface that has held raw meats.

Use an instant-read thermometer to cook meats to the proper internal temperature. Remember to insert the thermometer horizontally through the side of thin items such as burgers or steaks in order to get an accurate reading.

Sautéed Pork Chops with Braised Sauerkraut

MAKES 4 SERVINGS   HANDS-ON TIME: 20 MINUTES   TOTAL PREPARATION TIME: 25 MINUTES

Rick Bzdafka, my cousin Allie's husband, grew up in Cleveland's Polish community. A terrific cook, Rick has earned particular renown within the family for his sauerkraut recipe, which he prepares every year to complement the Thanksgiving turkey. This untraditional combo initially struck the non-Poles among us as not just weird, but damn near subversive. In fact, it makes all the sense in the world. Rick's braised sauerkraut is sweet and sour and cuts right through the rich, fatty turkey and gravy.

Although supermarket pork chops are nowhere near as fatty as they used to be, they can still benefit from an acidic counterpoint. I think Rick's sauerkraut harmonizes beautifully with them.

2 tablespoons vegetable oil

4 plain or smoked pork loin chops (½ inch thick; about 1½ pounds)

Kosher salt and freshly ground black pepper

1 small onion

2 cups drained sauerkraut

2 teaspoons caraway seeds

¼ cup dry white wine

1 to 1½ cups Homemade Chicken or Vegetable Stock (pages 10 and 11, add preparation time) or canned broth

¼ cup firmly packed dark brown sugar

3 tablespoons cider vinegar

2 tablespoons Dijon mustard

1. Heat 1 tablespoon vegetable oil in a large skillet over high heat until hot. If using plain pork chops, season them on all sides with salt and pepper. Place the chops in the hot skillet. Reduce the heat to medium-high and sauté, turning once, for 3 to 4 minutes per side for plain chops (they should be barely pink in the center) and 2 to 3 minutes per side for smoked chops. Meanwhile, chop the onion (about ½ cup); rinse the sauerkraut and squeeze it dry.

2. When the chops are cooked, transfer them to a plate and cover them loosely with aluminum foil. Set them aside.

3. Heat the remaining 1 tablespoon vegetable oil in the same skillet over medium heat until hot. Reduce the heat to medium-low; add the onion and cook for 5 minutes, or until it has softened. Add the caraway seeds and cook for 1 minute more.

4. Increase the heat to high; add the white wine and 1 cup chicken stock to the skillet; bring it to a boil, scraping up the brown bits at the bottom of the pan. Stir in the sauerkraut, brown sugar, vinegar, and mustard. Reduce the heat to low and cook, stirring frequently, for about 5 minutes. Add the juices from the resting pork chops and as much additional chicken stock as necessary to create a moist sauerkraut sauce. Add the chops briefly to the pan and cook until hot; serve topped with the sauerkraut.

$\mathscr{S}$peedy Moussaka

MAKES 4 TO 6 SERVINGS   HANDS-ON TIME: 25 MINUTES   TOTAL PREPARATION TIME: 60 MINUTES

Prepared traditionally, the wonderful Greek casserole called moussaka, which is made of ground lamb, eggplant, and cream sauce, is anything but slim and speedy. Loving the dish as much as I do, I've figured out some ways to speed up the preparation time and make it taste less heavy. I brush the eggplant with a modest amount of olive oil and bake it rather than sautéing it in a lot of oil, and substitute a mix of ricotta, feta, and yogurt for the cream sauce. Call me a heretic, but I believe this version is every bit as good as the more time-consuming, heavier classic version.

1 medium eggplant

3 tablespoons extra virgin olive oil

Kosher salt

1 pound ground lamb, beef, or turkey (see Note)

1 medium onion

2 garlic cloves

2 tablespoons fresh oregano leaves or 1 teaspoon dried

½ cup fresh flat-leaf parsley leaves

1 cup dry red wine

¼ cup tomato paste

¾ teaspoon ground cinnamon

Freshly ground black pepper

6 ounces feta cheese

One 15-ounce container whole milk ricotta

¼ cup plain low-fat or full-fat Greek-style yogurt (see page 49)

1. Preheat the oven to 375°F. Lightly oil a large rimmed baking sheet and a 9-inch square baking pan or 10-inch oval casserole dish.

2. Peel the eggplant and cut it crosswise into ½-inch slices. Combine the olive oil with ¼ teaspoon salt and brush the mixture on both sides of the eggplant slices. Arrange the slices in one layer on the baking sheet and bake them until they are just tender, 12 to 15 minutes. Remove the eggplant from the oven and set it aside until it is cool enough to handle.

3. Meanwhile, heat a large skillet over medium-high heat until hot. Crumble the lamb into the skillet and cook, stirring frequently, until the lamb is no longer pink. Transfer the lamb to a bowl using a slotted spatula, draining as much fat as possible back into the skillet. Remove and discard all but 1 tablespoon lamb fat from the skillet.

4. While the lamb is cooking, coarsely chop the onion (about 1 cup). Heat the remaining 1 tablespoon lamb fat in the skillet over high heat until hot. Reduce the heat to medium, add the onion, and cook, stirring frequently, until the onion is golden, about 5 minutes. Press the garlic (about 2 teaspoons) into the skillet and cook for 1 minute more. Chop the oregano (1 tablespoon) and the parsley (about ¼ cup).

continued on next page

5. Return the lamb to the skillet and stir in the red wine, tomato paste, oregano, and cinnamon. Cook, stirring occasionally, for about 5 minutes, or until the wine has almost evaporated. Add salt and pepper to taste and set aside.

6. Crumble the feta cheese into a medium bowl. Stir in the ricotta and parsley. Set aside ½ cup of the mixture.

7. Arrange one-third of the eggplant in the oiled pan or casserole dish. Top it with the lamb mixture. Add another one-third of the eggplant, the ricotta mixture in the bowl, and then the final one-third of eggplant. Stir the yogurt into the reserved ricotta mixture and spread it over the eggplant. Bake for about 35 minutes, or until the moussaka is heated through and the top cheese layer has set. Spoon the moussaka onto plates and serve immediately.

NOTE: If using beef or turkey, it may be necessary to add some olive oil to the skillet before adding the meat.

I never ate much fish as a kid, but I've come to love it as an adult. It's not only tasty, low in fat, and healthful, it cooks up in no time at all. In short, it's the perfect choice for a quick weeknight meal.

But there are two problems with fish: first, they're very perishable, and second, many popular species are on the verge of extinction. Dealing with their perishability is easy: Buy them fresh, bring them right home, keep them well chilled while you store them, and cook them as soon as possible, preferably the same day that you buy them. (How do you know your fish are fresh? Take a whiff; you should smell nothing other than the faint aroma of the sea.)

Keeping up with exactly which fish are endangered and which are sustainable is tougher because the list keeps changing. So, even though I have recommended particular fish for particular recipes here, those same fish might not be the best choices in a year or two. It is a good idea, then, to check in regularly with folks who keep a close eye on the situation, such as the Monterey Bay Aquarium (www.mbayaq.org; click on "Save the Oceans" and then "Seafood Watch"). You might even want to print out an up-to-date, wallet-size guide to take with you when you go to the fish store or supermarket.

The fish and shellfish in this chapter include wild salmon, Pacific halibut, arctic char, American-farmed tilapia and catfish, black cod, mussels, clams, and shrimp, all of which have bright futures as of this writing. The recipes suggest some of the myriad ways to cook and sauce seafood: baked plain and baked breaded, sautéed plain and sautéed battered, and spiced up with ingredients from New England to Greece to the Middle East.

FACING PAGE: *Black Cod with Warm Roasted-Tomato Vinaigrette and Aioli.*

$\mathcal{B}$lack Cod with Warm Roasted-Tomato Vinaigrette and Aioli

MAKES 4 SERVINGS ▪ HANDS-ON TIME: 20 MINUTES ▪ TOTAL PREPARATION TIME: 25 MINUTES

If you've never before tried black cod, now's the time to start. Fans of Jewish deli food know this fish when it is cured and smoked, as sable. Prepared fresh, black cod is meltingly tender, thanks to its high fat content. In fact, if you like Chilean sea bass (which is now endangered because of overfishing), you'll love black cod. In this recipe, the acidic tomato vinaigrette and garlicky aioli are wonderful counterparts to the rich fish.

Warm Roasted-Tomato Vinaigrette (page 13, add preparation time) or store-bought dressing
¼ cup mayonnaise
1 garlic clove
⅓ cup Wondra or unbleached all-purpose flour
1¼ pounds black cod
Kosher salt and freshly ground black pepper
1 tablespoon extra virgin olive oil

1. Prepare the Warm Roasted-Tomato Vinaigrette. When the tomatoes for the vinaigrette come out of the oven, reduce the oven temperature to 350°F.

2. Meanwhile, for the aioli, place the mayonnaise in a small bowl, press the garlic (about 1 teaspoon) into it, and stir to combine; cover and refrigerate the aioli until you are ready to serve.

3. When the vinaigrette has been prepared, spread out the flour in a pie plate lined with wax paper or parchment. Cut the cod into 4 portions and season it on all sides with salt and pepper to taste. Working with one piece at a time, toss the cod in the flour, lifting the wax paper on both sides to move the piece around; shake off the excess flour.

4. Heat the olive oil in a large skillet with an ovenproof handle over medium-high heat until hot. Place the fish in the skillet and sauté, turning once, for about 2 minutes per side, or until golden. Place the skillet in the oven and bake for about 5 minutes, or until the fish is just cooked.

5. Transfer a piece of fish to each of 4 dinner plates. Top with the vinaigrette and a dollop of aioli.

Sautéed Tilapia with Spicy Mint Sauce

MAKES 4 SERVINGS ▪ HANDS-ON TIME: 15 MINUTES ▪ TOTAL PREPARATION TIME: 25 MINUTES

This recipe contains everything you need to bestow some serious charisma on a bland fish fillet: lime juice for acidity, fish sauce for saltiness, mint for herbal brightening, and jalapeño for heat. I've cast tilapia in the lead role here, but almost any fish—catfish, arctic char, black cod, even salmon—would shine if given this treatment. Feel free to experiment.

1 jalapeño chile (make sure it has heat; see page 6)
¼ cup fresh mint leaves
¼ cup fish sauce
3 tablespoons fresh lime juice
2 tablespoons sugar
⅓ cup Wondra or unbleached all-purpose flour
Four 6-ounce boneless, skinless tilapia fillets
Kosher salt and freshly ground black pepper
3 tablespoons vegetable oil
2 medium scallions

1. Thinly slice the jalapeño crosswise, including the ribs and seeds; thinly slice the mint leaves crosswise to make shreds (about 2 tablespoons). Whisk together ½ cup water, the fish sauce, lime juice, jalapeño, sugar, and mint to make the sauce.

2. Spread out the flour in a pie plate lined with wax paper or parchment. Season the tilapia with salt and pepper to taste. Working with one fillet at a time, toss the tilapia in the flour, lifting the wax paper on both sides to move the fillet around; shake off the excess flour.

3. Heat the vegetable oil in a large nonstick skillet over high heat until hot. Reduce the heat to medium-high; add the fillets and cook for 3 minutes per side, or until just cooked through. Transfer the fillets to 4 serving plates and keep warm.

4. Meanwhile, trim and thinly slice the scallions crosswise (about ¼ cup). Add the scallions to the skillet and sauté them for 1 minute; add the sauce and simmer for 2 minutes. Spoon some of the sauce over each portion of fish and serve.

all about TILAPIA

Tilapia is the generic name of a group of freshwater fish that have been an important part of the Mediterranean and northern African cuisines for millennia. Also known as St. Peter's fish, tilapia was introduced to the United States in 1959 and was targeted as a good candidate for aquaculture because it was easy to raise and a low-fat, mild-flavored fish that people everywhere would like. Since then its popularity has increased, and today it is one of America's top ten seafoods.

Arctic Char Baked in Walnut Sauce

The walnut sauce in this recipe is a nod to *muhammara,* a spicy mix of roasted red peppers, walnuts, and pomegranate syrup that's popular throughout Turkey, Syria, and Lebanon. Typically, it's eaten as a dip with bread, but I thought it might work as a tasty sauce for fish, especially if the fish is baked in the sauce, which guarantees that the flavors of the two will marry. The sauce also acts to insulate the fish so that it doesn't overcook and comes out very moist. Delish! Please note: I have substituted balsamic vinegar for pomegranate syrup; it is more readily available.

½ cup walnut pieces
1 small serrano chile
 or ½ jalapeño chile
 (make sure it has
 heat; see page 6)
One 12-ounce jar
 roasted red peppers
 (pimientos)
1 small onion
2 tablespoons extra
 virgin olive oil
2 garlic cloves
1 teaspoon ground
 cumin
1 teaspoon fennel seed
2 tablespoons balsamic
 vinegar
Kosher salt and freshly
 ground black pepper
Four 6- to 7-ounce
 arctic char fillets

1. Preheat the oven to 350°F. Spread out the walnuts on a rimmed baking sheet and toast until golden, 7 to 10 minutes. Remove the sheet to a cooling rack and let the walnuts cool to room temperature, then coarsely chop them (about ⅓ cup). Turn up the oven temperature to 375°F.

2. While the nuts are toasting, remove the ribs and seeds from the serrano and coarsely chop it (about 2 teaspoons). Puree the red peppers and the serrano in a blender with the pepper juices until smooth; add the walnuts and pulse until they are finely chopped. Lightly oil a shallow casserole big enough for the fish to fit into in one layer. Finely chop the onion (about ½ cup).

3. Heat the olive oil in a medium skillet over medium heat until hot. Reduce the heat to medium-low; add the onion and cook for 5 minutes, or until it has softened. Press in the garlic (about 2 teaspoons) and cook for 1 minute more. Add the cumin and fennel to the onion; cook, stirring, for 2 minutes. Remove the skillet from the heat and stir in the red pepper mixture, vinegar, ½ teaspoon salt, and ¼ teaspoon pepper.

4. Season the fish on both sides with salt and black pepper. Arrange the fillets in the shallow casserole. Pour the walnut sauce over the fish. Cover with aluminum foil and bake for 15 to 20 minutes, or until the fish is just cooked through. Divide the fish among 4 plates, spoon some sauce on top of each portion, and serve.

Halibut or Cod on Chickpea Puree with Egg Lemon Sauce

MAKES 4 SERVINGS ■ HANDS-ON TIME: 30 MINUTES ■ TOTAL PREPARATION TIME: 38 MINUTES

I was thinking of Greece here: fish with an egg lemon sauce. But if the garlicky chickpea puree isn't strictly Greek, it is certifiably Mediterranean. And, okay, I cheated by adding cornstarch to the egg lemon sauce as a thickener. I wanted this recipe to be no muss, no fuss, and without the cornstarch, the sauce has a good chance of curdling.

Ethnic inauthenticity aside, I'm very pleased with this recipe. Served hot at dinner, it made The Husband very happy one evening. Served cold at lunch, it made him equally happy the next day. Also, although I've specified Pacific cod or halibut here, almost any fish, from salmon to catfish, would fill the bill.

½ small onion
3 tablespoons extra virgin olive oil
½ garlic clove
¼ teaspoon cumin seeds
One 15½-ounce can chickpeas
½ cup Homemade Chicken Stock (page 10, add preparation time) or canned broth
¼ teaspoon sweet or hot paprika
1½ teaspoons fresh lemon juice
Kosher salt and freshly ground black pepper
Foolproof Egg Lemon Sauce (page 17, preparation time added)
½ cup Wondra or unbleached all-purpose flour
Four 6-ounce pieces Pacific cod or halibut fillet

1. Finely chop the onion (about ¼ cup). Heat 1 tablespoon olive oil in a medium skillet over medium heat until hot. Reduce the heat to medium-low; add the onion and cook for 5 minutes, or until it has softened. Press in the garlic (about ½ teaspoon) and add the cumin seeds; sauté for 2 minutes more.

2. Rinse and drain the chickpeas. Add the chickpeas, chicken stock, and paprika to the onion mixture; simmer for 5 minutes. Using a fork or potato masher, coarsely mash the chickpeas. Add the lemon juice and salt and pepper to taste; keep warm. Meanwhile, make the Foolproof Egg Lemon Sauce.

3. Spread out the flour in a pie plate lined with wax paper or parchment. Season the fish with salt and pepper to taste. Working with one piece at a time, toss the fish in the flour, lifting the wax paper on both sides to move the piece around; shake off the excess flour.

4. Heat the remaining 2 tablespoons olive oil in a large nonstick skillet over medium heat. Add the fish pieces to the skillet and sauté them for about 8 minutes total, or until the pieces are golden on both sides and just cooked through. Spoon one-quarter of the chickpea mixture into the center of each of 4 dinner plates. Top each chickpea mound with a piece of fish; spoon the Foolproof Egg Lemon Sauce over the fish and serve.

Cajun Catfish with Cucumber Yogurt Sauce

MAKES 4 SERVINGS ▪ HANDS-ON TIME: 20 MINUTES ▪ TOTAL PREPARATION TIME: 25 MINUTES

One of The Husband's favorite weeknight meals is good old blackened redfish. This Paul Prudhomme classic consists of redfish fillets dipped in a hot spice mix (heavy on the cayenne) and sautéed in a searingly hot cast-iron skillet.

We like it hot, but for this recipe I stole a trick from those cuisines that enjoy tempering their spicy dishes by serving them with dairy accompaniments—Mexican and Indian come to mind. Hence, the cucumber yogurt sauce, which provides a cool contrast to the spicy-hot catfish.

One 6-inch piece seedless (English) cucumber
1 cup plain low-fat or full-fat Greek-style yogurt (see page 49)
2 garlic cloves
Kosher salt and freshly ground black pepper
⅓ cup Wondra or unbleached all-purpose flour
1 tablespoon Creole Seasoning (page 20, add preparation time) or store-bought seasoning
Four 6-ounce catfish fillets
3 tablespoons vegetable oil

1. Peel, seed, and coarsely grate the piece of cucumber (about 1 cup). Stir together the cucumber and yogurt; press in the garlic (about 2 teaspoons) and add salt and pepper to taste. Set aside.

2. Combine the flour and Creole Seasoning (if you are using seasoning that doesn't include salt, add ¼ teaspoon salt) in a pie plate lined with wax paper or parchment. Working with one fillet at a time, toss the fish in the seasoned flour, lifting the wax paper on both sides to move the piece around; shake off the excess flour.

3. Heat the vegetable oil in a large skillet over medium-high heat. Add the fillets to the skillet and sauté them for 3 minutes per side or until just cooked through. Transfer the fillets to 4 serving plates and top each portion with some of the cucumber yogurt sauce.

Sautéed Salmon with Cream Cheese Béarnaise Sauce

MAKES 4 SERVINGS ▪ HANDS-ON TIME: 20 MINUTES ▪ TOTAL PREPARATION TIME: 25 MINUTES

I happen to love béarnaise (an eggy butter sauce flavored with tarragon), but it's pretty tricky for the home cook, and I couldn't imagine anyone attempting it on a weeknight. I was at the office paging through an old cookbook on artichokes when I came across a recipe for cream cheese béarnaise. This struck me immediately as a great idea. I didn't follow the recipe in the book; I have taken the idea and run with it.

Here I've teamed up cream cheese béarnaise with salmon, a classic beneficiary of traditional sauce béarnaise. It's so good, I was tempted to put it on everything. It would also make an awfully good dip, especially for artichokes.

1 medium shallot
2 tablespoons white wine vinegar
2 tablespoons dry white wine
2 teaspoons dried tarragon
Kosher salt
1 tablespoon plus 1 teaspoon fresh tarragon leaves
4 ounces ⅓-less-fat cream cheese (Neufchâtel)
¼ cup whole milk
Freshly ground black pepper
1 tablespoon vegetable oil
Four 6- to 7-ounce pieces skinless salmon fillet

1. Finely chop the shallot (about ¼ cup). Combine the shallot, vinegar, white wine, dried tarragon, and a hefty pinch of salt in a small saucepan. Bring the mixture to a boil; reduce the heat to low and simmer for 3 to 4 minutes, or until the liquid has been reduced to about 1 tablespoon. Meanwhile, chop the fresh tarragon (about 2 teaspoons).

2. Add the Neufchâtel, 1 tablespoon at a time, to the saucepan and whisk until it has been incorporated. Whisk in the milk, fresh tarragon, and salt and pepper to taste. Keep warm on low heat while you cook the salmon.

3. Heat the vegetable oil in a large nonstick skillet over medium heat until hot. Season the salmon on all sides with salt and pepper to taste and add to the skillet. Cook for 3 minutes per side, or until just tender. Transfer the salmon to 4 plates and serve each portion topped with a spoonful of the béarnaise sauce.

Barbecued Salmon with Pickled Cucumbers

MAKES 4 SERVINGS ■ HANDS-ON TIME: 20 MINUTES ■ TOTAL PREPARATION TIME: 20 MINUTES

Salmon is the red meat of the fish world, able to handle the kind of hearty preparations you'd usually reserve for chicken or steak. Take barbecue sauce, for example. Put it on fillet of sole, and the fish's flavor is smothered under the sauce's acid, heat, and sugar. Put it on salmon, as I have here, and the sharp sauce provides a welcome counterbalance to the salmon's richness, and the pickled cucumbers add some refreshing crunch.

A note of caution: Before you use a store-bought barbecue sauce in this recipe, check the label to make sure that it doesn't have a ton of sugar in it. A sweet barbecue sauce (and many of the store-bought brands are very sweet) would make this dish too heavy.

½ cup Basic Barbecue Sauce (page 15, add preparation time) or store-bought sauce

1½ pounds skinless salmon fillet

Kosher salt and freshly ground black pepper

Dill Pickle Cucumber Slices (page 22, add preparation time) or store-bought pickles

1. Prepare the Basic Barbecue Sauce. Place an oven rack in the middle of the oven and preheat the oven to 400°F. Lightly oil a rimmed baking sheet.

2. Cut the salmon into 4 portions; season the salmon with salt and pepper to taste. Coat the pieces on all sides with the Basic Barbecue Sauce and place them on the baking sheet. Bake for 10 to 12 minutes for medium, or to the desired doneness. Meanwhile, prepare the Dill Pickle Cucumber Slices.

3. To serve, transfer the salmon to serving plates and spoon the cucumber slices over them, about ⅓ cup on each.

how do i
KNOW WHEN FISH IS DONE?

The general rule for cooking fish is about 10 minutes for every inch of thickness. Many recipes tell you to cook fish until it flakes, but if you take it that far, the fish will be overcooked. I have a better way. All food cooks from the outside in (except in a microwave, but we don't need to explore that now), and fish is no exception. Raw fish flesh is dense; if you tried to stick a paring knife straight down through it, you would feel resistance. Cooked fish flesh is very tender— a knife glides right through it. Try testing the fish a little before the projected cooking time listed in the recipe. If your knife meets a lot of resistance, let the fish cook longer; if your knife meets just a little resistance in the center, take the fish out and let it sit, covered, for a minute. (All protein has some carryover cooking time.) If the knife goes through very easily, get the fish out of the oven or pan immediately.

$\mathcal{S}$autéed Beer-Batter Shrimp with Tartar Sauce

MAKES 4 TO 6 SERVINGS ▪ HANDS-ON TIME: 25 MINUTES ▪ TOTAL PREPARATION TIME: 25 MINUTES

When it comes to deep-frying, my favorite batter is beer batter. Supersimple—just equal parts beer and flour—beer batter makes a very light, crisp coating. But I'd never thought that you could sauté with it, rather than deep-fry, until I read a recipe for sautéed beer-batter shrimp in *Cooking Light*. Intrigued but skeptical, I tried it, adding my little trick of dusting the shrimp in flour to start, which helps the batter to adhere to the shrimp. Once I had my shrimp, I married it to good old tartar sauce, a nod to my roots in New England, where tartar sauce ends up on top of every kind of fried food. However, if you're not in the mood to whip up some tartar sauce, use soy sauce instead. You can think of this recipe as a kind of American tempura.

One 12-ounce bottle beer
1 cup plus ⅓ cup Wondra or unbleached all-purpose flour
1 teaspoon Dijon mustard
Kosher salt
Tartar Sauce (recipe follows) or soy sauce
3 tablespoons vegetable oil
1 pound large shrimp, peeled and deveined
Freshly ground black pepper

1. Preheat the oven to 300°F. Whisk together 1 cup beer, 1 cup flour, the mustard, and ¼ teaspoon salt until just smooth. Strain the batter into another bowl and let stand for 10 minutes. Reserve the extra beer. Meanwhile, make the Tartar Sauce.

2. Put ⅓ cup flour into a pie plate lined with wax paper or parchment. Check the batter; it should have the consistency of a thick pancake batter. If it seems too thick, whisk in up to ¼ cup more beer.

3. Heat 1½ tablespoons vegetable oil in a large nonstick skillet over medium-high heat. Working with half the shrimp at a time, toss them in the flour, lifting the wax paper on both sides to move them around. Transfer the shrimp to a strainer and shake off the excess flour. Coat the shrimp with the batter, letting the excess drip off, and add them to the skillet. Cook them, turning once, for 1 to 2 minutes per side, or until they are golden. (Most of the batter will stay on the side you first put down in the skillet.)

4. Sprinkle the cooked shrimp with salt, transfer them to a baking sheet, and keep them warm in the oven while you cook the remaining shrimp in the remaining oil. Serve with the Tartar Sauce or soy sauce for dipping.

continued on next page

TARTAR SAUCE: Whisk together ¾ cup mayonnaise, ¼ cup finely chopped dill pickle, 1 trimmed and chopped medium scallion (about 2 tablespoons), 1 tablespoon drained capers, 1 tablespoon fresh lemon juice, 1 teaspoon Dijon mustard, ½ teaspoon Worcestershire sauce, and ¼ teaspoon hot sauce.

how many
SHRIMP ARE IN A POUND?

Now that is a question that doesn't have a short answer. Shrimp are marketed in many forms. You can get them in the shell, shelled except for the tail, fully shelled, and ready to eat, to name a few. Although the price of shrimp on the wholesale market is set by the number of shrimp per pound, in retail the categories vary from market to market. A rule of thumb for shrimp is that you will get about 10 colossal, 11 to 15 jumbo, 16 to 20 extra large, 21 to 30 large, 31 to 35 medium, or 36 to 45 small raw shrimp in their shells per pound. If the shrimp are partially or fully shelled, you will get up to 20 percent more shrimp in the pound, but they will be more expensive.

Oven-Fried Fish Sticks

MAKES ABOUT 24 FISH STICKS, 4 SERVINGS ▢ **HANDS-ON TIME: 10 MINUTES** ▢ **TOTAL PREPARATION TIME: 30 MINUTES**

I must confess that I never ate fish sticks as a child (I don't know what my mother was thinking), but The Husband and his siblings ate them all the time. It was as close as any of them ever came to fresh fish. In truth, it's the unfishiness of fish sticks that may be the real source of their appeal. "Uncomfortable around fish?" wondered a smart recent TV commercial. "Try Mrs. Paul's Fish Sticks." Exactly. Fish sticks are breaded, deep-fried, frozen, and then baked. Pull 'em out of the oven, douse 'em with ketchup, and they're warm, sweet, and doughy. In effect, they are closer to hot dogs, or to French fries, than to a fish dish.

There's no reason fish sticks can't be delicious and nutritious, however, or as much fun as they ever were. I dreamed up this version on behalf of a public relations campaign that was looking for healthful recipes for kids using sustainable fish. These fish sticks are made with catfish or tilapia, both of which are plentiful. The sticks are dipped in Herb or Citrus Butter (page 19). You have your choice of three breadings: dry bread crumbs, Japanese panko bread crumbs, or cornflakes. *Ummmmm, fish sticks!*

1 pound boneless, skinless catfish or tilapia fillets

4 tablespoons Herb or Citrus Butter (page 19; add preparation time) or lightly salted butter

1 cup dry bread crumbs, panko bread crumbs, or cornflake crumbs

Kosher salt and freshly ground black pepper

Lemon wedges, for garnish

1. Preheat the oven to 450°F. When the oven is hot, put a rimmed baking sheet on the middle rack for 10 minutes to heat.

2. Meanwhile, cut the fillets into 3 × ½-inch sticks; melt the butter and cool. Spread out the crumbs in a pie plate lined with wax paper or parchment. Working with several sticks at a time, dip the fish sticks into the butter and then into the crumbs, lifting the wax paper on both sides to move the sticks around; shake off the excess crumbs.

3. Arrange the fish sticks on the hot baking sheet and bake them for 5 minutes. Turn over the sticks and bake them for 5 minutes more, or just until they have cooked through. Season the fish sticks with salt and pepper to taste and serve them with lemon wedges.

Kimchi or Tomatillo Salsa Clams

MAKES 4 SERVINGS ■ HANDS-ON TIME: 30 MINUTES ■ TOTAL PREPARATION TIME: 35 MINUTES

If you think about it, the liquor in which a clam swims is nature's own clam sauce, a great source of the clam's appeal, whether you eat them raw or steamed. When they're steamed, it's usually done in water or white wine, with nothing more added than a little fat and a few spices. The clam shells open up as the little critters start to sweat, and the clam liquor flows into the liquid in the pot. And there you have it: instant clam sauce extraordinaire.

In this case, the clam liquor joins your choice of one of two of my favorite purees from the Head Starts chapter of this book: kimchi or tomatillo salsa. Both of them greatly enhance an already terrific ingredient.

1 recipe Quick or Quicker Kimchi (page 21, add preparation time), a double recipe of Tomatillo Salsa (page 23, add preparation time), or 2 cups store-bought kimchi or salsa

1 large onion

2 tablespoons extra virgin olive oil

48 small cherrystone clams

1 loaf crusty bread

1. Prepare the Quick or Quicker Kimchi or Tomatillo Salsa.

2. Finely chop the onion (about 2 cups). Heat the olive oil in a large saucepan over medium heat until hot. Reduce the heat to medium-low; add the onion and cook for 5 minutes, or until it has softened. If using kimchi, coarsely chop it or pulse it in a food processor fitted with the chopping blade. Add the kimchi or tomatillo salsa to the saucepan and cook, stirring, for 3 minutes.

3. Meanwhile, scrub the clams, discarding any that don't close. Add the cleaned clams to the saucepan; cover and steam for 5 to 7 minutes, or until they open. Transfer the clams to a bowl as they open. Discard any clams that don't open after 6 to 8 minutes.

4. Divide the clams and sauce among 4 soup or pasta plates and serve with crusty bread to mop up the sauce.

Steamed Mussels with Hot Sausage

MAKES 4 SERVINGS ■ HANDS-ON TIME: 40 MINUTES ■ TOTAL PREPARATION TIME: 45 MINUTES

This is my version of one of the great Portuguese surf-and-turf specialties. The Portuguese team up steamed clams and chorizo. I team up steamed mussels and hot Italian sausage. (My dear daughter has pointed out that not everyone is as fond of spicy food as yours truly. If you're one of those folks, just substitute sweet Italian sausage instead.)

This is a very simple dish, but each ingredient makes itself known. The mussel broth, flavored with garlic, fresh parsley, and a hint of orange, is every bit as important as the sausage and the mussels themselves. You're going to want plenty of crusty bread on hand to sop it up.

3½ pounds mussels (preferably cultivated)
1 large onion
¼ cup extra virgin olive oil
1 garlic clove
8 ounces hot Italian sausage (or sweet, if you prefer)
1 cup dry white or red wine
½ teaspoon freshly grated orange zest
½ cup fresh flat-leaf parsley leaves
Toasted or grilled French bread, as an accompaniment

1. Scrub the mussels well with a brush under cold water and remove the beards. Discard any mussels that won't close. Chop the onion (about 2 cups).

2. Heat the olive oil in a large, deep saucepan or Dutch oven over medium heat until hot. Reduce the heat to medium-low; add the onion and cook for 5 minutes, or until it has softened. Press in the garlic (about 1 teaspoon) and sauté for 1 minute more.

3. Remove the sausage from the casings and crumble it into the onion mixture. Cook, breaking up any large pieces of sausage, for about 5 minutes, or until it is no longer pink.

4. Add the mussels, wine, and orange zest to the saucepan. Cover and cook for 4 to 6 minutes or until the mussels just open. Check frequently and transfer the mussels to a bowl as they open. Discard any mussels that don't open after 6 to 8 minutes.

5. Chop the parsley (about ¼ cup). Divide the mussels among 4 dishes, ladling some of the sauce over each portion. Top each with chopped fresh parsley and serve with toasted or grilled French bread.

11

VEGETARIAN CORNUCOPIA

Back in the early seventies when I was a student at the University of Michigan, I lived for several years with three of my girlfriends in a big old ramshackle house. We divvied up all of the housework, including the making of dinner. Out of a combination of hippie inclination and economic necessity, we were pretty exclusively vegetarian. Having grown up in a carnivorous family, this was quite a shift for me, but, to my surprise, I made it without a bump.

Over the years I've become increasingly fond of vegetarian fare. This is at least partly a natural consequence of the increasing diversity of our citizens. Given that many new immigrants come from countries that favor vegetables much more than we do in America, we've enjoyed a boom in the number of international ingredients, including produce, now available at our fingertips, as well as a boom in the number of tasty recipes employing these ingredients. These happy trends dovetail with the desire of many health-minded native-born Americans for more and more vegetarian options.

The recipes in this chapter take their inspiration from India, Korea, Mexico, and Puerto Rico, as well as the good old U.S. of A. All are vegetarian; some are vegan. All are conceived as dinner entrées, needing no more supplement than a salad or simple side dish.

Many of the other chapters in this book also contain vegetarian recipes. Just look for the V icon.

FACING PAGE: *Mushroom Enchiladas.*

$\mathscr{C}$lay Pot Vegetable Stew Ⓥ

MAKES 4 SERVINGS ▪ HANDS-ON TIME: 45 MINUTES ▪ TOTAL PREPARATION TIME: 45 MINUTES

There's a vegetarian restaurant on East 32nd Street in Manhattan's Little Korea that's recently become my favorite lunchtime getaway. It's called HanGawi. Walk in and big old noisy New York simply disappears as the door closes behind you. You take off your shoes, sit at a sunken table, and find yourself attended to by friendly waiters (a very welcome change from their surly counterparts at many midtown restaurants). It's quiet enough to enjoy a candid conversation with your lunch partner without worrying about eavesdroppers. Really, it's the most amazing little oasis.

The prime draw, however, is the food, and the star of the menu is the clay pot vegetable stew. It's a mix of vegetables and tofu so hearty that it's hard to believe there's no meat lurking beneath the mushrooms and sweet potatoes. Here is my version of that dish, and I think it came out respectably well. The depth of flavor is thanks to the miso, or "fermented soybean paste." Now, if I could only figure out how to re-create HanGawi's superpeaceful atmosphere in our dining room at home.

1 large onion
8 ounces shiitake
　　mushrooms
One 1½-inch piece fresh
　　ginger
3 tablespoons
　　vegetable oil
4 garlic cloves
1 medium sweet potato
　　or 3 medium carrots
3 medium parsnips
3½ cups Homemade
　　Vegetable Stock
　　(page 11, add
　　preparation time)
　　or canned broth
½ cup sake or mirin
2 tablespoons soy
　　sauce (low sodium,
　　if you prefer)
7 ounces firm tofu
5 ounces baby spinach
　　(about 8 cups,
　　packed)

1. Chop the onion (about 2 cups). Clean the mushrooms, remove and discard the stems, and cut the caps into halves or quarters if they are large (about 4 cups). Peel and Microplane-grate the ginger (about 1½ teaspoons).

2. Heat 2 tablespoons vegetable oil in a large saucepan over medium heat until hot. Reduce the heat to medium-low; add the onion and cook for 5 minutes, or until it has softened. Add the remaining 1 tablespoon vegetable oil; turn the heat up to medium, add the mushrooms, and cook, stirring, for 5 minutes, or until the mushrooms are just tender. Add the ginger and press the garlic (about 1 tablespoon plus 1 teaspoon) into the mixture; cook, stirring, for 1 minute.

3. Meanwhile, peel the sweet potato and cut it into ½-inch pieces (about 1½ cups); peel the parsnips and slice them crosswise ½ inch thick (about 1½ cups). Add the sweet potato, parsnips, vegetable stock, sake, and soy sauce to the saucepan. Bring the mixture to a boil and simmer, partially covered, for 15 to 20 minutes, or until the potato and parsnips are tender. Cut the tofu into ½-inch cubes (about 1¾ cups).

¼ cup white miso
1 tablespoon fresh
lemon juice
Kosher salt and freshly
ground black pepper

4. Stir the spinach into the stew and simmer for 1 to 2 minutes, or until it has just wilted. Add the tofu and heat gently for 1 minute. Ladle ½ cup of the broth into a small bowl and whisk in the miso until it is combined; add the mixture to the soup along with the lemon juice and simmer for 1 minute more. Add salt and pepper to taste. Ladle into bowls and serve.

what is
COMMUNITY SUPPORTED AGRICULTURE?

Community supported agriculture, or CSA, is a cooperative program in which members of a community pay to support a local farm (usually an organic farm) in return for a share in the farm's harvest during the growing season. In the middle of the winter members contribute a set fee to the farmer to start the cycle. Then, for a predetermined number of months (this varies according to the part of the country you live in, but it is usually early June up until the week before Thanksgiving), each week you pick up a surprise basket of freshly harvested fruits and vegetables. Some CSAs have meat, honey, flowers, eggs, cheese, and other products as well. The availability of CSAs around the country continues to grow. To learn more about CSA and to find a program in your area, search online for the Robyn Van En Center at Wilson College or for "community supported agriculture."

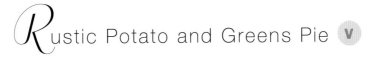

Rustic Potato and Greens Pie V

When I was working in *Gourmet's* test kitchen in the mid-eighties and we styled a dish to be photographed that didn't look perfect, we'd turn a negative into a positive by calling the dish "rustic" and bragging that it was "made by human hands." That's exactly the kind of thinking that went into this pie. Pastry impaired as I am, I can't help but love a pie that's as free-form and forgiving as this one.

You start by making my very simple food-processor pie dough. Roll it out into a rough circle between sheets of plastic wrap and drop it into a pie plate. Spoon the filling into the middle of the pie, then fold in the edges, free-form style. Bake it up and you're done. Family and friends will be amazed: "What, you made a savory pie on a weeknight?" Yes, you did.

This baby's real versatile, too. The eggs and potatoes, along with the cheese, are the binders, but you could substitute any number of other vegetables for the greens, including blanched broccoli and sautéed zucchini, carrots, mushrooms, leeks, and so on. Likewise, you can use the lower-fat versions of the cheeses or other cheeses altogether.

Basic Butter Pastry (page 28, add preparation time; you'll need just ½ recipe) or store-bought pastry for a single crust pie

¾ pound small boiling potatoes, such as Yukon gold or Red Bliss

1 medium onion

2 pounds cooking greens, such as chard, spinach, collards, mustard, or a mixture

2 tablespoons extra virgin olive oil

2 garlic cloves

2 ounces Gruyère cheese

1 ounce Parmigiano-Reggiano

1. Prepare the Basic Butter Pastry. Chill half while you make the filling. (Freeze the remaining half for another use.) Preheat the oven to 375°F.

2. Scrub the potatoes and cut them into 1½-inch pieces (about 2 cups); place them in a medium saucepan. Add cold salted water to cover by 1 inch. Bring the water to a boil over high heat; reduce the heat to low and simmer the potatoes for 15 to 20 minutes, or until they are tender when pierced with a knife.

3. Meanwhile, finely chop the onion (about 1 cup). Thoroughly rinse and spin dry the greens, remove the tough stems, and coarsely chop the leaves (about 24 cups). (If using chard, the stems will be tender; reserve them to stir-fry for another meal.)

4. Heat the olive oil in a large skillet over medium heat until hot. Reduce the heat to medium-low; add the onion and cook for 5 minutes, or until it has softened. Press in the garlic (about 2 teaspoons) and cook for 1 minute. Add half the greens and cook for

continued on next page

1 cup ricotta
⅛ teaspoon nutmeg
    (preferably freshly
    grated)
Kosher salt and freshly
    ground black pepper
2 large eggs

4 to 5 minutes, or until they have wilted. Remove the greens with tongs to a medium bowl. Repeat with the remaining half of the greens. Return the first batch of greens to the skillet and cook for 2 minutes more, or until any liquid that collected in the skillet has evaporated.

5. When the potatoes are done, drain and mash them with a potato masher. Combine the potatoes and the greens mixture in a large bowl and set aside to cool slightly.

6. Meanwhile, roll out the pastry between lightly floured sheets of wax paper to make a 12-inch round; pat the edges of the pastry to make the round even. Fit the pastry into a 9-inch pie plate; press against the sides of the plate, allowing the excess to hang over the edges. Put the pie plate in the fridge while you prepare the remaining ingredients.

7. Grate the Gruyère (about ½ cup) and Parmigiano-Reggiano (about ⅔ cup Microplane-grated or about ⅓ cup grated on the fine side of a box grater); fold the cheeses into the potato mixture along with the ricotta, nutmeg, and salt and pepper to taste.

8. Lightly beat the eggs; reserve 1 tablespoon. Stir the rest of the eggs into the potato mixture and spoon the filling into the pastry-lined pie plate. Gently lift the overhanging pastry over the filling, pleating as necessary to make it fit. (It will make a 1- to 1½-inch border covering the edges of the filling, which will be uncovered in the center.) Brush the pastry with the reserved 1 tablespoon egg.

9. Bake the pie for about 40 minutes, or until the filling is heated through and the pastry is golden. Let stand for 10 minutes before cutting.

Cheesy Corn Soufflé with Poblanos and Black Beans Ⓥ

MAKES 6 SERVINGS ▪ HANDS-ON TIME: 25 MINUTES ▪ TOTAL PREPARATION TIME: 45 MINUTES

This recipe features a roster of my favorite ingredients: poblano chile, corn, Cheddar cheese, salsa, and eggs. You can take advantage of the poblano roasting and resting time to do most of the prep, so don't be put off by the idea of starting the recipe by roasting a chile. However, if you can't find a fresh poblano in your supermarket, you can use a small can (4½ ounces) of chopped green chiles, drained, in its place. What is striking about this recipe is the successful coming together of a host of strong flavors. This one's a crowd-pleaser.

1 large poblano chile
4 ounces extra-sharp Cheddar cheese
2 large ears fresh corn or 2 cups thawed frozen corn kernels
One 15½-ounce can black beans
½ cup store-bought green or red salsa, or ½ cup Tomatillo Salsa (page 23, add preparation time)
Kosher salt
6 large eggs, at room temperature

1. Preheat the broiler to high. Butter a shallow 3-quart baking dish.

2. Put the poblano on a rimmed baking sheet and place it under the broiler, 4 inches from the heat. Broil, turning frequently, for 10 to 15 minutes, or until blackened on all sides. Transfer to a bowl, cover with plastic wrap, and let stand for 10 minutes. When cool, peel the chile and discard the seeds. Reduce the oven temperature to 425°F and place an oven rack in the middle of the oven.

3. Meanwhile, coarsely grate the cheese (about 1 cup), cut the kernels off the corn (about 2 cups), and rinse and drain the beans. Combine the beans, salsa, and ½ teaspoon salt in a food processor fitted with the chopping blade; pulse until finely chopped. Transfer the mixture to a large bowl. Add the poblano to the food processor; pulse 2 or 3 times until medium chopped. Add the poblano to the bean mixture and stir in the cheese and the corn.

4. Separate the eggs. Add 4 of the yolks to the bean mixture; reserve the remaining 2 for another use. Beat the egg whites and ⅛ teaspoon salt in an electric mixer until they form soft peaks. Stir one-quarter of the whites into the bean mixture and then fold in the remaining whites gently, until they are just incorporated. Pour the mixture into the prepared baking dish.

5. Bake for 15 to 20 minutes, or until the soufflé is puffed and golden. Serve immediately.

$\mathcal{V}$egetable Paprikash Ⓥ

MAKES 4 SERVINGS ▪ HANDS-ON TIME: 30 MINUTES ▪ TOTAL PREPARATION TIME: 35 MINUTES

Paprika, the defining spice in this recipe, is a powder made from red peppers. The peppers are now grown all over the world, but they emerged from the area bordering present-day Brazil and Bolivia and, as their seeds were dispersed by birds, made their way north. The Turks brought them to Hungary in the seventeenth century. Hungary's relatively warm climate allowed it to cultivate the most aromatic paprika peppers in Europe, and this is probably why the name the Hungarians gave the powder is the one by which we know it today. The excellence of native paprika is also why it's built into so many Hungarian dishes (whether or not the dish is called paprikash)—and why Hungarian cuisine is arguably the spiciest in Europe. Ranging in intensity from mild to hot, paprika in Hungary finds its way into recipes for everything from soups to stews, sauces, sweet pastries, and brandy. When I was growing up, Hungarian goulash was one of the pitifully few dishes I encountered that featured paprika. (The others were stuffed eggs and cottage cheese, and in both of those cases it was used more for its rust-red color than its peppery sweetness.)

It was only in recent years that I "discovered" paprika. It elbowed its way into my repertoire thanks to the innovative modern-day chefs of Spain. They feature it in sweet, hot, and smoked varieties, and now it is one of my favorite spices.

The Husband, a dedicated carnivore, loved this hearty, paprika-spiced vegetable stew. In effect, it's a goulash without the meat. For once he didn't miss the beef.

10 ounces cremini mushrooms

8 to 10 ounces small white mushrooms

1½ tablespoons extra virgin olive oil

1½ tablespoons unsalted butter

1 medium onion

1½ cups peeled baby carrots

2 tablespoons sweet paprika

½ to 1 teaspoon hot paprika

1. Clean and trim the mushrooms. If any are larger than 1 inch, halve them (about 6 cups). Heat half the olive oil and half the butter in a large skillet over medium heat until hot. Add the mushrooms and sauté until they begin to brown, 5 to 7 minutes. Meanwhile, thinly slice the onion (about 1 cup). Transfer the mushrooms to a bowl and set aside.

2. Heat the remaining half of the olive oil and half of the butter in the skillet over medium heat until hot. Reduce the heat to medium-low; add the onion and carrots and cook for 5 minutes, or until the onion has softened. Add both the sweet and hot paprika and cook for 1 minute. Stir in 3 cups vegetable stock and 1½ teaspoons salt. Cover and cook until the carrots are just tender, about 12 minutes.

4 cups Homemade
   Vegetable Stock
   (page 11, add
   preparation time) or
   canned broth
Kosher salt
1 large green bell
   pepper
¾ pound plum tomatoes
   (about 3 medium)
2 teaspoons unbleached
   all-purpose flour
½ cup fresh dill leaves
½ cup sour cream
Freshly ground black
   pepper
Cooked egg noodles, as
   an accompaniment

3. Meanwhile, coarsely chop the bell pepper (about 1½ cups) and the tomatoes (about 1½ cups). Whisk together the remaining 1 cup vegetable stock and the flour; whisk the mixture into the onion and carrots along with the reserved mushrooms, the bell pepper, and tomatoes. Bring to a boil over high heat; reduce the heat to low and simmer for 5 minutes. Chop the dill (about ¼ cup).

4. To serve, stir in the sour cream and 2 tablespoons dill. Heat almost to a boil; add salt and black pepper to taste. Spoon the stew over buttered egg noodles and sprinkle with the remaining dill.

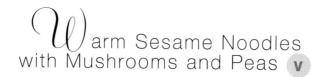

Warm Sesame Noodles with Mushrooms and Peas ⓥ

MAKES 6 SERVINGS ▪ HANDS-ON TIME: 20 MINUTES ▪ TOTAL PREPARATION TIME: 35 MINUTES

As far as I'm concerned, this recipe may be the best of all possible uses for the Peanut Sesame Sauce featured in the Head Starts chapter. If there's nothing to eat in the house but a package of fettuccine or spaghetti, the ingredients for the peanut sauce (peanut butter, hoisin sauce, scallions, and sesame oil), and some assorted leftovers, you still have the makings of a delicious meal. The sauce and the noodles are the crucial components; the rest of the ingredients are interchangeable. In fact, I'm convinced you could serve variations of this recipe once a week for a full year and no one would get bored, least of all the kids.

4 ounces shiitake
    mushrooms
8 ounces white
    mushrooms
1 recipe Peanut Sesame
    Sauce (page 16, add
    preparation time)
    or 1¾ cups store-
    bought peanut sauce
One 10-ounce package
    frozen green peas
2 tablespoons sesame
    seeds
7 ounces firm tofu
    (optional)
2 tablespoons
    vegetable oil
Kosher salt
1 pound fettuccine
½ pound snow peas
3 medium scallions
Freshly ground black
    pepper

1. Bring a large pot of salted water to a boil over high heat for the noodles. Clean the shiitakes, trim off and discard the stems, and slice the caps into ½-inch strips (about 1⅓ cups). Clean, trim, and slice the white mushrooms into ½-inch slices (about 2⅔ cups).

2. Prepare the Peanut Sesame Sauce. Thaw the green peas.

3. Place the sesame seeds in a large dry skillet over medium heat and toast until just golden, about 5 minutes; transfer to a small cup and set aside. Meanwhile, if using the tofu, cut it into ½-inch cubes. Heat the vegetable oil in the same skillet over high heat. Reduce the heat to medium-high; cook the tofu, stirring frequently, for about 4 minutes, or until golden on all sides. Add the shiitake mushrooms, white mushrooms, and a pinch of salt; sauté over medium-high heat for about 7 minutes, or until the liquid released by the mushrooms has evaporated.

4. Meanwhile, add the fettuccine to the boiling water. Cook until al dente, following the directions on the package. Trim the snow peas, remove their strings, and cut the snow peas diagonally in half. Trim and finely chop the scallions (a heaping ⅓ cup).

5. Add the snow peas and green peas to the fettuccine for the last 30 seconds of cooking time. Drain the fettuccine, snow peas, and green peas well, reserving 2 cups of the cooking liquid. Return the pasta and peas to the pot. Add the reserved cooking liquid to the pot along with the mushroom mixture, Peanut Sesame Sauce, and scallions. Add the sesame seeds and toss the mixture well. Season with salt and pepper to taste and serve.

DRIED PASTA BASICS

Always cook pasta in a large pot of boiling well-salted water: you need a lot of water so that the pasta doesn't come out gummy, and you need the water to be well salted because if you don't season the water and try to salt the pasta later, the pasta will not absorb the salt and it will taste bland. After you add the pasta to the pot, stir it well so that it doesn't stick together. Most dry pasta is done in anywhere from 8 to 12 minutes. Look to the package cooking times as a guideline, but start checking the pasta before the time is up. Take a piece of pasta out of the pot and break it in half; if you see a large white circle of uncooked dough in the center of the piece, put the pasta back in the water and cook it some more; if you see just a tiny circle, it is time to take the pasta out. Taste it as well; it should be al dente, with a tiny bite to it, a little bit of chewy resistance. Drain the pasta, saving some of the cooking water (a cup or two), and immediately add the pasta to the sauce. Ideally, you should finish cooking the pasta in the sauce; that way it absorbs more of the sauce flavor. You can add some of the reserved cooking liquid if the sauce seems too thick. One pound of pasta can feed four people nicely.

Three pasta no-nos:

- Do not add oil to the water. You don't want an oil slick on the pasta; this will prevent the sauce from sticking to it.

- Do not rinse the pasta; the sauce is sure to slither off. The residual starch on the drained pasta helps to make the sauce adhere.

- Do not ever make the pasta wait for the sauce. If you drain the pasta and park it, it will become one big mass. So make sure the sauce is almost done before you put the pasta into the pot of boiling water.

Mu Shu Vegetables with Pancakes ⓥ

MAKES 4 SERVINGS ▪ HANDS-ON TIME: 30 MINUTES ▪ TOTAL PREPARATION TIME: 35 MINUTES

This recipe is based on mu shu pork, the popular Chinese restaurant dish that combines deep-fried or stir-fried strips of pork with a colorful array of Chinese vegetables and some scrambled eggs, all of which are rolled up in a thin, cigarlike pancake and dipped in hoisin or plum sauce.

The simple removal of the pork leaves one with a wonderful vegetarian entrée. For the pancakes, you could make crêpes or substitute flour tortillas. (To warm the crêpes or tortillas, wrap them in aluminum foil and heat in a 300°F oven for 10 minutes.) Or just serve the vegetable mix on top of boiled white rice. The cashews add a tasty crunch.

8 thin pancakes (see Basic Crêpes, page 24, add preparation time) or use store-bought crêpes or flour tortillas or 3 cups boiled white rice

4 medium scallions

One 3-inch piece fresh ginger

3 garlic cloves

½ pound baby bok choy (2 or 3) or napa cabbage (about ⅓ head)

1 medium red bell pepper

8 ounces shiitake mushrooms

2 tablespoons vegetable oil

2 large eggs

Kosher salt

2 cups bean sprouts

½ cup unsalted roasted whole cashews

2 tablespoons sake, rice wine, or dry sherry

1. Prepare or warm the pancakes, tortillas, or rice and keep warm. Trim and thinly slice the scallions (about ½ cup); transfer them to a small bowl. Peel and Microplane-grate the ginger (about 1 tablespoon) and add to the bowl; press the garlic (about 1 tablespoon) into the bowl and stir to combine.

2. Slice the bok choy crosswise into ¼-inch strips (about 4¼ cups); thinly slice the bell pepper (about 1 cup). Clean the shiitakes, trim off and discard the stems, and thinly slice the caps (about 2⅔ cups).

3. Heat 1 tablespoon vegetable oil in a large skillet or wok over high heat until hot. Reduce the heat to medium; add the scallion mixture and cook for 1 minute. Add the mushrooms and bell pepper; cook until the mushrooms are tender, about 4 minutes.

4. While the mushroom mixture is cooking, lightly beat the eggs with a pinch of salt. Stir the bok choy and bean sprouts into the mushroom mixture and cook until they are just softened, about 2 minutes.

continued on next page

1 tablespoon hoisin sauce, plus more for serving
1 tablespoon soy sauce (low sodium, if you prefer)

5. Heat the remaining 1 tablespoon vegetable oil in a medium nonstick skillet over medium heat. Add the eggs, swirling the pan so that they coat the bottom of the pan, and cook until they are just set, like a pancake; turn the egg out onto a cutting board and coarsely chop. Coarsely chop the cashews.

6. Combine the sake, hoisin sauce, and soy sauce in a small bowl. Stir into the vegetables along with the chopped egg and cashews; cook just until everything is heated through, about 3 minutes. Serve with the pancakes or over rice. Pass additional hoisin sauce.

how do i
SELECT AND USE FRESH GINGER?

The younger fresh ginger is when it is harvested, the more juicy and tender it will be. Young ginger has a noticeably thin, translucent skin and is not as tough and fibrous as mature ginger. You are more likely to find it in Asian or gourmet markets. Supermarkets tend to stock more mature ginger, and although mature ginger is harder to grate, it will be flavorful as long as it is fresh. Avoid pieces of ginger that are shriveled or moldy and have thick, opaque skin. When a recipe calls for sliced or chopped ginger, it usually specifies a certain size piece of ginger in the ingredient list, but when you need a measured amount of grated ginger, it is sometimes hard to tell how much to buy. Because ginger is a natural product, each root varies somewhat in thickness, moisture, and fiber as well as in flavor. Although I can't guarantee it, I usually find that I can get about 1 tablespoon ginger from a firm, fresh root that is 1 to 1¼ inches in diameter and about 3 inches long after peeling. I always suggest grating ginger on a Microplane. Peel the ginger first and then be sure to grate over a plate or bowl. Add any juice that is collected, along with the grated ginger, to the dish you are cooking.

Hearty Kidney Beans and Rice Ⓥ

MAKES 6 TO 8 SERVINGS ▪ HANDS-ON TIME: 30 MINUTES ▪ TOTAL PREPARATION TIME: 40 MINUTES

My first cookbook featured a recipe for sofrito rice by Magda Alcayaga, my Guatemalan housekeeper. The addition of kidney beans converts that wonderful side dish into a hearty vegetarian entrée. You might want to top it off with some grated sharp Cheddar cheese or a spoonful of sour cream, but it is perfectly delicious without any gilding.

1 small onion
1 small tomato
½ red bell pepper
4 garlic cloves
½ cup firmly packed
    fresh cilantro leaves
    and stems
2 cups long-grain
    white rice
¼ cup vegetable oil
Kosher salt
⅛ to ¼ teaspoon
    cayenne pepper
½ cup pimiento-stuffed
    olives
Two 15½-ounce cans
    kidney beans
1 teaspoon ground
    cumin
1 teaspoon sweet or
    hot paprika
1 cup crushed tomatoes
    (preferably fire
    roasted)
1 cup Homemade
    Vegetable Stock
    (page 11, add
    preparation time)
    or canned broth
¼ cup drained capers
Freshly ground black
    pepper

1. To make the sofrito, coarsely chop the onion (about ½ cup), tomato (about ¾ cup), and bell pepper (about ¾ cup). Smash and peel the garlic. Combine the garlic with the onion, tomato, bell pepper, and cilantro in a blender or food processor fitted with the chopping blade. Add 2 tablespoons cold water and blend or process until smooth (about 1¼ cups).

2. Rinse and thoroughly drain the rice. Heat 2 tablespoons vegetable oil in a large saucepan over medium heat. Stir in ¼ cup of the sofrito and cook, stirring, for about 1 minute, or until fragrant. Stir in 1¼ teaspoons salt and the cayenne. Add 4 cups water and bring the mixture to a boil over high heat. Stir in the rice, bring back to a boil, and cook, uncovered, for about 10 minutes, until the water has been absorbed and holes appear on the surface of the rice.

3. Reduce the heat to low; cover the saucepan and cook for about 10 minutes more, or until the rice is fluffy and tender. Fluff the rice with a fork and set it aside for 5 minutes.

4. Meanwhile, prepare the beans. Heat the remaining 2 tablespoons vegetable oil in another large saucepan over medium heat. Add the remaining sofrito (about 1 cup) and cook for 5 minutes, stirring occasionally. Coarsely chop the olives; rinse and thoroughly drain the beans. Add the cumin and paprika to the saucepan and cook, stirring, for 1 minute.

5. Add the beans to the saucepan along with the crushed tomatoes, vegetable stock, olives, and capers; simmer for 10 to 15 minutes, or until the mixture is just slightly soupy. Add salt and black pepper to taste and serve over the sofrito rice.

$\mathcal{B}$lack Bean Tortilla Pizza

MAKES 4 SERVINGS ■ HANDS-ON TIME: 25 MINUTES ■ TOTAL PREPARATION TIME: 35 MINUTES

By the time my daughter, Ruthie, was five, she was such a black bean fanatic that the waiters at La Taza de Oro, a great little Puerto Rican restaurant in our neighborhood, used to ladle her up a bowl of them as soon as she and her dad walked into the spot. After a while, that was her name as far as they were concerned: Black Bean.

I can't claim that I ever achieved Ruthie's local notoriety, but I'm no slouch when it comes to black beans. I love their meatiness and the way they play so nicely with other ingredients. In this recipe, those ingredients include garlic, onion, and a chipotle chile. When I spread the bean mixture on cumin-and-oregano-scented tortillas, I like to think of them as little Mexican pizzas. When you top them off with your favorite cheese and a fresh herb salad, you've got yourself a very satisfying workweek dinner.

¼ cup extra virgin olive oil
¼ teaspoon ground cumin
¼ teaspoon dried oregano
Four 8-inch flour tortillas
1 small onion
2 garlic cloves
½ pound plum tomatoes (about 2 medium)
1 chipotle chile in adobo sauce, plus 2 teaspoons adobo sauce
One 15½-ounce can black beans
⅓ cup Homemade Vegetable Stock (page 11, add preparation time), canned broth, or water
Kosher salt and freshly ground black pepper
½ medium red bell pepper

1. Place an oven rack in the bottom shelf of the oven and preheat the oven to 375°F. Mix 3 tablespoons olive oil with the cumin and oregano.

2. Place the tortillas on 2 rimmed baking sheets; brush them with 1 tablespoon of the seasoned oil and bake them for 5 to 6 minutes, or until the surfaces are crisp. Let them cool slightly on the baking sheets.

3. Meanwhile, finely chop the onion (about ½ cup). Heat the remaining 1 tablespoon unseasoned olive oil in a medium skillet over medium heat until hot. Reduce the heat to medium-low; add the onion and cook for 5 minutes, or until it has softened. Press in the garlic (about 2 teaspoons) and cook for 1 minute more. Finely chop the tomatoes (about 1 cup). Increase the heat to medium, add the tomatoes to the onion mixture, and cook for 3 minutes, or until softened. Mince the chipotle.

4. Rinse and drain the black beans. Add the beans to the skillet along with the vegetable stock, chipotle, and adobo sauce. Cook for 3 to 5 minutes, mashing the bean mixture with a potato masher as it cooks, until the mixture is thick enough to mound. Add salt and black pepper to taste. Very thinly slice the bell pepper; halve the slices (about ½ cup). Coarsely grate the cheese (about 1 cup).

4 ounces Cheddar,
Monterey Jack, or
ricotta salata cheese
1 tablespoon fresh
lemon juice
1 cup fresh flat-leaf
parsley leaves
1 cup fresh cilantro
leaves

5. Turn the tortillas over so the crispier side is down. Divide the bean mixture among the tortillas and spread it to the edges. Top with the bell pepper and cheese. Bake the pizzas for 10 minutes, or until the cheese has melted and the edges of the tortillas are golden.

6. Meanwhile, whisk together the remaining 2 tablespoons seasoned olive oil, the lemon juice, and salt to taste in a medium bowl until the salt has dissolved. Stir in the parsley and cilantro.

7. Remove the pizzas from the oven, divide the parsley and cilantro salad among them, and serve.

$\mathcal{B}$aked Potatoes Stuffed with
Barbecued Green Beans and Cheddar Cheese ⓥ

MAKES 4 SERVINGS ▪ HANDS-ON TIME: 20 MINUTES ▪ TOTAL PREPARATION TIME: 1 HOUR 10 MINUTES

In my first cookbook, there was a recipe for Green Beans Stewed with Tomatoes and Mint. Called *fasolakia* in Greek, this dish was one of the stars of a great little Greek restaurant in Central Square in Cambridge that I used to frequent in the late seventies. It's true, of course, that stewing the beans makes their crunchiness go bye-bye, but the loss of crunch is more than made up for by increased tenderness, meatiness, and depth of flavor.

This recipe stars green beans stewed in barbecue sauce instead of tomato sauce. The beans make a tasty topping for a baked potato, especially when it's all finished off with grated sharp Cheddar cheese.

By the way, don't be surprised by how satisfying this dish is. A few years ago researchers compiled a food "satiation index." The humble baked potato was at the top of the list, ahead of both steak and ice cream.

4 medium russet
   potatoes (about
   2 pounds)
½ cup Basic Barbecue
   Sauce (page 15, add
   preparation time) or
   use store-bought
   sauce
1 small onion
2 plum tomatoes
2 tablespoons plus
   1 teaspoon extra
   virgin olive oil
1 garlic clove
½ pound green beans
Kosher salt and freshly
   ground black pepper
4 ounces sharp Cheddar
   cheese

1. Preheat the oven to 400°F. Scrub the potatoes and pierce each one several times with the tines of a fork. Place the potatoes on a rimmed baking sheet and bake them for about 60 minutes, or until they are very tender. Remove them to a cooling rack to cool slightly.

2. Prepare the Basic Barbecue Sauce.

3. Finely chop the onion (about ½ cup) and tomatoes (about 1 cup). Heat 1 tablespoon olive oil in a small skillet over medium heat until hot. Reduce the heat to medium-low; add the onion and cook for 5 minutes, or until it has softened. Press in the garlic (about 1 teaspoon) and add the tomatoes; cook for 1 minute more.

4. Meanwhile, trim the green beans and cut them into 2-inch pieces (about 1¾ cups). Add the beans and barbecue sauce to the skillet. Stir in just enough water to come slightly below the level of the beans (1 to 1¼ cups). Bring the mixture to a boil, cover it, and simmer for 30 to 40 minutes, or until the beans are very tender. Remove the lid and simmer until the sauce has reduced slightly. Add salt and pepper to taste.

5. Meanwhile, coarsely grate the cheese (about 1 cup). Place the potatoes on serving plates; cut each potato in half lengthwise not all the way through and mash the pulp lightly with a fork. Drizzle each with 1 teaspoon of the remaining olive oil and sprinkle with a little salt. Divide the beans and cheese evenly among the potatoes and serve.

$\mathcal{M}$ushroom Enchiladas Ⓥ

MAKES 4 SERVINGS ▪ HANDS-ON TIME: 25 MINUTES ▪ TOTAL PREPARATION TIME: 40 MINUTES

Funny thing about mushrooms: Although they're about 80 percent water to begin with, they have the spongelike ability to soak up a bunch more liquid besides. In this recipe, the mushrooms start by absorbing a very flavorful lime-and-cumin marinade. Then they're charred under the broiler along with tomatoes, onion, and garlic.

They're rolled in warm tortillas and topped with sour cream and avocado. The sour cream and avocado are a cooling complement to the spicy filling. If you'd like, you can swap in yogurt for the sour cream and basil for the cilantro.

1½ pounds portobello
    mushrooms (about
    6 medium to large)
3 tablespoons fresh lime
    juice
2 teaspoons ground
    cumin
Kosher salt
¼ cup plus 1 tablespoon
    vegetable oil
3 garlic cloves,
    2 unpeeled
¾ pound plum tomatoes
    (about 3 medium)
1 medium unpeeled
    onion
Freshly ground black
    pepper
Eight 8-inch flour
    tortillas
Half a 4½-ounce can
    chopped green chiles
1 ripe Hass avocado
½ cup fresh cilantro
    leaves
¾ cup sour cream

1. Place an oven rack 4 inches from the broiler heat source and pre-heat the broiler (see Note). Clean the mushrooms; remove and discard the stems (or reserve them for another use such as vegetable stock); scrape out the gills with a spoon and discard them. Slice the caps in half and then slice crosswise into ½-inch-thick strips (about 8 cups).

2. Whisk together the lime juice, cumin, and ¼ teaspoon salt in a medium bowl until the salt has dissolved; whisk in ¼ cup vegetable oil. Press in the peeled garlic clove (about 1 teaspoon) and whisk again. Transfer to a resealable plastic bag, add the mushroom slices, and knead gently to make sure the marinade is well distributed. Set aside the mushrooms to marinate while you prepare the tomatoes and onion.

3. Core the tomatoes; slice the onion 1 inch thick. Arrange the to-matoes, onion, and the remaining 2 unpeeled garlic cloves in one layer on a rimmed baking sheet; drizzle them with 1 tablespoon vegetable oil and sprinkle them with salt and pepper to taste. Broil them, turning them frequently, until the garlic is tender, about 10 minutes. Transfer the garlic to a bowl and continue to broil the tomatoes and onion, turning them frequently, until the tomatoes are tender and the onion is charred at the edges, 8 to 10 minutes more.

4. Meanwhile, wrap the tortillas in aluminum foil and warm them in the oven as far away as possible from the broiler (if your broiler is in the top of the oven, use the lowest rack of the oven under the broiler pan; if it is under the oven, use the highest rack). Drain the chiles. Halve, seed, peel, and medium chop the avocado (about 1 cup). Finely chop the cilantro (about ¼ cup).

5. When the tomatoes and onion have cooked, transfer them to the bowl with the garlic to cool slightly. Place the mushroom slices on the baking sheet and broil them, turning them frequently, until they are tender, 8 to 10 minutes. Transfer them to a medium saucepan when they are done.

6. Remove and discard the skins from the tomatoes, onion, and garlic. Transfer the vegetables to the bowl of a food processor fitted with the chopping blade; pulse until they are medium chopped. Add the mixture to the mushrooms along with the chiles (about 3 tablespoons) and salt and pepper to taste and stir well. Cook over medium heat until hot.

7. Spoon some of the mushroom mixture onto each of the 8 tortillas and roll up the tortillas. Transfer 2 tortillas to each of 4 dinner plates and top each tortilla with some of the sour cream, chopped avocado sprinkled with salt, and cilantro.

NOTE: If the heating element in your broiler does not cover enough space to cook the vegetables evenly, preheat the oven to 500°F and follow the same timing instructions.

Baked Cauliflower, Potato, and Pea Samosas ⓥ

MAKES 20 SAMOSAS, 4 SERVINGS ▪ HANDS-ON TIME: 45 MINUTES ▪ TOTAL PREPARATION TIME: 55 MINUTES

Whenever someone tells me he or she is no fan of vegetarian food, my advice is to try Indian vegetarian. A tradition that dates back to the rise of Hinduism more than two thousand years ago, Indian vegetarianism comprises a world of ingredients, techniques, and recipes, more than enough to open the mind of anyone who imagines that a vegetarian meal is bland and unsatisfying by definition.

The small stuffed and fried turnovers known in India as samosas are popular under other names throughout Asia, the Horn of Africa, and the Arabian Peninsula. Tradition requires that samosas be made with a special dough and folded in a particular way. I thought that would be too much bother on a weeknight, not to mention that nobody's going to deep-fry them at home. These are made of phyllo dough (one of my favorite cheating ingredients), folded into simple triangles, and then baked, not fried. They're delicious straight out of the oven, but they're even better after they've been dipped into the mint sauce.

½ pound small boiling potatoes, such as Yukon gold or Red Bliss
½ small head cauliflower
5 to 6 tablespoons vegetable oil (see Note)
Kosher salt
1 medium onion
½ serrano chile
One 1-inch piece fresh ginger
1 teaspoon cumin seeds
½ teaspoon ground coriander
½ teaspoon ground turmeric
Fresh Mint Chutney (recipe follows)
¼ cup fresh cilantro or basil leaves
½ cup thawed frozen peas

1. Preheat the oven to 450°F. Scrub the potatoes and cut them into 1½-inch pieces (about 1¼ cups); combine them with enough cold salted water to cover. Bring to a boil over high heat, reduce the heat to low, and simmer gently for 8 to 10 minutes, or until they are tender.

2. Coarsely chop the cauliflower (about 1⅔ cups); transfer to a bowl and toss with 1 tablespoon vegetable oil and ⅛ teaspoon salt. Arrange the cauliflower in one layer on a rimmed baking sheet and roast for 18 to 20 minutes, or until golden.

3. Finely chop the onion (about 1 cup). Remove the seeds and veins and finely chop the chile (about 1 teaspoon). Peel and Microplane-grate the ginger (about 1 teaspoon). Heat 2 tablespoons vegetable oil in a medium skillet over medium heat. Add the cumin seeds and cook, stirring, until they are fragrant. Reduce the heat to medium-low, add the onion, chile, ginger, coriander, and turmeric, and cook, stirring, about 10 minutes or until the onion is golden.

4. Meanwhile, prepare the Fresh Mint Chutney.

5. When the potatoes are done, drain them and transfer them to a medium bowl; mash them well with a potato masher. Finely chop

1 tablespoon fresh
lemon juice
½ teaspoon garam
masala (see Note,
page 92)
Five 16 x 12-inch phyllo
dough sheets

the fresh cilantro (about 2 tablespoons). Stir the cauliflower, peas, the onion mixture, cilantro, lemon juice, garam masala, and salt to taste into the potatoes. Set aside to cool. (You should have about 2 cups filling.)

6. Reduce the oven temperature to 375°F. When the vegetable filling has cooled, place the phyllo sheets in a stack and cover them with plastic wrap and a damp paper towel.

7. Place 1 phyllo sheet on an oiled work surface with a long side nearest you (keep the remaining sheets covered) and brush it with some of the vegetable oil. Cut it crosswise into four 4-inch-wide strips. Place about 1½ tablespoons of filling in the lower right-hand corner of each of the 4 strips, about ½ inch from the edge. One at a time, fold up the right corner of the strip to form a right triangle and continue folding, as if you were folding a flag.

8. Place the triangles, seam side down, on a large rimmed baking sheet; brush the tops with vegetable oil and cover the triangles with plastic wrap. Continue with the remaining phyllo sheets and filling to make 20 samosas.

9. Remove the plastic wrap from the samosas and bake them in the center of the oven for 12 to 15 minutes, or until they are puffed and golden. Serve them warm with the Fresh Mint Chutney.

FRESH MINT CHUTNEY: Combine 1 cup fresh mint leaves; 4 scallions, trimmed and coarsely chopped; ½ small serrano chile, coarsely chopped with seeds (a heaping teaspoon); 2 tablespoons fresh lime juice; 2 tablespoons water; 2 teaspoons brown sugar; ¾ teaspoon ground cumin; and ¾ teaspoon kosher salt in a food processor fitted with the chopping blade. Process until finely chopped.

NOTE: Substitute 2 to 3 tablespoons melted butter for vegetable oil to brush the phyllo, if desired.

AN ONION PRIMER

All members of the genus *Allium,* onions add flavor to any dish they join. Onions come to the market either fresh or dried (known as storage onions) and most are available year-round. Fresh onions such as scallions, leeks, chives, ramps, and garlic scapes should be refrigerated. Storage onions such as yellow, red, white, pearl, cipolline, sweet onions, and shallots, as well as garlic, should be stored somewhere cool and dry, but preferably not in the refrigerator.

LEEKS: Better known in Europe until the mid-twentieth century, leeks are a long stalk, 1 to 2 inches in diameter, white on the bottom and green on the top. They are mild in flavor and are good anywhere onions are used. It is essential to split the stalk and wash it thoroughly because sand often collects between the many layers of a leek.

CHIVES: Thin, deep green hollow stems, chives have a mild flavor and are usually snipped or sliced crosswise and added to soups, sauces, and salads just before serving.

RAMPS: Aka "wild leeks." Ramps appear in the springtime in fields and forests from the East Coast to the Midwest and as far south as Georgia. Their flavor is somewhere between that of onions and very fresh garlic, but with greater intensity.

GARLIC SCAPES: The long green flower stems put out by garlic bulbs when they first start to grow. Farmers trim them off early in the year so that the bulbs will grow larger. They have a mild garlic flavor. Cut them into pieces and cook them in soups, stews, stir-fries, and sauces.

SCALLIONS: Also called green onions; see All About Scallions, page 293.

YELLOW ONIONS: The onions most available in the market. They come in all sizes and are medium to strong in flavor.

RED AND WHITE ONIONS: Similar to yellow onions, but usually milder in flavor. Red onions provide a different color option in a recipe.

PEARL OR BOILING ONIONS: Small yellow, red, or white onions often used in stews.

CIPOLLINE ONIONS: An Italian variety that is small to medium in size with a flattened top and bottom surface.

SWEET ONIONS: Special varieties that have been bred to be milder in flavor and higher in sugar than regular onions. Because they are higher in moisture as well as sugar, they are more perishable than storage onions. Each variety is available only during a short season. Examples of sweet onions are Vidalia, Texas Sweet, Walla Walla, and Maui.

SHALLOTS: Small clustered bulbs with a deep russet papery skin that are dried after harvest. They add a wonderful sweet note to sauces and vinaigrettes.

GARLIC: One of the world's favorite alliums, garlic is reputed to attract love, cure colds, and repel vampires, but what it is really good at is adding big flavor to my favorite dishes.

$\mathcal{E}$ggplant and Cheese Cannelloni Ⓥ

MAKES 8 CANNELLONI, 4 SERVINGS · HANDS-ON TIME: 50 MINUTES · TOTAL PREPARATION TIME: 1 HOUR 20 MINUTES

I developed this recipe for King Arthur Flour, the oldest flour company in the country (and a sponsor of *Sara's Weeknight Meals* on public television). King Arthur challenged me to use its flour in a recipe for something other than bread. I immediately thought of cannelloni. *Cannelloni* literally means "big tubes" in Italian. The tubes start out either as large sheets of pasta or as *crespelle,* the Italian version of crêpes, then they're rolled around a savory filling, topped with a sauce, and baked.

These cannelloni are made with crêpes, which are far faster to work with than pasta sheets. For the filling, I chose a mixture of cheeses (you can substitute the low-fat versions of any of them if you'd like) and my mom's eggplant recipe, which is sliced eggplant brushed with olive oil or vinaigrette and baked. (Baked eggplant absorbs far less fat than sautéed eggplant.) Even though this recipe is meatless, it is more than substantial enough to fill you up on a cold fall or winter night.

1 recipe Basic Crêpes (page 24)
1 medium eggplant
3 tablespoons extra virgin olive oil
Kosher salt and freshly ground black pepper
2 ounces Parmigiano-Reggiano
4 ounces mozzarella
2 ounces Italian fontina cheese
3 ounces whole milk ricotta
2 cups Quick Tomato Sauce (page 14, add preparation time) or your favorite store-bought sauce
½ cup fresh basil leaves

1. Prepare the Basic Crêpes batter; set it aside to rest. Preheat the oven to 375°F. Lightly oil a large rimmed baking sheet.

2. Peel the eggplant and cut it crosswise into 16 slices, each about ½ inch thick. Brush both sides of the eggplant slices with olive oil, sprinkle with salt and pepper to taste, and arrange them in one layer on the baking sheet. Bake the eggplant until just tender, 12 to 15 minutes. Remove the pan from the oven and set it aside until the eggplant is cool enough to handle.

3. Meanwhile, prepare the cheese filling. Microplane-grate the Parmigiano-Reggiano (about 1⅓ cups) or grate it on the fine side of a box grater (about ⅔ cup). Coarsely grate the mozzarella (about 1 cup) and the fontina (about ½ cup). Set aside ½ cup mozzarella. Combine the Parmigiano-Reggiano, the remaining ½ cup mozzarella, the fontina, and ricotta (a generous ⅓ cup) in a medium bowl; season the cheese filling with salt and pepper to taste.

4. Cook the crêpes and set them aside on a cooling rack until they are just cool enough to handle.

continued on next page

5. To make the cannelloni, spread out several crêpes at a time on a work surface. Arrange two eggplant slices in the middle of each crêpe and top with one-eighth of the cheese mixture. Tuck in the sides of the crêpes and roll the crêpes up, enclosing the cheese and eggplant.

6. Spread ½ cup tomato sauce in the bottom of a shallow 9-inch square baking dish or pan. Add the cannelloni, seam side down, as they are finished. When all are in the dish, top with the remaining sauce and the reserved ½ cup mozzarella. Bake until the sauce is bubbly and the cheese has melted, about 30 minutes.

7. To serve, thinly slice the basil crosswise (about ¼ cup). Transfer 2 cannelloni to each of 4 plates and top with some of the basil.

what is
the best way

TO STORE FRESH HERBS?

Put leafy herbs, such as basil, parsley, dill, and cilantro, in a glass or glass measuring cup with water in the bottom (like cut flowers), cover loosely with a plastic bag over the top, and store in the fridge. They will keep for a week if set up this way. Woody herbs, such as rosemary and thyme, should be wrapped in paper towels, placed in a plastic bag, and refrigerated in the crisper.

12

SIDE DISHES WITH STAR QUALITY

Most of us make the same dozen main dishes for dinner over and over again. The same is true for side dishes. Let's face it: We do it because these recipes are dependable and likable, but after a while they can become boring as hell.

This chapter is meant not only to introduce you to a new slate of side dishes, but to get you thinking differently about what a side dish *is*. It includes one bread, two salads, a few potato dishes, pancakes, and a variety of vegetable recipes (none steamed). Look here for recipes to round out meals made from recipes in other chapters in the book, especially the ones from the poultry, meat, and fish chapters that are not complete meals in themselves. Or you can also assemble a whole meal out of two or three of these sides. I don't know about you, but I often find the so-called side dish more alluring than the main.

However you use them, almost all of these recipes require very little hands-on time, and you will be pleased to have created a break from the usual steamed vegetables.

FACING PAGE: *Celery and Parsley Salad with Parmigiano-Reggiano and Walnuts.*

Garlicky Green Beans and Shiitakes

MAKES 4 SERVINGS   HANDS-ON TIME: 15 MINUTES   TOTAL PREPARATION TIME: 18 MINUTES

Years ago *Gourmet* ran a wonderful recipe for broccoli with garlic sauce. It quickly became a staple at our house, even though the garlic sauce contained several tablespoons of oyster sauce. (Don't tell Ruthie!) This recipe applies the basic elements of that recipe to green beans and shiitake mushrooms, with the oyster sauce contributing salt as well as depth of flavor. I think this sauce and procedure would work well with any number of other vegetables, including carrots, cauliflower, and beets.

6 garlic cloves
2 tablespoons
    vegetable oil
1 pound green beans
8 ounces shiitake
    mushrooms
Kosher salt
½ cup Homemade
    Chicken or Vegetable
    Stock (pages 10 and
    11, add preparation
    time) or canned broth
3 tablespoons oyster
    sauce
¼ teaspoon crushed
    red pepper flakes
    (optional)
½ teaspoon toasted
    sesame oil

1. Smash the garlic cloves and peel them. Combine the vegetable oil and garlic in a large cold skillet; turn on the heat to medium-low and cook for 5 to 7 minutes, or until the garlic is golden. Remove the garlic with a slotted spoon and discard. Leave the oil in the pan.

2. Meanwhile, trim and halve the green beans crosswise (about 3½ cups). Clean the shiitakes, remove and discard the stems, and cut the caps into 1-inch pieces (about 2⅔ cups). Reheat the garlic oil over medium-high heat until very hot. Add the green beans and a hefty pinch of salt and stir-fry for 3 minutes.

3. Add the shiitakes, reduce the heat to medium, and sauté them for 3 minutes. Add the chicken stock, oyster sauce, and red pepper flakes, if using; cover and cook for 3 minutes, or until the beans and mushrooms are tender. Stir in the sesame oil and serve.

how to make
YOUR FRUITS AND VEGETABLES LAST LONGER

No one likes to open the fridge and find fruits and vegetables that are past their prime. Here are some ways to make the best use of your produce dollar:

- Store fruits and vegetables separately. Some fruits (like apples and pears) give off ethylene gas, which can make vegetables go bad faster.

- Water is the enemy. Don't put any fruit or vegetable in the fridge if it is wet (those misting machines in the supermarket produce shelves can make the produce quite wet). If produce is wet when you get home, dry it well and store it in a resealable plastic bag lined with a paper towel.

- Don't wash fruits or vegetables until right before you use them.

- If you are not going to get to a fruit or vegetable before it goes bad, freeze it. Most vegetables should be blanched in water briefly before freezing.

$\mathcal{S}$piced Peas and Onion Ⓥ

This one takes me back, way back, to the Thanksgivings of my youth, when my mom made sure that Birds Eye Peas and Pearl Onions in Lightly Seasoned Sauce occupied a bowl of honor on the groaning board. I loved them then, but these days I'm inclined to season my veggies myself.

You might figure that this recipe is too simple to be good, but you'd be wrong. The toasted cumin and mustard seeds, combined with thinly sliced caramelized onion, really jazz up good old frozen peas. Indeed, this is a classic case of less is more. We're doing very little here other than letting good ingredients speak for themselves.

One 10-ounce package frozen green peas
1 medium onion
2 tablespoons vegetable oil
1 teaspoon yellow mustard seeds
½ teaspoon cumin seeds
Kosher salt and freshly ground black pepper

1. Thaw the peas and pat them dry. Halve and thinly slice the onion (about 1 cup). Heat 1 tablespoon vegetable oil in a medium skillet over medium heat. Reduce the heat to medium-low; add the onion and sauté, stirring occasionally, until it is well browned, about 10 minutes. Remove to a bowl.

2. Add the remaining 1 tablespoon vegetable oil to the skillet and heat over high heat. Add the mustard and cumin seeds; cover immediately and cook, shaking the pan, for 30 seconds. Remove the pan from the heat and set aside until the seeds stop popping.

3. Add the peas to the pan and cook just until hot. Return the onion to the pan and cook until it is hot; season with salt and pepper to taste and serve.

Shredded Butternut Squash with Dates and Pistachios (V)

MAKES 4 SERVINGS ■ HANDS-ON TIME: 20 MINUTES ■ TOTAL PREPARATION TIME: 20 MINUTES

Ever since I discovered the shredding disc of a food processor, my life as a chef has been divided into pre-shredder and post-shredder, with every vegetable I see assessed for its shredability. What makes the shredder so sexy? It's just a great, great time-saver. Not only is it much quicker to shred something than to chop or cut it up by hand, it's much quicker to cook something that's already been shredded. For example, it takes 45 minutes to boil up beets. You can shred and sauté them in 3 minutes.

In this recipe, I've combined butternut squash with Middle Eastern flavors—dates, pistachios, mint, and lemon—for a tasty mix of sweet and sour. If you're looking for alternatives to squash, either sweet potatoes or carrots would fill the bill, and both of them are a heck of a lot easier to peel.

1 medium butternut
　squash (1½ pounds)
2 medium shallots
⅓ cup shelled natural
　pistachios
3 large dates
2 tablespoons vegetable
　oil
4 large mint leaves
1 to 1½ tablespoons
　fresh lemon juice
Kosher salt
Cayenne pepper

1. Peel the butternut squash and cut it into pieces that will fit into the feeding tube of a food processor. Fit the processor with the shredding disc and shred the squash (about 3½ cups). Finely chop the shallots (about ⅓ cup); coarsely chop the pistachios (about ⅓ cup); and pit and coarsely chop the dates (about ¼ cup).

2. Heat the vegetable oil in a large skillet over medium heat until hot. Add the shallots and cook for 1 minute, stirring. Add the butternut squash, turn up the heat to medium-high, and cook for 3 minutes, stirring, until the squash is tender. The mixture will become soft, like a puree. Shred the mint (about 2 teaspoons). Stir in the pistachios, dates, mint, and lemon juice. Add salt and cayenne to taste.

$\mathcal{E}$damame Mash

MAKES 4 SERVINGS ■ **HANDS-ON TIME: 10 MINUTES** ■ **TOTAL PREPARATION TIME: 30 MINUTES**

We served Edamame Mash in the *Gourmet* dining room for years. I'd been a big, big fan right along, but I always left its preparation to Jennifer Day, my *chef de cuisine*. One day I asked Jenn what was in the recipe besides fresh soybeans and discovered, to my horror, that the answer was "a lot of cream." No wonder it tasted so good!

Given that frozen edamame is so readily available these days and that it's so good for you, I wanted to include an edamame recipe in this book. I settled on a less fattening version of *Gourmet*'s Edamame Mash, swapping in buttermilk for the cream in the original. Buttermilk is thick and creamy despite the fact that its butterfat content is on a par with low-fat milk's. Then I went right ahead and supplemented the buttermilk with a few tablespoons of butter. But you don't have to. It's very tasty without it.

4 cups fresh peeled edamame or one 16-ounce bag frozen
½ cup buttermilk
1 to 2 tablespoons unsalted butter
Kosher salt and freshly ground black pepper

1. Bring a medium saucepan of salted water to a boil over high heat. Add the edamame and cook for 20 to 25 minutes, or until very soft. (*Note:* This is longer than the package directions tell you to cook them, but they need to be very soft in this recipe to be mashed.)

2. Drain the edamame and transfer to a food processor fitted with the chopping blade. Add the buttermilk, butter, and salt and pepper to taste and puree to the desired consistency. Transfer the mixture back to the saucepan and heat just until hot.

all about EDAMAME

Edamame is the Japanese name for green soybeans that have been harvested a bit before maturity so that they are fresh, green, and moist. Soybeans have been a part of the Asian diet for thousands of years, but they didn't come west to Europe until about three hundred years ago. America discovered soybeans in the early twentieth century and gradually experimented with all the ways this useful plant could become a part of our culture. In recent years the fresh green pods and the shelled beans have become a favorite snack. If you buy edamame fresh in the pods, just put them in a large pot of boiling salted water and cook them for 5 to 7 minutes, or until the small green beans inside the pods no longer taste raw. If you buy the beans frozen, follow the package directions.

$\mathcal{P}$an-Seared Asparagus ⓥ

MAKES 4 SERVINGS ▪ HANDS-ON TIME: 13 MINUTES ▪ TOTAL PREPARATION TIME: 15 MINUTES

Fresh asparagus is one of the great joys of the spring and summer months, but I've given up eating it boiled or steamed. It's largely water to begin with, and cooking it in water only makes it more watery. Happily, there are several other ways to get the best out of this vegetable. Grilling or roasting asparagus at high heat caramelizes and concentrates its sweetness. Sautéing it in a skillet over high heat, as in this recipe, also works, particularly when you finish it off with freshly grated Parmigiano-Reggiano and a spritz of lemon.

1½ pounds asparagus
½ ounce Parmigiano-Reggiano
2 tablespoons extra virgin olive oil
Kosher salt
1½ teaspoons fresh lemon juice
Freshly ground black pepper

1. Trim off the woody ends of the asparagus. If the stalk is ⅓ inch in diameter or more, lay the asparagus flat on a work surface and peel it from just under the head to the bottom using a vegetable peeler. Slice the stalks diagonally into 2-inch pieces (about 4 cups). Microplane-grate the cheese (about ⅓ cup) or grate on the fine side of a box grater (about 2½ tablespoons).

2. Heat the olive oil in a large skillet over high heat; add the asparagus and a pinch of salt. Cover and cook, stirring frequently, until the asparagus is starting to brown and is almost tender, about 2 minutes. (If the asparagus is very thin or very thick, adjust the time.) Remove from the heat and stir in the cheese, lemon juice, and pepper to taste.

$\mathcal{C}$elery and Parsley Salad
with Parmigiano-Reggiano and Walnuts Ⓥ

MAKES ABOUT 4 CUPS, 4 SERVINGS   HANDS-ON TIME: 20 MINUTES   TOTAL PREPARATION TIME: 20 MINUTES

Too many Americans think of parsley as no more than a garnish. The Italians know better. They put it in and on just about everything: meatballs, stuffing, pasta dough, sauces, and salads. In large quantities, too, not just a delicate little sprinkle here and there.

This salad is a tasty demonstration of the ability of parsley to command the center of the plate, or at the least to stand side by side with a simpatico partner: in this case, celery. Toss it with some lemon juice, olive oil, walnuts, and freshly shaved Parmigiano-Reggiano, and see if you're not convinced that parsley can be a star.

½ cup walnuts
6 medium celery stalks
1 ounce Parmigiano-
    Reggiano
1 tablespoon plus
    1 teaspoon fresh
    lemon juice
½ teaspoon kosher salt
3 tablespoons extra
    virgin olive oil
2 cups fresh flat-leaf
    parsley leaves

1. Preheat the oven to 350°F. Spread out the walnuts on a rimmed baking sheet and toast until golden, 7 to 10 minutes. Remove to a cooling rack and let the walnuts cool to room temperature. Coarsely chop the walnuts (about ⅓ cup).

2. Meanwhile, very thinly slice the celery crosswise (about 3 cups) and shave the cheese (about ⅓ cup).

3. In a large bowl, whisk together 1 tablespoon lemon juice and the salt until the salt has dissolved; gradually whisk in the olive oil. Taste and add more lemon juice if desired. Add the celery, parsley, cheese, and toasted walnuts to the dressing and toss until combined.

Cucumber and Tomato Salad
with Yogurt and Toasted Cumin Seed Dressing ⓥ

MAKES ABOUT 3 CUPS, 4 SERVINGS ▪ HANDS-ON TIME: 15 MINUTES ▪ TOTAL PREPARATION TIME: 15 MINUTES

I love Indian food. I think it's because of the masterful way the Indians incorporate spices. Usually, any given Indian dish includes a raft of spices, but in this recipe, there's only one: cumin seeds, toasted and crushed to magnify their flavor. They are potent enough to make even a common combination of ingredients—cucumber, tomato, and yogurt—seem fresh and exotic.

This salad would go especially well with a spicy dish because its sugar and dairy naturally tame a chile's heat. But it would also be a delightful side dish with many of the poultry, meat, or fish dishes in this book.

1 teaspoon cumin seeds
1 cup plain low-fat or full-fat Greek-style yogurt (see page 49)
1 teaspoon sugar
1 teaspoon kosher salt
¼ teaspoon freshly ground black pepper
One 5- to 6-inch piece seedless (English) cucumber
¾ pound plum tomatoes (about 3 medium)

1. Heat the cumin seeds in a small dry skillet over medium-high heat until they begin to brown and smell fragrant, about 2 minutes. Transfer the seeds to a small bowl and crush them with a spoon. Add the yogurt, sugar, salt, and pepper to the cumin seeds in the bowl.

2. Medium chop the cucumber with the skin left on (about 1½ cups); seed and medium chop the tomatoes (about 1½ cups). Combine the cucumber and tomatoes in a medium bowl. Just before serving, add the yogurt dressing to the cucumber and tomato salad and toss well.

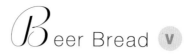eer Bread Ⓥ

MAKES 8 SERVINGS   HANDS-ON TIME: 10 MINUTES   TOTAL PREPARATION TIME: 30 TO 35 MINUTES

I had no idea about the widespread popularity of beer bread until Debbie Bickford, a long-time fan of my show, e-mailed her family's version to me, along with this introduction: "Hope you will enjoy this simple bread. It looks lumpy, but the lumps are yummy. My granddaughter likes it for the butter."

The first time I made Debbie's recipe, it was so ridiculously simple, I thought it was a joke. Then I ate it and I understood it was a miracle. So little effort, so much flavor. In fact, it was so good, it inspired me to come up with a few variations of my own: beer bread made with cornmeal or whole wheat flour, and beer bread with onion.

A cook named Farmgirl Susan, who writes for a Web site called A Year in Bread, wrote well about the recipe's versatility: "Beer bread is delicious warm or at room temperature and goes well with just about anything. You can even use it to make sandwiches. It also freezes beautifully."

There are home cooks in the South who whip up a batch of biscuits for every meal. I'm thinking this beer bread could become my frequent side for weeknight meals.

8 tablespoons (1 stick)
    unsalted butter
3 cups unbleached
    all-purpose flour
3 tablespoons sugar
1 tablespoon baking
    powder
1 teaspoon table salt
One 12-ounce bottle
    good-quality beer

1. Place an oven rack in the upper third of the oven and preheat the oven to 350°F. Place the butter in a 13 × 9 × 2-inch baking dish or pan and set it in the oven while the oven is preheating.

2. Stir together the flour, sugar, baking powder, and salt in a medium bowl. Stir in the beer until it is just incorporated. (The dough will be sticky and heavy.)

3. Pour 6 tablespoons melted butter out of the pan into a cup; tilt the pan to coat the bottom and sides with the remaining butter. Spoon the bread dough into the pan and spread evenly; drizzle the 6 tablespoons melted butter over the top. Bake for 20 to 25 minutes, or until the bumpy top is golden brown.

4. Remove the bread from the oven to a cooling rack; cut the bread into rectangles and serve warm.

ONION BREAD: Prepare the dough as above. Thinly slice a small onion and separate it into rings (about ½ cup). Toss it with the 6 tablespoons melted butter and arrange it over the top of the dough.

CORN BREAD: Prepare the dough as above, substituting 1 cup cornmeal for 1 cup of the flour.

WHOLE WHEAT BREAD: Prepare the dough as above, substituting 1 cup whole wheat flour for 1 cup of the all-purpose flour.

how can i

GET THE AROMA OF ONION OR GARLIC OFF MY HANDS?

Although Julia Child always recommended moistening your hands, rubbing them with salt, and then washing them with soap and water, the most widely mentioned remedy for onion and garlic aroma on your hands is to moisten your hands and rub them on something stainless steel. In most kitchen shops, you can find little metal bars made especially for the purpose, but you could even use the stainless steel faucet at your kitchen sink. My favorite remedy for cleaning up fishy hands is rubbing them with toothpaste, and that does a pretty good job on onion and garlic, too.

Leek, Cheddar, and Chive Pancakes Ⓥ

MAKES ABOUT 12 PANCAKES, 4 SERVINGS HANDS-ON TIME: 25 MINUTES TOTAL PREPARATION TIME: 35 MINUTES

Potato pancakes, aka latkes, are savory and served for dinner. Flour pancakes are sweet and served for breakfast. Or at least that's what I thought until now. These flour pancakes are savory dinnertime pancakes, and they're darned good, even if I do say so myself. They're also substantial enough that you'd have a meal if you paired them up with just a bit of protein—a slice or two of Canadian bacon, say, or a few sautéed shrimp—and a salad.

1 medium leek
1 tablespoon olive oil plus extra for brushing the griddle
4 ounces sharp Cheddar cheese
3 tablespoons unsalted butter
1½ cups unbleached all-purpose flour
1 teaspoon sugar
1 teaspoon baking powder
1 teaspoon table salt
1 cup whole milk
½ cup sour cream or yogurt
1 large egg
2 tablespoons snipped fresh chives

1. Preheat the oven to 250°F. Trim the leek and split it lengthwise. Cut it crosswise into ½-inch pieces (about 1 cup); rinse thoroughly and spin dry. Heat the 1 tablespoon olive oil in a small skillet over medium heat. Reduce the heat to medium-low, add the leek, and cook, stirring occasionally, for about 10 minutes, or until it is just turning golden.

2. Meanwhile, coarsely grate the cheese (about 1 cup) and melt the butter. Stir together the flour, cheese, sugar, baking powder, and salt in a large bowl. Whisk together the milk, sour cream, egg, butter, and chives in a small bowl. Add the leek and the milk mixture to the flour mixture and gently stir just until combined.

3. Heat a nonstick griddle or skillet brushed with oil over medium heat until hot. Add the batter ¼ cup at a time to make as many pancakes as will fit in the pan without touching. Cook for 3 minutes, or until the tops are covered with bubbles and the bottoms have begun to brown. Carefully turn the pancakes and cook for 2 minutes more, or until the bottoms have begun to brown. Transfer the pancakes to a rimmed baking sheet and keep warm in the oven. Repeat brushing with additional vegetable oil as needed, until all the batter has been cooked. Serve right away.

$\mathcal{S}$hredded Root Vegetable Latkes ⓥ

MAKES ABOUT 12 LATKES, 4 SERVINGS ▪ **HANDS-ON TIME: 25 MINUTES** ▪ **TOTAL PREPARATION TIME: 25 MINUTES**

Sometimes in the fall I buy a bunch of root vegetables for a particular recipe and fail to use them all up. Suddenly there's a lone parsnip or turnip hanging out in my vegetable drawer. How to rescue those worthy orphans? Use them in this recipe, in essence, nothing more than a fancy-schmancy potato latke. The key tool here is the shredding disc of your food processor, which makes it a snap to shred not only the root vegetables, but also the potatoes.

Traditionally, latkes are topped off with a dollop of sour cream. You can add it or not; these taste just fine without it.

1 pound assorted root
    vegetables, such
    as turnips, beets,
    parsnips, and carrots
½ pound boiling
    potatoes, such as
    Yukon gold or Red
    Bliss
1 small onion
1 large egg
⅓ cup unbleached
    all-purpose flour
Kosher salt and freshly
    ground black pepper
4 to 6 tablespoons
    vegetable oil
¼ to ½ cup sour cream

1. Preheat the oven to 250°F. Peel and coarsely shred the root vegetables, potatoes, and onion (about 3½ cups, packed, combined) in a food processor fitted with the shredding disc (or grate by hand if you don't have a food processor). Transfer the vegetables to a small bowl. Add the egg, flour, ½ teaspoon salt, and ¼ teaspoon pepper and toss well.

2. Heat 2 tablespoons vegetable oil in a large skillet over medium heat. Use a ¼-cup measure to drop mounds of the vegetable mixture into the skillet and to flatten them to 4-inch rounds. Cook until the bottoms are golden brown, about 5 minutes. Turn and brown the other sides, 4 to 5 minutes. Transfer the latkes to a rimmed baking sheet and keep warm in the oven. Repeat, adding vegetable oil as needed, until all the vegetable mixture has been cooked.

3. Sprinkle the latkes with salt and pepper to taste and serve them with sour cream.

Potato and Spinach Sauté with Mustard Seeds ⓥ

MAKES 4 SERVINGS ■ HANDS-ON TIME: 15 MINUTES ■ TOTAL PREPARATION TIME: 40 TO 45 MINUTES

I wish I reached for mustard seeds more often. They add slight heat and crunch to a recipe, like this vegetable sauté. Here the potatoes are cubed and slowly cooked until they're nice and golden on all sides. This takes a while, but—except for the occasional stir—it is unattended time. Then they're combined with quickly wilted spinach, onion, and the mustard seeds. If you've never cooked with mustard seeds before, you may be persuaded by their assertiveness and charm in this recipe to find a permanent home for them in your pantry.

1 pound boiling potatoes, such as Yukon gold or Red Bliss
¼ cup vegetable oil
Kosher salt
1 small onion
1½ teaspoons yellow mustard seeds
1 garlic clove
½ teaspoon cayenne pepper
5 ounces baby spinach (about 8 cups, packed)
Freshly ground black pepper

1. Scrub the potatoes and cut them into ½-inch cubes. Heat 2 tablespoons vegetable oil in a large nonstick skillet over medium-high heat until hot. Add the potatoes and cook over medium heat, stirring occasionally, for 20 to 25 minutes, or until they are golden and tender. Add salt to taste and transfer the potatoes to a bowl.

2. Meanwhile, chop the onion (about ½ cup). After the potatoes have been transferred to the bowl, reduce the heat to medium, add the remaining 2 tablespoons vegetable oil and the mustard seeds to the pan, and cook for about 10 seconds, or until the mustard seeds start to become fragrant and pop. Reduce the heat to medium-low; add the onion and cook for 5 minutes, or until it has softened. Press in the garlic (about 1 teaspoon) and add the cayenne; cook for 1 minute more.

3. Increase the heat to medium-high and add the spinach; cook, stirring, for about 3 minutes, or until the spinach has wilted. Return the potatoes to the skillet; add salt and black pepper to taste and cook just until heated through.

Rosemary Potatoes Cooked in a Bag (V)

This recipe is damn near miraculous, and it's completely delicious. You just throw all the ingredients into an aluminum foil package and toss the package into the oven. Forty-five minutes later it's done, and there's not even a pot to wash.

1½ pounds boiling potatoes, such as Yukon gold or Red Bliss
1 small onion
2 tablespoons fresh rosemary leaves or 1 teaspoon dried
3 tablespoons unsalted butter or extra virgin olive oil
1 teaspoon kosher salt
1 garlic clove

1. Preheat the oven to 425°F. Scrub and halve the potatoes lengthwise, then slice them crosswise ½ inch thick (about 4 cups). Thinly slice the onion (about ½ cup), chop the rosemary (about 1 tablespoon), and melt the butter, if using. Combine the potatoes, onion, butter, rosemary, and salt in a large bowl. Press in the garlic (about 1 teaspoon) and toss until the potatoes are evenly coated.

2. Cut an 18-inch square sheet of heavy-duty aluminum foil and transfer the potato mixture to it; fold the edges of the foil together and press the foil tightly against the potatoes. Place the package on a rimmed baking sheet and bake for 40 to 50 minutes, or until the potatoes are tender.

13
FIVE-INGREDIENT MAINS

I'll be honest with you: Although I loved the idea of this chapter—the fewer the ingredients, the faster dinner gets to the table—the *execution* of it was murder for me. I know, of course, that plenty of cuisines operate on the assumption that a few excellent ingredients, excellently prepared, are all you ever really need. But I've never rolled like that. I felt like I was in a straitjacket. It was truly difficult for me to limit the number of ingredients in a recipe, and even so, you'll notice a little cheating in the garnish department. (By the way, salt and pepper don't count.)

I decided not only to limit the number of ingredients, but to make sure that those ingredients I did use cooked up quickly: pasta and rice, seafood, pork tenderloin, ham steak, and duck breast. With these strictures in place, it was very gratifying to discover how little time it takes to rustle up such delicious entrées as Roasted Salmon with Hot Mustard Cracker Topping, Baked Chicken Wings with Creamy BBQ Dipping Sauce, and Peppery Broccoli with Feta Cheese and Angel Hair Pasta.

In the end, when five ingredients worked, they *really* worked. Taste-wise, the exercise helped me to relearn an old lesson: Sometimes less is more. Time-wise, it confirmed the obvious: Less is always better.

FACING PAGE: *Scallop, Basil, and Prosciutto Kebabs.*

Cheesy Breaded Pork Tenderloin Steaks

MAKES 4 SERVINGS ■ HANDS-ON TIME: 10 MINUTES ■ TOTAL PREPARATION TIME: 20 MINUTES

I love pork tenderloin. As long as it's not overcooked, it'll turn out juicy, flavorful, and tender every time. This recipe dresses it up with a little cheesy crunch, courtesy of a coating of bread crumbs and some nice, sharp Parmigiano-Reggiano. A quick sauté in extra virgin olive oil and these bad boys are good to go in minutes.

1 pork tenderloin, trimmed (1 to 1¼ pounds)
1 ounce Parmigiano-Reggiano
½ cup seasoned Italian bread crumbs
1 large egg
3 tablespoons extra virgin olive oil
Lemon wedges, for garnish (*shhh,* this does not count as an ingredient)

1. Slice the pork diagonally at a 45-degree angle into 8 pieces, each about ¾ inch thick. Don't worry if the pieces are not all the same size. Just make sure they are all ¾ inch thick. Microplane-grate the cheese (about ⅔ cup) or grate on the fine side of a box grater (about ⅓ cup).

2. Combine the bread crumbs and cheese in a shallow bowl. Lightly beat the egg with 1 tablespoon water in another shallow bowl. Dip each piece of pork into the beaten egg, letting the excess drip off, and then into the bread crumbs, packing the crumbs on all sides.

3. Heat 1½ tablespoons olive oil in a large skillet over high heat. Reduce the heat to medium and add the pork pieces. Cook for 3 minutes; turn the slices, add the rest of the olive oil to the pan, and cook for 3 minutes more, or until the pork is golden.

4. Remove the skillet from the heat and let the pork stand in the pan for 5 minutes. Transfer 2 pieces of pork to each of 4 plates and serve with a lemon wedge.

all about MUSTARD

Mustard has been used for centuries in different parts of the world as a condiment and preservative. Although in most cases only two kinds of mustard seeds—the milder yellow or white seeds and the more intense brown seeds—have been ground to produce mustard powder, the wide range of liquids with which they have been mixed to make prepared mustard has produced shelves of different flavors in the condiment section of our supermarkets.

American yellow mustard (aka ballpark mustard), the mildest choice, is made from white mustard seeds, combined with vinegar, sugar, and turmeric for color. The famous French Dijon mustard is made from brown mustard seeds moistened with white wine. German mustard is usually based on coarsely ground brown mustard seeds and beer. Colman's English mustard, a simple mixture of ground brown and white seeds and water, is much hotter than American mustards. Chinese mustard is usually the hottest and can be made at home by stirring a bit of water into finely ground mustard seeds.

Most people have their favorites. Although I tend to use mostly Dijon mustard, there are some recipes in which nothing but English or Chinese mustard will do.

Sautéed Duck Breasts
with Apricot–Szechuan Peppercorn Sauce

MAKES 4 SERVINGS   HANDS-ON TIME: 15 MINUTES   TOTAL PREPARATION TIME: 25 MINUTES

My first job out of cooking school was at The Harvest, a restaurant in Harvard Square in Cambridge. (It's the only restaurant I ever worked at that's still standing.) Our chef was Laura Boehmer, who was way ahead of her time when it came to using international ingredients. We were serving recipes with wonton skins, harissa, and ground sumac in the late seventies.

One of Laura's signature dishes was roast duck with sweet-and-sour apricot sauce flavored with Szechuan peppercorns—another avant-garde ingredient back in the day. No relation to black pepper or a chile pepper, Szechuan pepper is a fragrant pod grown widely throughout Asia that has a slightly lemony, woodsy aroma all its own. Generally, it's toasted, which will nicely perfume your kitchen, before being combined with other ingredients. It is Laura's apricot sauce that graces this recipe; its acidity is a great counterpoint to the rich duck.

Of course, it's much quicker to sauté some breasts than it is to roast a whole duck. Whether or not you eat the skin, be sure to cook the breasts with the skin on; they'll turn out much juicier that way. Although my family would say you're nuts not to eat the skin, I have to note that duck meat without skin is as lean as turkey white meat.

1 teaspoon Szechuan
    peppercorns (see
    Sources, page 359)
4 Pekin duck breast
    halves
Kosher salt and freshly
    ground black pepper
⅓ cup apricot preserves
2 tablespoons distilled
    white vinegar
¼ teaspoon toasted
    sesame oil

1. Heat a large skillet over medium-high heat until hot. Add the Szechuan peppercorns and toast them, stirring continuously, for 2 to 3 minutes, or until they are fragrant. Transfer them to a small cup and let them cool; then crush them with a spoon and set them aside.

2. Score the skin on each duck breast half in a crisscross pattern. Season the breast halves on all sides with salt and black pepper to taste and place them, skin side down, in the same hot skillet. Reduce the heat to medium and cook for about 10 minutes, or until the skin looks very crispy. Do not remove the fat as you go; the liquid fat in the pan helps to render out the fat in the skin.

3. When the duck skin is crisp, remove the duck to a plate, pour off almost all the fat from the pan, and reserve the fat for another use (such as sautéing potatoes). Return the duck to the skillet, meat

side down, and cook for 2 to 3 minutes more for medium-rare. Remove the duck to a clean plate, skin side up; cover it loosely with aluminum foil and set it aside for 5 minutes.

4. Meanwhile, make the sauce: Combine the preserves, vinegar, and crushed Szechuan peppercorns in a small saucepan. Cook, stirring constantly, just until the preserves have melted; remove the pan from the heat and stir in the sesame oil, any duck juices from the plate, and salt to taste.

5. To serve, slice the duck diagonally into ¼-inch-thick slices and arrange on 4 serving plates. Stir any juices from carving the duck into the sauce. Spoon some of the sauce over each serving of duck.

DUCK BREAST OPTIONS

The ever-increasing availability of duck is a great pleasure to a duck lover like me. These days there are five breeds of duck grown for meat in the United States: Pekin, Muscovy, Moulard, Mallard, and Rouen. Ducks are usually sold whole, but a few varieties are sold in parts. If you're looking for breasts, as in Sautéed Duck Breasts with Apricot–Szechuan Peppercorn Sauce, you can find both Pekin and Moulard. Pekins have a relatively mild taste, and the skin crisps up beautifully when cooked. Moulard duck breast, also called magret, is a crossbreed of Muscovy and Pekin. It is larger than the Pekin and has a big, steaklike flavor. A full (double) magret breast will feed four people, while a full (double) Pekin is big enough for only two. I love them both, but my family prefers the milder flavor and crispier skin of the Pekin. That's why, in this case, the Pekin gets the nod.

Ham Steak with Hot Raisin Sauce

MAKES 4 SERVINGS   HANDS-ON TIME: 10 MINUTES   TOTAL PREPARATION TIME: 20 MINUTES

Ham with raisin sauce is a good old-fashioned Granny-type recipe. Pork is often paired with fruit because the acid in the fruit provides a tasty counterbalance to the fat in the pork. Ham steaks, cut from the leg, team up very happily with raisins and apple cider. Where I diverge from Granny—and bring the heat—is with the addition of Colman's mustard. It was enough to turn the trick with The Husband, who otherwise shuns what he calls "the promiscuous coupling" of sweet with his savory.

2 tablespoons
    vegetable oil
1½ pounds ham steak
1 cup cider or
    apple juice
¾ cup golden raisins
1½ to 2 teaspoons
    prepared English
    mustard (preferably
    Colman's)

1. Heat the vegetable oil in a large skillet over medium-high heat until hot. Pat the steak very dry and add it to the skillet; cook it for 2 to 3 minutes per side, or until it is golden on both sides and heated through. Transfer the steak to a plate using tongs and cover loosely with aluminum foil.

2. Add the cider and raisins to the skillet and simmer for 4 to 6 minutes, or until the cider has reduced by half. Stir in the mustard and any ham juices from the plate.

3. To serve, divide the ham into 4 portions and top each portion with some of the raisin sauce.

$\mathcal{B}$aked Chicken Wings
with Creamy BBQ Dipping Sauce

MAKES 4 SERVINGS   HANDS-ON TIME: 12 MINUTES   TOTAL PREPARATION TIME: 30 MINUTES

Baked chicken wings are so good that it's virtually impossible to mess them up. I don't really think they need any sauce, but inspired by a dish, rock shrimp with a creamy spicy sauce, from one of my favorite restaurants in New York, Nobu, I just couldn't resist. The inspiration was more essence than substance: The only ingredient shared by Nobu's recipe and mine is mayonnaise. I love mayonnaise, especially when, as here, it's used in unexpected ways.

3 pounds chicken wing drummettes (about 24 drummettes)
Kosher salt and freshly ground black pepper
¾ cup mayonnaise
¼ cup Basic Barbecue Sauce (page 15, add preparation time) or store-bought sauce
1 tablespoon sherry vinegar
1 garlic clove

1. Place an oven rack in the middle of the oven and preheat the oven to 450°F. Season the wings with salt and pepper to taste and arrange them in one layer on a rack in a roasting pan. Bake them, turning them halfway through the cooking time, for 20 to 25 minutes, or until they are crispy and cooked through.

2. Meanwhile, for the dipping sauce, combine the mayonnaise, Basic Barbecue Sauce, vinegar, and salt and pepper to taste; press in the garlic (about 1 teaspoon) and stir together. Serve each portion of wings with a ramekin or little bowl of dipping sauce and plenty of napkins.

THE WIDE WORLD OF VINEGAR

When I was a teacher at Peter Kump's New York Cooking School (now known as the Institute of Culinary Education) in New York City, part of the first class curriculum was to make a vinaigrette. I explained the basic ratio of three parts oil to one part acid and then asked everyone in the class to make a vinaigrette using olive oil in those proportions. Everyone was instructed to pick a different acid. I thought all acid was created equal and that the three-to-one ratio worked across the board. I was wrong; each acid required a different proportion to balance the flavors. Rice vinegar is quite tame, and balsamic, because of its sugar content, needs very little oil to balance it in a salad dressing. Champagne vinegar is generally milder in flavor than white wine or red wine vinegar, and sherry vinegar and apple cider vinegar are quite acidic and full bodied. Fresh lemon juice, which is often used in salad dressings, can vary greatly in acid content. So the next time you make a vinaigrette or reach for an acid to add to a recipe, remember that a tablespoon of one kind is not going to be exactly interchangeable with a tablespoon of another. Don't rely on that formula of three to one. Rely instead on your taste buds and what tastes like a good balance of oil and vinegar to you.

Scallop, Basil, and Prosciutto Kebabs

MAKES 4 SERVINGS ■ HANDS-ON TIME: 15 MINUTES ■ TOTAL PREPARATION TIME: 22 MINUTES

Here's a little surf and turf haiku. I tested it exactly one time, and everyone agreed it was perfect as it was, a rare occurrence. The sole tricky part of this recipe is the broiling, if only because the temperatures on home broilers tend to be inconsistent, as are the distances from the oven shelf to the broiler. So be sure to keep a close eye on these kebabs as they broil. Obviously, it's better to check them sooner rather than later, because overcooked scallops are tough and dry. If your broiler turns out to be completely unreliable, go ahead and sauté the kebabs instead.

16 sea scallops (about 1½ inches in diameter; 1¼ pounds)
1 tablespoon fresh lemon juice
Kosher salt
2 tablespoons extra virgin olive oil
8 thin slices prosciutto di Parma (about 4 ounces)
16 large basil leaves

1. If the scallops still have the tough muscle that attaches them to the shell, trim it off. Pat the scallops dry with paper towels.

2. Whisk together the lemon juice and a hefty pinch of salt in a medium bowl until the salt has dissolved; whisk in the olive oil. Add the scallops and toss until they are well coated.

3. Cut the prosciutto slices in half crosswise and fold them into strips about 1½ inches wide (the same width as the scallops) and 3 to 4 inches long. Arrange the strips on a work surface and place a basil leaf in the center of each strip. Top the leaf with a scallop and wrap the prosciutto around the scallop to enclose it. Thread 4 prosciutto-wrapped scallops onto each of 4 metal skewers. (If using wooden skewers, soak them for 20 minutes in water before threading the scallops.)

4. Preheat the broiler to high. Arrange the skewers on a broiler pan and broil 4 inches from the heat source for 3 minutes per side, or until just cooked through, and serve immediately.

Roasted Salmon with Hot Mustard Cracker Topping

MAKES 4 SERVINGS · HANDS-ON TIME: 10 MINUTES · TOTAL PREPARATION TIME: 20 MINUTES

The Husband and I have taken to eating rice crackers as a way of staving off the impulse to devour our own hands during the terrible hour before dinner. These crackers come in a bunch of flavors. (My favorite is wasabi.) They're thin and crispy. And the best part: sixteen of them (one portion) clock in at a total of only 110 calories.

In this recipe, our wasabi rice crackers provide a tasty, crunchy crust for the salmon, requiring only a little "glue" to keep them in place. One of the few five-ingredient recipes to which I wasn't dying to add something, this little wonder, in my opinion, is perfect as is.

⅓ cup sour cream
1½ teaspoons prepared English mustard (preferably Colman's)
½ teaspoon packed light brown sugar
35 to 40 wasabi rice crackers
Four 6-ounce pieces center-cut salmon fillet, skin removed
Kosher salt

1. Preheat the oven to 400°F. Combine the sour cream, mustard, and brown sugar. Coarsely crush the rice crackers (about 1 cup).

2. Season the salmon on all sides with salt. Arrange the pieces in one layer in a shallow baking pan, skinned side down. Spread the top of each piece with the sour cream mixture and top with some of the crushed crackers. Bake the salmon for 10 to 12 minutes, or until barely cooked through, and serve right away.

HOOK-AND-LINE-CAUGHT FISH

Today you will see the words *line-caught fish* in your fish market and on restaurant menus. For decades the fishing industry has used fishing strategies that are more efficient for it and less responsible for the future of our seafood supply. Commercial fishing vessels have employed nonselective fishing methods such as trawling, purse seines, and long-line fishing that harvest and destroy a great deal of sea life (known as bycatch) that isn't their intended product. Hook-and-line fishing is a more environmentally responsible method of fishing and reflects techniques used in the past. Fishermen monitor their lines and harvest fish quickly so that any unwanted catch can be released while it can still survive, and the fishermen can still make a living. Be sure to look for "line-caught" fish in your market or favorite restaurants.

Baked Shrimp Stuffed with Italian Sausage

MAKES 4 SERVINGS · HANDS-ON TIME: 15 MINUTES · TOTAL PREPARATION TIME: 20 MINUTES

Bruce Aidells is one of my favorite cookbook authors and a renowned expert on charcuterie, salumi, and gourmet sausages. A recipe called Shrimp Stuffed with Sausages in Bruce's *Complete Sausage Book* pairs up the two main ingredients so cleverly that they stay glued together. As a longtime fan of surf and turf, I was intrigued and inspired. Heck, I was more than inspired; I stole his idea.

My addition to Bruce's recipe is the drizzling sauce. I'm not sure Bruce would approve, but I just had to include one more element. I think you'll be amazed at what you can do with just these five ingredients.

¾ pound jumbo shrimp, peeled and deveined

6 ounces hot or sweet Italian sausage (about 2 links)

¼ cup soy sauce (low sodium, if you prefer)

1 tablespoon seasoned rice vinegar

½ teaspoon toasted sesame oil

1. Preheat the oven to 450°F. Arrange the shrimp on a lightly oiled unrimmed baking sheet with all the shrimp facing the same direction to form a series of *C*s. Remove the casings from the sausages and put about 1 tablespoon sausage in the hollow formed by the *C* of each shrimp; press down so that the shrimp and sausage filling together make a solid round. Bake the stuffed shrimp for 10 minutes, or until they have cooked through.

2. Meanwhile, whisk together the soy sauce, rice vinegar, and sesame oil in a small bowl. Drizzle the sauce over the shrimp before serving.

uffalo Rice

MAKES 4 SERVINGS ▪ **HANDS-ON TIME: 25 MINUTES** ▪ **TOTAL PREPARATION TIME: 25 MINUTES**

It was Jenn Day, my *chef de cuisine* at *Gourmet,* who came up with the basic concept for this little gem: Buffalo chicken wing pasta—cubed chicken breasts sautéed in butter and tossed with hot sauce, blue cheese, and pasta. But I already had enough pasta recipes in this chapter, so I used rice instead, which also teams up beautifully with chicken, blue cheese, and hot sauce.

In keeping with this chapter's five-ingredient maximum, I use the rice cooking water as the liquid in this recipe, and it's plenty flavorful that way. If you wanted to substitute chicken stock for the water, well, just remember you're always alone in the kitchen.

1 cup long-grain
   white rice
8 ounces boneless,
   skinless chicken
   breast halves
3 tablespoons unsalted
   butter
Kosher salt
2 tablespoons hot sauce
4 ounces blue cheese
1 cup celery leaves, for
   garnish (optional;
   okay, I'm cheating)

1. Bring 6 cups salted water to a boil over high heat. Add the rice and cook for 15 to 17 minutes, or until it is tender. Drain the rice in a strainer, reserving 1 cup of the cooking liquid.

2. Meanwhile, cut the chicken into ½-inch cubes. Melt the butter in a large skillet over medium heat. Add the chicken and a pinch of salt and cook, stirring occasionally, for 3 to 5 minutes, or until just cooked through. Remove the chicken from the heat, toss with the hot sauce, and set aside in the skillet. Crumble the blue cheese (about 1 cup).

3. Once the rice has cooked, stir it into the chicken in the skillet along with the reserved 1 cup cooking liquid and the blue cheese. Divide the chicken and rice among 4 serving plates and top with the celery leaves, if using.

$\mathcal{P}$enne alla Vodka, Classic and Lite Ⓥ

MAKES 4 SERVINGS   HANDS-ON TIME: 15 MINUTES   TOTAL PREPARATION TIME: 25 MINUTES

The very name of this dish declares how untraditional it is. The penne is Italian, the vodka is Russian, and just how, when, and where they came together for the first time is a matter of dispute. Suffice it to say, however, it didn't happen much before the middle of the twentieth century.

Even more mysterious is the question of what, if anything, the vodka adds to this simple dish of pasta, tomato cream sauce, and hot pepper. I mean vodka really has no flavor. The answer, of course, is that vodka is alcohol, and alcohol is a superb conductor of flavor; it amplifies the intensity of the ingredients. Believe me, the same dish minus the vodka would seem bland by comparison.

My daughter, Ruthie, is a big fan of penne alla vodka. I love it, too, but I wanted to figure out a way to make it less fattening than usual, so, for the lite version, I exchanged the cream for milk thickened with flour. This pushes the number of ingredients required to six, but, really, in the interest of good health, who's counting? And the flavor remains big.

¾ cup canned tomato puree or crushed tomatoes (preferably fire roasted)
⅔ cup vodka
Kosher salt
Hefty pinch of crushed red pepper flakes (okay, extra ingredient—pretend it is like black pepper and doesn't count)
1 cup heavy cream (see Low-Fat Version, below)
1 pound penne
3 ounces Parmigiano-Reggiano
Freshly ground black pepper

1. Bring a large pot of salted water to a boil over high heat for the pasta.

2. Combine the tomato puree, vodka, ¼ teaspoon salt, and red pepper flakes in a medium saucepan. Bring to a boil over high heat, reduce the heat to low, and simmer for 5 minutes. Add the cream, return the mixture to a boil, and simmer until slightly thickened, about 15 minutes.

3. Add the penne to the boiling water and cook until al dente, following the package directions. Drain the pasta, reserving 1 cup of the cooking liquid. Return the pasta to the cooking pot.

4. Microplane-grate the cheese (about 2 cups) or grate on the fine side of a box grater (about 1 cup). Stir the sauce into the pasta along with the cheese, salt and pepper to taste, and enough of the cooking liquid to achieve the desired consistency. Spoon into shallow bowls and serve.

LOW-FAT VERSION: Instead of using the heavy cream, heat 1 cup whole or low-fat milk in a small saucepan over medium heat until steaming. Whisk together 1½ tablespoons unbleached all-purpose flour and another ¼ cup milk in a small bowl to make a smooth paste; whisk it into the hot milk and bring the mixture to a simmer, whisking constantly. Simmer for 2 minutes, then add to the tomato and vodka mixture in place of the cream and simmer for 10 minutes. Continue as directed above.

PAIRING PASTAS

These days the pasta section of any market offers an exciting array of choices. While it is great to have all those sizes and shapes to choose from and tempting to try something new each time, pastas come in many shapes for a reason. Pairing the pasta with a particular sauce can usually produce a better result. Here are some guidelines: Fine, delicate pastas, such as angel hair and very thin spaghetti, are happier with a thin sauce or a vegetable-filled broth, while a more robust pasta, such as tagliatelle, penne, or farfalle, stands up to a chunky sauce or one with seafood or vegetables in it. A creamy sauce or one with a lot of complexity pairs well with a shaped pasta, such as radiatore, orecchiette, or fusilli, that will catch the sauce in its curves and ruffles.

Peppery Broccoli with Feta Cheese and Angel Hair Pasta Ⓥ

MAKES 4 SERVINGS HANDS-ON TIME: 10 MINUTES TOTAL PREPARATION TIME: 20 MINUTES

During my first pregnancy, all the advice books seemed to say that if I truly wanted to give birth to a superbaby, I'd better eat broccoli three times a day. Normally, this wouldn't have been a terribly burdensome prospect, but I utterly lost my appetite—including my taste for broccoli—about four months into both my first and second pregnancies. Instead (get out your handkerchiefs), I had to force-feed myself Coffee Heath Bar Crunch ice cream just to keep my weight up. Somehow both kids came out fine, but afterward I was happy to resume my broccoli-eating ways.

Thank goodness the kids grew to like it, too. That's how I know that a simple dish like this—a whole head of broccoli, flavored with crushed red pepper flakes and feta cheese—makes a fine weeknight meal for the whole clan.

1 bunch broccoli (about 1½ pounds)
12 ounces angel hair pasta
2 cups Homemade Vegetable or Chicken Stock (pages 11 and 10, add preparation time) or canned broth
½ to 1 teaspoon crushed red pepper flakes
6 ounces feta cheese
Kosher salt

1. Bring a large pot of salted water to a boil over high heat. Cut the broccoli tops into bite-size florets; trim and peel the stems and slice them ½ inch thick (about 7 cups total). When the pot of water comes to a boil, add the broccoli. Cook for 3 minutes; remove the broccoli to a bowl using a slotted spoon.

2. Add the angel hair to the boiling water and cook until al dente, following the package directions. Drain well and return the pasta to the cooking pot.

3. Meanwhile, combine the vegetable stock and red pepper flakes to taste in a small saucepan and bring to a boil over high heat. Crumble the cheese (about 1½ cups).

4. Add the broccoli, vegetable stock, and cheese to the drained pasta. Heat over medium heat until hot; add salt, if needed, and serve.

Farfalle with Mushrooms and Bacon

As has often been noted, mushrooms are mostly water, but somehow the process of dehydrating and then rehydrating them manages to produce a deep, concentrated mushroom flavor in the water used to soak them. Indeed, you want to keep dried mushrooms on hand in the cupboard at all times because they produce, in effect, an instant sauce.

In this recipe, pasta is the neutral background against which the mushroom liquid and the tomato sauce (assisted by the bacon and cheese) take a bow. Serve it with a simple green salad and you have a meal.

2 ounces dried porcini
   or other dried
   mushrooms, or
   a mixture
4 ounces Parmigiano-
   Reggiano
4 ounces bacon
One 24- to 26-ounce
   jar prepared tomato
   sauce
1 pound farfalle or other
   shaped pasta
Kosher salt and freshly
   ground black pepper

1. Bring 2 cups water and the mushrooms to a boil in a small saucepan over high heat. Remove the pan from the heat and set aside to let the mushrooms soak for 15 minutes, or until they have softened.

2. Meanwhile, bring a large pot of salted water to a boil over high heat for the pasta. Coarsely grate the cheese (about 1⅓ cups).

3. Heat a large skillet over medium heat until hot. Cut the bacon slices in half crosswise. Reduce the heat to medium-low; add the bacon to the pan and cook, turning once, for 8 to 10 minutes, or until crisp. Remove the bacon to paper towels to drain. Set aside the skillet and bacon fat (about 2 tablespoons).

4. Gently lift the mushrooms out of the soaking liquid with your hands to let any sand sink to the bottom of the pan. Put the mushrooms in a bowl; pour the liquid through a strainer lined with a coffee filter or dampened paper towel set over a bowl and reserve. Rinse the mushrooms thoroughly to remove any remaining sand; cut any large mushrooms into bite-size pieces. Add the mushrooms, their reserved liquid, and the tomato sauce to the bacon fat in the skillet. Bring the mixture to a boil and simmer while the pasta is cooking.

5. Meanwhile, when the pot of water comes to a boil, add the farfalle. Cook until al dente, following the package directions. Drain the pasta well, reserving 1 cup of the cooking liquid. Return the pasta to the cooking pot. Add the mushroom-tomato sauce; cheese; some of the reserved cooking liquid, if desired; and salt and pepper to taste. Crumble the bacon over the mixture; toss well and serve.

14

TWO FOR ONE

What if you could prepare a no-fuss meal on a weeknight that gave you a head start on an even quicker meal the next night? This chapter allows you to do exactly that. Each recipe leaves behind fully cooked components for the fridge or freezer, all ready to refashion into a new meal a day or two later.

This kind of utility speaks to my favorite way to cook, which is to open the fridge, pull out the leftovers, add a little of this and a little of that, and then sit down to a delicious new meal, as if by magic. I provide you with more direction than that in this chapter, but you should definitely consider getting into the habit of always cooking more than you can eat in one meal, knowing that you can repurpose the extra food in a later recipe. There are all sorts of one-size-fits-all dishes, including risotto, fried rice, and baked pasta, that can comfortably serve as the basis for a new meal the next day.

In the following pages, I turn one night's roast pork tenderloin into the next night's delicious sandwich, lamb chops into a burger, steak with a cherry pepper sauce into a pasta sauce, celery root soup into a mussel sauce, marinated baked chicken into nachos, and simple sautéed fish into a decadent fish casserole.

FACING PAGE: *My Banh Mi.*

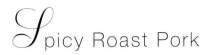

Spicy Roast Pork

MAKES 4 SERVINGS   HANDS-ON TIME: 20 MINUTES   TOTAL PREPARATION TIME: 40 MINUTES

Whenever I'm looking for a lean cut of pork, I reach for the tenderloin. Not only is it *very* lean, it is, as named, ridiculously tender, just as long as you don't overcook it.

I didn't much mess with the meat in this recipe except to lather it with sriracha (hot chili sauce) and seasoning, then counterbalance the heat by topping the cooked tenderloin with a cooling cucumber salad.

Why sriracha instead of, say, Tabasco (which I often reach for)? Because I was thinking ahead to the second half of this one-two punch: the banh mi sandwich (page 292). Like the banh mi, which has come to us courtesy of Vietnam, the Thai-based sriracha is of Asian provenance. Until a few years ago, Americans almost never encountered it, except in Thai or Vietnamese restaurants. Now it's fairly ubiquitous. (Just recently The Husband was offered some at a flea market crêperie in Pompano Beach, Florida.) See What Is Sriracha? (page 123) to learn more.

Two 1- to 1¼-pound
   pork tenderloins,
   trimmed and
   patted dry
¼ cup hot chili sauce
   (preferably sriracha)
2 teaspoons sugar
1 teaspoon kosher salt
Dill Pickle Cucumber
   Slices (page 22)

1. Preheat the oven to 400°F. Place the tenderloins in a lightly oiled roasting pan. Mix together the hot chili sauce, sugar, and salt. Spread the mixture over the tenderloins and roast the pork for about 25 minutes or until the center is still slightly pink (145°F on an instant-read thermometer).

2. Meanwhile, prepare the Dill Pickle Cucumber Slices; wrap and refrigerate the remaining piece of cucumber called for in the recipe to make My Banh Mi the next day.

3. Remove the tenderloins from the oven when they have finished cooking. Cover them loosely with aluminum foil and set them aside for 10 minutes. Slice and serve one tenderloin with the pickled cucumbers. Wrap and refrigerate the remaining tenderloin to make My Banh Mi the next day.

FACING PAGE: *Union Square Greenmarket, New York City.*

y Banh Mi

MAKES 4 SERVINGS ▪ **HANDS-ON TIME: 25 MINUTES** ▪ **TOTAL PREPARATION TIME: 25 MINUTES**

My brother Peter is a New York State Civil Court judge when he's on the clock and a devoted chowhound in his off-hours. One day about five years ago I went to meet Pete for lunch, and he took me to a little hole-in-the-wall a short walk from his chambers in downtown Manhattan. Called Sau Voi Corp., this strange little shop sold a variety of goods: brassieres stacked up like nesting yarmulkes, lottery tickets, Vietnamese music CDs, pornographic DVDs, and a selection of nondescript prepared food, tightly wrapped in plastic, that looked, in Pete's words, "like it had been sitting there since before World War II."

The shop also sold—and continues to sell—fresh banh mi sandwiches. Banh mi, in the words of the *New York Times*'s Julia Moskin, is the "classic street-vendor Franco-Vietnamese sandwich." In the hundred years or so since the Vietnamese began customizing the basic French sandwich of pâté on a baguette, the banh mi has mutated in dozens of brilliant ways, especially during its decade or so here in the States. Ms. Moskin, who ventured that "New York in 2009 is starting to look like the year of the banh mi," went on to note that "[American banh mi] are so rich in history, complex in flavor, and full of contradictions that they make other sandwiches look dumb."

Certainly, I've been a fan of them ever since my first bite at the Sau Voi Corp. This recipe is my interpretation, using liverwurst as a stand-in for the pâté. If you don't like liverwurst, you're welcome to use some French country pâté. Or leave it out altogether. There are plenty of other things going on here.

3 tablespoons
    unseasoned rice
    vinegar
1 tablespoon sugar
Kosher salt
One 5-inch piece
    seedless (English)
    cucumber (reserved
    from Spicy Roast
    Pork, page 291)
2 medium carrots
One 4-inch piece daikon
2 medium scallions

1. Whisk together the rice vinegar, 2 teaspoons sugar, and ¼ teaspoon salt in a medium bowl. Thinly slice enough of the reserved cucumber with the skin left on to make 1 cup. Coarsely shred (preferably using the shredding disc of a food processor) the carrots and daikon (about ¾ cups each). Trim and slice the scallions (about ¼ cup); halve, seed, and finely chop the jalapeño (about 2 tablespoons). Stir the cucumber, carrots, daikon, scallions, and jalapeño into the vinegar mixture.

1 large jalapeño chile
(make sure it has
heat; see page 6)
¾ cup mayonnaise
2 tablespoons hot chili
sauce (preferably
sriracha; see page
123)
1 Spicy Roast Pork
tenderloin (reserved
from previous recipe)
Four 6-inch baguette
pieces
¼ pound thinly sliced
cooked ham
¼ pound sliced
liverwurst (optional)

2. Meanwhile, combine the mayonnaise with the hot chili sauce and the remaining 1 teaspoon sugar. Thinly slice the pork tenderloin.

3. Split the baguette pieces horizontally. Spread the cut surfaces with the mayonnaise mixture. On the bottom half of the baguette pieces, arrange the pork, ham, liverwurst (if using), and pickled vegetable mixture. Add the top halves of the baguette pieces and serve.

all about SCALLIONS

As I was writing this book, I noticed that I was using more scallions than ever before. Mildly oniony, crunchy, and colorful, they were the right choice when a recipe just needed a little something. The name *scallion* comes from the ancient seaport town of Ascalon (modern-day Ashkelon in Israel). While there is a true green onion variety known as the scallion that has descended from those Mediterranean ancestors, the ones we find in the market may also be immature onions or leeks or the tops of shallots. At an early stage of development there is not a big difference in flavor among cousins in the onion family, so it is not essential to know the difference, but if you are curious, you can tell which branch of the family your bunch comes from. True scallions and baby leeks tend to be straight from top to bottom and come with roots attached. Baby onions have already started to form a bulb and are rounded at the bottom; they also usually have their roots. Shallot tops are easy to recognize because they have no roots

$\mathcal{G}$rilled Lamb Chops with Steak Butter

MAKES 4 SERVINGS ■ HANDS-ON TIME: 9 TO 15 MINUTES ■ TOTAL PREPARATION TIME: 44 TO 50 MINUTES

Ariane Daguin is the owner of a wonderful New Jersey–based food company called D'Artagnan. It is dedicated, in the Web site's words, "to putting the finest foie gras, meat, game, truffles, and mushrooms on the tables of American gastronomes." Although we're dear friends now, we got off on the wrong foot with Ariane when The Husband and I first met her in New York in the early eighties. Newly arrived in America, the daughter of a French chef, Ariane was naturally imbued with an appreciation for a wide variety of cuts of meat. Many of these were relatively tough, but they were also relatively cheap and terrifically flavorful. Most of them were also unavailable in America at the time. Why? Ariane had a theory. "Americans don't like to chew," she said.

Well! The Husband and I were duly offended, but in retrospect, Ariane was probably right. Twenty-five years later, America is much more like France, and Americans much more like the French. Who cares if the meat is a little chewier as long as the flavor is booming?

Consider lamb. I love lamb chops, but the usual supermarket choices are quite pricey. Increasingly, however, you can find chops cut from the shoulder. Although these are indeed chewier than other chops, they are much more affordable and flavorful as can be, which is why this recipe calls for shoulder chops. Alternatively, you're welcome to use lamb steaks cut from the leg if you can find them. They dress up very nicely with a little bit of flavored butter. I specify the Steak Butter here, but any of the flavored butters contained in the first chapter would work as well.

2½ pounds lamb shoulder chops (½ inch thick; either round bone or blade) or leg of lamb steaks
¼ cup extra virgin olive oil, plus extra if cooking in a skillet
2 tablespoons fresh lemon juice
1 teaspoon kosher salt
½ teaspoon freshly ground black pepper
2 garlic cloves

1. Cut the lamb into 6 equal portions.

2. Combine the olive oil, lemon juice, salt, and pepper in a large resealable plastic bag; press in the garlic (about 2 teaspoons) and add the lamb. Seal the bag and knead until the chops are evenly coated with the marinade. Set them aside to marinate at room temperature for 30 minutes.

3. Preheat a grill pan over high heat until hot. Remove the lamb from the bag, pat it very dry with paper towels, and grill it (you may need to do it in 2 batches) on the grill pan for 2 to 3 minutes per side for medium-rare. Or cook the lamb in olive oil in a skillet over high heat for 2 minutes per side.

continued on next page

4 tablespoons Steak Butter (see page 19) cut into 4 pieces, at room temperature

4. Transfer 4 lamb chop portions to 4 serving plates; top each chop with a tablespoon of the butter. Cover loosely with aluminum foil, set them aside for 5 minutes, then serve.

5. Meanwhile, transfer the remaining 2 lamb chop portions to a plate and set them aside, uncovered, to cool to room temperature. Then transfer them to a bowl (cover with plastic wrap) or a resealable plastic bag with their juices and refrigerate them for use the next day.

how can i
COOK MEATS TO PERFECT DONENESS?

Using an instant-read thermometer is a good start, but meat continues to cook once it is off the heat. It is important when cooking meat to remove it to the serving platter when it is 5°F below the temperature you want it to reach. Cover it loosely with a sheet of aluminum foil and let it stand for 5 minutes. The temperature will rise 5° to 10°F, depending on the size of the piece of meat and the temperature of the oven. There's an added bonus: The juices will redistribute throughout the meat, so they won't be lost when you carve it. When cooking steaks, get in the habit of pressing them gently to judge the doneness. The firmer they are, the more done they will be in the center.

Herbed Lamb and Feta Burgers

MAKES 6 SERVINGS ■ HANDS-ON TIME: 25 MINUTES ■ TOTAL PREPARATION TIME: 25 MINUTES

This recipe is slightly miraculous: You take just a little more than three-quarters of a pound of cooked lamb shoulder chops and turn them into a delicious entrée for six with the simple addition of bread crumbs, feta cheese, and an egg. Indeed, you can use this recipe as a template for repurposing the same amount of leftover cooked pork chops or beefsteak, so try to remember it the next time those ingredients accumulate in the fridge.

1 medium onion

3 tablespoons extra virgin olive oil

2 cooked lamb chop portions (reserved from Grilled Lamb Chops with Steak Butter, page 295)

2 tablespoons fresh oregano or basil leaves

4 ounces feta cheese

1 large egg

¾ cup plain dry bread crumbs

¼ teaspoon freshly ground black pepper

1. Chop the onion (about 1 cup). Heat 1 tablespoon olive oil in a large skillet over medium heat until hot. Reduce the heat to medium-low; add the onion and cook for 5 minutes, or until it has softened. Transfer the onion to a small bowl and set it aside to cool slightly. Reserve the skillet.

2. Meanwhile, cut the lamb off the bone, discarding the bone, and cut the meat into 1-inch pieces. Transfer the pieces to a food processor fitted with the chopping blade; add the oregano and pulse 6 to 8 times until the meat is chopped into medium-fine pieces.

3. Finely crumble the feta (about 1 cup). Beat the egg lightly in a medium bowl; stir in the lamb mixture, ¼ cup bread crumbs, the onion, cheese, and pepper. Shape the mixture into 6 burgers. The burgers will be soft and a little wet.

4. Spread out the remaining ½ cup bread crumbs in a pie plate or soup plate. Heat the remaining 2 tablespoons olive oil in the reserved large skillet over medium heat until hot. Gently dip the burgers into the bread crumbs to coat them lightly on all sides; shake off any excess crumbs. Add the burgers to the skillet and cook for 3 minutes per side, or until golden and heated through. Serve right away.

Top Blade Steaks with Cherry Pepper Sauce

MAKES 4 SERVINGS ■ HANDS-ON TIME: 25 MINUTES ■ TOTAL PREPARATION TIME: 25 MINUTES

I think of top blade steaks, cut from the animal's shoulder, as belonging to the same category as lamb shoulder chops: They are cheaper, chewier, and more flavorful than more tender cuts. Their one shortcoming is a ribbon of tough gristle running down the middle of the steak. You can deal with this gristle in either of two ways: Cut it out in a single operation after you've cooked the steak or eat around it bite by bite. To me, this little inconvenience is peanuts when stacked up against the steak's low price and big flavor.

A quick way to chop all the tomatoes called for here is to throw them into a food processor and then pulse them a few times. If you can't find cherry peppers, use pickled jalapeños. Whichever chile you use, add it to your taste. Three out of four of my hard-to-please taste-testing panelists thought I'd specified exactly the right amount of spicy hotness. Ruthie thought it was too darned hot.

This recipe deliberately requires you to make more sauce than necessary for the steaks. The leftover sauce is earmarked for the pasta in the recipe on page 300.

6 top blade, top chuck, chuck 7-bone, chuck arm, or chuck blade steaks (½ to ¾ inch thick; at least 2 pounds total)
Kosher salt and freshly ground black pepper
¼ cup extra virgin olive oil
2 pints cherry tomatoes
1 medium onion
1 garlic clove
1 teaspoon sweet paprika
4 pickled cherry peppers
½ cup dry white or red wine

1. Pat the steaks dry and season with salt and black pepper to taste. Heat 2 tablespoons olive oil in a large skillet over high heat. Reduce the heat to medium-high; add the steaks and cook them for 2 to 3 minutes per side for medium-rare. Transfer the steaks to a platter and cover them loosely with aluminum foil.

2. Meanwhile, coarsely chop the tomatoes (about 3 cups) and finely chop the onion (about 1 cup). Add the remaining 2 tablespoons olive oil to the skillet and heat over medium heat until hot. Reduce the heat to medium-low; add the onion and cook for 5 minutes, or until it has softened. Press in the garlic (about 1 teaspoon) and add the paprika; cook, stirring, for 1 minute. Stir in the tomatoes and simmer for 8 minutes, stirring occasionally.

3. Meanwhile, seed and coarsely chop the cherry peppers (about ⅓ cup). Add the wine to the skillet and simmer the mixture for 3 minutes, or until the liquid has reduced by half.

1 cup Homemade
Chicken Stock (page
10, add preparation
time) or canned broth
2 tablespoons sherry
vinegar
2 tablespoons unsalted
butter

4. Add the chicken stock, vinegar, and cherry peppers to the skillet and simmer for 5 minutes, or until the mixture has reduced to sauce consistency. Add the meat juices from the platter and the butter; swirl until the butter has melted. Add salt and black pepper to taste.

5. Remove, cover, and refrigerate 3 cups of the sauce and 2 of the steaks to make Orzo with Spicy Tomato Sauce (page 300) the next day. Transfer the remaining 4 steaks to dinner plates, top them with the remaining sauce, and serve.

Orzo with Spicy Tomato Sauce

MAKES 4 SERVINGS   HANDS-ON TIME: 15 MINUTES   TOTAL PREPARATION TIME: 20 MINUTES

Let's say you were so enthused about the Top Blade Steaks with Cherry Pepper Sauce that you ended up eating all six of the steaks you prepared. You might think you were in rough shape as you contemplated making this recipe out of the (mostly nonexistent) leftovers. Not so. Remember the leftover spicy tomato sauce? It's even better the day after. If you are, indeed, steakless, you probably have leftover protein in the fridge—bacon, chicken, shrimp—any of which can be substituted. Or bulk up the dish with some extra vegetables. (Even frozen ones. I won't tell.)

1 pound orzo
2 cooked steaks
    (reserved from Top
    Blade Steaks with
    Cherry Pepper
    Sauce, page 298)
1 tablespoon extra virgin
    olive oil
3 cups Cherry Pepper
    Sauce (reserved from
    previous recipe)
3 ounces Parmigiano-
    Reggiano
Kosher salt and freshly
    ground black pepper

1. Bring a large pot of salted water to a boil. Cook the orzo until al dente, following the package directions. Drain well and return the orzo to the cooking pot.

2. Meanwhile, cut the meat from the 2 steaks into ½-inch cubes (a scant 2 cups). Heat the olive oil in a medium skillet over medium heat until hot; add the meat and sear for 1 to 2 minutes. Transfer the meat to a bowl.

3. Add the reserved sauce to the skillet and bring the mixture to a boil over medium heat, stirring frequently. Microplane-grate the cheese (about 2 cups) or grate on the fine side of a box grater (about 1 cup).

4. To serve, add the meat, sauce, and ½ cup cheese to the orzo; add salt and black pepper to taste. Serve the remaining cheese on the side.

$\mathcal{P}$eruvian Baked Chicken Thighs

MAKES 4 SERVINGS ▪ **HANDS-ON TIME: 15 MINUTES** ▪ **TOTAL PREPARATION TIME: 1 HOUR 20 MINUTES**

Several years ago the *Gourmet* dining room was charged with making lunch for a battalion of travel writers on behalf of the Peru Tourism Bureau. Obviously, the food had to be authentically Peruvian, and it had to be delicious. I figured that there had to be at least one great Peruvian restaurant in cosmopolitan New York whose help I could enlist; in fact, there is a chain of them called Pio Pio. I went to the one on Manhattan's Upper West Side. Everything on the menu was good, and inexpensive, but I zeroed in on their specialty, *pollos a la brasa,* aka rotisserie chicken. It was so special and so specifically Peruvian that I ended up serving the Pio Pio chicken to our travel writers, who loved it. Given that the *Gourmet* dining room virtually never served food we hadn't made ourselves, this exception to the rule will have to remain our little secret.

This is Pio Pio's *pollos a la brasa* adapted, in the interest of saving time, for cut-up chicken. Their whole chicken is marinated for 8 to 24 hours before roasting on the spit. This one is marinated for 30 minutes and baked, but the meat still manages to pick up plenty of flavor. You can make this dish using white-meat chicken if you prefer; just cut down slightly on the cooking time. Meanwhile, don't be fooled by the simplicity of this recipe. It's completely delicious.

¾ cup fresh cilantro leaves

½ cup soy sauce (low sodium, if you prefer)

3 tablespoons distilled white vinegar

1½ tablespoons vegetable oil

1 tablespoon ground cumin

1½ teaspoons hot paprika

¾ teaspoon dried oregano

¼ to ½ teaspoon cayenne pepper

6 cloves garlic

12 small bone-in chicken thighs with skin (about 4 pounds)

Green Sauce (recipe follows)

1. Combine the cilantro, soy sauce, vinegar, vegetable oil, cumin, paprika, oregano, and the desired amount of cayenne in a blender; press in the garlic (about 2 tablespoons) and puree for the marinade. Combine the marinade and the chicken in a resealable plastic bag and set aside at room temperature for 30 minutes, turning the bag once.

2. Place an oven rack on the top shelf of the oven and preheat the oven to 450°F. Drain the chicken, discarding the marinade, and pat the chicken dry. Arrange the chicken on a rack in a shallow roasting pan. Roast for 20 to 30 minutes, or until crispy and cooked through. Let rest for 10 minutes before serving (Reserve 4 baked thighs for Chicken and Tomatillo Salsa Nachos, page 302.) Top each portion with some of the Green Sauce.

GREEN SAUCE: Combine 3 large scallions, trimmed and halved, ¼ cup sliced serrano chile with seeds and ribs, 1 tablespoon fresh lemon juice, 2 ounces crumbled goat cheese (½ cup), 1 tablespoon vegetable oil, ½ teaspoon salt, ¼ teaspoon black pepper, and ½ cup half-and-half in a blender and purée until smooth.

Chicken and Tomatillo Salsa Nachos

MAKES 4 SERVINGS ∎ HANDS-ON TIME: 20 MINUTES ∎ TOTAL PREPARATION TIME: 30 MINUTES

Given the strength of its component parts, it's no wonder that this recipe is so versatile. If you want to make the nachos without making the Peruvian Baked Chicken Thighs, you can use any leftover cooked chicken instead or even some store-bought rotisserie chicken. If you don't want to prepare the salsa yourself, you can substitute a store-bought brand. If you can't find green (tomatillo) salsa, you can use red salsa.

But there's no substitute for the Homemade Baked Tortilla Chips. You won't miss the fat in which they're usually fried and you'll love the spices. In fact, you might be inspired to prepare these chips as a stand-alone snack, a healthful and economical alternative to the supermarket varieties.

By the way, you can easily double or triple the recipe for the nachos and serve them to a crowd.

Homemade Baked
Tortilla Chips
(page 29)
1 cup Tomatillo Salsa
(page 23, add
preparation time) or
store-bought salsa
4 chicken thighs,
reserved from
Peruvian Baked
Chicken Thighs
(page 301)
6 ounces Monterey Jack
or Cheddar cheese
2 medium scallions
1 cup sour cream

1. Prepare the Homemade Baked Tortilla Chips. Leave the oven set to 400°F.

2. Prepare the Tomatillo Salsa.

3. Meanwhile, remove and discard the skin and bones from the chicken; finely shred the meat (about 1¾ cups). Coarsely grate the cheese (about 1½ cups). Trim and thinly slice the scallions (about ¼ cup).

4. When the tortilla chips are cool, arrange them in one layer on a large ovenproof platter and top them with the chicken and cheese. Bake them for 5 to 8 minutes, or until the chicken is hot and the cheese has melted. Top the nachos with the Tomatillo Salsa, sour cream, and scallions; serve immediately.

$\mathscr{S}$autéed Fish Fillets Meunière with Citrus Butter

MAKES 4 SERVINGS ▪ **HANDS-ON TIME: 15 MINUTES** ▪ **TOTAL PREPARATION TIME: 40 MINUTES**

Sole meunière was the first meal Julia Child ate on French soil, the meal that changed her life. *Vanity Fair*'s Laura Jacobs has described it as "the simplest, purest, most implicitly French preparation of fresh fish. All it requires is butter, flour, parsley, lemon, precision, history, and heat." A cornerstone of classic French cuisine, sole meunière was also one of the first recipes I was taught at cooking school.

Working at restaurants, I learned that it's a good idea to start this dish by soaking the fish in milk, which strips it of any unpleasant fish funk and also helps to make the flour stick.

Like sole, any fish fillets cooked meunière are delicious served with nothing more than a wedge of lemon. If you want to fancy it up a bit, transfer the fillets to a plate after they're sautéed, throw a few tablespoons of butter into the pan, cook until golden, and drizzle it onto the fish. Or top it off with my Citrus Butter. You'll win either way.

2½ pounds firm, skinless, mild-flavored fish fillets, such as tilapia or catfish

2 cups milk

1 cup Wondra or unbleached all-purpose flour

Kosher salt and freshly ground black pepper

2 tablespoons unsalted butter

2 tablespoons extra virgin olive oil

4 tablespoons Citrus Butter (page 19, add preparation time)

1. Cover the fish with the milk, cover, and chill for 30 minutes. Spread out the flour in a pie plate lined with wax paper or parchment.

2. Drain the fish, discard the milk, and cut four 5- to 6-ounce pieces from the thick ends of 4 fillets. Set aside the remaining fish. Season the 4 pieces on all sides with salt and pepper to taste. Heat 1 tablespoon butter and 1 tablespoon olive oil in a large nonstick skillet. Toss the 4 fillet pieces in the flour, lifting the wax paper on both sides to move the fish around; shake off the excess flour. Place the pieces in the skillet and sauté them, turning once, for 3 to 4 minutes per side, or until they are golden and almost cooked through. Transfer the fillets to dinner plates, top each with a tablespoon of the Citrus Butter, and serve.

3. Meanwhile, season the fish trimmings and remaining fillets with salt and pepper to taste. Coat them with the flour remaining from above. Add the remaining 1 tablespoon butter and 1 tablespoon olive oil to another skillet; add the fish trimmings and remaining fillets to this skillet and cook, turning once, for 2 to 3 minutes per side, or until just cooked through. Break the fish into chunks with a spatula, then transfer it to a refrigerator container or medium bowl, cover it, and refrigerate it for use in Whitefish Imperial (page 304).

hitefish Imperial

MAKES 4 SERVINGS ■ HANDS-ON TIME: 15 MINUTES ■ TOTAL PREPARATION TIME: 35 MINUTES

Whitefish Imperial is a slightly less decadent (and much less expensive) version of crab imperial, a dish that is the definition of decadence. Cookbook author and cooking show host John Shields describes crab imperial this way:

> [It is] the pièce de résistance of Chesapeake Bay Blue Crab dishes . . . a richly spiced crab casserole that is served in individual portions. It is reserved for the most special of family occasions and is the showpiece selection at fine Chesapeake dinnerhouses. Restaurant reputations are often made—and unmade—on the basis of their success with this dish.

Like its inspiration, this recipe is made with a mayonnaise cream sauce and spices, and then baked. It is comfort food and, as noted, only slightly less rich than the original.

Note: You cannot use low-fat mayonnaise in this recipe. It will separate.

1 tablespoon unsalted butter
1 tablespoon unbleached all-purpose flour
2 teaspoons seafood seasoning (preferably Old Bay Seasoning)
¾ cup low-fat milk
¼ cup plus 2 tablespoons mayonnaise
1 tablespoon fresh lemon juice
1 teaspoon Worcestershire sauce
1 teaspoon Dijon mustard
¼ teaspoon hot sauce
2 cups cooked fish (about 1 pound; reserved from Sautéed Fish Fillets Meunière with Citrus Butter, page 303)
1 tablespoon drained capers
Kosher salt and freshly ground black pepper
¼ teaspoon sweet or hot paprika

1. Preheat the oven to 375°F. Grease four 8-ounce ramekins and place them on a rimmed baking sheet.

2. Melt the butter in a small saucepan over medium-low heat. Add the flour and seafood seasoning; stir until smooth. Add the milk gradually, whisking until smooth; bring the mixture to a boil. Remove from the heat.

3. Stir ¼ cup mayonnaise into the sauce along with the lemon juice, Worcestershire sauce, mustard, and hot sauce. Break the fish into small pieces and gently stir it into the sauce along with the capers and salt and pepper to taste.

4. Divide the mixture among the ramekins. Top each with some of the 2 tablespoons mayonnaise and a sprinkle of paprika. Bake until heated through and the mayonnaise on top begins to brown, about 20 minutes. Serve right away.

$\mathcal{C}$elery Root and Potato Soup with Blue Cheese and Apples Ⓥ

MAKES 4 SERVINGS ▪ HANDS-ON TIME: 35 MINUTES ▪ TOTAL PREPARATION TIME: 55 MINUTES

Typically, you find the basic ingredients here—celery, apples, and walnuts—in a Waldorf salad. I added the blue cheese as a bonus, but by all means leave it out if you're not a fan. Or garnish the soup with goat cheese and walnuts. In fact, this soup is very versatile. If you're not partial to Waldorf salad flavors, you can go in any number of different directions instead, adding ham, sausage, chicken, carrots, or spinach.

By the way, you'll notice that there's no thickener and no cream in this recipe. There's no need for them because the celery root and potatoes, when pureed, produce all the creamy thickness you could ask for.

½ cup walnut pieces
2 small Golden Delicious apples
2 pounds celery root (see page 306)
1 medium onion
2 tablespoons unsalted butter or vegetable oil
1½ pounds Yukon gold potatoes
6 cups Homemade Vegetable or Chicken Stock (pages 11 and 10, add preparation time) or canned broth
3 ounces Maytag or other good-quality blue cheese

1. Preheat the oven to 350°F. Spread the walnuts out on a rimmed baking sheet and toast until golden, 7 to 10 minutes. Remove to a cooling rack and let cool to room temperature, then finely chop the nuts. Transfer to a bowl and set aside until ready to serve.

2. Meanwhile, peel and core the apples and cut them into 16 wedges; cut the wedges crosswise into ½-inch pieces (about 2¼ cups). Peel and thinly slice the celery root (about 6 cups) and the onion (about 1 cup). Heat 1 tablespoon butter in a large heavy saucepan over medium heat until bubbly. Add the apple pieces and cook, stirring constantly, until they begin to brown; transfer them to a bowl, cover, and set aside. Melt the remaining 1 tablespoon butter in the saucepan. Reduce the heat to medium-low; add the onion and cook for 5 minutes, or until it has softened.

3. Scrub, peel, and thinly slice the potatoes (about 4 cups). Add the vegetable stock, celery root, and potatoes to the saucepan and bring to a boil over high heat. Reduce the heat to low, cover, and cook for about 20 minutes, or until the celery root and potatoes are tender.

continued on next page

4. Transfer the soup to a blender in small batches and blend until smooth; transfer to a large bowl. Stir the soup in the bowl; transfer 2 cups to a tight container and refrigerate for use the next day in Linguine with Mussels and Celery Root Sauce (page 307).

5. Return the remaining soup to the pan and reheat. Crumble the blue cheese (about ¾ cup). Serve the soup garnished with the sautéed apples, crumbled blue cheese, and toasted walnuts.

what is CELERY ROOT?

Celery root, or celeriac, is the product of a special variety of celery that is cultivated just for the root. Although the gnarled, brown ball covered with fine root hairs wouldn't win any prizes for beauty, its flavor intensity gives it star power. A small root can deliver big celery taste to soups, sauces, and salads. In the supermarket, select celery root that is small, clean, and firm. Large roots tend to be porous in the center. Peel and slice, chop, or shred the root just before use and toss it with some lemon juice, if you are serving it raw.

$\mathcal{L}$inguine with Mussels and Celery Root Sauce

MAKES 4 SERVINGS   **HANDS-ON TIME: 35 MINUTES**   **TOTAL PREPARATION TIME: 40 MINUTES**

This recipe was a little gift from the gods of chance. The first time I made Celery Root and Potato Soup, I had some left over and I stashed it in the fridge. The next day, I was rummaging around for some lunch and found not only the leftover soup, but a batch of mussels in tomato sauce left over from a recipe tested at work. *Boing!* I combined the two leftovers, heated the mixture up, and happily wolfed it down. Then I realized I could stretch it even further if I treated the combination as a sauce, not a soup, and tossed it with linguine. Done.

2 pounds mussels (preferably cultivated, 40 to 70 mussels)

1 small onion

1 tablespoon extra virgin olive oil

One 14½-ounce can chopped tomatoes (preferably fire roasted)

2 tablespoons drained capers

½ teaspoon freshly grated lemon zest

1 tablespoon fresh lemon juice

Kosher salt

¼ teaspoon crushed red pepper flakes

1 pound linguine or spaghetti

2 cups Celery Root and Potato Soup (reserved from recipe on page 305)

Freshly ground black pepper

1. Bring a large pot of salted water to a boil. Scrub the mussels well with a brush under cold running water and remove the beards. Discard any that won't close. Chop the onion (about ½ cup).

2. Heat the olive oil in a large saucepan or Dutch oven over medium heat until hot. Reduce the heat to medium-low; add the onion and cook for 5 minutes, or until it has softened. Add the tomatoes, capers, lemon zest, lemon juice, ½ teaspoon salt, and the red pepper flakes. Bring the mixture to a boil over high heat. Reduce the heat to medium and cook, stirring occasionally, for 10 to 15 minutes, or until the sauce thickens slightly.

3. Add the mussels to the sauce; cover and cook for 5 to 7 minutes or until the mussels just open. Check frequently and transfer the mussels to a large bowl as they open. Discard any mussels that don't open after 6 to 8 minutes. Set the mussels aside until cool enough to handle.

4. Meanwhile, add the linguine to the boiling water and cook until al dente, following the package directions.

5. While the pasta is cooking, remove the mussels from their shells; discard the shells. Whisk the Celery Root and Potato Soup into the tomato sauce. Bring the mixture just to a boil over low heat. Stir the mussels into the sauce and cook just until they are hot; season with salt and black pepper to taste.

6. Drain the pasta thoroughly and divide it among 4 pasta bowls. Spoon the mussels and sauce over the pasta.

15

SUNDAY-NIGHT COMFORT MEALS

This is the one chapter that is not rush, rush, rush. There has to be one night of the week when you have a little more time than usual to make dinner, and that night is usually Sunday. Even so, while a few of these recipe require a little more prep than I would expect anyone to do on a weeknight, most of them don't require additional hands-on time as much as they do additional time to soak or marinate or cook in the oven or on the stove top.

But all of them fall into the category of comfort food, which is the kind of food you want on a Sunday night. Why? Because a lot of us tend to get a little blue on Sunday in anticipation of another week of school or work, even people like me who mostly stay on the sunny side of life. A favorite and familiar dish, made with love and care, and eaten with family and friends, can turn a meal into an occasion.

These recipes include meatballs, mac and cheese, vegetarian baked pasta, codfish stew, a couple of rib recipes, braised lamb chops, and pork carnitas. On a Sunday night, a meal like this can become an oasis, an opportunity to refresh yourself and prepare for the journey that begins again bright and early the next morning.

FACING PAGE: *Bibimbap.*

Deviled Bones

MAKES 6 SERVINGS   HANDS-ON TIME: 20 MINUTES   TOTAL PREPARATION TIME: 3 HOURS 15 MINUTES TO 3 HOURS 45 MINUTES

Surely you would have guessed, even if I hadn't told you, that deviled bones is a British recipe. It just sounds so gothic, doesn't it? This dish has been around since the heyday of Boswell and Johnson, when it was made with the leftover bones of a standing rib roast, which were coated with mustard and bread crumbs and baked. Apparently, this preparation was so delicious that the Brits started applying it to first-run short ribs, not just leftover prime ribs. What's so devilish about it? The mustard's heat.

The only downside to this recipe is that you have to braise the short ribs first and then add the crumb mixture. But this is unattended cooking time, and the end result—tender meaty ribs with crispy mustard crumbs—is well worth it. Try this with the Edamame Mash (page 259).

5 pounds meaty beef short ribs with the bones
Kosher salt and freshly ground black pepper
3 cups Homemade Chicken Stock (page 10, add preparation time) or canned broth
½ cup dry red wine
3 tablespoons Wondra or unbleached all-purpose flour
4 tablespoons Steak Butter (page 19, add preparation time) or salted butter
1 cup panko bread crumbs
2½ tablespoons Dijon mustard

1. Preheat the oven to 425°F. Season the short ribs on all sides with salt and pepper to taste. Arrange them in one layer in a roasting pan and roast for 30 minutes.

2. Remove the ribs from the oven; reduce the oven temperature to 350°F. Drizzle the chicken stock and red wine over the ribs; cover the pan very tightly with a lid, parchment, or aluminum foil, and return it to the oven for 2½ to 3 hours, or until the ribs are very tender.

3. Remove the ribs from the oven. Discard the bones, transfer the ribs to a bowl, and cover with aluminum foil. Strain the pan juices into a gravy separator and pour off the fat. Transfer 2 cups of the liquid to a saucepan, reserving the remaining pan juices for another use (such as soup). Bring the liquid to a boil over high heat. Whisk together ¼ cup water and the flour in a small bowl. Gradually whisk the flour mixture into the boiling pan juices and simmer the sauce for about 5 minutes.

4. Meanwhile, melt the Steak Butter and combine it with the panko. Preheat the broiler to high. Arrange the ribs in one layer on a rimmed baking sheet. Spread each rib with some of the mustard and top with the panko mixture. Broil the ribs for 1 to 2 minutes, watching carefully, until the crumbs just begin to brown.

5. To serve, spoon some of the sauce among 6 plates; divide the ribs on top. Serve the remaining sauce on the side.

$\mathcal{B}$raised Lamb Chops and Potatoes

MAKES 4 SERVINGS   HANDS-ON TIME: 30 MINUTES   TOTAL PREPARATION TIME: 2 HOURS 30 MINUTES

Braising is one of my favorite cooking techniques. You take a bunch of flavorful ingredients, throw them into a pot together, and gently cook them until the flavors merge into something new. The resulting whole is always greater than the sum of its parts.

In this recipe, the parts are lamb, potatoes, and tomatoes, which are substantial enough on their own so as not to need more than a single side dish to fill out the meal. I recommend the Celery and Parsley Salad with Parmigiano-Reggiano and Walnuts (page 261) and some crusty bread.

By the way, if you can't find, or don't like, sun-dried tomatoes, just substitute three medium plum tomatoes, thickly sliced. Sprinkle them with salt and layer them underneath the potatoes.

½ cup sun-dried tomatoes or ¾ cup sun-dried tomatoes packed in oil

4 shoulder lamb chops (preferably round-bone; about 1½ to 2 pounds)

Kosher salt and freshly ground black pepper

2 tablespoons extra virgin olive oil

1 large onion

3 garlic cloves

1¼ pounds large boiling potatoes, such as Yukon gold or Red Bliss

2 tablespoons fresh rosemary leaves or 1 teaspoon dried

1 cup dry red wine

2 cups Homemade Chicken Stock (page 10, add preparation time) or canned broth

1. Preheat the oven to 350°F. If using dried tomatoes not packed in oil, cover the tomatoes with hot water in a bowl; let stand until plumped, about 10 minutes, and then drain them.

2. Trim any excess fat from the lamb and season it with salt and pepper to taste. Heat 1 tablespoon olive oil in a large Dutch oven over medium-high heat until hot. Working in batches, brown the lamb for 2 to 3 minutes per side. Transfer the lamb to a bowl. Meanwhile, thinly slice the onion (about 2 cups) and garlic (about 2 tablespoons).

3. Add the remaining 1 tablespoon olive oil to the Dutch oven and reduce the heat to medium. Add the onion and cook for 8 to 10 minutes, or until it is golden, adding water, if necessary, to keep it from getting too dark. Add the garlic and cook for 1 minute more. Scrub and thinly slice the potatoes (about 4 cups). Cut the sun-dried tomatoes in half. Chop the rosemary (about 1 tablespoon).

4. Remove the onion mixture to a small bowl and stir in the sun-dried tomatoes, rosemary, ½ teaspoon salt, and ½ teaspoon pepper.

5. Add the red wine to the Dutch oven. Bring it to a boil, scraping up the brown bits at the bottom of the pan, and cook until reduced by half. Stir in the chicken stock and bring to a simmer. Carefully return the lamb with any lamb juices from the bowl to the Dutch oven, in one layer. Top with half the onion mixture and all the potatoes; sprinkle the potatoes liberally with salt and add the remaining onion mixture.

6. Cover the last layer of onion directly with a sheet of parchment or aluminum foil. Put the lid on the Dutch oven, transfer it to the oven, and braise for 2 hours, or until the lamb is very tender. Divide the chops among 4 plates and spoon some of the potatoes and onion mixture and cooking liquid on top of each one.

which POTATO?

Not every potato is right for every recipe. The two main categories of potatoes are baking and boiling. Baking potatoes, also called russet potatoes (the most famous is the Idaho), are high in starch and come out fluffy and light when they are baked. They're also great mashed. Given their starchy goodness, baking potatoes are the ones you want if you're making gnocchi or if you need a thickener for soup.

But if you're making a potato salad, you should reach for a boiling potato, like Red Bliss. Boiling potatoes hold their shape when they're cooked, and they have the added benefit of a thin skin, which means there's no need to peel them.

Some potatoes are considered all-purpose. The most famous of these is the Yukon gold, so named because of its naturally golden color, which somehow persuades us that it tastes like butter. They can be baked or broiled.

Having suggested that there is a perfect potato for every recipe, I hereby give you license to use any kind if the perfect potato isn't at hand when you need it. I never met a potato I didn't like.

Carnitas

MAKES 4 TO 6 SERVINGS   HANDS-ON TIME: 30 MINUTES, IF MAKING TORTILLAS; 15 MINUTES, IF USING STORE BOUGHT   TOTAL PREPARATION TIME: 2¾ TO 3 HOURS

Like many another chef, I've recently fallen head over heels for pork. What took me so long? Maybe it's because my mom never cooked pork when I was growing up (except for bacon). Maybe it's because when I actually started eating pork, it was at the height (or depth) of the National Pork Board's campaign to reposition the product as "the other white meat." Or maybe it's simply because I'd never been properly introduced to Latin-style pork: fatter cuts, like pork shoulder, combined with savory seasonings, then cooked slow and low.

Take carnitas, for example. "Carnitas, literally 'little meats,' are one of the splendid specialties of central Mexico, especially the state of Michoacan," writes Marilyn Tausend in *Cocina de la Familia*. "Pieces of pork are boiled in seasoned oil until tender on the inside and with a crispy exterior. They are usually shredded, daubed with salsa, and crammed into a freshly made tortilla. It is a dish that gives strength to weary spirits."

The depth of feeling expressed in that description reminds me of an episode of *The Simpsons* in which Homer waxes rhapsodic about pork after Lisa announces she's going to become a vegetarian.

Homer: Are you saying you're never going to eat any animal again? What about bacon?

Lisa: No.

Homer: Ham?

Lisa: No.

Homer: Pork chops?

Lisa: Dad, those all come from the same animal.

Homer: Heh heh heh. Ooh, yeah, right, Lisa. "A wonderful, magical animal."

The only labor-intensive parts of this recipe are cutting the meat into 1-inch cubes and, if you so choose, making homemade tortillas. The rest of the prep is simple. I cooked up a huge batch of it for a recent family reunion. None of my relatives is Hispanic and none of them has ever before reminded me of Homer Simpson. But they all dug into their carnitas with gusto.

continued on next page

2 pounds boneless pork shoulder
3 garlic cloves
2 tablespoons fresh oregano leaves or 1 teaspoon dried
2 tablespoons fresh thyme leaves or 1 teaspoon dried
1 Turkish bay leaf
½ teaspoon ground cumin
Kosher salt and freshly ground black pepper
1½ cups Homemade Chicken Stock (page 10, add preparation time) or canned broth
Vegetable oil, if needed
Masa to make 8 to 12 homemade tortillas, or store-bought corn tortillas
1 ripe Hass avocado
1 to 1½ cups fresh tomato salsa, homemade or store bought
1 cup fresh cilantro sprigs

1. Cut the pork into 1-inch cubes. Press the garlic (about 1 tablespoon). Chop the oregano (about 1 tablespoon) and thyme (about 1 tablespoon).

2. Combine the pork, garlic, oregano, thyme, bay leaf, cumin, ½ teaspoon salt, and ¼ teaspoon pepper in a deep heavy skillet (preferably cast iron). Add the chicken stock and 1½ cups water.

3. Bring the mixture to a boil over high heat; reduce the heat to very low and cover the skillet with parchment paper or aluminum foil and then the lid. Cook at a bare simmer for 1½ hours, or until the pork is very tender. Add water as needed to keep the pork partially covered with liquid.

4. Remove the cover from the skillet and simmer the pork, uncovered, stirring occasionally, for about 30 minutes, or until all the liquid has evaporated and the pork has cooked in its own fat and turned golden. If there is not enough fat left in the pan to brown the pork, add 1 to 2 tablespoons vegetable oil. Remove and discard the bay leaf.

5. Meanwhile, prepare homemade tortillas following the instructions on the masa package or wrap store-bought corn tortillas in aluminum foil and warm in a preheated 300°F oven. Halve, seed, peel, and coarsely chop the avocado.

6. To serve, top the tortillas with the pork, salsa, chopped avocado, and cilantro sprigs.

erk Spareribs

MAKES 4 SERVINGS   HANDS-ON TIME: 20 MINUTES   TOTAL PREPARATION TIME: 22 HOURS

I had my first happy encounter with jerk sauce in Jamaica, the land of its birth, a decade or so ago. I like what Helen Willinsky, the author of *Jerk: Barbecue from Jamaica,* had to say about it: "To eat jerk is to feel the African, Indian, and calypso cultures that produced it. It is not a predictable flavor, but rather a hot, spicy, uncontrolled festival that engages all your senses." The spices in question include scallions, onions, thyme, Jamaican pimiento (allspice), cinnamon, nutmeg, chile peppers, and salt. Applied at first to pork only, jerk now routinely graces barbecued chicken, seafood, and beef as well.

In this recipe, I've married the jerk sauce to pork spareribs. When it comes to cooking the ribs, I am a humble student of the fierce competitors at the annual Memphis in May World Championship Barbeque Cooking Contest. These gladiators disagree about any number of details, but everyone respects a basic rule: Low and slow is the way to go, so the tender meat will fall off the bone and into your mouth like a dream come true. These ribs need to marinate for a *looong* time and cook for 6 hours, so plan accordingly.

1 medium onion

4 medium scallions

1 Scotch bonnet chile

6 garlic cloves, smashed

⅓ cup fresh lime juice

½ cup vegetable oil

3 tablespoons soy sauce (low sodium, if you prefer)

1 tablespoon ground allspice

2 tablespoons fresh thyme leaves

1 tablespoon packed dark brown sugar

2 teaspoons kosher salt

½ teaspoon ground nutmeg

½ teaspoon ground cinnamon

5 to 6 pounds pork spareribs (preferably St. Louis style)

1. Coarsely chop the onion (about 1 cup); trim and chop the scallions (about ½ cup); remove the stem on the chile, and smash the garlic. Combine the onion, scallions, Scotch bonnet, garlic, lime juice, vegetable oil, soy sauce, allspice, thyme, brown sugar, salt, nutmeg, and cinnamon in a blender and puree until smooth.

2. Remove the silver skin from the ribs and cut them into 6- to 8-rib lengths. Combine the ribs with the pureed marinade in 2 resealable plastic bags; seal the bags and knead until the ribs are evenly coated with the marinade. Refrigerate for 16 hours, turning occasionally.

3. Put an oven rack in the middle of the oven and preheat the oven to 250°F. Remove the ribs from the marinade, allowing the excess to drip off. Discard the marinade. Arrange the ribs, meat side up, in a baking pan. Put the pan in the oven, cover with aluminum foil, and roast the ribs for 2 hours. Uncover the pan and roast for 4 hours more, or until the meat is very tender. Serve right away with plenty of napkins.

$\mathcal{S}$unday-Night Stir-fry Pork and Noodles

MAKES 4 SERVINGS ■ HANDS-ON TIME: 45 MINUTES ■ TOTAL PREPARATION TIME: 45 MINUTES

Chinese stir-fry recipes require that all the ingredients be sliced, diced, and premeasured before you even turn on the burner. Why? Because the ingredients spend so little time in the pan that if you peeled and Microplaned the ginger while you were cooking the pork, for example, the pork would blacken before you had a chance to add the ginger.

The extra hands-on time here is well worth it, given the finished recipe's many lovely layers of flavor and texture. When I told Ruthie that this dish was going to live in the Sunday Night Comfort Meals chapter, she said, "Perfect. It's noodles with a hearty sauce, and that's where it belongs."

Note: If you have the time, throw the pork into the freezer for 30 minutes before you slice it. It's much easier to slice if it's partially frozen.

1 pork tenderloin (about 1 pound)
1 tablespoon plus 2 teaspoons cornstarch
1 tablespoon sake, rice wine, or dry sherry
1 tablespoon seasoned rice vinegar
1 tablespoon soy sauce (low sodium, if you prefer)
One 1½-inch piece fresh ginger
4 ounces shiitake mushrooms
1 small head napa cabbage
6 medium scallions
½ pound linguine
¼ cup vegetable oil
½ teaspoon crushed red pepper flakes
1 garlic clove
1 cup Homemade Chicken Stock (page 10, add preparation time) or canned broth

1. Bring a large pot of salted water to a boil. Trim any fat and the silver skin from the tenderloin. Cut the tenderloin in half lengthwise, then very thinly slice it crosswise.

2. Whisk together 1 tablespoon cornstarch, the sake, rice vinegar, and soy sauce in a medium bowl. Add the pork to the bowl and toss to coat the pieces evenly. Set the pork aside to marinate while you prepare the rest of the ingredients.

3. Peel and Microplane-grate the ginger (about 1½ teaspoons). Clean the shiitakes, trim off and discard the stems, and cut the caps into 1-inch pieces (about 3 cups). Halve and core the cabbage; slice it crosswise into ½-inch strips (about 6 cups). Trim and thinly slice the scallions (about ¾ cup).

4. When the pot of water has come to a boil, add the linguine. Cook until al dente, following the package directions. Drain the pasta well, reserving 1 cup of the cooking liquid; return the drained pasta to the cooking pot.

5. Heat 2 tablespoons vegetable oil in a large skillet over high heat until very hot; add the pork and stir-fry for 2 minutes. Add the ginger and red pepper flakes to the skillet. Press in the garlic (about 1 teaspoon) and stir-fry for 30 seconds more. Transfer the pork to a bowl.

3 tablespoons oyster
sauce
1 tablespoon hoisin
sauce
1 teaspoon toasted
sesame oil
¼ teaspoon five-spice
powder (optional)
Kosher salt

6. Add the remaining 2 tablespoons vegetable oil to the skillet and heat over medium heat until hot. Add the shiitakes and cook for 4 minutes, or until they are light golden.

7. Meanwhile, whisk together the remaining 2 teaspoons cornstarch and ¼ cup chicken stock in a medium bowl until smooth. Whisk in the remaining ¾ cup chicken stock, the oyster sauce, hoisin, sesame oil, and five-spice powder, if using.

8. When the shiitakes have cooked, add the cabbage and scallions to the skillet and cook for 2 minutes more, or until they have wilted. Stir in the cornstarch mixture and cook, stirring, until the mixture comes to a boil and thickens. Add some of the reserved pasta cooking water until the mixture reaches a nice saucy consistency.

9. Add the cabbage mixture and the pork to the linguine and toss well. Cook over medium heat just until everything is hot. Add salt to taste and serve immediately.

how do you
USE TOASTED SESAME OIL?

Toasted sesame oil is best added to a recipe as a condiment for flavoring just before serving; a little goes a long way, so don't overdo it. A frequent ingredient in stir-fry dishes, it is also a last-minute addition to a bowl of peas, carrots, broccoli, leafy greens, mashed potatoes, noodles, or rice, and I add it to marinades and salad dressings. Toasted sesame oil is not used for cooking because the amount of oil usually needed to cook a dish would add too much flavor, and the oil itself burns more easily than most cooking oils. Sesame oil, like other nut and seed oils, tends to go rancid quickly and should be stored in a cool place away from light. Store it in the fridge to make sure it will be good the next time. It will keep for several months in the refrigerator. If it solidifies, just put the bottle into a bowl of hot water and it will liquefy quickly.

Roast Chicken Stuffed with Zucchini and Cheese

MAKES 4 SERVINGS   HANDS-ON TIME: 40 MINUTES   TOTAL PREPARATION TIME: 1 HOUR 20 MINUTES

No matter which method you use to cook it, chicken has a tendency to dry out. One way to ensure that the meat stays juicy is to put a layer of moist stuffing between the meat and the skin. This stuffing, made of zucchini and cheese, not only keeps the chicken meat incredibly moist, but also provides great flavor. This recipe has become a new family favorite.

1 medium zucchini
   (about ½ pound)
Kosher salt
½ medium onion
2 tablespoons extra
   virgin olive oil
1 garlic clove
1 teaspoon fresh thyme
   leaves
1½ ounces Parmigiano-
   Reggiano
2 slices firm white bread
¼ cup whole milk ricotta
Freshly ground black
   pepper
One 3½-pound chicken
Foolproof Egg Lemon
   Sauce (page 17, add
   preparation time;
   optional)

1. Coarsely grate the zucchini (about 2 cups); toss it with ¼ teaspoon salt and set it aside in a strainer to drain for 15 minutes. Meanwhile, finely chop the onion (about ½ cup). Place an oven rack in the middle of the oven and preheat the oven to 450°F.

2. Heat 1 tablespoon olive oil in a large skillet over medium heat until hot. Add the onion and cook for 6 to 8 minutes, or until it is golden. Press in the garlic (about 1 teaspoon) and cook for 1 minute more. Finely chop the thyme (about ½ teaspoon). Squeeze the zucchini by small handfuls to remove excess liquid.

3. Stir the thyme and well-drained zucchini into the skillet and sauté for 2 minutes over medium heat; transfer the mixture to a medium bowl and set aside.

4. Microplane-grate the Parmigiano-Reggiano (about 1 cup) or grate on the fine side of a box grater (about ½ cup). Pulse the bread in a blender to make 1 cup bread crumbs. Add the bread crumbs, the Parmigiano-Reggiano, the ricotta, and ¼ teaspoon pepper to the zucchini mixture. Add salt to taste.

5. Place the chicken in a shallow roasting pan. Gently loosen the skin on the breasts and thighs, trying not to tear it; rub the skin with the remaining 1 tablespoon olive oil and season with salt and pepper. Stuff the zucchini mixture evenly under the loosened skin of the chicken. (This is a messy project; just do your best.)

6. Roast the chicken for 10 minutes. Reduce the oven temperature to 375°F and roast the chicken for 20 minutes. Cover the chicken loosely with foil and roast for 25 to 30 minutes more, or until a meat thermometer inserted into an inner thigh registers 165°F.

7. Remove the chicken from the oven and set it aside for 10 minutes before carving. Meanwhile, prepare the Foolproof Egg Lemon Sauce, if using, and serve with the chicken.

Velvet Chicken with Sugar Snap Peas and Cashews

MAKES 4 SERVINGS   HANDS-ON TIME: 1 HOUR   TOTAL PREPARATION TIME: 1 HOUR

In the mid-eighties, when I was still working in the test kitchen at *Gourmet* but before I switched to my job as chef of the dining room, I became a huge fan of velveting, the Chinese method of marinating protein. First you coat the food with a mixture of egg whites, cornstarch, and salt. Then, after 30 minutes or so, you quickly deep-fry it. Finally, you stir-fry it. These steps prevent overcooking and seal in flavor. They also give the food a tempting, glossy appearance and a smooth, velvety texture. Hence the name of the process.

If you'd prefer not to deep-fry your velveted protein, you can poach it in water, as I've done here. The rest of the recipe is a typical stir-fry: vegetables (bell pepper and snap peas), sauce (black bean, soy sauce, and sake), and flavorings (ginger, garlic, and scallion). There are a lot of ingredients in this dish, and they're all tasty, but what people will remember is that velvety chicken.

1 large egg white

1½ tablespoons plus 1 teaspoon cornstarch

2 tablespoons sake, rice wine, or dry sherry

Kosher salt

1 pound boneless, skinless chicken breast halves

1 medium scallion

One 1-inch piece fresh ginger

3 garlic cloves

¾ cup Homemade Chicken Stock (page 10, add preparation time) or canned broth

1 tablespoon black bean chili or garlic sauce (preferably Lee Kum Kee brand)

1 tablespoon soy sauce (low sodium, if you prefer)

1. Whisk together the egg white, 1½ tablespoons cornstarch, 1 tablespoon sake, and 1 teaspoon salt in a medium bowl. Cut the chicken into 1-inch cubes and add to the mixture; toss until the chicken is well coated. Cover and refrigerate for 30 minutes.

2. Meanwhile, trim and thinly slice the scallion (about 2 tablespoons) and peel and Microplane-grate the ginger (about 1 teaspoon); combine in a small bowl. Press the garlic (about 1 tablespoon) into the bowl.

3. Bring a large pot of salted water to a boil over high heat. Whisk together the remaining 1 teaspoon cornstarch and ¼ cup of the chicken stock in a small bowl. Whisk in the remaining ½ cup chicken stock, the remaining 1 tablespoon sake, the black bean sauce, soy sauce, rice vinegar, and sugar.

4. Remove the strings from the peas. When the water has come to a boil, add half the peas and cook them for 30 seconds; remove them with a slotted spoon and pat them dry. Repeat with the remaining peas. Thinly slice the bell pepper (about 1⅓ cups).

1 tablespoon unseasoned rice vinegar
½ teaspoon sugar
½ pound sugar snap peas
1 medium red bell pepper
2 tablespoons vegetable oil
½ cup raw cashew pieces
Cooked white rice, as an accompaniment

5. Reduce the boiling water to a simmer. Stir the chicken to recoat the pieces. Using a slotted spoon, add the chicken to the water and cook for 1 to 2 minutes, or until the pieces are white on the outside. Drain them thoroughly and set them aside.

6. Heat the vegetable oil in a large skillet over medium heat until hot. Add the cashews; cook for 1 to 2 minutes, or just until they begin to brown. (Be careful; they brown quickly.) Remove the cashews from the oil using a slotted spoon and drain on paper towels.

7. Add the bell pepper to the skillet; cook, stirring, for 1 minute. Add the scallion mixture to the skillet; cook for about 20 seconds. Whisk the chicken stock mixture and stir it in; bring it to a boil.

8. Add the chicken and simmer over medium-low heat for 1 to 2 minutes, or until the chicken is cooked through. Stir in the peas and cashews and cook until hot. Serve with white rice.

all about

THICKENING A SAUCE

Whether you reach for the flour, cornstarch, or arrowroot, you can make a perfect thickened sauce, but the thickener you choose will determine its appearance. Flour (either all-purpose or Wondra) will make an opaque sauce; cornstarch will make a translucent sauce; and arrowroot will make a transparent sauce. The thickening power of each varies, but there is an easy formula to help you get the right amount each time: First, measure the liquid you want to thicken. It takes 1 tablespoon of flour for every cup of liquid to make a thin sauce, 2 tablespoons of flour per cup of liquid to make a medium sauce, and 3 tablespoons flour per cup of liquid to make a thick sauce. If you want to use cornstarch, it takes only ½ tablespoon for a thin sauce, 1 tablespoon for a medium sauce, and 1½ tablespoons for a thick sauce. With arrowroot, use a scant ½ tablespoon for a thin sauce, a scant 1 tablespoon for a medium sauce, and a scant 1½ tablespoons for a thick sauce. Flour will give you a sauce that is more tolerant of heat and can be gently reheated. Cornstarch and arrowroot should be cooked only briefly and can break down if reheated too long. To make an easy sauce, you can whisk flour, cornstarch, or arrowroot with a little bit of cold liquid, then whisk that mixture into the pot of boiling liquid you want to thicken. Or, if you are using flour, you can heat it gently with an equal amount of butter (aka roux) and then whisk in the liquid and bring the sauce to a boil.

$\mathscr{C}$hicken Escabeche

MAKES 4 SERVINGS   HANDS-ON TIME: 20 MINUTES   TOTAL PREPARATION TIME: 2 HOURS 50 MINUTES

Escabeche, from a Persian word meaning "acid food," is a venerable marinade made of olive oil, vinegar or citrus, onions, garlic, black peppercorns, and bay leaves. Applied to fish, seafood, chicken, and vegetables, it probably originated as "a fish dish in the medieval Arab world that was carried through Spain, France and Italy, across the Atlantic to Central and South America and then all the way over to the Philippines," according to Rick Bayless in *Mexico: One Plate at a Time.* It's also found under slightly different names in other countries: *escovitch* in Jamaica, *savoro* in Greece, and *scabetche* in North Africa.

There are two main reasons why *escabeche* (pronounced "es-cah-*bay*-chay") is so widely beloved: It's easy to make and it's deeply flavorful. You just throw the ingredients into a heavy saucepan or Dutch oven, slide it into the oven, and forget about it. In this case, the chicken is thoroughly imbued with the flavors of the cooking liquid, and the result is a kind of pickled stew that's equally wonderful served hot or cold.

3 medium onions

3 medium carrots

2 jalapeño chiles (make sure they have heat; see page 6)

4 garlic cloves

2 tablespoons fresh oregano leaves or 1 teaspoon dried

1 cup extra virgin olive oil

½ cup white wine vinegar

Kosher salt

1 Turkish bay leaf

3½ pounds cut-up chicken (8 to 10 pieces)

Freshly ground black pepper

Cooked white rice, as an accompaniment

1. Preheat the oven to 350°F. Thinly slice the onions (about 3 cups), carrots (about 1⅓ cups), and the jalapeños crosswise with the seeds and ribs (about ¼ cup). Combine them in a large Dutch oven; press the garlic (about 1 tablespoon plus 1 teaspoon) into the Dutch oven. Chop the oregano (1 tablespoon) and add to the Dutch oven along with the olive oil, vinegar, 1½ teaspoons salt, and the bay leaf; toss to combine.

2. Season the chicken pieces with salt and pepper to taste. Add the chicken to the Dutch oven and toss with the vegetables. Cover the pan first with a sheet of parchment or aluminum foil and then with the lid.

3. Bake the chicken and vegetables for 2½ hours, or until the chicken is very tender. Pour the contents of the Dutch oven into a large strainer or colander placed over a large bowl. Remove and discard the bay leaf; set the chicken and vegetables aside.

4. Pour the liquid from the bowl into a gravy separator or use a large spoon to remove and discard the fat. Return the remaining liquid to the Dutch oven and boil it until it has reduced by one-third. Season the sauce with salt and pepper to taste; return the chicken and vegetables to the Dutch oven and heat until hot. Serve with rice as an accompaniment.

Mexican Meatballs

MAKES 4 SERVINGS   HANDS-ON TIME: 40 MINUTES   TOTAL PREPARATION TIME: 65 MINUTES

This is not a traditional recipe, it's just me adding some of my favorite Mexican ingredients—fresh and smoked jalapeños (aka chipotles), salsa, cumin, and oregano—to ground turkey meatballs in tomato sauce. Is it a stretch for me to claim that this dish is sort of the Mexican version of Italian spaghetti and meatballs, except served on rice? Perhaps. Then again, a rose by any other name . . .

1 medium onion
3 tablespoons vegetable oil
1 medium jalapeño chile (make sure it has heat; see page 6) or pickled jalapeño chile
2 teaspoons fresh oregano leaves or ⅓ teaspoon dried
2 garlic cloves
½ teaspoon ground cumin
Kosher salt
1 slice firm white or whole wheat bread
1 large egg
1 pound ground turkey
1 small chipotle chile in adobo sauce
1 cup fresh or jarred salsa
One 8-ounce can tomato sauce (preferably fire roasted)
½ cup beer
Cooked white rice, as an accompaniment

1. Finely chop the onion (about 1 cup). Heat 1½ tablespoons vegetable oil in a large skillet over medium heat until hot. Reduce the heat to medium-low; add the onion and cook for 5 minutes, or until it has softened. Meanwhile, finely chop the jalapeño (about 1½ tablespoons). Chop the oregano (about 1 teaspoon).

2. Press the garlic (about 2 teaspoons) into the skillet; add the jalapeño, oregano, cumin, and a pinch of salt and cook, stirring, for 2 minutes. Transfer the mixture to a medium bowl and set aside for 5 minutes to cool slightly. Wipe out and reserve the skillet. Pulse the bread in a blender or food processor to make ½ cup fresh bread crumbs. Beat the egg lightly in a small bowl.

3. Add the turkey, bread crumbs, egg, and 2 teaspoons salt to the cooled vegetable mixture. Form into 12 balls using wet hands. Heat the remaining 1½ tablespoons vegetable oil in the reserved skillet over high heat until hot; reduce the heat to medium-high. Add the meatballs and cook until they have browned on all sides, about 3 minutes. Meanwhile, mince the chipotle (about 1½ teaspoons).

4. Add the salsa, tomato sauce, beer, and chipotle to the skillet. Bring to a boil over high heat; reduce the heat to low. Cover and simmer the meatballs for 15 minutes. Uncover and simmer for 5 to 10 minutes more, or until the sauce has thickened and the meatballs are cooked through. Serve the meatballs and sauce over the rice.

African Salt Cod and Tomato Stew

MAKES 4 SERVINGS   HANDS-ON TIME: ABOUT 25 MINUTES   TOTAL PREPARATION TIME: ABOUT 13 HOURS

Human beings all over the world have been eating salt cod under one name or another for at least the last five hundred years. One of the oldest ways of preserving fish, salting allowed the fish to travel long distances under all kinds of conditions without spoiling, rendering it an important product of international commerce in the process. Salt cod is used today in cuisines from Europe and the Mediterranean to West Africa, Brazil, and the Caribbean. The Husband is a huge fan of brandade, a French puree of salt cod, potato, garlic, and olive oil.

Delicious as it is, preparing salt cod is time-consuming: It must be soaked for hours, to plump up the fish and leach out the excess salt. I looked to Africa for inspiration for this recipe, a thick chowderlike stew flavored with Scotch bonnet chile and cilantro. (Don't worry. The sugar tempers the pepper's heat.) A green salad and some crusty bread would round out the meal nicely.

1 pound salt cod
1 large onion
4 tablespoons extra virgin olive oil
1 pound boiling potatoes, such as Yukon gold or Red Bliss
1½ pounds plum tomatoes (about 6 medium)
½ to 1 Scotch bonnet or habanero chile
1 tablespoon firmly packed dark brown sugar
1 garlic clove
½ cup dry white wine
¼ cup fresh cilantro leaves
Lemon wedges, for garnish

1. Combine the cod with cold water to cover in a medium bowl. Cover and soak in the refrigerator for 12 hours, changing the water several times. Drain and rinse the cod; cut it into 1-inch pieces. Slice the onion (about 2 cups).

2. Heat 1 tablespoon olive oil in a large skillet over medium heat until hot. Add the onion and cook for about 8 minutes, until it is golden; remove it to a bowl using a slotted spoon.

3. Meanwhile, scrub the potatoes and cut them into 1-inch cubes. Add 2 tablespoons oil to the skillet along with the potatoes and cook, stirring occasionally, for about 5 minutes, or until the potatoes are golden but not cooked through. Transfer the potatoes to the bowl with the onion, using a slotted spoon.

4. Chop the tomatoes (about 3 cups); finely chop the Scotch bonnet (1 to 2 teaspoons). Add the remaining 1 tablespoon olive oil to the skillet along with the tomatoes, chile, and brown sugar. Press the garlic (about 1 teaspoon) into the mixture and cook for 5 minutes.

5. Return the onion and potatoes to the skillet; add the cod and white wine, cover the pan tightly, and simmer the stew over low heat for 30 minutes, stirring occasionally. Chop the cilantro (about 2 tablespoons) and sprinkle it over the stew. Serve garnished with lemon wedges.

$\mathcal{S}$hrimp Dumplings in Chinese Chicken Stock

MAKES 4 SERVINGS   HANDS-ON TIME: 35 MINUTES   TOTAL PREPARATION TIME: 45 MINUTES

The Jewish people are justly proud of the restorative powers of their chicken soup, but I think the Chinese can give 'em a run for their money. What makes the Chinese version so special? Gingerroot, which reputedly has the power to settle your stomach and clear out your sinuses. Throw in shrimp dumplings, and Chinese chicken stock becomes the ultimate comfort food. My thanks to cookbook author Eileen Yin Fei Lo, who turned me on to Chinese chicken stock during one of her visits to my show on the Food Network.

9 medium scallions

One 2-inch piece fresh ginger

3 garlic cloves

6 cups Homemade Chicken Stock (page 10, add preparation time) or canned broth

1 teaspoon black peppercorns

6 ounces snow peas

1 small red bell pepper

¼ cup drained sliced water chestnuts

½ pound peeled and deveined medium shrimp

1½ tablespoons soy sauce (low sodium, if you prefer)

2 teaspoons cornstarch

32 wonton wrappers (3½ by 3 inches)

1. Cut 6 scallions crosswise into thirds and thinly slice the remaining 3 (a heaping ⅓ cup). Peel and coarsely slice the ginger and smash the garlic. Combine the chicken stock, scallion thirds, ginger, garlic, and peppercorns in a medium saucepan and bring the mixture to a boil over high heat. Cover the pan, reduce the heat to low, and let the mixture simmer for 20 minutes.

2. Meanwhile, bring a large pot of salted water to a boil over high heat. Trim the snow peas and thinly slice the bell pepper (about ¾ cup). Coarsely chop the water chestnuts.

3. Combine the shrimp, water chestnuts, two-thirds of the sliced scallions, the soy sauce, and cornstarch in a food processor fitted with the chopping blade; pulse until finely chopped but not pureed.

4. Place 4 wonton wrappers on a work surface; mound a slightly rounded tablespoon of the shrimp mixture on each. Moisten the edges, top with another wrapper, and press firmly around the edges to seal the dumplings. Repeat three times to make 16 dumplings.

5. When the water has come to a boil, add the dumplings, 4 to 6 at a time. Return the water just to a simmer and gently cook for 3 to 4 minutes, or until the wonton wrappers are tender. Using a slotted spoon, remove the dumplings to 4 pasta or soup plates.

6. When the chicken stock mixture has simmered for 20 minutes, strain it, discarding the solids, and return it to the saucepan. Add the snow peas and bell pepper and return it to a boil. Ladle the chicken stock and vegetables over the dumplings. Garnish with the remaining sliced scallions.

Odd Lots Mac and Cheese

MAKES 6 LARGE SERVINGS   HANDS-ON TIME: ABOUT 30 MINUTES   TOTAL PREPARATION TIME: 55 MINUTES

I don't know about you, but my fridge tends to fill up with odd assortments of small chunks of cheese: a leftover bit of Brie, some blue cheese bought for guests a week earlier, an end piece of cream cheese used for bagels last Sunday, a slice of mozzarella that didn't make it onto a sandwich. You don't want to toss these odds and ends, but you can't figure out how to use them.

Recently, I had a eureka moment: Why not throw them all together into a big pot of macaroni and cheese? Most cheeses play very nicely together. As long as there are some good melting cheeses in the mix, any combo will do.

This recipe is for straight make-it-and-eat-it mac and cheese. It will seem a little soupy when it's freshly done, but I like it that way. If you don't, just let it sit in the pot for 10 minutes and it will become more noodle-y. If you prefer it crunchy, preheat the oven to 400°F; pour the mac and cheese into a shallow casserole or gratin dish; top it with bread crumbs, or crushed potato chips or crackers; and bake it for 10 minutes, or until the crust is golden.

1 quart whole milk
6 tablespoons (¾ stick) unsalted butter
6 tablespoons unbleached all-purpose flour
8 ounces assorted cheeses (see Note)
1 tablespoon Worcestershire sauce
1 teaspoon dry mustard
1 teaspoon Tabasco sauce
Kosher salt
1 pound elbow macaroni
Freshly ground black pepper

1. Bring a large pot of salted water to a boil over high heat. Heat the milk in a large saucepan over medium heat until it is hot.

2. Melt the butter over medium-low heat in a medium saucepan. Add the flour and cook, whisking, for 5 minutes. Whisk in the hot milk in a stream; bring the mixture to a boil. Reduce the heat to low and simmer for 5 minutes.

3. Coarsely shred, cut up, or crumble the cheeses and whisk them into the milk mixture. Whisk together the Worcestershire, mustard, Tabasco, and 1 teaspoon salt and whisk into the sauce. Cook over low heat, stirring frequently, until the cheeses have melted; keep the cheese sauce warm.

4. When the pot of water comes to a boil, add the macaroni. Cook until al dente, following the package directions. Drain the macaroni, return it to the pot, and add the cheese sauce. Stir well, add salt and pepper to taste, and serve. Or set aside for 5 to 10 minutes and let the mixture firm up before serving.

NOTE: Hard cheeses and semihard cheeses such as Cheddar, Monterey Jack, and Swiss should be coarsely grated; soft cheeses such as Brie, goat, and cream cheese should be cut up or crumbled. The mix should include some flavorful cheeses; if all the cheeses are bland, the macaroni and cheese will be bland. If desired, the amount of cheese can be increased by 4 ounces.

$\mathcal{L}$entil and Eggplant Pastitsio Ⓥ

MAKES 6 SERVINGS   HANDS-ON TIME: 45 MINUTES   TOTAL PREPARATION TIME: 1 HOUR 10 MINUTES

As I noted in the introduction to the Vegetarian Cornucopia chapter, my college house-mates and I were first introduced to vegetarian food in the seventies. Our bibles then were Frances Moore Lappé's *Diet for a Small Planet* and volumes one and two of Anna Thomas's *The Vegetarian Epicure.* Any cookbook becomes a favorite if it ends up introducing you to two or three delicious and dependable recipes, but it seemed to us that just about every recipe in these three cookbooks was a gem.

One of the best recipes was the pastitsio from the first volume of *The Vegetarian Epicure,* which replaced the ground meat in the standard version of this classic Greek casserole with lentils and eggplant. This is my adaptation of that recipe. Even die-hard carnivores will find it comforting and filling.

1 cup lentils
Kosher salt
1 medium onion
¼ cup extra virgin olive oil
2 garlic cloves
1 small Italian eggplant or 2 Japanese eggplants (about 8 ounces)
2 teaspoons fresh oregano leaves or ⅓ teaspoon dried
One 8-ounce can tomato sauce (preferably fire roasted)
½ cup dry red wine
½ teaspoon ground cinnamon
Pinch of cayenne pepper
Freshly ground black pepper
2 cups whole milk

1. Bring the lentils, 4 cups water, and ¾ teaspoon salt to a boil in a medium saucepan over high heat. Reduce the heat to low and simmer, uncovered, until the lentils are just tender, 20 to 25 minutes.

2. While the lentils are cooking, finely chop the onion (about 1 cup). Heat 2 tablespoons olive oil in a large skillet over medium heat until hot. Reduce the heat to medium-low; add the onion and cook for 5 minutes, or until it has softened. Press in the garlic (about 2 teaspoons) and cook for 1 minute more.

3. Peel the eggplant and cut it into ½-inch pieces (about 2 cups). Increase the heat to medium-high; add the remaining 2 tablespoons olive oil and the eggplant to the skillet and cook, stirring occasionally, for 5 minutes, or until the eggplant is golden.

4. Chop the oregano (about 1 teaspoon). Stir the tomato sauce, red wine, oregano, cinnamon, and cayenne into the eggplant mixture. Bring it to a boil over high heat; reduce the heat to low and simmer for 10 minutes, or until slightly thickened. Drain the lentils and add them to the eggplant mixture. Add salt and black pepper to taste.

3 tablespoons unsalted
   butter
3 tablespoons Wondra
   or unbleached all-
   purpose flour
2 ounces feta cheese
⅛ teaspoon freshly
   grated nutmeg
1½ cups (6 ounces)
   elbow macaroni
1 ounce Parmigiano-
   Reggiano

5. Place an oven rack in the middle of the oven and preheat the oven to 350°F. Oil a 9-inch square baking pan or shallow 2-quart baking dish. Bring a large pot of salted water to a boil for the pasta.

6. Gently warm the milk. Rinse out the saucepan in which the lentils were cooked; add the butter and place the pan over medium-low heat until the butter is melted. Whisk in the flour and cook, whisking, for 3 minutes. Gradually whisk in the milk and simmer for 5 minutes. Crumble the feta cheese (about ½ cup) and add it to the milk mixture along with the nutmeg, and salt and black pepper to taste.

7. When the pot of water comes to a boil, add the macaroni. Cook until al dente, following the package directions; drain (about 4 cups). Microplane-grate the Parmigiano-Reggiano (about ⅔ cup) or grate on the fine side of a box grater (about ⅓ cup). Arrange one-half of the macaroni in the bottom of the baking pan. Top with half the lentil mixture and sprinkle one-third of the Parmigiano-Reggiano on top. Repeat with the remaining macaroni, lentil mixture, and one-third more of the Parmigiano-Reggiano. Top with the feta cheese sauce and smooth it to cover the lentil mixture. Top with the remaining Parmigiano-Reggiano. Bake the pastitsio for 20 to 25 minutes, or until bubbling around the edges.

ibimbap Ⓥ

MAKES 4 SERVINGS ■ **HANDS-ON TIME: 41 MINUTES** ■ **TOTAL PREPARATION TIME: 55 MINUTES**

Bibimbap is a Korean dish composed of warm white rice topped with sautéed and seasoned vegetables and chile pepper paste. It's often garnished with a raw or fried egg and sliced beef. Popular, flavorful, and healthful, *bibimbap* is simple to prepare. Each one of the ingredients is something special in itself.

I first encountered *bibimbap* when I was grazing for lunch in the Condé Nast cafeteria last year. It was the fried egg on top that initially caught my eye, but I was also happy to see so many vegetables in one dish. It wasn't hard to re-create the recipe at home, and everyone took to it right away, just as I had. Feel free to substitute any of the vegetables in your fridge for the ones I list. Likewise, I recommend brown rice or wheat berries, neither of which is traditional, but you're certainly welcome to use white rice. For me, the key components are the rice, the miso sauce, and my favorite, the fried egg.

1 cup brown rice or
  wheat berries
Sesame Miso Sauce
  (recipe follows)
4 ounces shiitake
  mushrooms
2 large carrots
4 tablespoons
  vegetable oil
Kosher salt and freshly
  ground black pepper
5 ounces baby spinach
  (about 8 cups,
  packed)
1 tablespoon sesame
  seeds
8 ounces firm tofu
4 large eggs
4 medium scallions
Thai chili sauce or hot
  sauce of your choice
Quick or Quicker
  Kimchi (page 21, add
  preparation time) or
  store-bought kimchi

1. Cook the rice or wheat berries in boiling salted water following the package directions (you should have about 3 cups).

2. Meanwhile, prepare the Sesame Miso Sauce. Clean the shiitakes, remove and discard the stems, and slice the caps (about 1⅓ cups). Coarsely grate the carrots, preferably using the shredding disc of a food processor (about 1½ cups).

3. Preheat the oven to 300°F. Heat 1 tablespoon vegetable oil in a large nonstick skillet over medium heat. Add the carrots, season them with salt and pepper to taste, and sauté them for 2 minutes, or until they are just tender. Transfer them to a rimmed baking sheet.

4. Add another 1½ tablespoons vegetable oil to the skillet. Add the mushrooms and a pinch of salt; cook for 4 minutes, or just until tender. Add the spinach and another pinch of salt to the mushrooms and cook for 3 minutes, or just until wilted. Stir in the sesame seeds and transfer the mixture to the baking sheet with the carrots.

5. Cut the tofu into four ⅓-inch slices; cut the slices in half. Add ½ tablespoon vegetable oil to the pan; increase the heat to high. Add the tofu and cook for about 3 minutes per side, until golden brown; transfer the tofu to the baking sheet. Put the baking sheet in the oven to keep warm while you fry the eggs.

6. Add the remaining 1 tablespoon vegetable oil to the pan. Crack the eggs, one at a time, into a cup or ramekin and add quickly to the pan. Fry until cooked to the desired degree of doneness. Trim and slice the scallions (about ½ cup).

7. To serve, mound ¾ cup hot rice in the center of each of 4 pasta bowls. Arrange 2 slices of the tofu on top along with 1 egg and one-quarter each of the carrots and the spinach mixture. Sprinkle the scallions over the top and drizzle with the Sesame Miso Sauce and Thai chili sauce. Top with a spoonful of kimchi, if desired.

MAKES ABOUT ⅔ CUP

SESAME MISO SAUCE: Combine 1 tablespoon water with 3 tablespoons vegetable oil; 2 tablespoons seasoned rice wine vinegar; 2 tablespoons red or white miso; 2 tablespoons finely grated fresh ginger; 1½ tablespoons well-stirred tahini; 1 tablespoon sake, rice wine, or dry sherry; and 2 tablespoons sugar in a blender and blend until smooth. Cover and refrigerate until ready to serve. May be kept in the refrigerator for up to 5 days; shake before using.

16

DON'T SKIP DESSERT

This is really my cooking partner Joanne's chapter. Although I'm happy to dig into dessert when it appears in front of me, I don't miss it if it isn't offered. But Joanne has a sweet tooth, as well as the genius to find new ways to delight it. Happily, she has also kept our weeknight mission in mind, meaning that all of these delicious desserts are simple and easy to make. There is pudding and pudding cake, a fruit tart, a turnover, cupcakes, cookies, fruit pot stickers, warm chocolate cheesecake, hot banana split crêpes, and the best chocolate brownies ever. Believe me, no one's jumping up from the table before dinner's over if they know any of these tasty treats is on its way.

FACING PAGE: *Butterscotch Pudding Cake*

ruit Pot Stickers Ⓥ

MAKES 12 POT STICKERS, 4 SERVINGS ■ HANDS-ON TIME: 20 MINUTES ■ TOTAL PREPARATION TIME: 35 MINUTES

I'd been using wonton wrappers to make pot stickers for years when it struck me that there's no law requiring the filling to be savory; you could fill them with anything, including something sweet. In this recipe, I've used plums and nectarines, but virtually any fruit would work. Indeed, you could adapt and readapt this recipe all year long according to whatever is in season.

What won't change, however, is how to cook a pot sticker. But first some history. In *Chinese Cooking for Dummies* by my pal Martin Yan, pot stickers are the legendary result of "an imperial chef's carelessness." One day this chef let the dumplings cook too long, leaving the bottoms far more browned and crispy than usual. Although he was sure the emperor would cut off his head, he received praise instead. When the emperor asked for the name of this marvelous new dish, the relieved chef promptly dubbed them pot stickers.

1 large plum or
   1 medium nectarine
2 tablespoons sugar
½ tablespoon fresh
   lemon juice
12 wonton wrappers
   (3½ by 3 inches)
½ tablespoon
   vegetable oil
½ tablespoon unsalted
   butter
Sweetened whipped
   cream or vanilla ice
   cream (optional)

1. Cut the plum or nectarine lengthwise into 6 wedges and then halve each piece crosswise to make a total of 12 pieces. Toss the fruit with 1 tablespoon sugar and the lemon juice in a medium bowl.

2. Spread out the wonton wrappers on a work surface. Place a piece of plum in the center of each. Reserve any juices in the bowl. Brush the edges of each wrapper with water; lift two opposite corners of each wrapper and press together above the center of the piece of plum; bring the other two opposite corners up and press them together. You should have shaped the wonton into a little pyramid with the piece of plum inside. Pinch the wrapper together very tightly at the seams to make sure it is well sealed.

3. Heat the vegetable oil and butter in a large nonstick skillet over medium heat until bubbly, then arrange the pot stickers, seam sides up, in the skillet. Cook them for 2 to 3 minutes, or until the bottoms are pale golden. Add ⅓ cup water, reduce the heat to low, cover the skillet with a lid, and cook for 5 minutes.

continued on next page

4. Sprinkle the remaining 1 tablespoon sugar over the pot stickers and cook, covered, for 1 to 2 minutes more, or until the liquid has evaporated. (Add more water and cook for 1 to 2 minutes more if the wonton wrappers are not tender.) Remove the lid and continue to cook until the bottoms of the pot stickers are crisp and golden. Gently loosen the pot stickers from the pan and lift them out onto a serving plate. Stir ¼ cup water into any juices left in the bowl in which the fruit was tossed. Add the mixture to the skillet, bring it to a boil, scraping up the brown bits at the bottom of the pan, and drizzle the liquid over the pot stickers. Serve hot with a spoonful of sweetened whipped cream or vanilla ice cream, if desired.

Homemade Chocolate or Malted Milk Pudding and Pops ⓥ

MAKES ABOUT 2½ CUPS, 4 SERVINGS PUDDING OR 6 FROZEN POPS ■ HANDS-ON TIME: 20 MINUTES ■
TOTAL PREPARATION TIME: 20 MINUTES, PLUS COOLING OR FREEZING TIME

Everybody loves pudding, but how many of us make it from scratch? Why bother when you can whip it up right out of the box, right? But this recipe is plenty easy, too, and unlike pudding from a box, it has no additives. It also has huge flavor. In fact, this is four recipes in one—chocolate pudding, malted milk pudding, and the same two flavors as frozen pudding pops (shades of Bill Cosby). They're also great at any temperature: hot out of the saucepan, cold out of the fridge, or frozen on a stick. (That actually makes six recipes in one, doesn't it?)

CHOCOLATE PUDDING AND POPS

4 ounces bittersweet chocolate
½ cup sugar
¼ cup natural (not Dutch process) unsweetened cocoa powder
2 tablespoons cornstarch
¼ teaspoon table salt
2 cups whole milk
2 large egg yolks
1 teaspoon pure vanilla extract

1. Medium chop the chocolate and set it aside. Whisk together the sugar, cocoa powder, cornstarch, and salt in a heavy medium saucepan. Gradually whisk in the milk and egg yolks. Cook the mixture, whisking constantly, over medium heat until it just starts to boil. Reduce the heat to low and continue to cook for 1 minute, still whisking constantly.

2. Remove the pudding from the heat. Whisk in the chopped chocolate and the vanilla and whisk until the chocolate has melted. Strain the pudding through a medium-mesh strainer into a bowl. Divide the pudding among 4 serving dishes or six ½-cup ice pop molds. Let the puddings cool for 10 to 15 minutes. Serve warm, or cover and refrigerate until ready to serve. Puddings will keep for 3 days in the fridge. Wrap and freeze the pudding pops. Pops will keep for up to 1 month in the freezer.

continued on next page

MALTED MILK PUDDING AND POPS

⅓ cup sugar
⅓ cup malt powder
  (see Note)
3 tablespoons
  cornstarch
¼ teaspoon table salt
2 cups whole milk
2 large egg yolks
2 teaspoons pure vanilla
  extract
1 cup malted milk balls

1. Whisk together the sugar, malt powder, cornstarch, and salt in a heavy medium saucepan. Gradually whisk in the milk and egg yolks. Cook the mixture, whisking constantly, over medium heat until it just starts to boil. Reduce the heat to low and continue to cook for 1 minute, still whisking constantly.

2. Remove the pudding from the heat and whisk in the vanilla. Strain the pudding through a medium-mesh strainer into a bowl. Divide the pudding among 4 serving dishes or six ½-cup ice pop molds. Coarsely chop the malted milk balls; transfer them to a re-sealable plastic bag and set them aside at room temperature until ready to serve. Let the puddings cool for 10 to 15 minutes. Serve warm, or cover and refrigerate until ready to serve. Just before serving, sprinkle the chopped malted milk balls onto the puddings. Puddings will keep for 3 days in the fridge. Wrap and freeze the pudding pops. Pops will keep for up to 1 month in the freezer.

NOTE: Malt powder is available in most supermarkets.

$\mathcal{B}$utterscotch Pudding Cake V

When I was a kid and we visited Cambridge, my parents used to take me to an old-fashioned ice cream parlor in Harvard Square. They served a butterscotch sundae made of coffee ice cream, hot butterscotch sauce, and whipped cream. Boy, it was good!

This pudding cake reminds me of those sundaes. When it's baked, it separates into a layer of cake and a layer of hot, rich butterscotch pudding sauce. It's a snap to make, and you can finish it off with whipped cream or vanilla ice cream or, if you're like me, with coffee ice cream.

4 tablespoons (½ stick) unsalted butter

1 cup unbleached all-purpose flour

¾ cup packed light brown sugar

2 teaspoons baking powder

½ teaspoon table salt

½ cup whole milk

2 teaspoons pure vanilla extract

Sweetened whipped cream, or vanilla or coffee (my favorite) ice cream (optional)

1. Place an oven rack in the middle of the oven and preheat the oven to 350°F. Lightly grease an 8-cup shallow baking dish or pan. Melt the butter in the microwave or in a small saucepan over low heat. Bring 1¼ cups water just to a boil over high heat.

2. Stir together the flour, brown sugar, baking powder, and salt in a medium bowl until there are no brown sugar lumps. Add the milk, the melted butter, and vanilla. Stir just until combined; transfer the stiff batter to the greased baking dish.

3. Set the baking dish in the oven and carefully pour the boiling water over the surface of the batter. Bake for 30 to 35 minutes, or until the cake on the top has a crisp, golden surface and the pudding sauce on the bottom bubbles (sometimes through the top surface).

4. Set aside for 5 to 10 minutes to cool slightly. Serve warm with whipped cream or ice cream, if desired.

$\mathcal{J}$oanne's New-and-Improved Blueberry Tart Ⓥ

MAKES 6 TO 8 SERVINGS ▪ HANDS-ON TIME: 15 MINUTES ▪ TOTAL PREPARATION TIME: 15 MINUTES

Bake a blueberry, and it tends to break down and turn into a sort of thin jam. This never struck me as a problem—it still tastes great—but Joanne undertook a mission to create a tart that celebrated the blueberry's texture as well as its taste. She achieved it in this recipe by putting a mix of cooked blueberries and raw blueberries into a prebaked pie shell. The raw blueberries, flavored with the sauce of the cooked blueberries, seem to explode in your mouth. It's not a small thing. For added thrills, top off this tart with a dollop of vanilla ice cream, vanilla yogurt, or whipped cream. Heaven.

Basic Butter Pastry (page 28, add preparation time; you'll need just ½ recipe) or store-bought pastry for a single-crust pie
⅔ cup sugar
2 tablespoons cornstarch
¼ teaspoon table salt
4 cups blueberries
1 teaspoon freshly grated lemon zest
2 tablespoons fresh lemon juice

1. Preheat the oven to 400°F. Prepare the Basic Butter Pastry. Roll out one-half of it between lightly floured sheets of wax paper to make an 11-inch round. (Freeze the other half for another use.) Fit the round into a 9-inch tart pan with a removable bottom, press it against the sides of the pan, and trim off any overhanging pieces. Pierce the bottom and sides of the pastry thoroughly with the tines of a fork. (This will prevent the crust from puffing up.) Bake the crust for 10 to 12 minutes, or until it is dark golden.

2. Stir together the sugar, cornstarch, and salt in a small saucepan. Gradually stir in ⅔ cup water. Add ¾ cup blueberries and cook over medium heat, stirring constantly, until the mixture comes to a full boil, the berries have popped, and the sauce has thickened. Remove from the heat and stir in the lemon zest and lemon juice.

3. Combine the thickened sauce with the remaining 3¼ cups blueberries in a medium bowl; transfer to the baked tart crust and spread the blueberries to fill the shell. Let cool to room temperature and serve, or cover and refrigerate until ready to serve. The tart will keep in the fridge for 3 days.

$\mathcal{L}$emony Pear Turnovers

MAKES 12 TURNOVERS, 6 SERVINGS ■ HANDS-ON TIME: 15 MINUTES ■ TOTAL PREPARATION TIME: 25 MINUTES

As I've confessed many a time, I count myself among the sad legions of the pastry impaired. That doesn't mean I don't *love* pastry; it just means I struggle to make it. Anyway, whenever pastry is called for, I start looking for an easy-to-use stand-in. One of my favorites is plain old white bread. Not the kind that's better wadded up and hurled at a likely target in a food fight than actually eaten. I'm talking about "homemade style" white bread that boasts enough integrity to be rolled out, like pastry, into a square.

My less-than-noble motives aside, bread and fruit go together nearly as happily as pastry and fruit; think of every fruit-filled bread pudding you've ever enjoyed. These "turn-overs" are made with baked pears. (Baking intensifies a pear's flavor.) If you want to fancy them up a little, you can complement the filling with some almond paste or a few dried cherries or cranberries.

2 tablespoons unsalted butter
1 ripe Bartlett pear
¼ teaspoon freshly grated lemon zest
1 tablespoon fresh lemon juice
2 tablespoons plus ½ teaspoon sugar
12 slices homemade-style white bread

1. Preheat the oven to 350°F. Lightly grease an unrimmed baking sheet. Melt the butter in the microwave or in a small saucepan over low heat and set aside.

2. Peel and thinly slice the pear. Cut the slices crosswise into quarters and toss them with the lemon zest, lemon juice, and 2 tablespoons sugar in a small bowl.

3. Trim off and discard the crusts from the bread; cover the slices with plastic wrap. One at a time, place the bread slices between sheets of wax paper or plastic wrap and roll with a rolling pin until they are very thin.

4. Divide the pear slices among the bread slices. Moisten the edges of the bread squares with water. Matching two opposite points, fold half of each bread slice over to enclose the pear slices and make a triangle; firmly press the edges together.

5. Arrange the turnovers on the baking sheet, brush them with the melted butter, and sprinkle them with the remaining ½ teaspoon sugar. Pierce the top of each turnover with the tines of a fork. Bake the turnovers for about 10 minutes, or until they are golden and the pears are tender.

Three-Ingredient Apple Crisp ⓥ

If you don't count the salt (and you shouldn't), you might wonder how the heck anyone can make a delicious apple crisp with just three ingredients. The answer is by starting with granola, which comes fully loaded with oats, nuts, sugar, and dried fruit. (Is this cheating? Don't tell anyone.)

⅓ cup apricot preserves or sweetened fruit spread
4 large Golden Delicious apples (about 2 pounds)
Table salt
2 cups sweetened granola

1. Preheat the oven to 350°F. Lightly grease a shallow 6-cup baking dish. Melt the preserves in the microwave or in a small saucepan on the stove.

2. Peel, core, and thinly slice the apples; toss them with the preserves and a pinch of salt in the baking dish and spread them out to make an even layer. Sprinkle the granola evenly over the apples. Cover the dish loosely with a sheet of greased aluminum foil and bake for 30 minutes.

3. Remove the aluminum foil and bake for about 15 minutes more, or until the apples are tender. Serve warm or cold.

Raspberry Almond Rugelach

MAKES 32 COOKIES ■ HANDS-ON TIME: 35 MINUTES ■ TOTAL PREPARATION TIME: ABOUT 2 HOURS

To get an idea about what rugelach means to a certain generation of Jewish Americans, there's no better guide than Philip Roth. *American Pastoral,* his 1997 novel, begins with a reunion of the Weequahic (New Jersey) High School's 1950 graduating class. At the end of the evening, everyone is given a coffee mug containing a handful of rugelach, "each a snail of sugar-dusted pastry dough, the cinnamon-lined chambers microscopically studded with midget raisins and chopped walnuts." Like Proust's madeleine, Roth's rugelach somehow inspires his narrator to remember everything.

Of course, you don't have to be Jewish to love rugelach. The crescent-shaped pastries are still available at fine Jewish delis and bakeries everywhere, and with a variety of fillings: raisins, walnuts, almonds, cinnamon, chocolate, marzipan, poppy seeds, apricots, and raspberry. Unlike macaroons, which are identified with the Passover holiday, rugelach are not special-occasion sweets.

Using my Basic Butter Pastry and my techniques for rolling out dough, the pastry impaired should be able to sail through this recipe without too much trauma. To begin with, this dough is made with a food processor, which is much faster than doing it by hand. Second, rolling out the dough between lightly floured sheets of plastic wrap eliminates the dough's tendency to break apart or to get too soft, which causes it to stick to the rolling surface or to the rolling pin. Also, each of these rugelach ends not as a tricky little triangle, but as a simple little roll, a distinct time-saver.

This recipe yields 32 rugelach, but you might want to put half aside in the freezer, all rolled up and ready to be sliced for the oven, and bake them when the mood strikes for a quick and delicious delicacy.

Basic Butter Pastry
    Sweet Variation
    (page 28)
One 7-ounce package
    almond paste
2 to 2½ tablespoons
    seedless red
    raspberry jam

1. Place an oven rack in the middle of the oven and preheat the oven to 350°F. Line 2 baking sheets with parchment or aluminum foil coated with nonstick cooking spray.

2. Prepare the Basic Butter Pastry Sweet Variation using 1 teaspoon pure vanilla extract. Flatten the dough into 2 equal disks and chill for 1 hour.

continued on next page

3. Roll out 1 disk of dough between 2 large sheets of plastic wrap dusted with flour to make an 8-inch square. Remove the top sheet of plastic wrap. Roll out half the almond paste between 2 sheets of plastic wrap to make a paper-thin 8- by 7-inch rectangle. Remove the top sheet of plastic wrap and invert the almond paste onto the pastry, leaving ½ inch uncovered on two opposite sides. Spread half the jam (about 1 tablespoon) over the almond paste.

4. Starting from one of the uncovered sides of the pastry, loosely roll up to make a log. Arrange the log of dough seam side down on a cutting board and cut it crosswise to make 16 cookies. Arrange the cookies on one of the prepared baking sheets. Repeat with the remaining disk of dough, the almond paste, and jam.

5. Bake the rugelach for 20 to 22 minutes, or until they are firm in the center and just beginning to brown on the edges. Transfer to a rack to cool; let cool to room temperature and serve, or store in an airtight container. The rugelach will keep for 1 week.

 Quick Brownies **v**

Joanne really outdid herself on this one. These brownies are ridiculously good, as gooey and chocolaty as anyone could wish. Best of all, they require only 15 minutes of hands-on time. Try not to make them every night of the week.

8 tablespoons (1 stick) unsalted butter

¾ cup sugar

⅔ cup natural (not Dutch process) unsweetened cocoa powder

⅓ cup unbleached all-purpose flour

½ teaspoon baking powder

¼ teaspoon table salt

2 large eggs

1 teaspoon pure vanilla extract

½ cup semisweet chocolate chips

½ cup chopped walnuts (optional)

1. Preheat the oven to 350°F. Generously grease a 9-inch square baking pan. Melt the butter in the microwave or in a small saucepan over low heat; let cool slightly.

2. Combine the sugar, cocoa powder, flour, baking powder, and salt in a medium bowl. Add the eggs, melted butter, and vanilla and stir with a fork until a lumpy batter forms. Stir in the chocolate chips and the walnuts, if using.

3. Transfer the batter to the baking pan and bake until the center appears set, about 25 minutes. Transfer to a rack to cool; let cool for 15 minutes. Cut into 16 squares and serve warm.

$\mathcal{H}$ot Banana Split Crêpes Ⓥ

MAKES 4 SERVINGS ■ HANDS-ON TIME: 25 MINUTES ■ TOTAL PREPARATION TIME: 25 MINUTES

You want to eat these on a special occasion, or on a Sunday night to fortify you against the week ahead.

You'll notice that the hands-on time for this baby is longer than for most of the other dessert recipes. If that's a red flag, not to worry. You can make one (or more) parts of the recipe, toss the rest, and still end up plenty happy. Forget the crêpes, for example, and mound the ice cream right on top of the caramelized banana. Or just use raw bananas as you would in a standard banana split. Or, forget the crêpes, caramel, *and* banana and pour the killer chocolate sauce directly onto the ice cream. You will still be wholly satisfied.

4 Basic Crêpes
(page 24, add
preparation time)
or use store-bought
crêpes
Chocolate Sauce
(recipe follows)
4 ripe medium bananas
(about 1½ pounds)
1 cup strawberries
4 tablespoons (½ stick)
unsalted butter
½ cup half-and-half
⅓ cup packed light
brown sugar
⅛ teaspoon table salt
1 teaspoon pure vanilla
extract
1 pint vanilla ice cream
½ cup salted peanuts
(optional)

1. Make the Basic Crêpes. Prepare the Chocolate Sauce. Peel the bananas and cut them in half crosswise; split the halves lengthwise. Hull and quarter the strawberries.

2. Melt the butter in a large skillet over medium-high heat until the foam subsides. Add the bananas, increase the heat to high, and sauté them for about 3 minutes, turning them until they are golden; transfer them to a plate using a slotted spoon.

3. Add the half-and-half, brown sugar, and salt to the skillet and cook until the mixture begins to thicken, about 3 minutes; stir in the vanilla. Add the bananas and turn them until they are well coated; remove the skillet from the heat.

4. Place 1 crêpe on each of 4 dessert plates; spoon one-quarter of the bananas and sauce onto each crêpe and roll up. Top each with a scoop of ice cream and some strawberries, Chocolate Sauce, and peanuts, if using.

CHOCOLATE SAUCE: Combine ¾ cup water, ⅓ cup sugar, and ¼ teaspoon salt in a small saucepan. Bring to a boil over medium heat. Whisk in ½ cup natural (not Dutch process) unsweetened cocoa powder; reduce the heat to low and simmer until the mixture thickens slightly, 3 to 4 minutes. Remove the saucepan from the heat and stir in ¼ cup semisweet chocolate chips and 1 teaspoon pure vanilla extract; stir until the chips are melted.

$\mathcal{P}$umpkin Coconut Bars ⓥ

MAKES 12 BARS ▪ HANDS-ON TIME: 15 MINUTES ▪ TOTAL PREPARATION TIME: 35 MINUTES

For a lot of folks, the first recipe they ever cooked was printed on the back of a box, a package, or a can. Nestlé Semi-sweet Chocolate Morsels gave us Toll House Chocolate Chip Cookies. Lipton Onion Soup Mix turned into Lipton Onion Dip. Campbell's Cream of Mushroom Soup became Classic Green Bean Casserole. After all, why not depend on the makers of a favorite product to have some good ideas about how to use that product?

It was that kind of thinking that led Joanne to the inspiration for this dessert. Reading a recipe for pumpkin pie filling on the back of a can of pumpkin puree last Thanksgiving, she thought, "If we use a simple cookie crumb crust instead of a pie dough, we can turn this filling into tasty pumpkin pie bars with no sweat." The very first version was delicious, but I thought we could jazz it up even more. So we exchanged coconut milk for the milk in the filling, and gingersnap cookies for the vanilla shortbread cookies in the crust. It turned out very well.

Forty 2-inch gingersnaps
2 tablespoons unsalted butter
¾ cup unsweetened coconut milk
2 large eggs
⅔ cup packed light brown sugar
1 teaspoon ground cinnamon
1 teaspoon pure vanilla extract
½ teaspoon ground ginger
½ teaspoon table salt
One 15-ounce can pumpkin puree (not pie filling)

1. Preheat the oven to 375°F. Butter a 13 × 9 × 2-inch baking pan. Grind the gingersnaps in a food processor fitted with the chopping blade to make crumbs (about 2 cups). Melt the butter in the microwave or in a small saucepan over low heat.

2. Stir together the gingersnap crumbs and melted butter in a medium bowl; pat the crumbs evenly into the bottom of the pan. Bake for 5 minutes, until the crumbs begin to darken.

3. Meanwhile, whisk together the coconut milk, eggs, brown sugar, cinnamon, vanilla, ginger, and salt until smooth. Stir in the pumpkin puree and spread the mixture evenly over the crumbs.

4. Bake for about 20 minutes, or until the center has set. Transfer to a rack and let cool slightly. Cut into 12 bars and serve warm; refrigerate any leftovers.

how to make
YOUR OWN COCONUT MILK

It is easy to find unsweetened coconut milk in the international aisle of your supermarket these days, both full fat and lite, and it works just fine in most recipes. But the flavor of home-made coconut milk is truly superior. Sometime, when you have a little time on a weekend, make some coconut milk; it won't be the last time you do it.

You'll need:

1 large coconut without any cracks and containing liquid
(shake it to make sure you hear liquid swishing around)

2 cups water

1. Pierce the softest eye of the coconut with an ice pick or metal skewer; drain the liquid and reserve it for another use.

2. Bake the coconut in a 400°F oven for 15 minutes. Break the coconut with a hammer (or wrap it in a clean kitchen towel and smash it down on a hard surface such as a concrete floor (this is getting violent, isn't it?) until it breaks into several pieces.

3. Remove the flesh from the shell, levering it out carefully with the point of a strong knife. Peel off the brown membrane with a vegetable peeler and cut the coconut meat into small (about 1-inch) pieces. In a blender or food processor fitted with the chopping blade, grind the coconut meat in batches, transferring it to a bowl as it is ground.

4. Bring the water to a boil in a 2- to 2½-quart saucepan over medium-high heat; add the coconut. Cook the coconut for 2 minutes, then remove the pan from the heat. Let the mixture stand, covered, for 10 minutes.

5. Blend the coconut mixture in a food processor or blender until it is very thick. Strain the coconut mixture through a fine sieve set over a bowl, pressing hard on the solids. Working over the bowl, squeeze small handfuls of solids to extract as much milk as possible.

6. Coconut milk keeps, covered and chilled, for 3 days or frozen, in an airtight container, for 6 months.

Makes about 2 cups

$\mathcal{C}$arrot Cupcakes Ⓥ

MAKES 12 CUPCAKES ■ HANDS-ON TIME: 10 MINUTES; 15 MINUTES, IF USING CREAM CHEESE GLAZE ■
TOTAL PREPARATION TIME: 30 TO 35 MINUTES

I love carrot cake, but I love carrot cupcakes even more: first, because a cupcake encased in its own wrapper is going to stay fresher longer; second, because everyone feels special when he or she gets a personal little dessert.

I've thought of a couple of different ways to jazz up the standard cream cheese frosting: with lemon or with candied ginger. Both bestow a touch of class on the humble carrot.

3 medium carrots
1 cup unbleached all-purpose flour
½ cup packed light brown sugar
1½ teaspoons baking powder
½ teaspoon table salt
½ teaspoon ground cinnamon
¼ teaspoon ground allspice
⅔ cup vegetable oil
2 large eggs, beaten lightly
2 tablespoons dark seedless raisins
2 tablespoons chopped walnuts
Lemon or Ginger Cream Cheese Glaze (recipes follow; optional) or 2 tablespoons confectioners' sugar

1. Put an oven rack in the middle of the oven and preheat the oven to 350°F. Place paper liners in 12 cupcake pan cups. Coarsely grate the carrots, preferably using the shredding disc of a food processor (about 1 cup).

2. Combine the flour, brown sugar, baking powder, salt, cinnamon, and allspice in a medium bowl. Make a well in the center of the dry ingredients and add the carrots, vegetable oil, eggs, raisins, and walnuts. Stir with a fork until the dry ingredients are completely moistened.

3. Divide the batter among the cupcake cups. Bake the cupcakes for 20 to 25 minutes. Remove from the oven and let cool on cooling racks.

4. Meanwhile, make one of the cream cheese glazes, if using. Just before serving, glaze the cupcakes or sift confectioners' sugar over the tops. Store any leftovers in the refrigerator.

LEMON CREAM CHEESE GLAZE: Soften 1½ ounces cream cheese in a small bowl. Stir in 1 cup unsifted confectioners' sugar, ½ teaspoon freshly grated lemon zest, and 1½ to 2½ teaspoons fresh lemon juice until smooth.

GINGER CREAM CHEESE GLAZE: Soften 1½ ounces cream cheese in a small bowl. Stir in 1 cup unsifted confectioners' sugar, ½ teaspoon pure vanilla extract, and 1 to 2 teaspoons water until smooth. Stir in 1 tablespoon finely chopped crystallized ginger.

Oatmeal Almond Cookies Ⓥ

MAKES 32 COOKIES ▪ HANDS-ON TIME: 15 MINUTES ▪ TOTAL PREPARATION TIME: 30 TO 35 MINUTES

You'll notice that there's no complicated technique involved in the making of this recipe. In fact, there is no technique involved at all. It's what we in the industry refer to as a "dump recipe": You dump all the ingredients into a food processor and mix 'em up. Then you press the mixture into a baking sheet, bake it, cut it, and eat it with deep pleasure. That's it. Sounds hard to believe, but trust me: These are really great cookies.

1 cup packed light
  brown sugar
8 tablespoons (1 stick)
  unsalted butter,
  softened
1 large egg
1 teaspoon pure almond
  extract
1 cup self-rising all-
  purpose flour
1 cup old-fashioned
  rolled oats
1 cup sliced natural
  almonds

1. Preheat the oven to 350°F. Cover a large rimmed baking sheet with aluminum foil; coat the foil with vegetable oil or nonstick cooking spray.

2. Combine the brown sugar, butter, egg, and almond extract in the bowl of a food processor fitted with the chopping blade; process until smooth. Add the flour and pulse until a soft dough forms. Add the oats and almonds and pulse 4 or 5 times to combine.

3. With oiled hands, pat the mixture out onto the baking sheet to make a 12 × 10-inch rectangle. Bake for 15 to 20 minutes, or until firm and golden. Remove to a cooling rack and cut into 32 rectangles while still hot. Let cool to room temperature and break the cookies apart where cut. Store in an airtight container. The cookies will keep for 1 week.

what if i
DON'T HAVE SELF-RISING FLOUR?

Self-rising flour was one of the first shortcuts offered to home bakers by flour companies that then went on to make "mixes" of all sorts. Self-rising flours are either regular all-purpose flour or cake flour to which baking powder and salt have been added. If you have a recipe that calls for self-rising flour and you don't have any in your pantry, just add 1½ teaspoons baking powder and ¼ teaspoon table salt to each cup of either plain all-purpose or plain cake flour you use. One interesting question that was sent to the Kitchen Shrink page on my Web site was from someone who had put self-rising flour and plain flour in unmarked canisters and wondered how to tell them apart. That was easy to answer. Just taste them. The salty one is self-rising.

Warm Chocolate Cheesecake (V)

MAKES 4 SERVINGS ■ HANDS-ON TIME: 15 MINUTES ■ TOTAL PREPARATION TIME: 35 TO 40 MINUTES

Although I'm not a fool for traditional cheesecake, I'm very partial to this chocolate version, especially when it's eaten warm. It is deeply chocolate and it boasts the slight tang of cream cheese. Its texture changes completely, depending on when it's eaten: It's creamy right out of the oven and quite firm after it's been refrigerated (although the kids tend to dog it before it makes it to the fridge). I like it in its natural state, ungarnished. Ruthie likes to sprinkle fresh raspberries on it.

One 3.5-ounce bar bittersweet chocolate
8 ounces full-fat or ⅓-less-fat cream cheese (Neufchâtel)
1 teaspoon pure vanilla extract
¼ cup plus 2 tablespoons sugar
2 teaspoons unbleached all-purpose flour
1 large egg

1. Preheat the oven to 350°F. Butter four ½-cup ramekins and place them on a rimmed baking sheet.

2. Coarsely chop the chocolate and melt it in the top of a double boiler or in a metal bowl set over a saucepan of simmering water. Combine the chocolate with the cream cheese and vanilla in the bowl of a food processor fitted with the chopping blade. Process until well blended.

3. Stir together the sugar and flour, add it to the processor, and blend it into the chocolate mixture. Add the egg and pulse until smooth. Divide the batter among the ramekins.

4. Bake for 20 to 25 minutes, or until the centers are set. Transfer to a cooling rack to cool slightly before serving.

how can i

MELT CHOCOLATE WITHOUT ITS SCORCHING OR HARDENING?

Chocolate is very sensitive to heat, and it is best to melt it slowly. I like to melt it in the top of a double boiler or in a metal bowl set over water that has come to a boil and then been removed from the heat. Be patient, and when it looks as if much of the chocolate has melted, remove it from the hot water and stir it until it is all melted and smooth. You can also set a heatproof glass measuring cup into the pan of hot water and add the chocolate to the cup. Be careful not to let any of the water splash into the cup because, while you can melt chocolate with a liquid as long as you have at least 1 tablespoon of liquid per ounce of chocolate, small amounts of a liquid will cause chocolate to "seize" and become hard and lumpy. If that does happen, you may be able to save the chocolate by quickly stirring in ½ teaspoon vegetable oil per ounce of chocolate. You can also melt chocolate in a microwave, but be sure to use 50% power and microwave for short intervals (20 seconds) at a time. Stir, and if you don't have a turntable in your microwave, turn the dish frequently.

SOURCES

KALUSTYAN'S

www.kalustyans.com
123 Lexington Avenue
New York, NY 10016
800-352-3451, 212-685-3451
Spices (including Szechuan peppercorns), garam masala, pappadams, beans, grains, *lentilles du Puy,* condiments, international ingredients of all kinds

ADRIANA'S CARAVAN

www.adrianascaravan.com
800-316-0820
Chiles, fresh and dried mushrooms, spices, herbs, grains, oils, vinegars, hot sauces, condiments, international ingredients of all sorts

ZINGERMAN'S

www.zingermans.com
422 Detroit Street
Ann Arbor, MI 48104
888-636-8162, 734-663-3354
Specialty meats, cheeses, breads, spices, herbs, condiments

PENZEYS SPICES

www.penzeys.com
12001 West Capitol Drive
Wauwatosa, WI 53222 (and other locations)
800-741-7787, 414-760-7307
Herbs, spices (including Szechuan peppercorns), condiments, and other seasonings

THE SPICE HOUSE

www.thespicehouse.com
1031 North Old World Third Street
Milwaukee, WI 53203 (and other locations)
888-488-0977, 414-272-0977
Herbs, spices (including Szechuan peppercorns), condiments, and other seasonings (including wasabi powder)

PEPPERS

www.peppers.com
Midway Galleria
18701 Ocean Highway
Rehoboth Beach, DE 19971
800-998-3473, 302-644-6900
Hot sauces, ground pure chile powders, salsas, salad dressings, barbecue sauces, spice rubs

KENYON'S GRIST MILL

www.kenyonsgristmill.com
21 Glen Rock Road
P.O. Box 221
West Kingston/Usquepaugh, RI 02892
800-753-6966, 401-783-4054
Stone-ground cornmeal and johnnycake meal

NIMAN RANCH

www.nimanranch.com
1600 Harbor Bay Parkway, Suite 250
Alameda, CA 94502
510-808-0330
Natural beef, pork, lamb, poultry, smoked and cured meats

FACING PAGE: *Mamoun's Falafel, MacDougal Street, New York City.*

JAMISON FARM
www.jamisonfarm.com
171 Jamison Lane
Latrobe, PA 15650
800-237-5262
Natural lamb

D'ARTAGNAN
www.dartagnan.com
280 Wilson Avenue
Newark, NJ 07105
800-327-8246, Ext. 0
Duck and duck products, organic poultry,
sausages, game, mushrooms

BROWNE TRADING COMPANY
www.brownetrading.com
Merrill's Wharf
262 Commercial Street
Portland, ME 04101
800-944-7848, 207-775-7560
Smoked salmon, trout, and other fish; fresh
seafood; truffle products

DURHAM'S TRACKLEMENTS
www.tracklements.com
212 East Kingsley Street
Ann Arbor, MI 48104
800-844-7853, 734-930-6642
Smoked salmon and trout

MEXGROCER.COM
www.mexgrocer.com
4060 Moreno Boulevard, Suite C
San Diego, CA 92117
877-463-9476
Mexican ingredients and cooking equipment

THE SPANISH TABLE
www.spanishtable.com
1426 Western Avenue
Seattle, WA 98101 (and other locations)
206-682-2827
Spanish and Portuguese ingredients (including
chorizo) and cookware

LA TIENDA
www.tienda.com
3601 La Grange Parkway
Toano, VA 23168
800-710-4304, 888-331-4362, 757-566-9606
Spanish ingredients (including chorizo and
piquillo peppers) and cookware

REAL WASABI
www.realwasabi.com
52A Persimmon Street
Bluffton, SC 29910
843-815-7442, 877-492-7224
Fresh wasabi

PACIFIC FARMS USA, LP
www.freshwasabi.com
P.O. Box 223
Florence, Oregon 97439
800-927-2248
Fresh wasabi and wasabi products

WWW.CHEFSCATALOG.COM
Kitchen gadgets and equipment (including the
Microplane)

RESOURCE CREDITS

PHOTO FOR HEAD STARTS (PAGE 8)
Beveled-edge bamboo cutting board from
www.tagltd.com

**INDIAN SCRAMBLED EGGS WITH
PAPPADAMS (PAGE 32)**
"Ceramic Contour" plate by Vance Kitira
International, www.vancekitira.com/
800-646-6360

TURKISH POACHED EGGS (PAGE 49)
"Garden Glaze" plates by Vance Kitira
International, www.vancekitira.com/
800-646-6360

"Mango" fork and spoon from www.iittala.com/
800-448-8252

APPETIZERS FOR DINNER (PAGE 56)
Platter designed by Monica Porter for Montes
Doggett, www.montesdoggett.com

SEAFOOD GAZPACHO (PAGE 74)
Cups and tray designed by Monica Porter for
Montes Doggett, www.montesdoggett.com

**SPRING SOUP WITH BREAD DUMPLINGS
(PAGE 86)**
"Garden Glaze" bowl by Vance Kitira
International, www.vancekitira.com/
800-646-6360

**RICE, RADISH, AND SNAP PEA SALAD
WITH SEARED BEEF (PAGE 120)**
"Ceramic Contour" plates by Vance Kitira
International, www.vancekitira.com/
800-646-6360

**SEARED SCALLOPS AND BUTTER
LETTUCE SALAD (PAGE 138)**
"Oyyo Petal" plate by Teroforma,
www.teroforma.com

Platter designed by Monica Porter for Montes
Doggett, www.montesdoggett.com

**SOBA NOODLES WITH ASIAN CLAM
SAUCE (PAGE 144)**
"Kartio" glasses from www.iittala.com/
800-448-8252

POLENTA LASAGNA (PAGE 156)
"Copper Fusion" fry pan in platinum by Chantal,
www.chantal.com/800-365-4354

SPICES (PAGE 160)
"Kitira Gourmet" slate board from Vance Kitira
International, vancekitira.com/800-646-6360

**CHICKEN SALTIMBOCCA WITH
ARTICHOKE SAUCE (PAGE 164)**
Napkin from www.tagltd.com

HENS KOTOPOULO (PAGE 183)
"Corinth" plate at SimonPearce.com/
800-774-5277

REUBEN PIZZA (PAGE 190)
"Kitira Gourmet" slate board by Vance Kitira
International, www.vancekitira.com/
800-646-6360

**BLACK COD WITH WARM ROASTED-
TOMATO VINAIGRETTE (PAGE 208)**
"Barre" plate at SimonPearce.com/800-774-5277

SAUTÉED BEER BATTER SHRIMP (PAGE 218)

Plate by Home Essentials & Beyond, www.homeessentials.com

Platter (with lemons) designed by Monica Porter for Montes Doggett, www.montesdoggett.com

MUSHROOM ENCHILADAS (PAGE 224)

"Teema" plate from www.iittala.com/ 800-448-8252

Bowl from www.tagltd.com

CUCUMBER AND TOMATO SALAD WITH YOGURT (PAGE 263)

Tray and "Contempo" tea bowls by Vance Kitira International, www.vancekitira.com/ 800-646-6360

GRILLED LAMB CHOPS (PAGE 294)

Bowl by Sophie Conran for the Portmeirion Group, www.portmeirion.com

BIBIMBAP (PAGE 308)

"Ceramic Contour" bowls by Vance Kitira International, vancekitira.com/800-646-6360

"Aarne" glasses from www.iittala.com/ 800-448-8252

DEVILED BONES (PAGE 311)

"Lattice Blue/Orange" plate from J. Chew Porcelain, www.jchewporcelain.com

CARNITAS (PAGE 314)

"Barre" plates at SimonPearce.com/ 800-774-5277

RASPBERRY ALMOND RUGELACH (PAGE 346)

"Avva White" small cups by Teroforma, www.terforma.com

HERB STORAGE SHOT (PAGE 251)

"Flea Market Lantern" from www.tagltd.com

INDEX

and "Grilled" Cheese
Slices, 89
Tortilla Chips, Homemade
Baked, 29
Vegetable Paprikash, 232–33
Vegetable Stew, Clay Pot,
226–27
Vegetable Stock, Homemade,
11
White Bean, Marinated,
Toasts, *56,* 70
Zucchini Omelet, Open-
Faced, with Tomato Sauce
and Feta, 42–43
Velvet Chicken with Sugar Snap
Peas and Cashews,
322–23
Vietnamese flavors, in My Banh
Mi, *288,* 292–93
vinaigrettes:
acids for, 277
Grapefruit, 139
Roasted-Tomato, Warm, 13
vinegars, 277
balsamic, choosing, 79
rice, seasoned and
unseasoned, 7
Vodka, Penne alla, Classic and
Lite, 282–83

W

walnut(s):
Celery and Parsley Salad with
Parmigiano-Reggiano and,
252, 261
Ham and Beet Salad with
Crispy Johnnycake and
Goat Cheese Toasts,
132–33
Salmon with Asparagus and
Noodles, 159
Sauce, Arctic Char Baked in,
212

Waltuck, David, 181
Warm Chocolate Cheesecake,
356
Warm Roasted-Tomato
Vinaigrette, 13
Warm Sesame Noodles with
Mushrooms and Peas,
234–35
Warm Steak House Salad with
Blue Cheese Dressing,
130–31
wasabi, 67
Dressing, 129
Mayonnaise, 66
rice crackers, in Roasted
Salmon with Hot Mustard
Cracker Topping, 279
Watercress, Smoked Salmon,
and Hearts of Palm Salad
with Buttermilk Dressing,
141
wheat berries:
Bibimbap, 308, 332–33
with Creamy Cauliflower
Sauce, 150–51
white bean(s):
Brown Rice with Broccoli
Pesto, 154
Chicken Cassoulet, 166–67
Marinated, Toasts, *56,* 70
Whitefish Imperial, 304
Whole Wheat Bread, 265
Whole Wheat Linguine with
Salmon and Asparagus,
159
Willinsky, Helen, 317
wine, cooking with, 7
Wolfert, Paula, 166
Wondra, 181, 323
wonton wrappers:
Fruit Pot Stickers, *336,*
337–38
Shrimp Dumplings in Chinese
Chicken Stock, 327

Worcestershire sauce, in Steak
Butter, *8,* 19
World's Fair (1939), 24
wraps:
Lettuce, Ground Turkey and
Mint, *56,* 64
Omelet, Tahini Crab, 53
Peking Duck, *98,* 108–9

Y

yams vs. sweet potatoes, 81
Yan, Martin, 337
Year in Bread, A, 264
yeast, 27
yellow summer squash, in
Sunny Summer Soup with
Zucchini Crisps, 90–91
yogurt, 7
Cucumber Sauce, 214
Greek-style, 7, 49
Tandoori Chicken Wing
Drummettes, 171
and Toasted Cumin Seed
Dressing, 262, *263*
Turkish Poached Eggs with
Sage Oil and, 48, *49*

Z

Zingerman's, 359
zucchini:
Barley Provençale, 148–49
Crisps, Sunny Summer Soup
with, 90–91
Omelet, Open-Faced, with
Tomato Sauce and Feta,
42–43
Roast Chicken Stuffed with
Cheese and, 320–21
Roasted Vegetable and Fresh
Ricotta Sandwiches, *118,*
119